ROCKING THE SHIP OF STATE

D0064435

FEMINIST THEORY AND POLITICS
Virginia Held and Alison Jaggar, Series Editors

TITLES IN THIS SERIES

Rocking the Ship of State: Toward a Feminist Peace Politics, edited by Adrienne Harris and Ynestra King

Reproducing the World: Essays in Feminist Theory, Mary O'Brien

Sexual Democracy: Women, Oppression, and Revolution, Ann Ferguson

ROCKING THE SHIP OF STATE

Toward a Feminist Peace Politics

edited by

ADRIENNE HARRIS
Rutgers University

YNESTRA KING
Institute for Social Ecology

Westview Press
BOULDER, SAN FRANCISCO, & LONDON

Feminist Theory and Politics Series

Published in 1989 in the United States of America by Westview Press, Inc., 5500 Central Avenue, Boulder, Colorado 80301, and in the United Kingdom by Westview Press, Inc., 13 Brunswick Centre, London WC1N 1AF, England

Library of Congress Cataloging-in-Publication Data
Rocking the ship of state : toward a feminist peace politics / edited
by Adrienne Harris and Ynestra King.
     p. cm. — (Feminist theory and politics series)
   ISBN 0-8133-0710-4   ISBN 0-8133-0711-2 (pbk.)
   1. Women and peace. 2. Feminism. I. Harris, Adrienne.
II. King, Ynestra. III. Series.
JX1965.R63 1989
327.1′72′088042—dc19   89-30340
                                                                            CIP

Printed and bound in the United States of America

The paper used in this publication meets the requirements of the American National Standard for Permanence of Paper for Printed Library Materials Z39.48-1984.

10   9   8   7   6   5   4   3   2   1

To the memory of Barbara Deming
and
to all our children:
Katherine, Justin, Maiga, and Lyle
—*A.H.*
Laura, Toby, Andrew, Robbie, Hannah, and Lisa
—*Y.K.*

Contents

Acknowledgments

This project emerges out of the collective thinking of the group of women who are its contributors. It also springs from a political need to put feminist minds to work on the questions and problems that constitute the issue of "peace."

The group's work was supported for several years by the Institute for Research on Women at Rutgers University, with Lourdes Benería and Phyllis Mack as our particular guiding angels, and by a loan from the People's Life Fund.

At a later stage, the Canadian Broadcasting Corporation supported the production of a three-hour documentary, "Woman as Peacemaker," broadcast as part of the radio series *Ideas*. Adrienne wishes to thank Bernie Lucht and Lister Sinclair for their support of the documentary but especially to thank the producer, Sara Wolch, a loving and exacting critic. Sara's combination of demand and support profoundly aided the development and deepening of this analysis in which women and peace are linked.

Also, while we worked on this book, Ynestra cofounded the WomanEarth Feminist Peace Institute to develop connections between feminism, ecology and peace, and philosophy and spirituality. She thanks Starhawk, Gwyn Kirk, Luisah Teisch, Rachel Bagby and Rachel Sierra for their teachings, support, and struggle in making a multiracial, feminist peace movement more possible. Ynestra also thanks the Feminist International for Peace and Food for the Peace Tent at the United Nations Decade on Women held in Nairobi, a demonstration of global feminism in action, and the New York City Women's Pentagon Action. All these experiences contributed to the shaping of this book.

Within our original group Sara Ruddick and Ann Snitow have continued to provide editorial muscle, warm words over late night phone calls, and the soothing of many desperations.

Because this work has been brewing for a number of years, there is a wonderful host of friends and colleagues who have sharpened the analyses and work developed in this book. We thank Jessica Benjamin, Mary Marshall Clark, Muriel Dimen, Irene Dowd, Virginia Goldner, Linda Metcalf, Eileen Monahan, Grace Paley, Robert Sklar, Virginia Tiger, Marilyn Young, the WomanEarth Feminist Peace Institute, the Women's Studies Program at the University of Southern Maine, the Feminist International for Peace and Food, the Seminar on Motherist Movements of the Barnard College Women's Center, and the Seminar on Psychoanalysis and Gender at the New York Institute for the Humanities.

We also thank Elisse Morss, Katherine Tentler, and Susan Sklar for typing, transcribing, and editorial assistance.

At Westview Press, we thank Spencer Carr for calm and care and our editor, Jeanne Campbell, and copyeditor Jan Kristiansson. This book, we hope, is not standard academic fare. We wanted distinct voices—rhetoric and passion as well as argument and footnotes. We have all this distinct and different music, this play of contradiction and difference, and we thank Westview and the editorial staff for permitting this particular hybrid of academics and activism to flower.

To Alison Jagger and Virginia Held, the editors of this series, thanks for support and inspiration.

Adrienne Harris
Ynestra King

Introduction

ADRIENNE HARRIS and YNESTRA KING _____

A feminist is a person who used to be a woman until she saw the light.

A feminist peace activist is a person who used to be a woman and who in the interest of peace may become one again.[1]

Throughout this century, women have worked for peace on the basis of traditional and idealized visions of womanhood and femininity. As mothers, as preservers of life, as "angels of consolation," they spoke and acted in the name of peace. It was a brilliant strategy. Consigned to the relative powerlessness of the private sphere, women moved into public political life while maintaining the protective cover of their traditional role. Caretakers and spiritual centers in the domestic sphere, they thought they could take public power only by becoming housekeepers and moral mothers to the nation.

This powerful ideal of moral motherhood provided the rationale for middle class women's peace groups at the beginning of the twentieth century and in the period before and during World War I. Protest was conducted in a ladylike manner. Women took pains to present themselves as decorous and respectable. The appeal to peace was often made in the name of children.

But this political strategy, so powerful for a century of militant woman's peace movements, is now problematized in light of the critique of gender emerging from the feminist movement. When seen through the prism of modern feminism, the traditional woman's peace movement is based on constricting stereotypes and rigid sex roles that diminish everyone.

During the 1980s, a powerful feminist peace movement has emerged, intentionally locating itself on the contradictory terrain of women, peace, and feminism. Women's peace activities in Western Europe and the United States have been among the most visible and militant practices

1

in the current political landscape. At the same time, feminists have critiqued the very woman-based and woman-identified forms of political and social life that this movement draws on. What is emerging from this contradictory situation is a feminist peace movement, paradoxically grounded both in traditional women's culture and contemporary feminism. Rather than diminish this contradiction, this book has been developed on the premise that women's peace organizing is strengthened and transformed through confrontation with feminist questions of gender.

Moreover, the influence cuts both ways. Feminist theory and feminist political practice are transforming the ways women work for peace by transforming our understanding of gender, motherhood, and political discourse. Much of the passion that animates this book comes from activism and political practice, and thus the book is part of an abiding commitment to the idea that practice informs theory.

The militance and creativity of women's peace movements, as exemplified by the encampments at Greenham Common and Seneca, force a rethinking of theory as a political strategy akin to civil disobedience and guerrilla theater, a disruptive, presumptuous practice that seeks to undermine conventional authority and hierarchy. Sometimes this leads to conscious and subversive use of women's traditional place as mother and as Other, the outsider, the person at the margins of power. But at the same time, women are refusing to remain in the female ghetto, the place on the margins.

By taking a more powerful place in the political arena, feminist peace activists are changing the terms in which the public discourse on peace and disarmament is conducted. Just as it has contributed to the development of theory, the contemporary feminist peace movement has also provided a glimpse of the feminine political imagination in practice. The militant, evocative actions contemporary women are taking in the name of peace show that the powers of a particularly female imagination extend into the political world, disrupting the conduct and discourse of public political life.

Civil disobedience, the practice of militant nonviolence by women in peace actions, can be seen as a form of écriture féminine, or a new "feminine text." In this movement, the relationship of feminism and women's peace politics is a mutually enhancing one. The feminist analysis, with its critique of stereotypes and the rigidity of male and female roles, has shaped and transformed women's peace activities. Our contributors demonstrate how the feminist peace movement is intentionally using the powerful imagery of women as peacemakers and men as war-makers, not to perpetuate these fixed and ancient oppositions but to end this fatal dualism once and for all.

It is on this political territory that feminist peace politics is making a crucial contribution to feminist theory and practice in helping to reformulate the relationship between women and feminism and women and "femininity." In the traditional women's peace movements, political action was undertaken in deeply conventional female terms. Women Strike for Peace rolled a giant dishtowel covered with the names of antiwar signatories down Pennsylvania Avenue to the White House. Demonstrators were urged to dress neatly. Protest was conducted in white hats and gloves. In the contemporary scene, women's political actions synthesize conventional women's imagery with militance. Women encircle the Greenham base by weaving yarn to close the gates against the missiles.

There is a daring energy and physicality to women's civil disobedience in the current movements for peace. If traditional ideas or myths are used, the use is often ironic and self-conscious. New forms of action, unheard of in the earlier movements, make an appearance: a frank acknowledgment of righteous feminist rage and a spirited opposition to state power. Our collection will explore the continuities and discontinuities in this evolving praxis.

Another paradox explored in this book is the contradiction facing women's antimilitarist movements that also wish to support movements for social justice and against racism. These struggles, often waged as wars of national liberation, can appear in dramatic conflict with pacifist principles and a nonviolent stance. Definitions of feminism and priorities in the feminist agenda have often divided white women and women of color. A pacifist women's peace movement has sometimes been seen by women of color as a naive luxury when compared to movements for basic social justice and national liberation. Nonetheless, on the issues of peace and antiwar/anti-imperialist organizing, white women and women of color have much to say to each other. But the conditions of dialogue are only beginning to emerge. In this collection, we make no effort to resolve contradictions and differences prematurely but to further this dialogue.

* * *

This collection draws on several decades of activist experience as well as intellectual work. In small groups, separately and together, we have been at Seneca and at Greenham and have marched in demonstrations and political actions throughout the United States. Several of us, in an affinity group called Demeter's Daughters, sat in at the United Nations. Others have engaged in nonviolent civil disobedience protesting militarist economic interests on Wall Street and opposing apartheid at the South African Mission to the United Nations. Women in this collection have worked on reproductive rights, on welfare rights, and on civil rights and social justice actions. We have participated in organizations from the Student Nonviolent Coordinating Committee and Women Strike for Peace to the more recent Women's Pentagon Action and the Rainbow Coalition. We have been part of Third World liberation movements, anti–Vietnam War work, the Sisterhood of Black Single Mothers, and the black feminist struggle to save Medgar Evers College. We believe that the insight and expertise drawn from our participation in these movements provide a rich and original examination of the intersection of peace activism and feminism.

The last decade has been a time of stunning emergency: War weapons of unprecedented number and magnitude threaten planetary annihilation. But this has coincided with the reemergence of a women's peace movement, this time a feminist peace movement. Military and economic warfare against Nicaragua is escalating. At the point of publication, a curious mix of hope and danger prevails. Many movements of national liberation remain gravely in danger in Latin America. Apartheid is still supported by the United States. Black resistance and uprising in South Africa are being met with increasingly violent oppression by the South African government. Domestic incidences of racism lay bare how little real change there has been in U.S. social and political life. A modest treaty, limited arms control, and the fascinating possibilities of *glasnost'* are occasions of hope and promise. Above all, these developments speak to the steady power and vision of peace movements, in particular women-based movements.

Yet militarism continues to shape our economic priorities. On the more personal and local level, jobless and alienated young people, many of them black and Hispanic, hear the seductive appeal of "career" army. Nowhere are the irony and tragedy of this more apparent than in the current popular response to Vietnam War memorials. Recently the streets of major cities have been filled with the veterans of the Vietnam War— so many ruined and defeated faces in parades in which peace signs and U.S. flags flash side by side in a bizarre and contradictory iconography. In the films that began to appear in the 1980s, there was a struggle to control and define this experience. Conventional ideas and images of patriotism and brave soldiering were set against the deep irrationality of war-making and war policies.

The massive use of resources and capital to fund the military has depleted social, medical, and educational programs to a staggering degree. In this country, the thousands of homeless are living witnesses to the moral and financial bankruptcy of mental health facilities, social welfare programs, low-income housing, and employment opportunities. The loss of jobs, programs, and resources is creating a new, primarily female, poverty class. What is less often noted is the drastic effect of the militarization of culture on every aspect of our daily lives, beyond the violence of war and war-making economic priorities.

The militarization of culture is of particular concern to feminists who have spent the last twenty years challenging the authority of men in society and working to reshape social life in ways that respect the full humanity of everyone. Sexual repression and a conscious manipulation of traditional family values by a well-financed, resurgent, right-wing fundamentalist movement go hand in hand with increasing authoritarianism in every aspect of daily life. We can see this repression in the increase in violence against women, particularly against feminist women and their programs; the impact of economic privation and unemployment on the mental health of working men and women; the increase in spousal battery and child abuse; changing patterns in the assault and rape of women in public spaces; and, at the most public level, the recent bombing of abortion clinics.

With apparent ease, the U.S. public is accepting a level of disregard for other human beings and a resurgence of a Darwinian social philosophy. Militarized culture establishes itself in the life of citizens as xenophobia, a refusal to recognize the humanity of others within this country, just as soldiering abroad depends on denying the humanity of "alien" peoples.

Our objective in this book is to balance and relate history, theory, and practice to each other. This book has been made with a clear-eyed commitment to the full range of tensions and triumphs that feminist peace politics affords. Feminist peace politics entails a commitment to a particular process in the conduct of political life, which Dorothy Dinnerstein has named the "double vision," the steadiness to see short- and long-term projects at the same time. We must act with a clear sense of danger to life on this planet but also take time to do it right. We must hunker down by the campfire, fantasize, and conjure a peaceful and just future, create conditions that free the imagination, and do the painstaking work of analysis. Vision and critique must go forward in tandem. There is much in women's quotidian lives and much in feminist peace practices that combine a sense of emergency and the capacity for lifelong patience. Throughout the book, this double vision is maintained and explored.

Feminist Visions

In Part 1, writers consider the experience of women as children, the practice of women as mothers, and feminist critiques of gender as important sources of insight into the conduct, dynamics, and motivation of a feminist peace politics. Dorothy Dinnerstein connects men's fear of women and the "womanly" aspects in themselves to the asymmetry of our early child care arrangements, in which child care is almost exclusively women's work. According to Dinnerstein, men's fear and hatred of women are outcomes of a child's earliest attachment to a mother who seems both endlessly bountiful and all powerful. Following this analysis, the twin issues of war and ecological devastation can be understood as manifestations of the deep-rooted fear and hatred men direct at women. Dinnerstein argues powerfully that war-making and the pillaging of the earth—of Mother Nature—follow from patriarchal and masculine assertions of domination and control.

Zala Chandler addresses the issues of peace movements and racism and argues that peace work must be renamed such that antiracism is a central component of peace practices, not an addenda. The debates between white women peace activists and women of color require us to see that these two distinct movements trace their history from traditions of nonviolence.

Ann Snitow discusses "maximizing" and "minimizing" tendencies in modern feminism. The first is a strain within the women's movement that seeks to deepen, empower, and maximize women's culture and women's unique experiences. This tendency has been the source of major mass political movements and sustained political action. At the same time, the tendency toward minimizing the differences between men and women argues that the dissolution of gender stereotypes is a necessary condition for social liberation and peace. Snitow seeks to bind these oscillations in feminist thought by developing the view that gender is kinetic and malleable. She argues for a feminist peace politics that draws on the shared condition of women but never rigidifies gender truths.

Sara Ruddick and Adrienne Harris investigate how the idea and ideals of "femininity," "women," and "mother" are raised to the level of cultural icon and used ideologically in the service of war-making and how they must be rehabilitated for peace. These chapters, and the one by Snitow, seek to integrate current feminist analyses of gender with feminist political action.

Gwyn Kirk, coordinator of Greenham Women Against Cruise Missiles, translates her experience at the peace camp at Greenham Common in England into a rich meditation on the particular power and character of feminist civil disobedience and nonviolence.

Feminism Challenges Militarism

In Part 2, the writers focus the inquiring, critical eye of feminism on the state and militarism. Feminist critiques of strategic arms control and of the militarization of the economy seek to transform the general public discourse on war-making and arms proliferation and challenge the technological "rationality" that dominates modern social and political life. Defense planning and economic planning are two domains crucial to the maintenance and promotion of war-making and global oppression from which women are excluded or marginalized. In this section, our contributors seek to transform the very terms of public debate on these issues by shaking the gates of patriarchy and of the technological rationality that dominates modern social and political life, just as the women have shaken the gates of Greenham and Seneca.

Nancy Hartsock writes about the pathological power of militarism on male psychic life. Through an analysis of the *Iliad,* she demonstrates that the masculine idealization of heroism is men's answer to the problem of mortality. According to Hartsock, men need war and combat to achieve full manhood as it is now constituted.

Carol Cohn demonstrates the terrifying irrationality of arms control planning and the masculine worship of technology. She asserts that a feminist confrontation with this world of missiles and abstract war-making requires us to become "techno-bilinguals" in a rather risky, complicated way. We must learn the language of military apparatus and deterrence but recognize that speaking the language can shape thinking about weapons. According to Cohn, we have to find a new way of speaking that will render the "feminine" and the feminist position visible and credible in a public discourse on disarmament and arms control. To this end she charges us with the curious task of learning the technology and analysis of defense strategists without losing our bearings. (In the work of Cohn, Hartsock, and others, the sanctity and rationality of "the Word" is challenged, providing us with an understanding of reasonableness that is both old and new, a feminist ideal of reason that is not abstracted from the totality of action, moral choice, and the whole person.)

Barbara Omolade analyzes the impact of the military on the black community. Her experiences as a black woman, as a feminist, and as a civil rights activist inform her understanding of the role of the military within the black community. She explores how military recruitment operates like an oscillating current, alternately empowering young black males and then inducting them into a racist and violent environment in which they will suffer disproportionate numbers of deaths in wartime. She poses the dilemma facing poor women, many of them black: If your kid is nineteen, jobless, futureless, and at risk from the lethal trouble of urban streets, do you not long for the crisp authority of the military regimen to bring some shape to a future that otherwise seems empty and alienated?

Finally, this part offers a feminist critique of the militarization of the economy. Lourdes Benería and Rebecca Blank chart the stunning inroads military spending has made on social programs. They also explore the deep irrationality of our current economic life and conjure feminist visions of a plausible and possible conversion to a peacetime economy.

Organizing for Peace: Triumphs and Troubles

The writers in Part 3 examine the history, the scope, and the current condition of women's peace movements. From the vantage point of actual participation in the important women's peace actions of the past thirty years, these women, fully versed in feminism and feminist theory, analyze and interpret these political forms and movements for a contemporary audience.

Phyllis Mack's chapter concentrates on the social and political movements initiated by St. Francis, the Quakers, and Mahatma Gandhi, and she suggests we look for the power of the feminine and the womanly in these movements led by men. She reads these movements for the potency of feminine imagery as tools for political change and for galvanizing popular consciousness.

Amy Swerdlow, a participant in Women Strike for Peace and the primary historian of that movement, writes about the power and limitations of this motherist organization of the 1960s and 1970s. Rhoda Linton writes about the feminist culture and forms of decisionmaking at the Seneca peace camp. Gwyn Kirk analyzes the activities around the Greenham peace camps. Both make important feminist contributions to the understanding of political forms and organizations and political theory. Both assert that women's peace camps are laboratories of gender testing and that they transform the character and political work of women.

In an Afterword, Ynestra King, a feminist peace activist and founder of the Women's Pentagon Action, examines several key actions in the history of feminist peace politics. She argues for militant nonviolent direct action as a critical feminist strategy. She asserts that, in addition to cultural transformation (a strength of feminist practice), we must be able to confront state power in some way consistent with feminist politics while continuing to evolve both our understanding of peace and a politics of joy in life.

This anthology addresses the difficult but central questions for peace politics raised by feminist theory and practice and by contemporary analyses of gender. The resulting chorus is not sweet and harmonious. There are contradictions, difficult choices, vigorous differences. Rather than providing declarative or rhetorical answers, the women writing here are participating in a feminist process of respectful dialogue that honors the complexity of women's experience as it relates to war and peace. But the chapters in this book are held together by the hope and conviction that feminism and the struggle for peace and social justice can and must be woven together in the process of moving toward peace.

Notes

1. These two epigrams were the collective invention of the Rutgers Study Group on Peace and Disarmament.

PART ONE

Feminist Visions

What Does Feminism Mean?

DOROTHY DINNERSTEIN

Webster[1] defines feminism as "a. the theory that women should have political, economic and social rights equal to those of men; b. the movement to win such rights for women." But in a human realm whose dictionaries define as a "theory"—i.e., a debatable idea—the notion that women should have such rights, feminism must define itself in terms far broader than this: other core changes, in such a realm, are inseparable from change in our uses of gender. Women whose energies are focussed on achieving equality within the status quo—within a short-term future, that is, in which present social reality continues otherwise essentially unaltered—are hoping for what cannot happen.

Indeed "status quo" is itself a weird misnomer for our present collective condition. The reality we inhabit—the reality within which I write this and you read it: our driven predatory depersonalized human realm, fragile and frantic, blind with passion to prevail, fanatically greedy, rigidly and mortally coercive—is surely anything but stable. We are moving fast—nosediving—toward ecological catastrophe and/or nuclear Armageddon. If we cannot pull out of this nosedive the short-term future can evaporate at any moment. And to pull out of it—to avert the death of living earthly reality—means mustering a huge, a miraculous, spurt of human growth and change: fast change: change within persons and within intimate groups, and change in the nature of the larger societal units (cultural, economic, political and regional) on whose level the developments we call historic take place.

What happens in those larger societal units happens in three-way interaction with what happens within persons and within intimate groups. It would be folly, I think, to suppose that we can mastermind the outcome, or even identify all the crucial features, of this process. An

13

adequate overview of the changes that would make it possible for earthly life to go on now is not within our mental reach: our pooled intelligence— even with the prosthetic extensions which it has so cleverly devised for itself, and of which it is so stupidly proud—falls far short of that task.[2] Such an overview might well tell us that there is no chance—none at all—for this planet's organic fuzz to outlive the twentieth century. What I am discussing here, then, are some *necessary* conditions for a living earthly future. What the *sufficient* conditions are is another question, and maybe we're lucky not to know the answer to it. *Without hope— open-eyed hope, which by definition embodies uncertainty and counsels action, not blind hope, which is passive and shuns available fact—we are already dead.* And an equal-rights feminist stance oriented to an otherwise unchanged social reality *is* blind hope: hope resigned, on some silent level of feeling, to the truth of what it denies: the imminence of world murder. It is a business-as-usual strategy: a self-deceptive device for whiling away time: a blind to-do: a solemn fuss about concerns that make no sense if we have no future, as the end of earthly life (an end that is bound to come sometime, but why now? and why at human hands?) draws closer. Surely one should, at every moment, choose: fiddle frankly while Rome burns (because music is intrinsic to the moment: like love, it fulfills itself by being made: sing "I am! I am!" while bearing witness to your world's annihilation) or try to put the fire out. Business as usual, which carries intrinsic reference to a future, is blank denial: the most primitive of those defense mechanisms that Freud challenged us to outgrow.

Feminism is a living movement, I am saying, a movement honest with itself, only insofar as it embodies active radical try-to-put-the-fire-out hope: long-shot optimism, based on the widest knowledge we have— tentative, partial knowledge—and on love for the widest reality that human feeling at its mammalian core can authentically embrace—earthly life: optimism that has faced the possibility of failure, and felt through— come to terms with, and put in its proper place—the silent hatred of Mother Earth which breathes side by side with our love for her, and which, like the hate we feel for our human mothers, poisons our attachment to life.

Central to a humanly whole feminist vision is awareness that our traditional uses of gender form part of an endemic mental and societal disorder: part of the everyday psychopathology, the normal taken-for-granted mishugas, that is killing our world. Not only do our old sexual arrangements maim and exploit women, and stunt and deform men: the human way of life that they support moves, by now, toward the final matricide—the rageful, greedy murder of the planet that spawned us—and seems bent on reaching out into space for new planets to kill. In doing what we do with gender we humans not only constrict and distort ourselves; we also rape and desecrate earthly nature, and threaten to lay waste, as fast as we can get to it, to whatever may be alive in outer space. I say "we humans," not "those men," because while it is of course mainly men, not women, whose military and economic games threaten to de-create what our grandparents called Creation, they play these games with tacit female consent. Maybe we could not stop them if we tried. But so far we have not—not on the scale which could make such effort realistic rather than purely symbolic/ expressive—found ways to try.

As girls, we were trained—shaped, schooled—to become the responsibly nurturant members of the human family, alert to the needs of vulnerable, dependent beings.[3] Now—grown up; rejecting that old male-female division of responsibility, but equipped still with the traditional skills we were taught; demanding that men and boys must learn them too, but aware that time is short and such learning inexorably slow; knowing that the public realm, which men still rule, is in mortal trouble, and the earth itself a vulnerable being: a vitally endangered creature, needy, damaged already, and dependent on human protection from further human assault—now, at this moment, we crazy feminists may well be the most sanely conscious little part of our ailing lifeweb. From the perspective of this consciousness, what feminism most urgently means is something very much broader than the right to equal pay for equal work, or to orgasm (although such rights are of course part of it). It means *withdrawing from old forms of male-female collaboration, not only because they restrict female access to some major sources of power, status, and pleasure,[4] but now, most centrally, because they express and support the insanity that is killing the world.* And it means *mobilizing the wisdoms and skills with which our female history has equipped us, and focussing them upon the chance that this world-murder can be interrupted— stopped; reversed—and human life reordered: reworked into forms harmonious with those we now threaten to smash:* forms as shapely as trees and stately as gorillas; as elegant as giraffes and exuberant as coral reefs; as gaily wise as elephants and whales; as loving and free as lions and housecats; as green as grass, and brave as flowers.

The core meaning of feminism, I am saying, lies, at this point, in its relation to earthly life's survival. Equal rights goals matter, first of all, because they have to do with psychic growth: fast growth: growth away from the infantilisms, male and female, which support and are supported by our old uses of gender, and toward human responsibility: responsibility for our own self-creation; for our complex and internally contradictory bodily and psychic traits; for the place we have carved out for ourselves in the earthly lifeweb; and for the life and death power over nature that has come to lie in our ingenious, unwise hands. Feminism is a crucial human project—a project worthier of adult passion than war or the manufacture of plastic bottles—only insofar as it moves us toward the outgrowing of the mental birth defect, the normal psychopathology, that makes us so deadly a danger, now, to the living realm that spawned us: the birth defect that makes us—clever inventive affectionate tool-using ape-cousins who "dreamed ourselves into existence"[5]: sociable playful mammals who laugh, weep, talk, talk, and talk—an ecological cancer, and a nuclear time bomb, in the body of the earth.

At the heart of this birth defect, I think—at the core of human malaise—is scared refusal to know that we *did* in fact create ourselves: that we *are*, in fact, collectively self-made beings, responsible for our own existence: culture-dependent two-legged primates whose crucial biological assets—our brains and our hands—are usable only insofar as we acquire, through learning, the prosthetic equipment which, over eons, we ourselves (our human and proto-human ancestors, that is) seem, collectively, to have fashioned: perishable equipment, easily lost forever: equipment upon which we so heavily rely that without it the creatures we have slowly become as we brought it slowly into being would be too disabled to reconstruct it: tools, skills, language and the concepts it carries, and pooled knowledge of earthly fact: detachable equipment, progressively elaborated, refined and extended, the beginnings of which seem apt to have taken shape in tandem—in back and forth interdependence—with the evolution of our complex central nervous systems, our upright bodies, and our subtle, versatile hands.

This human fear of facing human self-creation—this core refusal of our collective responsibility: responsibility for what we are, for the realm we have made, and for the earthly lifeweb that has nurtured our existence: all of which we now seem about to wipe out—stands face to face, at this point, with what the psychically androgynous Lewis Mumford, at eighty,[6] begged us to mobilize: "mammalian tenderness and human love." It is a confrontation implicit in every part of world-conscious human life—and central, I think, in feminism, which is (among other things) a bid for female sharing of public power. *The question for women is what kind of public power we want to share: the kind that is killing the world or the kind that is focussed on keeping the world alive.*

These differing modes of power—life-hostile power, bent on damaging what it cannot kill or control (polluting, maiming, reducing it; desecrating or degrading it; boxing it in) and nurturant power, which cherishes the freedom and integrity and health of what it loves—seeem to have coexisted, till this century, in fragile balance.[7] World War I, followed in my lifetime by Hitler, Hiroshima, and the steadily growing weight of world-killing machinery since Hiroshima—the stockpiled thunderbolts of a crazed and dimwitted Jove: enough of them by now to denude the

---

Box A

Some people—these days probably most—*shut* the world out. Partly or wholly, they even now deny the real probability of earthly life's destruction, and in that way—on some dark split-off mental level, maybe willingly—increase that possibility: being alive and human can get to feel like more trouble than it's worth. Others, maddened by assault on their need to prevail, seem wholly and overtly willing to *wipe* the world out. Anger at reality's refusal to confirm infantile omnipotence can be either active or passive, that is: it can be either assaultive or withdrawing. In this respect the quiet apathy of the apolitical masses and the reckless bellicosity of an active Reaganite have much in common.

(As I write—mid-April '86—the leaders of a large nation and a small one stand poised to provoke the U.S.-USSR confrontation that could in fact wipe the world out: the mighty and crazy Reagan and the punier and equally crazy Khadafi, each cheered on by countless puffed up little followers.* We watch them play planetary chicken, try to believe it's true, and can't quite do so: if I really believed it, could I sit here writing? Still, if we survive this moment's crisis—as we will have done if the book of which this chapter is part is printed and you, reader, sit breathing as you read it—our descent into nothingness remains in principle reversible.)

---

*Wall stickers reading "U.S. #1" materialize hourly, like dandelions, and I grope for the words of the song whose melody floats in my head. I catch them: "Deutschland, Deutschland über Alles."

---

earth of life how many times over?—heralded a fateful tipping of that fragile balance.

Can this tipping conceivably still be righted? reversed? The runaway societal-technologic trends that underlie it are of course fueled in large part by malignant human impulses, impulses to realize the old enraged eye-closing thumb-sucking infantile-omnipotent dream of making the world go away: of shutting it out or wiping it out, since it refuses to obey the baby's wishes (see Box A).

Still, what fuels a trend need not wholly steer history. Clearly, "amazing inventions for death"[8] are metastasizing, and international political machinery is moving us—heavily; steadily—toward extinction. But human impulses toward the protection of life, impulses more volatile than political machinery, more flexible and agile, can—may?—at the same time be gathering momentum; we may yet mobilize Eros, put Thanatos in its proper psychic place[9] and turn the deathly tide.

Feminism has bearing on this gathering of momentum—feminism is a vital part, that is, of current history—only insofar as feminism spells out, and embodies in its practice, the links between change in our uses of gender and reversal of our descent into nuclear and/or ecological hell. Maybe—who knows?—we can still manage this reversal. But doing so means outgrowing normal human psychopathology: surmounting, in other words, ordinary moral cowardice and mental sloth. It means repudiating violence, active and passive, and renouncing coercive exploitative lifeways: using our rage, like our shit, not for ammunition as our monkey cousins do, but humanly: to fertilize green growth. It means mobilizing the core interest and empathy which (alongside anger, fear and cannibalistic cravings) we feel toward each other: our impulse to understand and comfort and forgive each other: our built-in attraction to the humanly created human realm (the realm to whose presence our large brains, upright posture and clever hands refer, just as our eyes refer to light and our ears to sound): and our protective filial concern for earthly nature.

Such mobilization would take all the strengths we could muster. It would draw on the traditional talents which women and men, respectively, now embody: talents whose exercise in our present extremity might hasten their merging (and thereby deepening) inside each human skin. It would call forth the energy we need—all of us, in all the earth's nations—to start changing our old uses of gender, uses that now support the infantile violence and greed, the infantile fusion of irresponsibility and felt omnipotence, that are killing our world. And it would foster those new strengths, those new forms of resourcefulness, which would start to take shape as we worked out new modes of community and primary-group life. (See Box B).

Men for example—far more, on balance, than women—have traditionally felt responsible for the public realm. They have embodied skills for speaking out in this realm: skills for foreseeing and summarizing historic events; for articulating moral and philosophical principles; for organizing broad collective action. With some impressive and instructive exceptions, it is men, throughout recorded political and religious history, who have been the main leaders and rulers, the main prophets and priests.

Indeed it is mainly men—a few highly gifted men: in our own time, men like Freud, Mumford, Norman Brown—who have been in a position to articulate in the public realm the counterconsiderations that women in private life—many women, ordinary women—have all along embodied: the counterconsiderations which, taken, seriously, limit human enthusiasm

Box B

It feels crazy to be writing this. How—by what benign wildfire contagion—could it happen? Yet how could we live if we agreed there was no chance it could happen? Maybe non-activists' secret hope is that something the crazy activists do will turn the unthinkable tide, with whose approach all of us (in our varying, but mostly numb and silent ways) are obsessed. And surely what activists have to hope— what saner hope is possible?—is that this "something" will be the massive worldwide burst of constructive energy that Freud challenged us to muster:[10]

> The fateful question for the human species seems to me to be whether and to what extent their cultural development will succeed in mastering the disturbance of their communal life by the human instinct of aggression and self-destruction. It may be that in this respect precisely the present time deserves a special interest. Men have gained control over the forces of nature to such an extent that with their help they would have no difficulty in exterminating one another to the last man. They know this, and hence comes a large part of their current unrest, their unhappiness and their mood of anxiety. And now it is to be expected that the other of the two "Heavenly Powers," eternal Eros, will make an effort to assert himself in the struggle with his equally immortal adversary. But who can foresee with what success and with what result?[11]

for human (mainly male human) exploit: the doubts that women, within safe boundaries, have all along powerlessly ventilated in a running critique, a subordinates' critique, sealed off from the flow of formal historic event to which it refers. This societal safety valve, this "court jester" mechanism, has channelled off potentially subversive female energy, and at the same time vicariously ventilated truant male misgivings, letting the male-steered stream of public event move undeflected—and with substantial tacit female consent, we must remember (see Box C)— toward what by now looks like all-but-inevitable nuclear and/or ecological hell. Can this sealed-off subordinate critique become part of that stream of overt public event in time to redirect its flow? Maybe it can; but for this to happen, the critique itself must be extended. What a few male critics of male exploit have all along been saying in public, and innumerable female court jesters in private—that history-making is shot through with crazy, life-hostile urges—omits mention of a basic concomitant of those lethal urges: if we want to renounce them, we must change what we do with gender. Since such change means abolition of

---

Box C

It is vital, clearly, that this tacit female consent be withdrawn: that our old complicitous grumble (maternal, but cowed; unimpressed, but self-deprecating; worried, but sheepishly proud of our big boys; amused by their silly bravado, but protective of their tender egos; afraid *for* them, but afraid *of* them; angry and contemptuous, but deferent; doubtful, but dazzled) become active, unqualified resistance. Those bully boys are killing us, and our children, and the earth's innocent plants and beasts—and we, human and standing by, share by default their guilt. Standing by, we are co-responsible for their lying and their stealing, their predation and pollution, their ravaging assault on everything that lives: co-responsible, by default, for the murder of earthly reality.

---

male privilege (privilege to which wise and kind men, as well as mean and foolish ones, are deeply addicted) men are understandably slow to grasp its bearing, now, on earthly life's fate.

Indeed we female jesters ourselves, once we start to grasp this bearing, must either put up or shut up. Self-respect tells us to choose: throw away our clown hats, dive deep, and surface as feminist survival activists—or praise our lords and pass the final ammunition. What becomes clear is that the misgivings women have all along been ventilating—the critique we have ambivalently mumbled, in private, about the realm where "with streaming banners noble deeds are done"—must now be articulated in a more responsible, actively insurgent public context: a context embodying change in our old uses of gender. Central to such change, wherever women and men live together, is movement toward male sharing of the life-maintaining, nurturant work that women have all along done: intimate, personal work that will be in important ways transformed—as will work in the world-making public realm as well—when that public realm's demands are fused with the demands of fragile, growing young life.

Such change will necessarily take time. But its beginning, if that beginning is strong, announces a deep turn toward life. It is a commitment to the future which alters the present, like pledging allegiance or planting trees.

We are feminists, then, for many reasons; but feminism matters now, most centrally, because the old uses of gender that it challenges have kept human beings, no matter how busily and well they work at their everyday tasks, humanly feckless. They have helped both sexes stay infantile, helped us deny collective responsibilities which we can escape

---

Box D

Enthusiasm for space travel is rooted, I think, in hostility to earthly life. And how I wish that folks possessed by this enthusiasm could just buzz off and leave this boring green ball to those of us who want no other home!

If—*if*—space journeys were launched from a thriving, sturdy, earthly lifeweb—from a mother-planet unthreatened by human short-sightedness life-hatred and greed—I would ask only that astonautical enthusiasts go away, enjoy their hobby, and leave the rest of us in peace: that self-important cosmic comings and goings be governed by some simple rules of courtesy and justice: that they be paid for by folks who want them to happen and can afford the wild expense, not by hungry children and lonely impoverished old women and displaced demoralized Native Americans and desperate migrant farm workers; and that they manage not to be the noisy nuisance they now are to planetary homebodies like me.

As things are, astronautical ardor smells vile to me. It stinks of matricide: of sweet baby boys gone ugly.

---

at this point only by dying off (or by moving off into space, some folks must dimly feel; but see Box D).

The possibility that we may after all pull through this emergency—that there may after all continue to be a warm brainy human race, rooted in a sweet earthly lifeweb—depends on the rate at which we can break through the collective developmental stalemate, the collective refusal of responsibility, of which our old uses of gender are a core expression: refusal of responsibility for our own self-creation, and refusal of responsibility to keep the lovely living earth—now mortally imperiled by our foolish cleverness, our callow nastiness, our silly self-conceit, our brute compulsion to prevail—alive.

What survival now demands, in sum, is fast steps—fast giant steps—toward growing up. And a necessary condition for such growth is change in our uses of gender. This is a kind of change which most men, bound and blinded by caste privilege, tend to resist: although—or because?—it promises to deepen their humanity, to free them from warping constraints, they by and large fear it. So the task of initiating these fast giant steps—the task of mobilizing human life-love and starting to outgrow the species-specific mental birth defect of which our uses of gender are part and our assault on the ecosphere an expression: the task of focussing human energy on protection of the lifeweb for whose fate we have by now, willy-nilly, made ourselves responsible—is at this point largely in female hands. What happens next may well depend on us.

Notes

1. *Webster New Collegiate Dictionary* (Springfield, Mass.: G and C. Merriam, 1979).

2. See Gerald Barney, ed., *The Global 2000 Report to the President,* vols. 1 and 2 (Washington, D.C.: Council on Environmental Quality and the Department of State, 1981); and Institute for Progress Toward a Sustainable Society, *Worldwatch State of the World* (New York: Norton, 1986). These useful surveys suggest both the dimensions of our survival problems and the impossibility of knowing whether or not coordinated human effort could still, at this point, bring them under control.

3. Nancy Chodorow, *The Reproduction of Mothering* (Berkeley: University of California Press, 1978); Carol Gilligan, *In A Different Voice* (Cambridge, Mass.: Harvard University Press, 1982); Sara Ruddick, "Preservative Love and Military Destruction: Some Reflections on Mothering and Peace," in Joyce Trebilcot, ed., *Mothering: Essays in Feminist Theory* (Totowa, N.J.: Rowman and Allenheld, 1984).

4. And constrict male existence, of course, in ways at least equally maiming, so maiming that the victim is typically unaware of the constriction.

5. Lewis Mumford, "Animal into Human," pp. 409–421, in *Interpretations and Forecasts: 1922–1972* (New York: Harcourt Brace Jovanovich, 1973).

6. Mumford, "Animal into Human."

7. Lewis Mumford described this unsteady balance in *The City in History* (New York: Harcourt, Brace and World, 1961), and in *The Myth of the Machine* (New York: Harcourt, Brace and World, 1966). Sigmund Freud analyzed its psychic roots in *Civilization and Its Discontents* (New York: Norton, 1961). Norman Brown continued that analysis in *Life Against Death* (New York: Vintage Books, 1959). Women writers of widely varying perspectives and sensibilities (Colette, Virginia Woolf, and Simone de Beauvoir, for example, throughout their work) have compared its expression in female and male experience.

8. "Unity Statement—Women's Pentagon Action," in Leonie Caldecott and Stephanie Leland, eds., *Reclaim the Earth* (London: The Women's Press, 1983).

9. That is, a more tolerable place. What this place should be for humans (as compared with other intelligent beings who seem in some way aware of death: apes, whales, and elephants, for instance, who have memory, foresight, and imagination but not, apparently, culture or history—not the consciousness, that is, of a cumulatively evolving social reality) is a question for which our old religious answers have never been wholly adequate. If they had been, we would not have been moving, all along, toward our present mortal crisis. It is a question whose meaning we need time to come to better terms with—more time than we now seem likely to have. Yet even a small step toward such a coming to

terms, a sense of movement in that direction, might at this moment be crucial. (Ref. Brown: "using the death instinct"—whatever that is—"to die with.")

10. Dorothy Dinnerstein, *The Mermaid and the Minotaur* (New York: Harper Colophon Books, 1976).

11. Sigmund Freud, *Civilization and Its Discontents*.

TWO

Antiracism, Antisexism, and Peace
(Sapphire's Perspective)

ZALA CHANDLER

Can you imagine a summer firestorm clashing with the coming winter winds? How enraged She[1] would be! "How dare He[2] trample on the beauty and warmth I have brought to this place called Earth!" Sapphire would think as She experienced the chill of the coming winter winds. His coldness might make Her doubt, for a moment, Her powers. But then She would know them again. And She would strut and cite them. Call upon them with thunder and lightning to hold her up/forward. For Sapphire *knows* Her accomplishments . . . Her powers. She has studied them over and over again in Her lessons of life. She knows that She has birthed some of the greatest warriors, creators, givers of life of Mother Earth, including the African sun/storms/sapphires/diamonds named Cleopatra, Candace, Nzingah, Tubman, Sojourner, Mandela, Assata, and more. *All* great reasons for Her self-assuredness . . . Her beliefs in the possibilities of tomorrow . . . peace with dignity and justice.

Can you *really* imagine a summer firestorm clashing with the coming winter winds? If yes, then you can understand "Sapphire's perspective." It is the perspective of a knowing, wild woman who dares not accept all of the rules of the old way. It is the perspective of a proud, creative, woman-warrior who resists domination in all its forms. It is the perspective of an African woman born and raised in the United States (with all that implies), a condition that compels me to write this piece.

Should the questions of feminism, antiracism, and peace be on the African-American national and international agenda? Of course they must! As a people who have concentrated energies on gaining justice and equality in the United States, African-Americans, both in a conscious and a nonconscious fashion, represent the "cutting edge" for feminism, antiracism, and peace. Why?

The history of all African people in the Americas is a history of resistance and struggle. From Nat Turner to Rosa Parks, David Walker to Malcom X, Sojourner Truth to Angela Davis, Fannie Lou Hammer to Assata Shakur et al., black people have resisted and struggled against oppression in the United States. In particular, objective history attests to the fact that the African female has played a tremendous role in that resistance.

The African woman slave, like the African man slave, bore the whip and picked the cotton and created new industrial tools as part of this nation's working/slave class. The African woman and man of that era did not argue about who was the "most oppressed" or the "more equal" because their collective human misery and their equal work responsibilities mandated a different understanding and expenditure of energy. And out of this period, this class, this "understanding," came the likes of Sojourner Truth and Harriet Tubman, two of the most well-known freedom fighters/resisters of slavocracy.

Sojourner Truth and Harriet Tubman stood tall and firm against slavery, and their lives were early answers to many of the current questions of feminism and antiracism. For them, there was never a lasting question concerning the role of women. They were mothers to us all. For them, there was never a lasting question concerning the role of African slaves in the United States. The slaves *must* resist! The slaves must rebuild in new images! Sojourner's and Harriet's understanding of peace, as exhibited by their roles in regard to the Civil War, was that lasting peace would be possible once all men and women enjoyed/shared equality and justice as human beings. While their ultimate goal was peace, they knew that it could come only after their people's liberation. Thus, their very lives serve to show us that many of the questions arising in the current white women's movement and the peace movement have long been addressed, although not necessarily answered in its final forms, within the African-American community. Perhaps a glance at some of the major questions that have confronted the African-American community would help to reaffirm and/or reject certain principles and tactics for those of us currently in that community and, at the same time, help to clarify some of the issues plaguing the other movements for change in this country.

Should African-Americans Unify and Resist Oppression?

Yes. When the survival of a people becomes synonymous with resistance, then there is little other choice. Further, when we objectively look at the history of the United States of America, we see that the survival of the African race within its boundaries has in and of itself been a form of resistance. Gerda Lerner stated in her book, *Black Women in White America,* "Over and over again, in their 350 years of history, Black people in White America have had to struggle for sheer survival. Not only physical and economic survival, but spiritual survival was at stake as generation after generation sought to come to terms with an implacably hostile and exploitative environment."[3] The statistics on lynchings, infant mortality, hunger, deteriorated housing, deliberate miseducation, imprisonment, police brutality, depression, alcohol, and other drugs within the African community in the United States support the understanding that African people have survived in the United States in spite of the intentions of the European population who settled and developed here. According to the information provided by such statistics, some would not expect the African population in the United States to flourish at all. In fact, the realities of black existence in the United States led numerous black leaders, including W.E.B. DuBois, Ida B. Wells, Mary Church Terrell, and Malcolm X, to consider petitioning the United Nations and charging the United States with genocide. That we have been able to grow and develop is a testimony to our determination and will to survive against all odds.

But resistance must go far beyond the state of mere survival. It must seek and implement concrete change. And in ebbs and flows the African-American community has stood up to resist openly and confront the system of oppression in the United States, making changes and moving forward inch by inch. The general condition of the community and the overall gains that have been made through the years as a result of community action have forced a basic understanding in the black community that absolutely nothing has been gained by Africans here without a struggle, without sacrifice, without commitment, without unity. Indeed, this history has proven that, as Frederick Douglass said, "Power concedes nothing without a demand."[4] And demands become meaningless without various forms of unity and a willingness to act.

Should the African-American Woman Participate in a Movement for Feminism?

From this question derives another: Should we separate from and/or be critical of our African-American men? How silly these questions seem to many activist African-American women who have not been tainted by the media perception and projection of what it means to be a "feminist"[5] in this country. How can we not be feminist? And, at the same time, how can we possibly separate from our fathers, our brothers, our lovers, our sons, our friends? We cannot struggle for just a *part* of us to be free. We must struggle for *all* of us to be free! Thus, our sense of feminism includes both the "self" and the whole in its consideration of changing the world.

History has given testimony to the fact that the majority of African-American women do not want to be a part of any movement that seeks to exclude African men. At the same time, our growing consciousness, through struggle, makes us more and more intolerable of sexist behavior. In simple terms, we do not want to be dominated—by anyone! Therefore, the conscious African woman recognizes that we must be critical of ourselves and our counterpart, the African man. The main item on our agenda, however, must be the telling of the black woman's stories and the changing of the black woman's condition because black women are the only ones with the ability and determination to do so. (This follows a historical logic: No dominated human being or group has been freed of the shackles of oppression until he/she/they took the initiative and mobilized the leadership needed to do so.)

The ruling power structure—white males—has a great deal to gain by a confusion among black men and women about what it means to be a feminist (in many of the same ways that the power elite benefits from confusing the majority white population about the goals of an antiracist movement in this country). There is no question that today's African woman in the United States, descendant of both queens and slaves, suffers tremendously by a permeating idea that gives men superiority over women and the European race superiority over the African one. There should also be no question that both the African male and the African female will benefit and move further toward justice when all of us can become feminist, in addition to being nationalist, and thus recognize the great strengths and contributions as well as rights of African women. Then, we will share, like Tubman and Turner, Walker and Sojourner, every aspect of our lives as each other's equals in struggle.

With African grandmothers facing the possibilities of a state hit squad serving public housing eviction notices (for example, Eleanor Bumpers in New York[6]) and unemployed African youth being fair game for restless, white males (for example, Bernard Goetz in New York[7]), today's African men and women in the United States can no more afford the luxury of arguing about who is "most oppressed" or "more equal" than could our slave ancestors. Black women must assume the responsibility of standing up for and promoting the rights of black women in the context of (not behind) fighting for the total liberation of the African nation in the United States.

The examples of the liberation struggles on the African continent have served to illustrate the role that women should and must play (and that men should and must accept) in a movement for the self-determination and freedom of a nation. For example, African leader Amilcar Cabral took a forward step in Guinea Bissau when, in 1965, his organization declared that women, who constituted more than 30 percent of the nation's population, must have equal rights and be encouraged to participate on the battlefront and in the leadership as equals to men. During that nation's fight for independence from colonial rule by Portugal, all able members of the population—male and female—were called upon to cook, clean, mend, produce, lead, and fight in the trenches for freedom.

The self-determination movement in Guinea Bissau was a revolution that promoted feminism in a very concrete way. The inclusion of a women's section as a fundamental part of the leadership within the independence movement in Guinea Bissau ensured that, at least for that time being, a feminist view and course of action would be presented simultaneously with the nationalist view and course of action. In the final analysis, the degree of the African male and female ability and willingness to recognize, support, and defend the rights and full participation of women in reordering an oppressive society has proven to be an important aspect of progress or regress within Africa. (The seemingly backwards steps regarding the role of women that some of the more progressive nations have taken since obtaining independence is something that should receive critical examination and offer vital lessons.)

What Role Does the "System" Play in the Antiracism, Antisexism, and Peace Movements in This Country?

To answer this question, we must settle upon some basic generalities. That so many covert activities have been launched by the government against people involved in movements for change—for example, the FBI versus the Black Panthers, the Socialist Workers party, and various peace groups—shows that the system has a vested interest in thwarting the antiracism, antisexism, and peace movements in this country.

Clearly, Harriet Tubman, who took up arms in her struggle for liberation, and Sojourner Truth, who used the platforms of this country to expose the plight of African people, understood that the bottom-line formula for ending the existing treatment of black people was the destruction of the system of slavocracy. Anything short of a total halt to slavery would represent a type of reform in which neither one of these freedom fighters was interested. This same analysis is applicable today.

Sexism and feminism, racism and racial equality, and war and peace cannot be defined or understood apart from an analysis of the very system of capitalism that has deliberately developed racism, sexism, and war to some of their most sophisticated forms in modern history. There cannot be any serious consideration of ending the evils of racism, sexism, and war without speaking of the termination of their root causes in the world systems of injustice.

An error that constantly plagues many of the movements for social change in the United States is the notion that sexism, racism, and war perpetuated worldwide by the United States can be ended in the United States without the destruction of capitalism. They cannot! Of course, this is not to say that we cannot or should not stand up tall for racial and sexual justice and peace prior to an end to capitalism. In fact, standing up is a part of the process of organizing, educating, agitating, and learning so that some real challenges to capitalism can be made. Fighting for reforms is an important tactic in the overall strategy for complete change—that is, for a more democratic and humane society.

Concerned (conscious) people can and must struggle against racism in the United States (and abroad, for that matter). Racism is one of the most evil and destructive institutions in the world. But the bottom line is that racism is as American as are apple pie and hot dogs. Witness the 1984 and 1988 Democratic party primaries and nominating conventions and the national elections in which Ronald Reagan and George Bush were chosen overwhelmingly by racism in this country. Movements can force reforms out of the system (see the civil rights movement), but there will be no end to racism without an end to capitalism because racism is systemic.

Likewise, people can and must struggle against sexism, but here again history has proven that those in power never give up that power until they are forced to do so. And this "power struggle" includes the fight against male domination and male privilege in significant areas within society. Although it is true that white males in the United States might make a few concessions (if they are given an offer they can't refuse!), and although they might even encourage women to put on suits and ties or hard hats if the conditions are ripe (as during World War II), these concessions have always been granted in such a manner so as to allow for their reversal when the pressures are lessened. In short, sexism cannot be eliminated in the United States without a total social rearrangement of the United States, including an end to patriarchal society. Sexism, too, is systemic.

What About Peace?

There is (or should be) absolutely no doubt that we must all be against the current military and nuclear buildup (with ultimate possibilities of nuclear war), and we must stand firm against national wars of aggression. In particular, the African-American community must recognize the necessity of standing up against the U.S. war machine and wars of aggression against other nations because the disproportionate numbers of black soldiers dying on the front lines in Vietnam, the funding of terrorism in Nicaragua, and the strategic U.S. affiliations with South Africa have helped us to see that peace is inextricably interwoven with racial justice at home and abroad.

The question then becomes why haven't more African-American people gotten involved in the antinuke and peace movements in this country? Perhaps the average African-American person does not have the time to worry about the dangers of nuclear war when the mere survival of the African race in the United States is an issue; in too many instances black men, women, and children can be killed at any point, in any place in these United States by either civilians or those in uniforms without the murderer even spending a night in jail, much less facing the possibility of spending life in prison (as was the case with the murderers of Medgar Evers, Emmet Till,[8] Eleanor Bumpers, and Michael Stewart,[9] to name a few); when the infant mortality rate in the black community is twice that of the rest of the nation; when 70 percent of black youth cannot find jobs; when 80 percent of the urban prison population is Black and Latino as compared to a less than 20 percent black U.S. population; when 70 percent of black youth drop out of high school prior to obtaining a high school diploma. These statistics don't begin to touch the day-to-day crisis/struggle for decent food, clothing, and shelter that makes peace important, on the one hand, but not a priority, on the other.

At the same time, however, African-American activists with consciousness recognize that war in recent years has hurt African, Asian, and Latin nations disproportionately to those whose inheritance is European, to say nothing of the fact that these wars have been fought to maintain the comfort and privilege of the world capitalist class and to prevent the self-determination of peoples in the resource-rich areas of Africa, Asia, and Latin America. Therefore, African-Americans have been and must be on the front line to stop U.S. aggression in the world. Support for the liberation struggles of Vietnam, South Africa, Angola, Guinea Bissau, and Zimbabwe is outstanding evidence of the internationalism of African-Americans.

Finally, there appears to be a double-edged sword when it comes to addressing the question of peace in a world situation that has provided African people worldwide with little choice except war for liberation. How can a "peace" movement honestly support, with integrity, those international movements that use war as a method of obtaining self-determination (self-rule)? Although many people are involved in the antinuke and peace movements as a matter of moral consciousness, they must understand that there is a difference, as Frederic Douglass so eloquently stated, between the slave master who is whipping his slave and the slave who snatches the whip from the master and commences to whip the master.

In most instances, the peoples of Africa, Asia, and Latin America attempted peaceful means—petitions, demonstrations, sit-ins—to obtain independence and control of their own destinies; but following peaceful attempt after attempt, and wanton murder of many of those who dared to stand up, they were forced to resort to armed struggle against domination. Therefore, the peace and antinuke movements are challenged with the responsibility of obstructing U.S. aggression against these nations while at the same time giving support to the legitimate rights of all the nations of the world to enjoy the rights and privileges of self-determination. The peace movement should never expect reciprocal laying down of arms by master and slave. *True* peace can only come at a point when nations no longer seek to dominate nations and when humans with blue eyes no longer seek to enslave humans with brown and/or black eyes. War and aggression, like racism and sexism, are systemic.

Because there are so many lessons to be learned from recent as well as past history, women in general and in the African-American community in particular must recognize and analyze what has been one of the greatest *movements* for antiracism, feminism, and peace in the recent history of this country—the 1984 and 1988 movements to have Reverend Jesse Jackson selected as the presidential candidate for the Democratic party. Jesse Jackson was the only candidate who had not just given lip service to the Equal Rights Amendment but actually developed a position paper expressing the need for equality of women and men in the United States. He was the only candidate who initially declared that he would select a female as a running mate for the vice-presidential seat (indeed, the movement for Jesse Jackson and his outspoken views on the rights and role of women forced the Democratic party in 1984 to select Geraldine Ferraro as the first female vice-presidential candidate in the United States). He was the *only* real peace candidate, advocating the total withdrawal of U.S. troops from Latin America and the rights of struggling people in Africa, Latin America, and Asia to have self-determination. He was the only candidate who suggested and stood for unity among all oppressed people in the United States—the people of the rainbow. The attention and articulation that he paid to poor and suffering people—black and white—were outstanding.

Clearly, the movement around Jesse Jackson was one that actually rocked the state. What started out as a joke for the rulers of the United

States actually became a concern as this movement for jobs, peace, and equality gathered momentum and the possibility of actual nomination. This movement was enough of a threat to require that every form of dirty journalism and smear tactics, including those that would stir up the great clouds of racism, be used to see that this man/this movement got stopped. Unfortunately, a number of the white liberals and progressives let themselves be easily turned around by this media operation, which has proven through history to be willing to distort time, place, and conditions in order to sway public opinion. In short, the movement for Jesse Jackson lost primarily because those folk who should have known better fell for the tricks of the capitalist-controlled media. And, worse, progress lost because racism reared its ugly head once again to keep white people, including the white women's feminist movement, from being supportive of this movement in a way that would have been a real statement to the power brokers of this country. If only the white majority, especially the white liberals and progressives, had dared join hands with the black community and nominated Jesse Jackson president, we might now be charting a less racist and sexist future for the United States.

In the final analysis, those women who define themselves as feminist *and* African nationalist must learn from recent and past history in order to better determine our future as women and as African people. We must be clear about who our friends are and who our enemies are so that we can develop viable tactics for changing the condition of all African peoples. Those women who are white and define themselves as feminist must consciously and actively divorce themselves from the privileges afforded them as a result of racism so that we all might have a better chance at a unity that would actually challenge white male privilege and its *system* of thought and action (patriarchal monopoly capitalism). In the words of a sister, freedom fighter Assata Shakur: "It is our duty to fight for our freedom. It is our duty to win. We must love each other and support each other. We have nothing to lose but our chains!"[10]

Notes

1. All of the She-made Gods who look like me.
2. White, ruling male and all of the He-made Gods who look like him.
3. Gerda Lerner, *Black Women in White America* (New York: Vintage Books, 1973), p. 287.
4. Frederick Douglass, "If There Is no Struggle, There Is no Progress," in Philip Foner, ed., *The Voice of Black America* (New York: Simon & Schuster, 1972), pp. 197–203.

5. A feminist is an activist on behalf of women's rights and interests. Feminism is the theory of the political, economic, and social equality of the sexes.

6. Eleanor Bumpers was a sixty-seven-year-old black grandmother residing in New York City who was shot to death by white New York City Housing police when she resisted eviction for nonpayment of one month's back rent. The police claimed that they were justified in killing her because she came at them with a knife as they were breaking down her door. The police shot two bullets into Ms. Bumpers's body. The first one shot off a part of the hand they claimed was holding the knife; the second one killed her. The police officer responsible was cleared of all charges.

7. Bernard Goetz, a white man, was acquitted of attempted murder charges and given a light sentence for illegal gun possession after he shot four black youth who, he claimed, looked as if they were planning to rob him when one of them asked him for a dollar. One boy, who was shot in the back, is paralyzed from the neck down. Witnesses stated that he did not say anything to Goetz.

8. Emmet Till was a fourteen-year-old Chicago school boy who was viciously murdered while he was spending his summer vacation with his great uncle in Mississippi. He was seized from his great uncle's house by a group of white men appearing in the middle of the night. They later testified in court that he had whistled at a white woman in a country store. Emmet Till's body was found brutally beaten, shot through the head, and tied to an iron cotton-gin wheel at the bottom of the Tallahatchie River. The two white men accused of abducting the boy were acquitted in a brief trial—at which the black press was kept segregated.

9. Michael Stewart was an unarmed young black artist who was beaten and choked to death while in police custody in New York City. Despite community protests, none of the eleven police officers involved has been convicted of his murder.

10. Assata Shakur, *From Somewhere in the Whirlwind* (pamphlet).

THREE

A Gender Diary

ANN SNITOW

What is this book about? Why a *women's* peace movement? Is peace a women's issue, more than other people's? Do women have a special relationship to peace, and if so, where does that relationship come from? Political history? Biology?

Some peace activists have argued that these questions don't much matter. For whatever reasons—and no doubt for many different ones—women keep initiating women-only peace actions. Since such women-only groups are an authentic political form with an eventful history, it may seem perverse to ask whether women *should* be drawn into them. Isn't it mean-spirited to complain about commitment?

Nonetheless, a number of feminists, myself included, felt uneasy about the new wave of women-only peace groups of the early 1980s. As feminist peace activist Ynestra King characterized the new spirit: "A feminist peace sensibility is forming; it includes new women's culture and traditional women's culture."[1] Some saw such a fusion between traditional female solidarity and new women's forms of protest as particularly powerful. Others felt that the two were at cross-purposes. Might blurring them actually lead to a watering down of feminism?[2] The idea that women are by definition more nurturant, life giving, and less belligerent than men is very old; the idea that such gender distinctions are social, hence subject to change, is much more recent, fragile, counterintuitive, and contested. Can the old idea of female specialness and the newer idea of a female outlook forged in social oppression join in a movement? And just how?

The book you are holding began in a study group that met for a time in 1983 to talk about women's peace politics. I was the irritating one in our group, always anxious about the nature of our project. I was the one who always nagged, "Why a women's *peace movement?"*

35

I argued with a patient Amy Swerdlow that women asking men to protect the children (as Women Strike for Peace asked Congress in 1961) was a repetition of an old, impotent, suppliant's gesture. Men had waged wars in the name of just such protection. And besides, did we want a world where only women worried about the children?[3] "So what's your solution?" the good-tempered group wanted to know. "Should women stop worrying about the children? Who trusts men to fill the gap?" Amy described how the loving women, going off to Washington to protest against nuclear testing, filled their suburban freezers with dinners so their families would miss them less.

Don't think I couldn't grasp that this nurturance was an assertion of the values of daily life meant to confront the culture of war. The women enacted an exaggerated Nurturant Mother in order to draw attention to its usually invisible counterpart, a Deadly Dad. With Women Strike for Peace, gender entered the committee room, where issues of gender certainly belong.

But I was one of the daughters of those mothers presenting that outsiders' piece of performance art, "Mothers Save the Planet for Their Children." I loved them for their love and—with all the stupid injustice of the young— resented them for their impotence. Were we, too, to have no public voice? I gave the group examples of how terrifying this had felt to me as a child, offering such overheated images as Claudia Koonz's description of the hysterical gender consciousness of the Nazis. Even moments before killing their prisoners, the Nazis instructed them, "Men to the right, women to the left."[4] I tried to explain the source of my resistance to the motherly rhetoric of the women's peace movement. During the 1960s, some of us had angrily offered to poison men's private peace, abort men's children. We proposed a bad girl's exchange: We'd give up protection for freedom, give up the approval we got for nurturance in exchange for the energy we'd get from open anger.

Of course, I knew what the group would ask me next, and rightly, too: "Whose freedom? Which rage? Isn't abandoning men's project of war rage enough? And is women's powerlessness really mother's fault?" Although I reminded the group that the new wave of feminists never blamed motherhood as much as the media claimed, we did run from it, like the young who scrawled the slogan on Paris walls in 1968: "Cours, comarade, le vieux monde est derrière toi." (Run, comrades, the past is just behind you.)

I was one of these poison daughters, and the group—full of mothers who had seen fractious children before—was tolerant, willing to entertain the daughters' rejection of the lives of the mothers.

This scene is caricature, but it begins to get at the mood of our group. When Rhoda Linton described how women planted rose bushes *inside* the barbed wire fences of military bases, I understood the elegance of this mixture of militant civil disobedience with love for the still-flowering earth.[5] I could read the symbolism of these acts—the white-gloved mothers in Washington, the daring, fence-climbing planters of vines and fig trees at the Seneca peace encampment—but this recognition of the expressive languages of women's peace politics didn't make that language mine.

I asked the members of the group how *they* proposed to end the organization of social life along gender lines. Didn't they think women's work must be done by men, too? If there is to be no more "women-only" when it comes to emotional generosity or trips to the laundry, there should certainly be no more "women-only" when it comes to the peace movement. Didn't they agree that peace is assumed to be a women's issue for all the wrong reasons? Maybe the most radical thing we could do would be to refuse the ancient women-peace connection. Because the army is a dense locale of male symbols, actions, and forms of association, let men sit in the drizzle with us at the gates of military installations. Let men join us in worrying about the children for a change. And so it went.

Until one day Ynestra King tactfully suggested that perhaps I was seeking a mixed group to do my peace activism. (Mixed is a code word for men and women working together.) I was horrified. We were laughing, I'm pleased to recall, as I confessed myself reluctant to do political work in mixed groups. The cliches about women in the male Left making the coffee and doing the xeroxing were all literally true in my case. (I blame myself as well; often I chose those tasks, afraid of others.) Only by working with women had I managed to develop an intense and active relationship to politics at all. Not only had my political identity been forged in the women only mold, but the rich networks I had formed inside feminism were the daily source of continued activism. Women-only (the abstraction, the childhood memory) was full of problems; women-only (the political reality in my life) was full of fascination, social pleasure, debates about meaning in the midst of actions taken, even sometimes, victories won.

On its face this clash of theoretical and practical positions may seem absurd, but it is my goal to explore such contradictions, to show why they are not absurd at all. Feminism is inevitably a mixed form, requiring by its very nature such inconsistencies. In what follows I try to show, first, that a common divide keeps forming in both feminist thought and action between the need to build the identity "woman" and give it solid political meaning and the need to tear down the very category woman and dismantle its all too solid history. Feminists often split along the lines of some version of this argument, and that splitting is my subject. Second, I argue that although a settled compromise between these positions is currently impossible, and although a constant choosing of sides is tactically unavoidable, feminists—and indeed most women—live in a complex relationship to this central feminist divide. From moment to moment, we perform subtle psychological and social negotiations about just how gendered we choose to be.

This tension—between needing to act as women and needing an identity not overdetermined by our gender—is as old as Western feminism. It is at the core of what feminism is. The divide runs, twisting and turning, right through movement history. The problem of identity it poses was barely conceivable before the eighteenth century, when almost everyone saw women as a separate species. Since then absolute definitions of gender difference have fundamentally eroded, and the idea "woman" has become a question rather than a given.

In the current wave of the movement, the divide is more urgent and central a part of feminism than ever before. On the one hand, many women moved by feminism are engaged by its promise of solidarity, the poetry of a retrieved worth. It feels glorious to "reclaim an identity they taught [us] to despise." (The line is Michelle Cliff's.) Movement passion rescues woman-only groups from contempt; female intimacy acquires new meanings and becomes more threatening to the male exclusiveness so long considered "the world."

But other feminists, often equally stirred by solidarity, rebel against having to be "women" at all. They argue that whenever we uncritically accept the monolith woman, we run the risk of merely relocating ourselves inside the old closed ring of an unchanging feminine nature. It may be a pleasure to be "we," and it may be strategically imperative to struggle as "we," but who, they ask, are "we"?[6]

Even if theorists emphasize the contingent and the historical and say, for example, that peace is an issue that affects women *differently* from men because of our different social position, we're trapped again in an inevitably oversimplified idea of "women." Are *all* women affected the same way by war? Or is class or age or race or nationality as important a variable? What do we gain, this second group of feminists wonders, when we name the way we suffer from war as a specifically *women's* suffering?

The political meaning of these sides changes, as does the place they hold in each woman's life. But no matter where each feminist finds herself in the argument about the meaning of women-only, all agree that in practical political work, separate women's groups are entirely necessary. Whatever the issue, feminists have gained a great deal by saying, "We are 'women,' and this is what 'women' want." This belief in some ground of shared experience is the social basis from which any sustained political struggle must come.

Even feminists like myself, anxious about any restatement of a female ideal—of peacefulness or nurturance or light—are constantly forced in practice to consider what activists lose if we choose to say peace is *not* a women's issue. We keep rediscovering the necessity to speak specifically as women when we speak of peace because the female citizen has almost no representation in the places where decisions about war and peace are made—the Congress, the corporation, the army.

For example, in 1979, President Jimmy Carter fired former congress-woman Bella Abzug from her special position as co-chair of his National Advisory Commission for Women because the women on the commission insisted on using that platform to talk about war and the economy. These, said the president, were not women's issues; women's role was to support the president. Carter was saying in effect that women have no place in general social debate, that women, as we learned from the subsequent presidential campaign, are a "special interest group."

What a conundrum for feminists: Because women have little general representation in Congress, our demand to be citizens—gender un-specified—can be made only through gender solidarity; but when we declare ourselves separate, succeed, for example, in getting our own government commission, the president turns around and tries to make that power base into a ghetto where only certain stereotypically female issues can be named. So, however separate *we* may choose to be, our "separate" has to be different from his "separate," a distinction it's hard to keep clear in our own and other minds, but one we must keep trying to make.

This case may seem beside the point to radicals who never vested any hope in the federal government in the first place. But the firing of Bella Abzug was a perfect public embodiment of the puzzle of women's situation. The idea that "women" can speak about war is itself the unsettled question, requiring constant public tests. It is no coincidence that Bella Abzug was one of the organizers of Women Strike for Peace in 1961. She must have observed the strengths and weaknesses in the public image of mothers for peace; then, on the coattails of feminism, she tried to be an insider, a congresswoman presumably empowered to speak—as a woman, or for women, or for herself—on any public topic. People with social memory were able to witness the problem that arises for the public woman, no matter *what* her stance. Feminism is potentially radical in almost all its guises precisely because it interprets this injustice, makes the Abzug impasse visible. Once visible, it begins to feel in-tolerable.[7]

By traveling along the twisting track of this argument, I have made what I think is a representative journey, what feminist historians such as Joan Kelly-Gadol and Denise Riley have called an "oscillation," which is typical of both feminist theory and practice.[8] Such oscillations are inevitable for the foreseeable future. In a cruel irony that is one mark of women's oppression, when women speak *as women* they run a special risk of not being heard because the female voice is by our culture's definition that-voice-you-can-ignore. But the alternative is to pretend that public men speak for women or that women who speak inside male-female forums are heard and heeded as much as similarly placed men. Few women feel satisfied that this neutral (almost always male) public voice reflects the particulars of women's experience, however varied and indeterminate that experience may be.

Caught between not being heard because we are different and not being heard because we are invisible, feminists face a necessary strategic leap of nerve every time we shape a political action. We weigh the kinds of powerlessness women habitually face; we choose our strategy—as women, as citizens—always sacrificing some part of what we know.

Because "separate" keeps changing its meaning depending on how it is achieved and in what larger context its political forms unfold, there is no fixed progressive position, no final theoretical or practical resting place for feminists attempting to find a social voice for women. Often our special womanness turns into a narrow space only a moment after we celebrate it; at other times, our difference becomes a refuge and source of new work, just when it looked most like a prison in which we are powerless. And finally, although women differ fundamentally about the meaning and value of "woman," we all live partly in, partly out of this identity by social necessity. Or as Denise Riley puts it, "Women are not women in all aspects of their lives."[9]

Peace is *not* a women's issue; at the same time, if women don't claim a special relationship to general political struggles, we will experience that other, more common specialness reserved for those named women: We will be excluded from talking about and acting on the life and death questions that face our species.

Names for a Recurring Feminist Divide

In every case, the specialness of women has this double face, although often, in the heat of new confrontations, feminists suffer a harmful amnesia; we forget all about this paradox we live with. Feminist theorists keep renaming this tension, as if new names could advance feminist political work. But at this point new names are likely to tempt us to forget that we have named this split before. In the service of trying to help us recognize what we are fated, for some time, to repeat, here's a reminder of past taxonomies.

MINIMIZERS AND MAXIMIZERS

The divide so central as to be feminism's defining characteristic goes by many names. Kate Stimpson cleverly calls it the feminist debate between the "minimizers" and the "maximizers."[10] Briefly, the minimizers are the feminists who want to undermine the category "woman," to minimize the meaning of sex difference. (As we shall see this stance can have surprisingly different political faces.) The maximizers want to keep the category (or feel they can't do otherwise), but they want to change its meaning, to reclaim and further elaborate the social being woman, and to empower her.

RADICAL FEMINISTS AND CULTURAL FEMINISTS

In *Daring to Be Bad: A History of the Radical Feminist Movement in America, 1967–1975,* Alice Echols sees this divide on a timeline of the current women's movement with "radical feminism" more typical of the initial feminist impulse in this wave, succeeded by "cultural feminism." Echols's definition of the initial burst of radical feminism shows that it also included cultural feminism in embryo. She argues that both strains were present from the first—contradictory elements that soon proclaimed themselves as tensions in sisterhood. Nonetheless, the earlier groups usually defined the commonality of women as the shared fact of their oppression by men. Women were to work separately from men not as a structural ideal but because such separation was necessary to escape a domination that only a specifically feminist (rather than mixed, Left) politics could change. Echols gives as an example Kathie Sarachild, who disliked the women's contingents at peace marches against the Vietnam War: "Only if the *stated* purpose of a women's group is to fight *against* the relegation of women to a separate position and status, in other words, to fight for women's liberation, only then does a separate women's group acquire a revolutionary character. Then separation becomes a base for power rather than a symbol of powerlessness."[11]

On the other side stands Echols's category "cultural feminism." In Echols's depiction of the divide, the cultural feminist celebration of being female was a retreat from radical feminism: "It was easier to rehabilitate femininity than to abolish gender."[12] She offers as a prime example of the growth of cultural feminism the popularity of Jane Alpert's "new feminist theory," published in *Ms* magazine in 1973 as "Mother Right":

Feminists have asserted that the essential difference between women and men does not lie in biology but rather in the roles that patriarchal societies (men) have required each sex to play. . . . However, a flaw in this feminist argument has persisted: *it contradicts our felt experience of*

the biological difference between the sexes as one of immense significance.
. . . The unique consciousness or sensibility of women, the particular
attributes that set feminist art apart, and a compelling line of research
now being pursued by feminist anthropologists all point to the idea
that *female biology is the basis of women's powers.* Biology is hence the
source and not the enemy of feminist revolution.[13]

Echols concludes that by 1973, "Alpert's contention that women were
united by their common biology was enormously tempting given the
factionalism within the movement."[14]

Ironically, then, the pressure of differences that quickly surfaced in
the women's movement between lesbians and straight women, between
white and black, between classes, was a key source of the new pressure
toward unity: The female body offered a permanence and an immediately
rich identity that radical feminism, with its call to a long, often negative
struggle of resistance, could not.

As her tone reveals, in Echols's account, radical feminism is a relatively
positive term, cultural feminism an almost entirely negative one. As I'll
explain later, I have a number of reasons for sharing this judgment.
Finally, however, it won't help us to understand recurring feminist
oppositions if we simply sort them into progressive versus reactionary
alignments. The divide is nothing so simple as a split between truly
radical activists and benighted conservative ones; or between real agents
for change and liberal reformers; or between practical fighters and
sophisticated theorists. The sides in this debate don't line up neatly in
these ways at all. Maximizers and minimizers have political histories
that converge and diverge. Nonetheless, a pretense at neutrality won't
get us anywhere either. I'm describing a struggle, and every account of
it contains its overt or covert tropism toward one side or the other.

ESSENTIALISTS AND SOCIAL CONSTRUCTIONISTS

We have only to move from an account of movement politics to one
of feminist theory to reverse Echols's scenario of decline. In academic
feminist discussion, the divide between the essentialists and the social
constructionists has been a rout for the essentialists. Briefly, essentialists
(such as Alpert) see gender as rooted in biological sex differences. Hardly
anyone of any camp will now admit to being an essentialist because
the term has become associated with a naive claim to an eternal female
nature. All the same, essentialism, like its counterpart cultural feminism,
is abundantly present in current movement work. When Barbara Deming
writes, "The capacity to bear and nurture children gives women a special
consciousness, a spiritual advantage rather than a disadvantage," she is
assigning an enduring meaning to anatomical sex differences. When

Andrea Dworkin describes how through sex a woman's "insides are worn away over time, and she, possessed, becomes weak, depleted, usurped in all her physical and mental energies . . . by the one who occupies her," she is asserting that in sex women are immolated as a matter of course, in the nature of things.[15]

Social construction—the idea that the meaning of the body is changeable—is far harder to embrace with confidence. As Ellen Willis once put it, culture may shape the body, but we feel that the body has ways of pushing back.[16] To assert that the body has no enduring, natural language often seems like a rejection of common sense. Where can a woman stand—embodied or disembodied—in the flow of this argument?

Writing not about gender in general but about that more focused issue of bodies and essences, sexuality, Carole Vance has raised questions about the strengths and vicissitudes of social construction theory. She observes that the social constructionists who try to discuss sexuality differ about what is constructed. Few would go so far as to say that the body plays no part at all as a material condition on which we build desire and sexual mores. But even for those social constructionists who try to escape entirely from any a priori ideas about the body, essentialism makes a sly comeback through unexamined assumptions. For example, how can social constructionists confidently say they are studying "sexuality"? If there is no essential, transhistorical biology of arousal, then there is no unitary subject, sexuality, to discuss: "If sexuality is constructed differently at each time and place, can we use the term in a comparatively meaningful way? . . . Have constructionists undermined their own categories? Is there an 'it' to study?"[17]

The same question comes up—often in a less self-conscious way—in discussions of gender. Feminists differ widely about the role of biology in determining what men and women are like. For example, does the idea that gender is socially constructed undermine the assumptions of feminist peace politics? Certainly, yes, when activists base their work on biological claims of female superiority. But many feminist peace activists respond adroitly to the questions raised by social construction by arguing that women's particular history and social role rather than their essentially more pacific nature are what make their peace activism special. Often, however, there is slippage between these two groups. The feminist peace movement, with its ethic of tolerance, is one of the few political communities in which social constructionists and essentialists coexist without much wrangling or noise. As Rhoda Linton once put it, "There's plenty of good work they can do together."

In the essentialist-versus-social constructionist version of the divide, we can see that one term in the argument is far more stable than the other. Essentialism, such as Jane Alpert's in "Mother Right," assumes a relatively stable social identity in "male" and "female," while, as Carole Vance argues, social construction is at its best as a source of destabilizing questions. By definition, social construction theory cannot offer a securely bounded area for the study of gender; instead it initiates an inspiring collapse of gender verities.

CULTURAL FEMINISTS AND POSTSTRUCTURALISTS

The contrast between more and less stable categories suggests yet another recent vocabulary for the feminist divide. In "Cultural Feminism Versus Post-Structuralism: The Identity Crisis in Feminist Theory," Linda Alcoff puts Echols's definition of cultural feminism up against what she sees as a more recent counterdevelopment: feminist poststructural theory. By speaking only of "the last ten years," Alcoff lops off the phase of radical feminism that preceded cultural feminism in movement history, thereby leaving the revisionist image of extreme essentialism (such as Mary Daly's in *Gyn/Ecology*) as the basic matrix of feminist thought from which a radical "nominalism" has more recently and heroically departed, calling all categories into doubt.[18] It is no accident that with attention to detail, Alice Echols can trace a political decline from radical feminism to cultural feminism between 1967 and 1975, while Linda Alcoff can persuasively trace a gain in theoretical understanding from cultural feminism to poststructuralism between 1978 and 1988. Put them together and both narratives change: Instead of collapse or progress, we see one typical oscillation in the historical life of the divide.

These two accounts are also at odds because they survey very different political locations: Echols is writing about radical feminist activism, Alcoff about developments in academic feminist theory. Although political activism has developed a different version of the central debate from that of the more recent academic feminism, both confront the multiple problems posed by the divide. Nor will a model work that goes like this: *thesis* (essentialism, cultural feminism), *antithesis* (poststructuralism, deconstruction, Lacanian psychoanalysis), *synthesis* (some stable amalgam of women's solidarity that includes radical doubts about the formation, cohesion, and potential power of the group).

Instead, the divide keeps forming *inside* each of these categories. It is fundamental at any level we care to meet it: material, psychological, linguistic. For example, U.S. feminist theorists don't agree about whether poststructuralism tends more often toward its own version of essentialism (strengthening the arguments of maximizers by recognizing an enduring position of female Other) or whether poststructuralism is instead the best tool minimalists have (weakening any totalizing, permanent concept such as "woman.")[19] Certainly, poststructuralists disagree among themselves, and this debate around and inside poststructuralism should be no surprise. In feminist discourse, a tension keeps forming between finding a useful lever in female identity and seeing that identity as hopelessly compromised, unavoidably inert.

I'm not regressing here to the good old days of an undifferentiated, undertheorized sisterhood, trying to blur distinctions others have usefully struggled to establish, but I do want to explore a configuration—the divide—that repeats in very different circumstances. For example, in an earlier oscillation both radical feminism and liberal feminism offered their own versions of doubt about cultural feminism and essentialism. Liberal feminists refused the idea that biology should structure women's public and sometimes even their private roles. Radical feminists saw the creation and maintenance of gender difference as the means by which patriarchs controlled women.[20] Although neither group had the powerful theoretical tools later developed by the poststructuralists, both intimated basic elements in poststructuralist work: that the category woman was a construction, a discourse about which there had been an ongoing struggle; and that the self, the "subject," was as much the issue as were social institutions. To be sure, these early activists often foolishly ignored Freud; they invoked an unproblematic self that could be rescued from the dark male tower of oppression; and they expected the radical deconstruction of gender hourly, as if the deconstruction of what had been constructed was relatively easy. Nonetheless, radical, philosophical doubts about the cohesion of woman have roots that go all the way down in the history of both liberal and radical feminism.

Recently I asked feminist critic Marianne DeKoven for a piece she and Linda Bamber wrote about the divide for the Modern Language Association in 1982. "Feminists have refined our thinking a great deal since then," she said. Yes, no doubt; but there is not much from the recent past that we can confidently discard. In fact, the Bamber/DeKoven depiction of the divide remains useful because we are nowhere near a synthesis that would make these positions relics of a completed phase. One side of the divide, Bamber says in her half of the paper, "has been loosely identified with American feminism, the other with French feminism."

But in fact these labels are inadequate, as both responses can be found in the work of both French and American feminists. Instead of debating French vs. American feminism, then, I want to define the two poles of our responses nonjudgmentally and simply list their characteristics under Column A and Column B.

Column A feminism is political, empirical, historical. A Column A feminist rebels against the marginalization of women and demands access to "positions that require knowledge and confer power." A Column A feminist insists on woman as subject, on equal pay for equal work, on the necessity for women to be better represented in political life, the media, history books, etc. Column A feminism assumes, as Marks and de Courtivron put it, "that women have (always) been present but invisible and if they look they will find themselves."

The Column B feminist, on the other hand, is not particularly interested in the woman as subject. Instead of claiming power, knowledge and high culture for women, Column B feminism attacks these privileged quantities as "phallogocentric." In Column B the feminine is valorized not as a subjectivity equal to masculine subjectivity but in metonymic association with "what . . . has been left out of Western Thinking/Writing." The feminine in Column B is part of the challenge to God, money, the phallus, origins and ends, philosophical privilege, the transcendent author, representation, the Descartian cogito, transparent language, and so on. . . . Whereas the Column A feminist means to occupy the center on equal terms with men, the Column B feminist, sometimes aided by Derrida, Lacan, Althusser, Levi-Strauss and Foucault, subverts the center and endorses her own marginalilty.[21]

No doubt Bamber and DeKoven would restate these terms now in the light of seven more years of good, collective feminist work, but I am trying to write against the grain of that usually excellent impulse here, trying to suggest a more distant perspective in which seven years become a dot.

Alcoff is only the latest in a long line of frustrated feminists who want to push beyond the divide, to be done with it. She writes typically, "We cannot simply embrace the paradox. In order to avoid the serious disadvantages of cultural feminism and post-structuralism, feminism needs to transcend the dilemma by developing a third course."[22] But "embracing the paradox" is just what feminism cannot choose but do. There is no transcendence, no third course. The urgent contradiction women constantly experience between the pressure to be a woman and the pressure not to be one will change only through a historical process; it cannot be dissolved through thought alone. This is not to undervalue theory in the name of some more solid material reality but to emphasize that the dualism of the divide requires constant work; it resists us. It's not that we can't interrupt current patterns or that trying to imagine our way beyond them isn't valuable, but that such work is continual.[23]

What is more, activists trying to make fundamental changes, trying to push forward the feminist discourse and alter its material context, don't agree about what sort of synthesis they want. Nor can activists turn to theorists in any direct way for a resolution of these differences. Activism and scholarship have called forth different readings of the divide, but neither of these locations remains innocent of the primary contradiction. There is no marriage of theoretical mind and activist brawn to give us New Feminist Woman. The recognition that binary thinking is a problem doesn't offer us any immediate solution.

In other words, neither cultural feminism nor poststructuralism suggests a clear course when the time comes around to discuss political strategy. Although we have learned much, we are still faced with the continuing strategic difficulty of *what to do*. As Michèle Barrett puts it, "It does not need remarking that the postmodernist point of view is explicitly hostile to any political project beyond the ephemeral."[24] The virtue of the ephemeral action is its way of evading ossification of image or meaning. Ephemerally, we can recognize a possibility we cannot live out, imagine a journey we cannot yet take. We begin: The category woman is a fiction; then, poststructuralism suggests ways in which human beings live by fictions; then, in its turn, activism requires of feminists that we elaborate the fiction woman as if she were not a provisional invention at all but a person we know well, one in need of obvious rights and powers. Activism and theory weave together here, working on what remains the same basic cloth, the stuff of feminism.

Some theorists, such as Alcoff, reach for a synthesis, a third way, beyond the divide, while others, such as Bamber and DeKoven, choose instead the metaphor of an inescapable, irreducible "doubleness"—a word that crops up everywhere in feminist discussion. To me, the metaphor of doubleness is the more useful; it is a reminder of the unresolved tension on which feminism continues to be built. Alice Walker evokes this state of mind in her definition of "womanist" (her word for a black feminist): "Appreciates and prefers women's culture, women's emotional flexibility. . . . Committed to survival and wholeness of entire people, male and female. Not a separatist, except periodically, for health."[25]

This is not to deny change, but to give a different estimate of its rate. Mass feminist consciousness has made a great difference; we have created not only new expectations but also new institutions. Yet, inevitably, the optimism of activism has given way to the academic second thoughts that tell us why our work is so hard. For, indeed, even straightforward, liberal changes—equal pay, day care—are proving far more elusive than feminists dreamed in 1970. We are moving more slowly than Western women of the late twentieth century can easily accept—or are even likely to imagine.

MOTHERISTS AND FEMINISTS

If the long view has a virtue beyond the questionable one of inducing calm, it can help feminists include women to whom a rapid political or theoretical movement forward has usually seemed beside the point—poor women, peasant women, and women who for any number of reasons identify themselves not as feminists but as militant mothers, fighting together for survival. In a study group convened by Temma Kaplan since 1985, Grass-Roots Movements of Women, feminists who do research about such movements in different parts of the world, past and present, have been meeting to discuss the relationship among revolutionary action, women, and feminist political consciousness.[26] As Meredith Tax describes this activism:

> There is a crux in women's history/women's studies, a knot and a blurry place where various things converge. This place has no name and there is no established methodology for studying it. The things that converge there are variously called: community organizations, working-class women's organizations, consumer movements, popular mass organizations, housewives' organizations, mothers' movements, strike support movements, bread strikes, revolutions at the base, women's peace movements. Some feminist or proto-feminist groups and united front organizations of women may be part of this crux. Or they may be different. There is very little theory, either feminist or Marxist, regarding this crux.[27]

The group has been asking, In what class circumstances do women decide to band together as women, break out of domestic space, and publically protest? What part have these actions actually played in gaining fundamental political changes? How do women define what they have done and why? Does it make any sense to name feminist thinking as part of this female solidarity? Is there reason to think some kind of feminist consciousness is likely to emerge from this kind of political experience? Is the general marginality of these groups a strength or a weakness?

Almost all the women we have been studying present themselves to the world as mothers (hence, motherists) acting for the survival of their children. Their groups almost always arise when men are forced to be absent (because they are migrant workers or soldiers) or in times of crisis, when the role of nurturance assigned to women has been rendered impossible. Faced with the imperatives of their traditional work (to feed the children, to keep the family together) and with the loss of bread, or mobility, or whatever they need to do that work, women can turn into a militant force, breaking the shop windows of the baker or the butcher, burning the pass cards, assembling to confront the police state, sitting in where normally they would never go—on the steps of the governor's house, at the gates of the cruise missile base.

As feminists, it interested us to speculate about whether the women in these groups felt any kind of criticism of the social role of mother itself, or of the structural ghettoization of women, or of the sexism that greets women's political efforts. As Marysa Navarro said of the women she studies, the Mothers of the Plaza de Mayo, who march to make the Argentine government give them news of their kidnapped, murdered children, "They can only consider ends that are mothers' ends."[28] The surfacing of political issues beyond the family weakened the Mothers of the Plaza de Mayo. Some wished to claim that party politics didn't matter and that their murdered children were innocent of any interest in political struggle. Others felt political activism had been their children's right, one they now wished to share. These argued that their bereavement was not only a moral witnessing of crime and a demand for justice but also a specific intervention with immediate and threatening political implications to the state.

This kind of difference has split the Mothers of the Plaza de Mayo along the feminist divide. To what extent is motherhood a powerful identity, a word to conjure with? To what extent is it a patriarchal construction that inevitably places mothers outside the realm of the social, the changing, the active? What power can women who weep, yell, mourn in the street have? Surely a mother's grief and rage removed from the home, suddenly exposed to publicity, are powerful, shocking. Yet as Navarro also points out, the unity of this image was misleading; its force was eventually undermined by differences a group structured around the monolith, mother, was unable to confront.

But, finally, to give the argument one more turn, many Plaza de Mayo women experienced political transformation through the mothers' network. No group can resolve all political tensions through some ideal formation. The mothers of the disappeared, with their cross-party unity, have been able to convene big demonstrations, drawing new people into the political process. Women can move when a political vacuum develops; by being women who have accepted their lot they can face the soldiers who have taken their children with a sense of righteous indignation even a usually murderous police find it hard to dispute. On whatever terms, they have changed the political climate, invented new ways to resist state terrorism.

Using examples such as these, the Grass-Roots study group gave rise to a particularly poignant exploration of the feminist divide. In each member's work we saw a different version of how women have managed the mixed blessing of their female specialness. Actions such as bread riots are desperate and ephemeral, but also effective. With these street eruptions, women put a government on notice; they signal that the poor can be pushed no further. It is finally women who know when the line has been crossed to starvation. But what then? The prices go down; the women go home—until the next time.

Women's movements for survival are like firestorms, changing and dissolving, resistant to political definition. We asked, Would a feminist critique of the traditional role of women keep these groups going longer? Or might feminist insights contribute to the splits that quickly break down the unity shared during crisis? Or, in yet another shift of our assumed values, why *shouldn't* such groups end when the crisis ends, perhaps leaving behind them politicized people, active networks, even community organizations capable of future action when called for? If the Left were to expand its definition of political culture beyond the state and the workplace, wouldn't the political consciousness of women consumers, mothers, community activists begin to look enduring in its own way, an important potential source of political energy? Perhaps, our group theorized, we're wrong to wish the women to have formed ongoing political groups growing out of bread riots or meat strikes. Maybe we'd see more if we redefined political life to include usually invisible female networks.

The more we talked, the more we saw the ramifications of the fact that the traditional movements were collectivist, the feminist ones more individualistic. Women's local activism draws on a long history of women's culture in which mutual support is essential to life, not (as it often is with contemporary, urban feminists) a rare or fragile achievement. The community of peasant women (or working women or colonized women or concerned mothers) was a given for the motherists; crisis made the idea of a separate, private identity beyond the daily struggle for survival unimportant. Here was another face of the divide: Collectivist movements are powerful, but they rarely raise questions about women's work. Feminism has raised the questions and claimed an individual destiny for each woman, but remains ambivalent toward older traditions of female solidarity. Surely our group was ambivalent. We worried that mothers' social networks could rarely redefine the terms of their needs. And rich as traditional forms of female association may be, we kept coming on instances in which the power of societies organized for internal support along gender lines was undermined by the sexism of that very organization.

For example, historian Mrinalini Sinha's research describes how the Bengali middle class of nineteenth-century India used its tradition of marrying and bedding child brides as a way of defining itself against a racist, colonial government.[29] The English hypocritically criticized

Bengali men as effeminate because they could not wait. Bengali men answered that it was their women who couldn't wait and that the way to control unbounded female sexuality—in which, of course, the English disbelieved—was to marry women at first menstruation.

In Sinha's account the voices of Bengali women are rarely heard, but the question of which sexism would control them—the English marriages of restraint or the Bengali marriages of children—raged around these women. Neither side in the quarrel had women's autonomy or power at heart. Both wanted to wage the colonial fight using women as the symbolic representatives of their rivalry. Because Bengali men wanted control of their women just as much as the English wanted control of Bengali men, the anticolonial struggle had less to offer women than it did men. In general, our group found that sexism inside an oppressed or impoverished community—such as rigidity about gender roles, or about male authority over women, or about female chastity—has cost revolutionary movements a great deal. Too often, gender politics goes unrecognized as an element in class defeat.[30]

Our group disagreed about the women's solidarity we were studying. Was it a part of the long effort to change women's position and to criticize hierarchy in general, or did motherist goals pull in an essentially different direction from feminist ones? And no matter where each one of us found herself on the spectrum of the group's responses to motherist movements, no resolution emerged of the paradox between mothers' goals and the goals of female individuals no longer defined primarily by reproduction and its attendant tasks. We saw this tension in some of the groups we studied, and we kept discovering it in ourselves. (Indeed, some of us were part of groups that used motherist rhetoric, as Ynestra King and I were of women's peace networks or Amy Swerdlow had been of Women Strike for Peace.)

Drawing hard lines between the traditional women's movements and modern Western feminist consciousness never worked, not because the distinction doesn't exist but because it is woven inside our movement. A motherist is in some definitions a feminist; in others, not. And these differing feminisms are yoked together by the range of difficulties to be found in women's current situation. Our scholarly distance from the motherists kept collapsing. The children's toy exchange network Julie Wells described as one of the political groupings that have built black women's solidarity in South Africa couldn't help striking us urban women in the United States as a good idea.[31] We, too, are in charge of the children and need each other to get by. We, too, are likely to act politically along the lines of association our female tasks have shaped. We sometimes long for the community the women we are studying took more for granted. At the same time, we couldn't help remarking on the ways those sustaining communities—say of union workers, or peasants, or ghettoized racial groups—used women's energy, loyalty, and passion as by right, while usually denying them say in the group's public life, its historical consciousness.

Culture offers a variety of rewards to women for always giving attention to others first. Love is a special female responsibility. Some feminists see this female giving as fulfilling and morally powerful. Others see it more negatively as a mark of oppression and argue that women are given the job of "life" but that any job relegated to the powerless is one undervalued by the society as a whole. Yet in our group there was one area of agreement: Traditional women's concerns—for life, for the children, for peace—*should* be everyone's. Beyond that agreement the question that recreates the feminist divide remained: *How* can the caring that belongs to mother travel out to become the responsibility of everyone? Women's backs hold up the world, and we ached for the way women's passionate caring is usually taken for granted, even by women themselves. Some Western feminists, aching like this, want to recognize and honor these mothers who, as Adrienne Rich writes, "age after age, perversely, with no extraordinary power, reconstitute the world."[32] Others, also aching, start on what can seem an impossible search for ways to break the ancient, tireless mother's promise to be the mule of the world.

EQUALITY AND DIFFERENCE

By now anyone who has spent time wrangling with feminist issues has recognized the divide and is no doubt waiting for me to produce the name for it that is probably the oldest, certainly the most all-encompassing: equality versus difference. Most feminist thought grapples unavoidably with some aspect of the equality-difference problem at both the level of theory and of strategy. In theory, this version of the divide might be stated: Do women want to be equal to men (with the meaning of "equal" hotly contested),[33] or do women see biology as establishing a difference that will always require a strong recognition and that might ultimately define quite separate possibilities inside "the human"?

Some difference feminists would argue that women have a special morality, or aesthetic, or capacity for community that it is feminism's responsibility to maximize. Others would put the theoretical case for difference more neutrally: that woman, no matter what she is like, is unassimilable; because she is biologically and therefore psychologically separable from man, she is enduring proof that there is no universally representative human being, no "human wholeness."[34] In contrast, the equality feminists would argue that it is possible for the biological difference to wither away as a basis for social organization, either by moving men and women toward some shared center (androgyny) or toward some experience of human variety in which biology is but one small variable.

Difference theory tends to emphasize the body (and, more recently, the unconscious, where the body's psychic meaning develops); equality theory tends to deemphasize the body and to place faith in each individual's capacity to develop a self not ultimately circumscribed by a collective law of gender. For difference theorists the body can be either the site of pain and oppression or the site of orgasmic ecstasy and maternal joy. For equality theorists, neither extreme is as compelling as the overriding idea that the difference between male and female bodies is a problem in need of solution. In this view, therefore, sexual hierarchy and sexual oppression are bound to continue unless the body is transcended or displaced as the center of female identity.

At the level of practical strategy, the equality-difference divide is just as ubiquitous as it is in theory. Willingly or not, activist lawyers find themselves pitted against each other because they disagree about whether "equal treatment" before the law is better or worse for women than "special treatment," for example, in cases about pregnancy benefits or child custody. (Should pregnancy be defined as unique, requiring special legal provisions, or will pregnant women get more actual economic support if pregnancy, when incapacitating, is grouped with other temporary conditions that keep people from work? Should women who give birth and are almost always the ones who care for children therefore get an automatic preference in custody battles, or will women gain more ultimately if men are defined by law as equally responsible for children, hence equally eligible to be awarded custody?[35]) Sometimes activists find themselves pressured by events to pit the mainstreaming of information about women in the school curriculum against the need for separate programs for women's studies. Or they find themselves having to choose between working to get traditionally male jobs (for example, in construction) or working to get fair pay in the women-only jobs they are already doing.

We rush to respond that these strategic alternatives should not be mutually exclusive, but often, in the heat of local struggles, they temporarily become so. No matter what their theoretical position on the divide, activists find themselves having to make painfully unsatisfactory short-term decisions about the rival claims of equality and difference.[36]

Regrettably, these definitions, these examples, flatten out the oscillations of the equality-difference debate; they obscure the class struggles that have shaped the development of the argument; they offer neat parallels where there should be asymmetries. Viewed historically, the oscillation between a feminism of equality and one of difference is a bitter disagreement about which path is more progressive, more able to change women's basic condition of subordination.

In this history each side has taken more than one turn at calling the other reactionary, and each has had its genuine vanguard moments. Difference gained some working women protection at a time when any social legislation to regulate work was rare; while equality lay behind middle-class women's demand for the vote, a drive Ellen DuBois has called "the most radical program for women's emancipation possible in the nineteenth century." At the same time, bourgeois women's demands that men should have to be as sexually pure as women finessed the divide between difference and equality and gave rise to interesting cross-class alliances of women seeking ways to make men conform to women's standard, rather than the usual way round—a notion of equality with a difference.[37] As DuBois points out, deciding which of these varied political constructions gave nineteenth century women the most real leverage to make change is difficult: "My hypothesis is that the significance of the woman suffrage movement rested precisely on the fact that it bypassed women's oppression within the family, or private sphere, and demanded instead her admission to citizenship, and through it admission to the public arena."[38] In other words, at a time when criticism of women's separate family role was still unthinkable, imagining a place outside the family where such roles would make no difference was—for a time—a most radical act.

Equality and difference are broad ideas and have included a range of definitions and political expressions. Equality, for example, can mean anything from the mildest liberal reform (this is piece-of-the-pie feminism, in which women are merely to be included in the world as it is) to the most radical reduction of gender to insignificance. Difference can mean anything from Mary Daly's belief in the natural superiority of women to psychoanalytic theories of how women are inevitably cast as "the Other" because they lack penises.[39]

Just now equality—fresh from recent defeats at the polls and in the courts—is under attack by British and U.S. theorists who are developing a powerful critique of the eighteenth and nineteenth century roots of feminism in liberalism. In what is a growing body of work, feminists are exploring the serious limitations of a tradition based on an ideal of equality for separate, independent individuals acting in a free, public sphere—either the market or the state. This liberalism, which runs as an essential thread through Anglo-American feminism, has caused much disappointment. Feminists have become increasingly aware of its basic flaws, of the ways it splits off public and private, leaves sexual differences entirely out of its narrative of the world, and pretends to a neutrality that is nullified by the realities of gender, class, and race. A feminism that honors individual rights has nonetheless grown leary of the liberal, capitalist tradition, which always puts those rights before community and before any caring for general needs. Liberalism promises an equal right to compete, but as Bell Hooks puts it, "Since men are not equals in white supremacist, capitalist, patriarchal class structure, which men do women want to be equal to?"[40]

These arguments against the origins and tendencies of equality feminism are cogent and useful. They have uncovered unexamined assumptions and the essential weakness in a demand for a passive neutrality of opportunity. But there are cracks in the critique of equality feminism that lead me back to my general assertion here that neither side of the divide can easily be transcended. The biggest complaint against a feminist demand of equality is that this construction means women must become conceptual men or, rather, that to have equal rights they will have to repress their biological difference, to subordinate themselves in still new ways under an unchanged male hegemony.[41] In this argument the norm is assumed to be male, and women's entry into public space is assumed to be a loss of the aspects of experience they formerly embodied—privacy, feeling, nurturance, dailiness. Surely, however, this argument entails a monolithic and eternal view both of public space and of the category "male." How successfully does public space maintain its male gender markers, how totally exclude the private side of life? (The city street is male, yet it can at times be not only physically but also conceptually invaded, say, by a sense of neighborhood or by a demonstration of mass solidarity.[42]) Does male space sometimes dramatically reveal the fact of women's absence? How well does the taboo on public women hold up under the multiple pressures of modernity? Even if margin and center are conceptual absolutes, to what extent do individual men and women experience moments in both positions?

Or, if we reject these hopeful efforts to find loopholes in the iron laws of gender difference, the fear that women will become men still deserves double scrutiny. Is the collapse of gender difference into maleness really the problem women face? Or are we perhaps quite close to men already in the moment when we fear absorption into the other?

None of this is meant as a refutation of the important current work that brings skepticism to the construction of our demands. When Wendy Chavkin notes that making pregnancy disappear by calling it a "disability" is one more way of letting business and government evade sharing responsibility for reproduction, she is right to worry about the invisibility of women's bodies and of women's work in reproduction, of which their bodies are one small part. When Alison Jaggar gives examples of how male norms have buried the often separate needs of women, she is sounding a valuable warning. When Myra Jehlen describes how hard it is for the concept of a person to include the particular when that particular is female, she is identifying the depth of our difficulty, men's phobic resistance to the inclusion of women into any neutral or public equation.

Nonetheless, I want to reanimate the problem of the divide, to show the potential vigor on both sides. On the one hand, an abstract promise of equality is not enough for people living in capitalism, where everyone is free both to vote and to starve. On the other, as Zillah Eisenstein has argued in *The Radical Future of Liberal Feminism*, the demand for equality has a radical meaning in a capitalist society that claims to offer it but structurally denies it.[43] Feminism asks for many things the patriarchal state cannot give without radical change. As Juliet Mitchell pointed out in her rethinking of the value of equality feminism, when basic rights are under attack, liberalism feels necessary again. At best, liberalism sometimes tips in action and becomes more radical than its root conceptions promise. Certainly, no matter which strategy we choose— based on a model of equality or of difference—we are constantly forced to compromise and must wish for some such synergy of effect from our efforts.[44]

It's not that we haven't gotten beyond liberalism in theory but that in practice we cannot *live* beyond it. In their very structure, contemporary court cases about sex and gender dramatize the fact of the divide, and media questions demand the short, onesided answer. Each "case," each "story" in which we act is different, and we are only at moments able to shape that difference, make it into the kind of "difference" we want.[45]

The Divide Is Not a Universal

After having said so much about how deep the divide goes in feminism, how completely it defines what feminism *is*, I run the risk of seeming to say that the divide has some timeless essence. In fact, I want to argue the opposite, to place Western feminism inside its two-hundred-year history as a specific possibility for thought and action that arose as one of the possibilities of modernity.

When Mary Wollstonecraft wrote one of the founding books of feminism in 1792, *A Vindication of the Rights of Woman*, she said what was new then and remains fresh, shocking, and doubtful to many now: that sex hierarchy—like ranks in the church and the army or like the then newly contested ascendency of kings—was social, not natural. Although women before her had named injustices and taken sides in several episodes of an ancient *querrelle des femmes*, Wollstonecraft's generation experienced the divide in ways related to how feminists experience it now. She saw the immense difficulty of women breaking through into participation in a male world, but she also could feel that there was no reasonable, eternal impediment to women's doing so. At one and the same time she could see gender as a solid wall barring her way into liberty, citizenship, and a male dignity she envied and could see how porous the wall was, how many ways she could imagine stepping through into an identity less absolute and more chaotic.

Modern feminists often criticize her unhappy compromise with bourgeois revolution and liberal political goals, but if Wollstonecraft was often an equality feminist in the narrowest sense, eager to speak of absolute rights and an idealized male individualism and to ignore the body, this narrowness was in part a measure of her desperation.[46] The body, she felt, could be counted on to assert its ever-present and dreary pull; the enlightenment promised her a mind that might escape. She acknowledged difference as an absolute—men are stronger—and then, with cunning, she offered men a deal:

> Avoiding, as I have hitherto done, any direct comparison of the two sexes collectively, or frankly acknowledging the inferiority of woman, according to the present appearance of things, I shall only insist that men have increased that inferiority till women are almost sunk below the standard of rational creatures. Let their faculties have room to unfold, and their virtues to gain strength, and then determine where the whole sex must stand in the intellectual scale.[47]

Wheedling a bit, Wollstonecraft made men the modest proposal that if women are inferior, men have nothing to fear; they can generously afford to give women their little chance at the light. This is a sly, agnostic treatment of the issue of equality versus difference. An experimental and groping spirit, Wollstonecraft *didn't know* how much biological difference might come to mean; that she suffered humiliation and loss through being a woman she did know, and all she asked was to be let out of the prison house of gender identity for long enough to judge what men had and what part of that she might want.

When Wollstonecraft wrote, difference was the prevailing wind, equality the incipient revolutionary storm. She feared that if women could not partake in the new civil and political rights of democracy, they would "remain immured in their families groping in the dark."[48] To be sure, this rejection of the private sphere made no sense to many feminists who came after her and left modern feminists the task of recognizing the importance of the private and women's different life there; yet it is a rejection that was absolutely necessary as one of feminism's first moves.

We in turn have rejected Wollstonecraft's call for chastity, for the end of the passionate emotions "which disturb the order of society";[49] we have rejected her confidence in objective reason and her desire to live as a disembodied self (and a very understandable desire, too, for one whose best friend died in childbirth and who was to die of childbed fever herself), but we have not gotten beyond needing to make the basic demands she made—for civil rights, education, autonomy. (How she hated the necessity of placating powerful men, a theme that preoccupies us, too, in sexual harassment cases she would have perfectly understood.)

Finally, what is extraordinary in *A Vindication* is its chaos. Multivalent, driven, ambivalent, the text races over most of feminism's main roads. It constantly goes back on itself in tone, thrilling with self-hatred, rage, disappointment, and hope—the very sort of emotions it explains are the mark of women's inferiority, triviality, and lascivious abandon. Though its appeals to God and virtue are a dead letter to feminists now, the anger and passion with which Wollstonecraft made those appeals—and out of which she imagined the depth of women's otherness, our forced incapacity, the injustice of our situation—feel thoroughly modern. Her structural disorganization comes in part from a circular motion through now familiar stages of protest, reasoning, fury, despair, contempt, desire.[50] She makes demands for women, then doubles back to say that womanhood should be beside the point. Her book is one of those that mark the start of an avalanche of mass self-consciousness about gender injustice.

So, in the midst of the hopeful excitement, the divide is there, at the beginning of our history. As Anne Phillips puts it, this tension is "built into the feminist project. Men and women are different; they are also unequal; feminists will continue to debate and disagree over how far the inequality stems from the difference, and how far the difference can or should be eliminated."[51]

If the divide is central to feminist history, feminists need to recognize it with more suppleness, but this enlarged perspective doesn't let us out of having to choose a position in the divide. On the contrary, by arguing that there is no imminent resolution of this central contradiction, I hope to throw each reader back on the necessity of finding where her own work falls and of assessing how powerful that political decision is as a tool for undermining the dense, deeply embedded oppression of women.

By writing of the varied vocabularies and constructions feminists have used to describe the divide, I do not mean to intimate that they are all one, but to emphasize their difference. Each issue calls forth a new configuration, a new version of the spectrum of feminist opinion, and most require an internal as well as external struggle about goals and tactics. Although it is understandable that we dream of peace among feminists, that we resist in sisterhood the factionalism that has so often disappointed us in brotherhood, still we must carry on the argument among ourselves. Better, we must actively embrace it. The tension in the divide, far from being our enemy, is a dynamic force that links very different women. Feminism encompasses central dilemmas in modern experience, mysteries of identity that get full expression in its debates. The electricity of its internal disagreements is part of feminism's continuing power to shock and involve large numbers of people in a public conversation far beyond the movement itself. The dynamic, feminist divide is about difference; it dramatizes women's differences from each other—and the necessity of our sometimes making common cause.

A Gender Diary

SOME STORIES, SOME DIALOGUES

In the early days of this wave of the women's movement, I sat in a weekly consciousness raising group with my friend A. We compared notes recently: "What did you think was happening? How did you think our own lives were going to change?" A. said she had felt, "Now I can be a woman; it's no longer so humiliating. I can stop fantasizing that secretly I am a man, as I used to, before I had children. Now I can value what was once my shame." Her answer amazed me. Sitting in the same meetings during those years, my thoughts were roughly the reverse: "Now I don't have to be a woman anymore. I need never become a mother. Being a woman has always been humiliating, but I used to assume there was no exit. Now the very idea 'woman' is up for grabs. 'Woman' is my slave name; feminism will give me freedom to seek some other identity altogether."

If, as I've said, the divide offers no third way, no high ground of neutrality, I certainly have not been able to present this overview so far without a constant humming theme beneath, my own eagerness to break the category woman down, to find a definition of difference that pushes so far beyond a settled identity that "being a woman" breaks apart. Although sometimes I have found the theoretical equality arguments I have described blinkered and reactive, when it comes to strategy, I almost always choose that side, fearing the romance of femaleness even more than the flatness and pretense of undifferentiated, gender-free public space.

I suspect that each one's emphasis—equality or difference—arises alongside and not after the reasons. We criticize Wollstonecraft's worship of rationality, but how willing are we modern ones to look at the unconscious, the idiosyncratic, the temperamental histories of our own politics? It is in these histories—private, intellectual, and social—that we can find why some women feel safer with the equality model as the rock of their practice (with difference as a necessary condition imposed on it), while other women feel more true to themselves, more fully expressed, by difference as their rock (with equality a sort of bottom-line call for basic reforms that cannot ultimately satisfy).

Why do I decide (again and again) that being a woman is a liability, while others I know decide (again and again) that a separate female culture is more exciting, more in their interests, more promising as a strategic stance for now than my idea of slipping the noose of gender, living for precious moments of the imagination outside it? An obvious first answer is that class, race, and sexual preference determine my choices, and surely these play their central part. Yet in my experience of splits in the women's movement, I keep joining with women who share my feminist preferences but who have arrived at these conclusions from very different starting points. If we're serious about recognizing and honoring the differences among women, we're going to have to accept the multiple sources of each one's choice, the complex stories that bring us to our resting place in any particular argument.

This is not to understate the importance of class, race, and sexual preference but merely to observe that these important variables don't segment feminism along the divide; they don't provide direct keys to each woman's sense of self-interest or desire; nor do they yield clear directions for the most useful strategic moves. For example, lesbian and straight women are likely to bring very different understandings and needs to discussions of whether women's communities work, whether the concept is constricting. Yet in my own experience, trust of women's communities does not fall out along the lines of sexual preference. Instead, up close, the variables proliferate. What was the texture of childhood for each one of us? What face did the world beyond home present?

In the 1950s, when an earlier, roiled life of gender and politics had subsided and the gender messages seemed monolithic again, I lived with my parents in the suburbs. My mother's class and generation had lived through repeated, basic changes of direction about women, family, and work, and my own engaged and curious mother passed her ambivalent reception of the world's mixed messages on to me in the food. With hindsight, I can see that gender, family, and class weren't the settled issues they seemed then. But the times put a convincing cover over continuing change. Deborah Rosenfelt and Judith Stacey describe this precise historical moment and the particular feminist politics born from it:

> The ultradomestic nineteen fifties [was] an aberrant decade in the
> history of U.S. family and gender relations and one that has set the
> unfortunate terms for waves of personal and political reaction to family
> issues ever since. Viewed in this perspective, the attack on the
> breadwinner/homemaker nuclear family by the women's liberation
> movement may have been an overreaction to an aberrant and highly
> fragile cultural form, a family system that, for other reasons, was
> already passing from the scene. Our devastating critiques of the
> vulnerability and cultural devaluation of dependent wives and mothers
> helped millions of women to leave or avoid these domestic traps, and
> this is to our everlasting credit. But, with hindsight, it seems to us that
> these critiques had some negative consequences as well. . . .
> Feminism's overreaction to the fifties was an antinatalist,
> antimaternalism movement.[52]

I am the child of this moment and some of the atmosphere of rage
generated by that hysterically domestic ideology of the 1950s can now
feel callow, young, or ignorant. Yet I have many more kind words to
say for the reaction of which I was a part in the early 1970s than
Rosenfelt and Stacey seem to. I don't think the feminism of this phase
would have spoken so powerfully to so many without this churlish
outbreak of indignation. Nothing we have learned since about the fragility
of the nuclear family alters the fundamental problems it continues to
pose for women. It is not really gone, although it is changing. And
although feminism seeks to preside over the changes, other forces are
at work, half the time threatening us with loneliness, half the time
promising us rich emotional lives if we will but stay home—a double
punch combination designed to make the 1950s look, by contrast, safe.
The 1950s were not safe, not for me anyway, and they don't become
so with hindsight.

It's hard to remember now what the initial feminist moves in this
wave felt like, the heady but alarming atmosphere of female revolt. As
one anxious friend wondered back then, "Can I be in this and stay
married?" The answer was often, "No," the upheaval terrifying. Some
of us were too afraid of the lives of our mothers to recognize ourselves
in them. But I remember that this emotional throwing off of the mother's
life felt like the only way to begin. Black women whose ties to their
mothers were more often a mutual struggle for survival rarely shared
this particular emotion. Audre Lord, for example, has said that "black
children were not meant to survive," so parents and children saw a
lifeline in each other it was harder for the prosperous or the white to
discern.[53] The usually white and middle-class women who were typical
members of early women's consciousness raising groups often saw their
mothers as desperate or depressed in the midst of their relative privilege.

Many had been educated like men and had then been expected to become—men's wives. We used to agree in those meetings that motherhood was the divide. Before it, you could pretend you were just like everyone else; afterward, you were a species apart—invisible and despised.

But if motherhood was despised, it was also festooned—then as now—with roses. Either way, in 1970, motherhood seemed an inevitable part of my future, and the qualities some feminists now praise as uniquely women's were taken for granted as female necessities. Everyone wanted the nice one, the sweet one, the good one, the nurturant one, the pretty one. No one wanted the women who didn't want to be women. It's hard to recover how frightening it was to step out of these ideas, to resist continuing on as expected; it's hard to get back how very naked it made us feel. Some of the vociferousness of our rhetoric, which now seems unshaded or raw, came partly from the anxiety we felt when we made this proclamation, that we didn't want to be women. A great wave of misogyny rose to greet us. So we said it even more. Hindsight has brought in its necessary wisdom, its temporizing reaction. We've gotten beyond the complaint of the daughters and have come to respect the realities—the worries and the work—of the mothers. But to me, "difference" will always represent a necessary modification of the initial impulse, a reminder of complexity, a brake on precipitate hopes. It can never feel like the primary insight felt, the first breaking with the gender bargain. The immediate reward was immense, the thrill of separating from authority.

Conversation with E.: She recalls that the new women's movement meant to her: You don't have to struggle to be attractive to men any more. You can stop working so hard on that side of things. I was impressed by this liberation so much beyond my own. Once again I felt the opposite. Oppressed and depressed before the movement, I found sexual power unthinkable, the privilege of a very few women. Now angry and awake, I felt for the first time what the active eroticism of men might be like. What men thought of me no longer blocked out the parallel question of what I thought of them, which made sexual encounters far more interesting than they had once been. Like E., I worried about men's approval less, but (without much tangible reason) my hopes for the whole business of men and women rose. For a brief time in the early 1970s, I had an emotional intimation of what some men must feel: free to rub up against the world, take space, make judgments. With all its hazards, this confidence also offered its delight—but only for a moment, of course. The necessary reaction followed at once: Women aren't men in public space. There is no safety. Besides, I had romanticized male experience; men are not so free as I imagined. Still, I remember that wild if deluded time—not wanting to be a man but wanting what men have, the freedom of the street. The feminist rallying cry, "Take Back the Night," has always struck me as a fine piece of movement poetry. We don't have the night, but we want it, we want it.

Another memory of the early 1970s: An academic woman sympathetic to the movement but not active asked what motivated me to spend all this time organizing, marching, meeting. (Subtext: Why wasn't I finishing my book? Why did I keep flinging myself around?)

I tried to explain the excitement I felt at the idea that I didn't have to be a woman. She was shocked, confused. This was the motor of my activism? She asked, "How can someone who doesn't like being a woman be a feminist?" To which I could only answer, "Why would anyone who likes being a woman need to be a feminist?"

Quite properly, my colleague feared woman hating. She assumed that feminism must be working to restore respect and dignity to women. Feminism would revalue what had been debased—women's contribution to human history. I, on the other hand, had to confess: I could never have made myself lick all those stamps for a better idea of what womanhood means. Was this, as my colleague thought, just a new kind of misogyny? I wouldn't dare say self-hatred played no part in what I wanted from feminism from the first. But even back then, for me, women hating—or loving—felt beside the point. It was the idea of breaking the law of the category itself that made me delirious.

The first time I heard "women" mentioned as a potentially political contemporary category I was already in graduate school. It was the mid 1960s, and a bright young woman of the New Left was saying how important it was to enlist the separate support of women workers in our organizing against the Vietnam War. I remember arguing with her, flushed with a secret humiliation. What good was she doing these workers, I asked her, by addressing them and categorizing them separately? Who was she to speak so condescendingly of "them"? Didn't she know that the inferior category she had named would creep up in the night and grab her, too?

I'm ashamed now to admit that gender solidarity—which I lived inside happily, richly every day in those years—first obtruded itself on my conscious mind as a threat and a betrayal. So entirely was I trapped in negative feelings about what women are and can do that I had repressed any knowledge of femaleness as a defining characteristic of my being.

I can see now that women very different from me came to feminist conclusions much like my own. But this is later knowledge. My feminism came from the suburbs, where I knew no woman with children who had a job or any major activities beyond the family. Yet, although a girl, I was promised education, offered the pretense of gender neutrality. This island of illusions was a small world, but if I seek the source for why cultural feminism has so little power to draw me, it is to this world I return in thought. During the day, it was safe, carefully limited, and female. The idea that this was all made me frantic.

S. reads the gender diary with consternation. In Puerto Rico where she grew up this fear of the mother's life would be an obscenity. She can't recognize the desire I write of—to escape scot free from the role I was born to. Latina feminists she knows feel rage, but what is this shame, she wants to know. In her childhood both sexes believed being a woman was magic.

S. means it about the magic, hard as it is for me to take this in. She means sexual power, primal allure, even social dignity. S. became a feminist later, by a different route, and now she is as agnostic about the meaning of gender as I am. But when she was young, she had no qualms about being a woman.

After listening to S., I add another piece to my story of the suburbs. As Jews who weren't spending much of their time being Jewish, we lived where ethnicity was easy to miss. (Of course, it was there, but I didn't know it.) In the suburbs, motherhood was white bread, with no powerful ethnic graininess. For better and worse, I was brought up on this stripped, denatured product. Magical women seemed laughably remote. No doubt this flatness in local myth made girls believe less in their own special self, but at the same time it gave them less faith in the beckoning ideal of mother. My gifted mother taught me not the richness of home but the necessity of feminism. Feminism was her conscious as well as unconscious gift to me.

It is not enough for the diary to tell about how one woman, myself, came to choose again and again a feminism on the minimalizers side of the divide. Somehow the diary must also tell how this decision can never feel solid or final. No one gets to stay firmly on her side; no one gets to rest in a reliably clear position. Mothers who believe their daughters should roam as free as men find themselves giving those daughters taxi fare, telling them not to talk to strangers, filling them with the lore of danger. Activists who want women to be very naughty (as the women in a little zap group we call No More Nice Girls want women to be) nonetheless warn them there's a price to pay for daring to defy men in public space.[54] Even when a woman chooses which shoes she'll wear today—is it to be the running shoes, the flats, the spikes?—she's deciding where to place herself for the moment on the current possible spectrum of images of woman. Whatever our habitual positions on the divide, in daily life we travel back and forth, or, to change metaphors, we scramble for whatever toehold we can.

Living with the divide: In a room full of feminists, everyone is saying that a so-called surrogate mother, one who bears a child for others, should have the right to change her mind for a time (several weeks? months?) after the baby is born. This looks like agreement. Women who have been on opposite sides of the divide in many struggles converge here, outraged at the insulting way one Mary Beth Whitehead has been treated by fertility clinics, law courts, and press. She is not a "surrogate" we say, but a "mother" indeed.

The debate seems richer than it's been lately. Nobody knows how to sort out the contradictions of the new reproductive technologies yet, so for a fertile moment, there's a freedom, an expressiveness in all that's said. Charged words such as "birth" and "mothering" and "the kids" are spilling all around, but no one yet dares to draw the ideological line defining which possibilities belong inside feminism, which are antithetical to it. Some sing a song of pregnancy and birth while others offer counterpuntal motifs of child-free lesbian youth, of infertility, all in different keys of doubt about how much feminists may want to make motherhood special, different from parenting, different from caring—a unique and absolute relation to a child.

But just as we're settling in for an evening that promises to be fraught, surprising, suggestive, my warning system, sensitive after eighteen years of feminist activism, gives a familiar twitch and tug. Over by the door, one woman has decided: Surrogacy is baby selling and ought to be outlawed. All mothering will be debased if motherhood can be bought. Over by the couch, another woman is anxiously responding: Why should motherhood be the sacred place we keep clean from money, while men sell the work of their bodies every day? Do we want women to be the special representatives of the moral and spiritual things that can't be bought, with the inevitable result that women's work is once again done without pay?

Here it is then. The metaconversation that has hovered over my political life since 1970 when I joined one of the first women's consciousness raising groups. On the one hand, sacred motherhood. On the other, a wish—variously expressed—for this special identity to wither away.

Only a little later in the brief, eventful history of this ad hoc Mary Beth Whitehead support group, a cleverly worded petition was circulated. It quoted the grounds the court used to disqualify Whitehead from motherhood—from the way she dyed her hair to the way she played patty-cake—and ended: "By these standards, we are all unfit mothers." I wanted to sign the petition, but someone told me, "Only mothers are signing." I was amazed. Did one have to be literally *a mother in order to speak authentically in support of Whitehead? Whether I'm a mother or not, the always obvious fact that I am from the mother half of humanity conditions my life.*

But after this initial flash of outrage at exclusion, I had other, second thoughts: Maybe I should be glad not to sign. Why should I have to be assumed to be a mother if I am not? Instead of accepting that all women are mothers in essence if not in fact, don't I prefer a world in which some are mothers—and can speak as mothers—while others are decidedly not?

To make a complicated situation more so: While I was struggling with the rights and wrongs of my being allowed to sign, several other women refused to sign. Why? Because the petition quoted Whitehead's remark that she knew what was best for her child because she was the mother. The nonsigners saw this claim as once again imputing some magic biological essence to motherhood. They didn't want to be caught signing a document that implied that mother always knows best. They supported Whitehead's right to dye her hair but not her claim to maternal infallibility.

I saw the purity of this position, recognized these nonsigners as my closest political sisters, the ones who run fast because the old world of mother right is just behind them. But in this case I didn't feel quite as they felt. I was too angry at the double standard, the unfair response to Whitehead's attempts to extricate herself from disaster. I thought that given the circumstances of here, of now, Mary Beth Whitehead was as good an authority about her still-nursing baby as we could find anywhere in the situation. It didn't bother me at all to sign a petition that included her claim to a uniquely privileged place. The press and the court seemed to hate her for that very specialness, yet they all relegated her to it, execrating her for her unacceptable ambivalence. Under such conditions, she was embracing with an understandable vengeance the very role the world names as hers. Who could blame her?

Eventually, I signed the petition, which was also signed by a number of celebrities and was much reported in the press. It is well to remember how quickly such public moments flatten out internal feminist debates. After much feminist work, the newspapers—formerly silent about feminism's stake in surrogacy questions—began speaking of "the feminist position." But nothing they ever wrote about us or our petition came close to the dilemma as we had debated it during the few intense weeks we met. Prosurrogacy and antisurrogacy positions coexist inside feminism. They each require expression because neither alone can respond fully to the class, race, and gender issues raised when a poor women carries a child for a rich man for money.[55]

Over time I've stopped being depressed by the lack of feminist accord. I see feminists as stuck with the very indeterminancy I say I long for. This is it then, the life part way in, part way out. We can be recalled to "woman" anytime—by things as terrible as rape, as trivial as a rude shout on the street—but we can never stay inside "woman" because it keeps moving. We constantly find ourselves beyond its familiar cover.

Gender markers are being hotly reasserted these days—U.S. defense is called "standing tough," while the pope's latest letter calls motherhood woman's true vocation. Yet this very heat is a sign of gender's instabilities. We can clutch aspects of the identity we like, but they often slip away. Modern women experience moments of free fall. How is it for you, there, out in space near me? Different, I know. Yet we share—some with more pleasure, some with more pain—this uncertainty.

Notes

I am indebted to the hard-working readers of an earlier draft, who are nevertheless not to blame for the times I have failed to profit from their excellent advice: Nancy Davidson, Adrienne Harris, Temma Kaplan, Mim Kelber, Ynestra King, Susana Leval, Eunice Lipton, Alix Kates Shulman, Alan Snitow, Nadine Taub, Meredith Tax, Sharon Thompson, and Carole Vance.

1. MARHO Forum, John Jay College, New York, March 2, 1984.

2. See, for example, the feminist essays critical of Greenham in *Breaching the Peace: a collection of radical feminist papers* (London: Onlywomen Press, 1983).

3. See Chapter 12.

4. Claudia Koonz, "Race, Sex, and Misogyny in Nazi Germany" (Presented at the Scholar and the Feminist 12, Barnard College, New York, March 30, 1985).

5. See Chapter 13, and Rhoda Linton and Michele Whitham, "With Mourning, Rage, Empowerment and Defiance: The 1981 Women's Pentagon Action," *Socialist Review* 12, nos. 3-4 (May-August 1982), pp. 11–36.

6. The "we" problem has no more simple solution than does the divide itself, but in spite of its false promise of unity the "we" remains politically important. In this piece, "we" includes anyone who calls herself a feminist, anyone who is actively engaged with the struggles described here.

7. Bella Abzug and Mim Kelber, *Gender Gap* (Boston: Houghton Mifflin, 1984). According to Kelber, Carter was outraged that the women of the commission were criticizing his social priorities; they were supposed to be on his side. Most of the commission resigned when Carter fired Abzug. When he reconstituted the commission somewhat later, the adjective national had been dropped from its name and it became the President's Advisory Commission for Women, with restricted powers and no lobbying function.

8. "In the United States, we oscillate between participating in, and separating from, organizations and institutions that remain alienating and stubbornly male dominant" (Joan Kelly, "The Doubled Vision of Feminist Theory," in Joan Kelly, *Women, History and Theory: The Essays of Joan Kelly* [Chicago: University of Chicago Press, 1984], p. 55). Also see Denise Riley, *War in the Nursery: Theories of the Child and Mother* (London: Virago, 1983).

9. Denise Riley, talk at the Barnard Women's Center, New York, April 11, 1985.

10. Catharine R. Stimpson, "The New Scholarship About Women: The State of the Art," *Ann. Scholarship* 1, no. 2 (1980), pp. 2–14.

11. Alice Echols, *Daring to Be Bad: A History of the Radical Feminist Movement in America, 1967–1975* (Minneapolis: University of Minnesota Press, forthcoming), typescript, p. 81 (Chap. 2).

12. Ibid., p. 273 (Chap. 6).

13. Ibid., p. 270 (Chap. 6).

14. Ibid., p. 273 (Chap. 6).

15. Barbara Deming, "To Those Who Would Start a People's Party," *Liberation* 18, no. 4 (December 1973), p. 24, cited in Echols, *Daring*, typescript, p. 272 (Chap. 6); Andrea Dworkin, *Intercourse* (New York: The Free Press, 1987), p. 67. Dworkin is not a biological determinist in *Intercourse*, but she sees culture as so saturated with misogyny that the victimization of women is seamless, total, as eternal in its own way as "mother right."

16. Ellen Willis, remarks at the NYU Symposium on the publication of *Powers of Desire: The Politics of Sexuality*, New York, December 2, 1983.

17. Carole S. Vance, "Social Construction Theory: Problems in the History of Sexuality," in Anja van Kooten Niekerk and Theo van der Meer, eds., *Homosexuality, Which Homosexuality?* (Amsterdam: An Dekker, Imprint Schorer, 1989).

18. Linda Alcoff, "Cultural Feminism Versus Post-Structuralism: The Identity Crisis in Feminist Theory," *Signs* 13, no. 3 (Spring 1988), especially p. 406.

19. Linda Alcoff sees poststructuralism as antiessentialist; in contrast, in *Feminist Studies* 14, no. 1 (Spring 1988), the editors Judith Newton and Nancy Hoffman introduce a collection of essays on deconstruction by describing differences *among* deconstructionists on the question of essentialism as on other matters.

20. See New York Radical Feminists, "Politics of the Ego: A Manifesto for N.Y. Radical Feminists," in Anne Koedt, Ellen Levine, and Anita Rapone, eds., *Radical Feminism* (New York: Quadrangle, 1973), pp. 379–383. The vocabulary of the manifesto, adopted in December 1969, seems crude now, its emphasis on "psychology" jejune; but the document begins with the task feminists have taken up since—the analysis of the interlocking ways in which culture organizes subordination.

21. Linda Bamber and Marianne DeKoven, "Metacriticism and the Value of Difference" (Paper presented at the MLA panel Feminist Criticism: Theories and Directions, Los Angeles, December 28, 1982), pp. 1–2.

22. Alcoff, "Cultural Feminism," p. 421.

23. One might make a separate study of third-course thinking. Sometimes this work is an important and urgent effort to see the limiting terms of a current contradiction, to recognize from which quarter new contradictions are likely to develop. Third-course writing at its best tries to reinterpret the present and offer clues to the future. (English theorists have called this prefigurative thinking.) But often this work runs the risk of pretending that new terms resolve difficulties, and, more insidiously, it often falls back covertly into the divide it claims to have transcended. I admire, although I am not always persuaded by, the third-course thinking in such pieces as Angela Miles, "The Integrative Feminine Principle in North American Radicalism: Value Basis of a New Feminism,"

Women's Studies International Quarterly 4, no. 4 (1981), pp. 481–495. I have more doubts about pieces such as Ann Ferguson, "Sex War: The Debate Between Radical and Libertarian Feminists," and Ilene Philipson, "The Repression of History and Gender: A Critical Perspective on the Feminist Sexuality Debate," *Signs* 10, no. 1 (Autumn 1984), pp. 106–118. These essays claim a higher ground, "a third perspective" (Ferguson, p. 108), that is extremely difficult to construct; their classifications of the sides of the divide reveal a tropism more unavoidable than they recognize.

24. Michèle Barrett, "The Concept of 'Difference,'" *Feminist Review* 26 (Summer 1987), p. 34.

25. Alice Walker, *In Search of Our Mothers' Gardens* (San Diego: Harcourt Brace Jovanovich, 1983), p. xi (epigraph). Also see, for example, Kelly, "The Doubled Vision of Feminist Theory"; and Adrienne Rich, "Compulsory Heterosexuality and Lesbian Existence," in Adrienne Rich, *Blood, Bread and Poetry* (New York: Norton, 1986), p. 60ff. Rich also uses the metaphor of the continuum to describe the range in women's lives among different levels of female community. In *The Daughter's Seduction: Feminism and Psychoanalysis* (Ithaca, N.Y.: Cornell University Press, 1982), Jane Gallop describes Julia Kristeva's effort to think beyond dualism: "A constantly double discourse is necessary, one that asserts and then questions" (p. 122).

26. Members of the study group, convened at the Barnard Women's Center: Margorie Agosin, Amrita Basu, Dana Frank, Temma Kaplan, Ynestra King, Marysa Navarro, Ann Snitow, Amy Swerdlow, Meredith Tax, Julie Wells, Marilyn Young.

27. Meredith Tax, "Agenda for Meeting at Barnard, May 3, 1986," p. 1.

28. Marysa Navarro, Grass Roots Meeting, May 3, 1986. Also see Shirley Christian, "Mothers March, but to 2 Drummers," *New York Times*, February 21, 1987.

29. Mrinalini Sinha, "The Age of Consent Act: The Ideal of Masculinity and Colonial Ideology in 19th Century Bengal," *Proceedings*, Eighth International Symposium on Asian Studies (1986), pp. 1199–1214; and Mrinalini Sinha, "Gender and Imperialism: Colonial Policy and the Ideology of Moral Imperialism in Late 19th Century Bengal," in Michael S. Kimmel, ed., *Changing Men: New Directions in Research on Men and Masculinity* (Newbury Park, Calif.: Sage, 1987), pp. 217–231.

30. At the Grass-Roots study group, Julie Wells and Anne McClintock offered the example of Crossroads in South Africa, a squatter community of blacks largely maintained by women but finally undermined by, among other things, a colonialism that placed paid black men in charge. Also see descriptions of ways in which women become connected with revolutionary movements in Maxine Molyneux, "Mobilization Without Emancipation? Women's Interests, the State, and Revolution in Nicaragua," *Feminist Studies* 11, no. 2 (Summer 1985), pp. 227–253; Temma Kaplan, "Women and Communal Strikes in the Crises of 1917–1922," in Renate Bridenthal, Claudia Koonz, and Susan Stuard, eds., *Becoming Visible: Women in European History*, 2nd ed. (Boston: Houghton Mifflin, 1987), pp. 429–449; and Temma Kaplan, "Female Consciousness and Collective Action: The Case of Barcelona, 1910–1918," *Signs* 7, no. 3 (1982), pp. 545–566.

31. Julie Wells, "The Impact of Motherist Movements on South African Women's Political Participation" (Paper presented at the Seventh Berkshire Conference on the History of Women, June 19, 1987).

32. Adrienne Rich, "Natural Resources," in Adrienne Rich, *The Dream of a Common Language: Poems, 1974–1977* (New York: Norton, 1978), p. 67.

33. Alison M. Jaggar gives an account of the contemporary feminist debate about the meaning and value of the demand for "equality" in "Sexual Difference and Sexual Equality," in Deborah L. Rhode, ed., *Theoretical Perspectives on Sexual Differences* (New Haven: Yale University Press, forthcoming). For some general accounts of the debate, also see Josephine Donovan, *Feminist Theory* (New York: Frederick Ungar, 1985); Hester Eisenstein, *Contemporary Feminist Thought* (Boston: G. K. Hall, 1983); Hester Eisenstein and Alice Jardine, eds., *The Future of Difference* (Boston: G. K. Hall, 1980); Zillah R. Eisenstein, *Feminism and Sexual Equality: Crisis in Liberal America* (New York: Monthly Review Press, 1984); Juliet Mitchell, *Women's Estate* (New York: Pantheon, 1971); Juliet Mitchell and Ann Oakley, eds., *What Is Feminism?* (New York: Pantheon, 1986). The debates about Carol Gilligan's *In a Different Voice: Psychological Theory and Women's Development* (Cambridge, Mass.: Harvard University Press, 1982), often turn on the equality/ difference problem. See John Broughton, "Women's Rationality and Men's Virtues: A Critique of Gender Dualism in Gilligan's Theory of Moral Development," *Social Research* 50, no. 3 (Autumn 1983), pp. 597–624; Linda K. Kerber, Catherine G. Greeno and Eleanor E. Maccoby, Zella Luria, Carol B. Stack, and Carol Gilligan, "On *In a Different Voice*: An Interdisciplinary Forum," *Signs* 11, no. 2 (Winter 1986), pp. 304–333; *New Ideas in Psychology* (Special Issue on Women and Moral Development) 5, no. 2 (1987); and Seyla Benhabib, "The Generalized and the Concrete Other: The Kohlberg-Gilligan Controversy and Feminist Theory," in Seyla Benhabib and Drucilla Cornell, eds., *Feminism as Critique* (Minneapolis: University of Minnesota Press, 1987), pp. 77–95. Similarly, the feminist response to Ivan Illich, *Gender* (New York: Pantheon, 1982), has tended to raise these issues. See, for example, Lourdes Benería, "Meditations on Ivan Illich's *Gender*," in B. Gustavsson, J. C. Karlsson, and C. Rafregard, eds., *Work in the 1980's* (London: Gower Publishing, 1985).

34. The phrase "human wholeness" comes from Betty Friedan, *The Second Stage* (New York: Summit Books, 1981), and the concept receives a valuable and devastating critique in Myra Jehlen, "Against Human Wholeness: A Suggestion for a Feminist Epistemology" (manuscript).

35. For the pregnancy issue, see "Brief of the American Civil Liberties Union et al," amici curiae, *California Federal Savings and Loan Association et al. V. Mark Guerra et al.,* Supreme Court of the United States, October Term, 1985, Joan E. Bertin, Counsel of record; Wendy Chavkin, "Walking a Tightrope: Pregnancy, Parenting, and Work," in Wendy Chavkin, ed., *Double Exposure: Women's Health Hazards on the Job and at Home* (New York: Monthly Review Press, 1984); Lise Vogel, "Debating Difference: The Problem of Special Treatment of Pregnancy in the Workplace" (Paper presented at the Women and Society Seminar of Columbia University, New York, January 25, 1988); Kai Bird and Max Holland, "Capitol Letter: The Garland Case," *The Nation*, July 5–12, 1986, p. 8; Wendy

Williams, "Equality's Riddle: Pregnancy and the Equal Treatment/Special Treatment Debate," *N.Y.U. Review of Law and Social Change* 13 (1984–1985); Herma Hill Kay, "Equality and Difference: The Case of Pregnancy," *Berkeley Women's Law Journal* 1 (1985). For the custody issue, see Katharine T. Bartlett and Carol B. Stack, "Joint Custody, Feminism and the Dependency Dilemma," *Berkeley Women's Law Journal*, Winter 1986–1987, pp. 501–533; Phyllis Chesler, *Mothers on Trial: The Battle for Children and Custody* (Seattle: Seal Press, 1986); Lenore J. Weitzman, *The Divorce Revolution: The Unexpected Social and Economic Consequences for Women and Children in America* (New York: Macmillan, 1985). The work of Nadine Taub, director of the Women's Rights Litigation Clinic, School of Law, Rutgers/Newark, has frequent bearing on both issues and on the larger questions in equality/difference debates. See Nadine Taub, "Defining and Combatting Sexual Harassment," in Amy Swerdlow and Hannah Lessinger, eds., *Class, Race and Sex: The Dynamics of Control* (Boston: G. K. Hall, 1983): pp. 263–275; Nadine Taub, "Feminist Tensions: Concepts of Motherhood and Reproductive Choice," *Gender and Transition* (forthcoming); Nadine Taub, "A Public Policy of Private Caring," *The Nation*, May 31, 1986, pp. 756–758; Nadine Taub and Wendy Williams, "Will Equality Require More Than Assimilation, Accommodation or Separation from the Existing Social Structure?" *Rutgers Law Review* 37, no. 4 (Summer 1985), pp. 825–844. The burgeoning feminist work on the new reproductive technologies also reproduces the divide. For complete references to all aspects of these debates, see Nadine Taub and Sherrill Cohen, *Reproductive Laws for the 1990s* (Clifton, N.J.: Humana Press, 1989).

36. If I had come up with an example of a feminist strategy that faced the power of the divide squarely yet at the same time undermined the oppression the divide represents, I'd choose recent feminist comparable worth legislation. Humble and earthshaking, comparable worth asserts two things: First, because women and men do different work, the concept "equal pay" has little effect on raising women's low wages; and, second, if work were to be judged by standards of difficulty, educational preparation, experience, and so on (standards preferably developed by workers themselves), then antidiscrimination laws might enforce that men and women doing work of comparable worth be paid the same. (Perhaps nurses and automechanics? Or teachers and middle managers?) The activists who have proposed comparable worth have singularly few pretentions. They are the first to point out that on its face, the proposal ignores the work women do in the family, ignores the noneconomic reasons why women and men have different kinds of jobs, ignores what's wrong with job hierarchies and with "worth" as the sole basis for determining pay. Yet this little brown mouse of a liberal reform, narrow in its present political potential and limited by its nature, has a touch of deconstructive genius. Without hoping to get women doing men's work tomorrow, the comparable worth model erodes the economic advantages to employers of consistently undervaluing women's work and channeling women into stigmatized work ghettoes where pay is always lower. With comparable worth, the stigma might well continue to haunt women's work, but women would be better paid. Men might start wanting a "woman's" job that paid well, while women might have new psychological incentives to cross gender work categories. Who knows, perhaps stigma might not catch up

as categories of work got rethought and their gender markers moved around. And if the stigma clung to women's work, if men refused to be nurses even if nurses were paid as well as construction workers, a woman earning money is an independent woman. She can change the family; she can consider leaving it. Comparable worth asserts the divide, yet, slyly, it goes to work on the basic economic and psychological underpinnings of the divide; it undermines the idea that all work has a natural gender. See Sara M. Evans and Barbara J. Nelson, *Wage Justice: Comparable Worth and the Paradox of Technocratic Reform* (Chicago: University of Chicago Press, 1989). The mixtures of progressive and conservative impulses that have characterized both sides of the divide at different moments get a nuanced reading from Nancy F. Cott in her historical study of American feminism, *The Grounding of Modern Feminism* (New Haven, Conn.: Yale University Press, 1987).

37. See, for example, July R. Walkowitz, *Prostitution and Victorian Society: Women, Class, and the State* (Cambridge: Cambridge University Press, 1980).

38. Ellen Dubois, "The Radicalism of the Women Suffrage Movement: Notes Toward the Reconstruction of Nineteenth-Century Feminism," in Anne Phillips, ed., *Feminism and Equality* (New York: New York University Press, 1987), p. 128.

39. See Mary Daly, *Gyn/Ecology: The Metaethics of Radical Feminism* (Boston: Beacon Press, 1978). Maggie McFadden gives an account of this range in her useful taxonomy piece, "Anatomy of Difference: Toward a Classification of Feminist Theory," *Women's Studies International Forum* 7, no. 6 (1984), pp. 495–504. Adrienne Harris has pointed out to me that essentialism comes and goes in feminist psychoanalytic discussions of the penis: "The concept slips, moves and breaks apart."

40. Bell Hooks, "Feminism: A Movement to End Sexist Oppression," in Phillips, *Feminism and Equality*, p. 62.

41. Taken together, Alison Jaggar's essays on the equality/difference debate offer a poignant (and I think continuingly ambivalent) personal account of how one feminist theorist developed doubts about the equality position. See Jaggar, "Sexual Difference and Sexual Equality"; Alison Jaggar, "Towards a More Integrated World: Feminist Reconstructions of the Self and Society" (Talk at Douglass College, New Brunswick, N.J., Spring 1985); Alison Jaggar, "Sex Inequality and Bias in Sex Differences in Research" (Paper for the Symposium of Bias in Sex Differences Research, American Association for the Advancement of Science Annual Meeting, Chicago, February 14–18, 1987).

42. See, for example, Christine Stansell, *City of Women: Sex and Class in New York, 1789–1860* (New York: Knopf, 1986).

43. Zillah Eisenstein, *The Radical Future of Liberal Feminism* (New York: Longman, 1981).

44. Mitchell, "Women and Equality" (1976), reprinted in Phillips, *Feminism and Equality*, pp. 24–43.

45. The feminist scandal of the Sears case offers a particularly disturbing example of the divide as it can get played out within the exigencies of a court case. See Ruth Milkman, "Women's History and the Sears Case," *Feminist Studies*

12 (Summer 1986), pp. 375–400; and Joan W. Scott, "Deconstructing Equality-Versus-Difference: Or the Uses of Poststructuralist Theory for Feminism," *Feminist Studies* 14, no. 1 (Spring 1988), pp. 33–50. In her introduction to *Feminism and Equality*, Anne Phillips offers a useful instance of how, in different contexts, the feminist ambivalence about liberalism emerges; she observes that in the United States, feminism began with equality models that revealed their inadequacy in practice, while in Britain, feminists began with a socialist critique of liberal goals that their own disappointments have modified in the equality direction.

46. See the now classic restoration of Mary Wollstonecraft by Juliet Mitchell, "Women and Equality." Also see two more recent, subtle readings of Wollstone-craft: Patricia Yeager, "Writing as Action: *A Vindication of the Rights of Woman*," *The Minnesota Review*, no. 29 (Winter 1987), pp. 67–80; Cora Kaplan, "Wild nights: pleasure/sexuality/feminism" (1983), reprinted in Nancy Armstrong and Leonard Tennenhouse, eds., *The Ideology of Conduct: Essays on Literature and the History of Sexuality* (New York: Methuen, 1987), pp. 160–184. An instance of Wollstonecraft's contemporaniety: Linda Nochlin makes precisely her arguments about gender; Nochlin sees it as a variable changeable as class or vocation in her ground-breaking essay, "Why Have There Been No Great Women Artists?" (1971), reprinted in Thomas B. Hess and Elizabeth C. Baker, eds., *Art and Sexual Politics: Why Have There Been No Great Women Artists?* (New York: Macmillan, 1971), pp. 1–39.

47. Mary Wollstonecraft, *A Vindication of the Rights of Woman*, ed. Carol H. Poston (New York: Norton, 1975), p. 35.

48. Ibid., p. 5.

49. Ibid., p. 30.

50. Shulamith Firestone, *The Dialectic of Sex: The Case for Feminist Revolution* (New York: William Morrow, 1970), strikes me as offering the best instance of this mixture of tones in contemporary feminism. Firestone dedicates her book to de Beauvoir, but her political fervor comes much closer to Wollstonecraft's.

51. Phillips, *Feminism and Equality*, p. 22.

52. Rosenfelt and Stacey, "Second Thoughts on the Second Wave," *Feminist Studies* 13, no. 2 (Summer 1987), pp. 350–351.

53. Audre Lord, talk at the MLA.

54. Since the Hyde Amendment restricting Medicaid abortions in 1979, No More Nice Girls has done occasional, ad hoc street events in New York City to dramatize new threats to women's sexual autonomy.

55. In a longer version of this chapter, I plan to offer three studies of feminist political work: a longer discussion of the Baby M case; a personal account of the internal feminist debates about pornography; and a discussion of the political mixtures typical of women's peace camps such as Greenham Common.

FOUR

Mothers and Men's Wars

SARA RUDDICK

The rhetoric that pervades dominant understandings of war and peace is dichotomous and split along gender lines—a perfect illustration of standpoint theory. Within militarist thinking, as well as within larger militarist cultures, a warrior's death—and murder—is set against a child's birth; male violence against feminine connection; military destruction against preservative love.

The soldier[1] male wears a double face. He is a victim:

> From my mother's sleep I fell into the State
> And I hunched in its belly till my wet fur froze.
> Six miles from earth, loosed from its dream of life,
> I woke to black flak and the nightmare fighters.
> When I died they washed me out of the turret with a hose.[2]

He is a monster killer:

> With loud sobs, she rushes up to the child who is lying next to the dead soldier, drops to her knees, and draws the limp little body to herself. The soldiers' guns are lowered again. . . . She raises her skinny fist to the sky, trembling with impotent rage. . . . Zing, zing, zing. A whole pack of bullets zips past. The woman is hit.[3]

Often he's both:

> In bombers named for girls, we burned
> The cities we had learned about in school—

Till our lives wore out; our bodies lay among
The people we had killed and never seen.[4]

Whether victim or killer, War is his. A woman's name is on his weapon, her body is riddled by his bullets; it is her life, sleep, and care from which he has "fallen." But she cannot share the war he makes and which makes him. And although he counts on her to preserve a place that survives his madness, he also has contempt for what he sees as her innocence and safety:

> We soldiers are in the habit of respecting only those who have stood their ground under fire. That is why so many of us inwardly turn away from women, even when outwardly we can't do without them.[5]

The representative heroine of maternal peacefulness is the *mater dolorosa* ("mother of sorrows"), familiar from the lithographs of Käthe Kollwitz. Scrounging for food to keep her children alive, weeping over the body of her son, nursing survivors, sadly rebuilding her home, reweaving the connections that war has destroyed—as she grieves over her particular loss, she mourns war itself. Where she gives birth and sustains life, his war only hurts and destroys.

Faced with the division between men's wars and the life that the *mater dolorosa* sustains, women, mothers, and feminists cast their lot:

> My heart is moved by all I cannot save:
> so much has been destroyed
>
> I have to cast my lot with those
> who age after age, perversely
>
> with no extraordinary power
> reconstitute the world.[6]

The Myth: The Masculinity of War and Women's Peacefulness

Even from the soberest perspective, there is much to be said for dividing the world between men's wars and the women's world which they threaten. War certainly seems to be men's business. It is mostly men who make civil and foreign battle plans, who invent weapons and supervise their construction. Men predominate among the spies, police chiefs, judges, and governors who construct a peacetime order guaranteed by the threat of violence. The world's generals and negotiators, bombardiers and captains, chiefs of staff, and defense secretaries have been and still are mostly men. More men than women shoot the pistol and work the missiles; certainly more men than women command them.

Traditionally, in most cultures, it has been men's lot to fight while women watch, suffer, applaud, ameliorate, and forgive. In war men become "warriors." If they are killed, they are killed in action. Their deaths represent a sacrifice that is in part chosen and thus is a testament to courage. A man makes war partly for the woman whom he protects, who is his audience. "She loved me for the dangers I had passed, / And I loved her that she did pity them."[7] Her admiring tears make his fighting possible; her danger from his enemy makes his fighting necessary. Raped or killed, her possessions plundered, "his" woman is the last prize and the sweetest revenge his enemy exacts from him.

Militarists use the myth of war's manliness to define soldierly behavior and to reward soldiers. Boot camp recruits are "ladies" until, trained in obedient killing, they become men. Misogyny is a useful element in the making of a soldier, as boys are goaded into turning on and grinding down whatever in themselves is "womanly." "Women are dinks. Women are villains."[8] Sexist language for women and—almost the same—their bodies is common in military disciplines, as many battle chants reveal. Even where misogyny and lust are absent, the warrior embodies a peculiarly masculine ideal of camaraderie and lonely herosim:

> The idea is manliness, crudely idealized. You liken dead friends to the pure vision of the eternal dead soldier. You liken living friends to the mass of dusty troops who have swarmed the world forever. And you try to find a hero.[9]

Rarely does anyone, man or woman, deny the manliness of war. The views of David Marlowe, chief of the department of psychiatry at the Walter Reed Army Research Institute, are representative. According to Marlowe, men's strength and physical endurance qualify them to fight. Physical characteristics shade into others that are first biochemical and then social or sociochemical. Men's famous propensity for aggression is an example:

> [Men and women] are indeed better and worse at doing certain kinds of things. One of these things is fighting, certainly in the forms required in land combat. The male's greater vital capacity, speed, muscle mass, aiming and throwing skills, his greater propensity for aggression and his more rapid rises in adrenaline make him more fitted for physically intense combat.[10]

Social-biochemical properties become frankly social and sexual:

> Not only is the capacity to carry out aggression—i.e., to fight—related to the nature of the male bond, but a greater part of the bond's sustaining power lies in the language of male sexual identity. . . . The soldier's world is characterized by a stereotypical masculinity. His language is profane, his professed sexuality crude and direct; his maleness is his armor, the measure of his competence, capability and confidence of himself.[11]

Erotic male friendship is actually feared in most militaries, while erotic "male bonding" is celebrated. This bonding becomes a condition of fighting, as men's love for each other is wound into their capacity to kill:

> Combat in all human groups is and has been an almost exclusively male preserve, and organized warfare has been, in a sense, the expression of male-bonded groups that constitute armies and their analogues. As Lionel Tiger put it, "males are prone to bond, male bonds are prone to aggress, and therefore aggression is a predictable feature of human groups of males."[12]

Even ostensibly antiwar movies, such as *Platoon* and *Full Metal Jacket*, manage to celebrate the manliness and men-lovingness of war.

Virtually no one denies that military thinking is imbued with masculine values. Yet a boy is not born, but rather becomes, a soldier. Becoming a soldier means learning to control fears and domestic longings that are explicitly labeled "feminine." The soldier earns the right to violence and sex; to fail is to remain "womanly" while losing the fight to women. This much has long been familiar. What is increasingly clear is that becoming a militarist means acquiring a distinctive way of thinking that has also been associated with masculinity. As feminist critics have noticed, philosophers often honor, even as they construct, conceptual connections between reason, war, and masculinity. As Plato warned, the struggle to become reasonable "mustn't be useless to warlike men"; on the contrary, philosophers see to it that those men and (sometimes) women who are called "reasonable" have "proved best [both] in philosophy and with respect to war."[13] Both philosophy and war require transcending the particular affections and concrete complexities of "womanly" material and domestic life. . . .

As the tendency to define reason in opposition to the feminine takes different historical and philosophical forms, so too the masculinity and abstractness of military thinking change with the changing economic and technological contexts of war. In nuclear defense establishments, a "language of warriors," a "techno-strategic rationality,"[14] is shared by armers and disarmers, chiefs of staff and chief negotiators. This rationality exhibits in near caricature the kinds of dichotomization and abstraction that, in other contexts, have been characterized as male. As Jean Bethke Elshtain points out, military theorists

> portray themselves as clear-sighted, unsentimental analysts describing the world as it is . . . a world of self-confirming theorems invites fantasies of control over events that we do not have. . . . Through abstracted models and logic, hyper-rationalism reduces states and their relations to games which can be simulated. . . . One of the legacies of war is a "habit of simple distinction, simplification, and opposition." . . . One basic task of a state at war is to portray the enemy in terms as absolute and abstract as possible in order to distinguish as sharply as possible the act of killing from the act of murder. . . . It is always "*the enemy*," a "pseudo-concrete universal."[15]

In her account of her sojourn among defense intellectuals, Carol Cohn tells of how she learned to speak, and then was trapped in, a military language marked by abstractions and euphemisms that protect the speaker and prohibit the listener from even imagining the physical suffering of nuclear holocaust.

> "Clean bombs" [so-called because they release a higher proportion of energy through explosive blast than through radiation] may provide the perfect metaphor for the language of defense analysts and arms controllers. This language has enormous destructive power, but without . . . the emotional fallout that would result if it were clear one was talking about plans for mass murder, mangled bodies, and unspeakable human suffering.[16]

In this language, Cohn says, the reference points, the agents and the victims, are not people but weapons and weapons systems.

> There is simply no way to talk about human death or human societies when you are using a language designed to talk about weapons. Human death just is "collateral damage"—collateral to the real subject which is the weapons themselves.[17]

Techno-strategic rationality is only an extension, albeit a stunning one, of the abstractness that characterizes military discourse as a whole. In militarist thinking, human bodies are subordinated to abstract causes, different bodies are organized around abstract labels of civilian or soldier, "the enemy" or ally, us or them. Weapons, positions, and targets have always been the primary referents of military strategy. When Olive Schreiner claimed that "no woman would say of a human body it is nothing," implying the militarists are committed to exactly this denial, she was contrasting women's speech with the strategic discourse of "conventional" militarists preparing for the first world war.[18]

If war is "masculine" and "abstract," peace seems "feminine" in exactly the way standpoint theorists predict. Women's peacefulness often begins in negation; alienated women insist that they stand outside men's wars and are repelled by otherwise respect-worthy men who have been transformed by war's rhetoric. Virginia Woolf's *Three Guineas*, a feminist antimilitarist tract from the fascist thirties, has assumed a central place in contemporary feminist peace politics:

> Inevitably, we look upon societies as conspiracies that sink the private brother, whom many of us have reason to respect, and inflate in his stead a monstrous male, loud of voice, hard of fist, childishly intent upon scoring the floor of the earth with chalk marks, within whose mystic boundaries human beings are penned, rigidly, separately, artificially. . . .
>
> Therefore if you insist upon fighting to protect me, or "our" country, let it be understood soberly and rationally between us that you are fighting to gratify a sex instinct which I cannot share; to procure benefits which I have not shared and probably will not share; but not to gratify my instincts, or to protect myself or my country. . . . As a woman I have no country, as a woman I want no country, my country is the whole world.[19]

For many women, a more or less conscious alienation from "men's wars" is positively grounded in a history of caring labor. Patriotic East German women declare their political identities maternally as they address their government:

> We women do not regard military service for women as an expression of our equality, but as standing in contradiction to our existence as women. We regard our equality as consisting *not* in standing together with *those* men who take up arms, but in solidarity with *those* men who have like us recognized that the abstract term "enemy" in practice means destroying human beings. . . . We feel that as women we have a particular mission to preserve life and to give our support to the old, the infirm and the weak.[20]

A Soviet dissident writing from exile sounds a similar message:

> It is natural for women, who give life, to be opposed to war and violence—war of any sort, be it in Vietnam or Afghanistan, and violence against any being. We do not distinguish between guns and nuclear bombs, because all are weapons used for the death and destruction of people.[21]

The Australian physician Helen Caldicott has made a similar maternalist position well known in the United States:

> Women all over the world are mobilizing for disarmament. . . . As mothers we must make sure the world is safe for our babies. . . . Look at one child, one baby. . . . I have three children, and I'm a doctor who treats children. I live with grieving parents. I understand the value of every human life. . . . I appeal especially to the women to do this [peace] work because we understand the genesis of life. Our bodies are built to nurture life.[22]

The same point has been reiterated by so many women from so many nations over so many years that it is hard to hear it afresh. Nor is it only women who expect peacefulness from others. Some men attribute to mothers a romantic peacefulness that few who know them would dare to match. American physician and writer Lewis Thomas provides an exuberant example:

> All the old stories, the myths, the poems comprehended most acutely by young children, the poking and nudging and pinching of very young minds, the waking up of very small children, the learning what smiles and laughter are all about, the vast pleasure of explanation, are by and large the gifts of women to civilization. . . . Put the women in charge I say. . . . Place the single greatest issue in the brief span of human existence, the question whether to use or get rid of thermonuclear weapons of war, squarely in the laps of the world's women. I haven't any doubt at all what they will do with this issue, possessing as they do some extra genes for understanding and appreciating children.[23]

There is a sober basis for this rhetoric. All of women's work— sheltering, nursing, feeding, kin work, teaching of the very young, tending the frail elderly—is threatened by violence. When maternal thinking takes upon itself the critical perspective of a feminist standpoint, it reveals a contradiction between mothering and war. Mothering begins in birth and promises life; military thinking justifies organized, deliberate deaths. A mother preserves the bodies, nurtures the psychic growth, and disciplines the conscience of children; although the military trains its soldiers to survive the situations it puts them in, it also deliberately endangers their bodies, minds, and consciences in the name of victory and abstract causes. Mothers protect children who are at risk; the military risks the children others protect. What Chinua Achebe sees in a Biafran mother's "ghost smile" and "singing eyes" is war's perversion of preservative love:

No Madonna and Child could touch
that picture of a mother's tenderness
for a son she soon would have to forget

The air was heavy with odours
of diarrhoea of unwashed children
with washed out ribs and dried up
bottoms struggling in laboured
steps behind blown bellies. Most
mothers there had long ceased
to care but not this one; she held
a ghost smile between her teeth
and in her eyes the ghost of a mother's
pride as she combed the rust-coloured
hair left on his skull and then—
singing in her eyes—began carefully
to part it. . . . In another life this
would have been a little daily
act of no consequence before his
breakfast and school; now she
did it like putting flowers
on a tiny grave.[24]

Women's war narratives—fictional or remembered—draw on the power of Kollwitz's *mater dolorosa*. Through her eyes war is a catastrophic destruction that swamps whatever purposes lie behind it. While the staunchest militarist knows that war brings suffering, the *mater dolorosa* stands for the refusal to subordinate pain to tales of victory and defeat. As in the best war stories, "The cold *brutality* of the deeds of war is left undisguised; neither victors nor vanquished are admired, scorned or hated."[25] The vision of war as suffering amid the ruins takes on new poignancy as we imagine wars worse than any we have known. Anne Marie Troger is among those who have noted a surprising continuity between stories German women now tell about their experiences in World War II and the political rhetoric of the disarmament movement. As she notes:

women's memories of the inferno of burning cities under carpet
bombing allows one to imagine nuclear war: destructive forces
operating beyond interference, with no visible enemy or front.[26]

The tales of Hiroshima survivors speak in our century for war itself:

I heard her voice calling "Mother, Mother." I went towards the sound.
She was completely burned. The skin had come off her head
altogether, leaving a twisted knot at the top. My daughter said,

"Mother, you're late, please take me back quickly." She said it was
hurting a lot. But there were no doctors. There was nothing I could do.
So I covered up her naked body and held her in my arms for nine
hours. At about eleven o'clock that night she cried out again "Mother,"
and put her hand around my neck. It was already ice-cold. I said,
"Please say Mother again." But that was the last time.[27]

Mothers need not wait for war to become antimilitarist. Although I
only occasionally alluded to war in parts 1 and 2, I believe that everyday
maternal thinking contrasts as a whole with military thinking. Just-war
theories control our perceptions of war, turning our attention from bodies
and their fate to abstract causes and rules for achieving them. Nuclear
thinking gives an illusion of control over events that are profoundly
unpredictable. For mothers, too, the dream of perfect control is dangerously seductive, but in identifying humility as a virtue they relinquish
the fantasy of dominating the world. The analytic fictions of just-war
theory require a closure of moral issues final enough to justify killing
and "enemies" abstract enough to be killable. In learning to welcome
their own and their children's changes, mothers become accustomed to
open-ended, concrete reflection on intricate and unpredictable spirits.
Maternal attentive love, restrained and clear-sighted, is ill adapted to
intrusive, let alone murderous, judgments of others' lives. If they have
made training a work of conscience and proper trust a virtue, if they
have resisted the temptation to dominate their children and abrogate
their authority, then mothers have been preparing themselves for patient
and conscientious nonviolence, not for the obedience and excessive trust
in authority on which military adventures thrive.

Indeed, as I will argue in detail in the next chapter, if military
endeavors seem a betrayal of maternal practice, nonviolent action can
seem a natural extension. Maternal "peacefulness" is not a sweet,
appeasing gentleness that gives peace a bad name and has little to do
with children living peacefully in the world. When mothers fight with
their children or on their behalf, when they teach their children ways
of fighting safely, without being trampled on or trampling others, they
engage in nonviolent action. Since children are vulnerable and the
vulnerable are subject to abuse and neglect, mothers may be more than
usually tempted by sadism, self-indulgent aggression, and self-protective
indifference to the real needs of others. If mothers refuse to abandon
or assault their children but, whatever their disappointment and anger,
learn ways to live without giving up on the connections they have
fostered or the lives they have tended, they exemplify the commitments
of nonviolence.

In the glare of war's destruction and the light of women's hope, what mother would hesitate to "cast her lot" with peacemakers? As suffragist Anna Shaw asked several wars ago:

> Looking into the face of . . . one dead man we see two dead, the man and the life of the woman who gave him birth; the life she wrought into his life! And looking into his dead face someone asks a woman, what does a woman know about war? What, what friends, in the face of a crime like that does a man know about war?[28]

Complications

Men's wars, women's peace; a warrior's murder, a child's birth. "It's up to women to change the world." "Put women in charge, I say!" Both the rhetoric and the theory run up against two facts: men are not so warlike and women are certainly not peaceful.

Consider first the "masculinity" of war. There is, undeniably, a disproportionate male presence in defense councils and on battlefields as well as a masculinist military ideology to justify it. The manliness of war is an outcome of many factors. Considered as a biological class, men *may* have a greater propensity toward aggressiveness than women, and this aggressiveness, which is given license in wars, *may* also motivate some of the men who engage in them. On the other hand, warfare, especially in its contemporary forms, seems to require, as much as physical aggression, a tolerance of boredom or the ability to operate a computer under stress, characteristics that are neither distinctly "masculine" or heroic. Freudian theorists explain why men tend to need and be comforted by the abstract thinking that creates enemies and the abstractions and fantasies of control expressed in rules of war. But these same Freudians point out that the tendencies toward abstraction and control vary in historical circumstances and that, in any case, men differ from each other as much as women do. A legend of heroically violent manliness is taught in patriotic homes, neighborhood movies, schools, and boot camps. There is, too, the sheer weight of history, of Fathers and Fathers before them who marched away, fought, and, if they returned, were set apart by their knowledge of the mysteries of danger and death. I would not deny that cumulatively, biological, psychological, and historical conditions provide partial and modest explanations of men's greater propensity for war. The problem is that men's compliance in war or active pleasure in battle has been confidently explained in so many ways that we are likely to forget that the masculinity of war is in large part a myth that sustains both women and men in their support for violence.

Very few of the men who take part in war can be said to "make war." Most are foot soldiers and workers in the service of grand campaigns they did not design, about which they were not consulted, and which they rarely comprehend. Even within the military, the proportion of suppliers and bureaucrats to active fighters is high. These soldiers who do engage in combat are usually very young men. Many are conscripted for battle; others fight only to escape intolerable civilian life. Some boys fight eagerly; many of the eager boys are as deluded by patriotic fervor and duty to others as they are by masculinist myths. That they often fight for "national interests" and "causes" from which they derive no benefit and which they barely understand should not detract from the principles and loyalty that motivate them.

If men were so eager to be fighters, we would not need drafts, training in misogyny, and macho heroes, nor would we have to entice the morally sensitive with myths of patriotic duty and just cause. Indeed, history suggests that men have an even more ambivalent relation to the fighting expected of them than women do to the mothering work for which they are said to be "naturally suited." Some men thrill to battle and to the sexually predatory violence it allows. Others partake with mixed feelings but minimal question—simply because fighting is expected of them. Some of these men later report that they took pleasure not only in excitement and camaraderie but also in destruction, cruelty, and the bizarre deaths around them. But there are others, as well as these same men on other days, who are ashamed and disgusted by the killing. Then, in every war, are men who with clear-sighted courage refuse to fight, often at great cost to themselves.

It would be ironic if women were to accept a central, heroic image from military mythology: the male soldier on the battlefield of soldiers, a killer who can be killed. If the soldier is an executioner, he is also victim. As he makes war, war makes and often maddens him. Before she wrote *Three Guineas*, Virginia Woolf created Septimus Smith, a romantically patriotic, white working-class Englishman who "had gone through the whole show, friendship, European War, death, had won promotion" and thus had also "developed manliness."

> For now that it was all over, truce signed, and the dead buried, he had, especially in the evening, these sudden thunder-claps of fear. He could not feel.[29]

Toni Morrison's Shadrack, a Black American soldier "blasted and permanently astonished by the events of 1917," is also haunted by memory. While Septimus kills himself, Shadrack establishes a national suicide day to control death. His near hallucinatory memory of "the soldier" is quite specific:

> He ran, bayonet fixed, deep in the great sweep of men flying across the field. Wincing at the pain in his foot he turned his head a little to the right and saw the face of a soldier near him fly off. Before he could register shock, the rest of the soldier's head disappeared under the inverted soup bowl of his helmet. But stubbornly, taking no direction from the brain, the body of the headless soldier ran on, with energy and grace, ignoring altogether the drip and slide of brain tissue down its back.[30]

Shadrack's memory is worth clinging to: a headless soldier, running with energy and grace, as his brain drips and slides down his back. War's manliness.

Women's peacefulness is at least as mythical as men's violence. Women have never absented themselves from war. Wherever battles are fought and justified, whether in the vilest or noblest of causes, women on both sides of the battle lines support the military engagements of their sons, lovers, friends, and mates. Increasingly, women are proud to fight alongside their brothers and as fiercely, in whatever battles their state or cause enlists them. There is nothing in a woman's genetic makeup or history that prevents her from firing a missile or spraying nerve gas over a sleeping village if she desires this or believes it to be her duty.

War is exciting; women, like men, are prey to the excitements of violence and community sacrifice it promises. War offers personal adventure and economic advantage to men and women. It may be, however, that women are especially enlivened by war's opportunities just because they are traditionally confined by domestic expectations in peacetime. Nonetheless, women usually justify their militarism as men do, in terms of loyalty, patriotism, and right. Even peace-loving women, like most men, support organized violence, at least in "emergencies." Like some men, some women are fierce and enthusiastic militarists; others, also like some men, see war as a natural catastrophe but collude with it, delegating to leaders political and military judgments they do not intend to understand. Most women, like most men, believe that violence must be met by violence and that the virtue of a cause justifies the horrors done in its name.

Although women and men support war for reasons that transcend gender, war also excites women in gender-related ways. It is sometimes forgotten that to the extent that it is masculine, war is also distinctly feminine. As Virginia Woolf exclaimed in 1941, "No, I don't see what's to be done about war. It's manliness; and manliness breeds womanliness—

both so hateful."[31] War offers its own redescription of the work that standpoint theorists celebrate. Doing the wash keeps the home fires burning, a kiss inspires a soldier, and daily child care is suffused with a patrio-erotic glow. Even as it excites its distinctive brand of self-congratulatory heroism in feminine women, war also offers the adventurous—or the same woman in her adventurous moments—real and imagined freedoms from feminine duty. In wartime a women may lead a charge up palace steps, carry secrets behind the lines, blow up the troop train, free prisoners, or torture them—and thereby enrich the romantic imagination of all women.

Perhaps many women do not succumb to the romance of war and are instead horrified by "giving over living sacrifices in the bodies of male children for the survival of the homeland."[32] Yet war affords even horrified women the opportunity "to engage in deeds that partake of received notions of glory, honor, nobility, civic virtue."[33] Not surprisingly, even regretful mothers often construe their military service in maternal terms. A German munitions maker in the second world war, like many of her counterparts elsewhere, pithily described her war acts as a plausible extension of peacetime love and duty: "Earlier I buttered bread for him, now I paint grenades for him, and think 'this is for him.'"[34] Similarly, an English woman working in an armaments factory during the Falklands war explained her military activities as a widening of peacetime maternal concern:

> Our attitude was that although it was unfortunate we were involved [in the war], once it was upon us we had to get on and do everything to back our boys. People were very willing to work overtime and do whatever was necessary, whether you've got a son involved or not, when it's the English, it's your boys isn't it? I mean it could be your boy next time.[35]

When war ends, mothers nurse the survivors just as, at first, they painted grenades and then put gold stars in their windows. How could they do otherwise? In a time of crisis, would they foster dissension within a family or community whose connectedness it has been their responsibility to sustain? Having applauded their children's efforts from the first somersault to their latest high school test, would they undermine their resolve when legal force combines with community excitement to draft them for war? If her son is killed while killing, should his mother deny herself the consolation of giving his "sacrifice" a point? For her own sake, for her children and family's sake, isn't it a mother's duty to accept, hopefully, justifications for violence?

Listen again to Adrienne Rich:

I have to cast my lot with those
who age after age, perversely

with no extraordinary power
reconstitute the world.

These lines are preceded by lines that speak of "the fibers of actual life
/ as we live it now," symbolized by incomplete, interrupted, unfinished
weaving:

this fraying blanket with its ancient stains
we pull across the sick child's shoulder

Or wrap around the senseless legs
of the hero trained to kill[36]

It is the same blanket that mothers wrap around a sick child and a
wounded killer. A pure maternal peacefulness does not exist and cannot
be invented.

The Hope

A pure maternal peacefulness does not exist; what does exist is far more
complicated: a deep unease with military endeavors not easily disen-
tangled from patriotic and maternal impulses to applaud, connect, and
heal; a history of caring labor interwoven with the romance of violence
and the parochial self-righteousness on which militarism depends. Nor
for all her power to move us is the *mater dolorosa* a reliable instrument
of peace. In many Western cultures women are portrayed as strong and
brave victims of circumstances over which they have little control. Their
sufferings and sacrifices are expected; they persevere in a violent world—
but they bear no responsibility for it. Although she reminds us unre-
lentingly of war's suffering and the loving connections she persistently
sustains, the *mater dolorosa* also equates war to natural catastrophes, like
hurricanes, and peace to a normal quietness that catastrophe interrupts.
It is the beginning of peace politics to realize that war is an activity
for which human beings plan, in which they consciously engage, and
in which, therefore, they can anticipate the suffering they later mourn.
If it is essential for developing a peace politics to keep one's eye on
suffering, it is equally important to identify the actions that knowledge
of suffering requires.

The dilemma of women's peacefulness is the dilemma of peace politics
itself. Peacemakers must make people look closely and persistently at
the myriad horrors of war; peace requires standing in solidarity with
war's victims. Yet the victims' part can too easily be the part of despair

and apolitical perseverance. It is good to persevere and right to admire those who do. But the peacemaking woman has to become as active, inventive, and angry as an ordinary, harassed, coping mother. Yet unlike that mother she must find a way to see and to resist the organized violence that "befalls" her and her people. She must identify threats to the protectiveness that in an ordinary way she has valued and created, starting with threats to her own children and then including as many other children as her imaginative knowledge allows.

Although mothers are not intrinsically peaceful, maternal practice is a "natural resource" for peace politics. For reasons both deep and banal it matters what mothers say and do. Women, and perhaps especially mothers, have serviced and blessed the violent while denying the character of the violence they serve. A peacemaker's hope is a militarist's fear: that the rhetoric and passion of maternity can turn against the military cause that depends on it. Mothers have supported their boys and their leaders, but in the contradiction of maternal and military aims there is a dangerous source of resistance. Because mothers have played their military parts well, their indifference, their refusal to endorse, could matter now. The question peacemakers face is how the "peacefulness" latent in maternal practice can be realized and then expressed in public action so that a commitment to treasure bodies and minds at risk can be transformed into resistance to the violence that threatens them.

Käthe Kollwitz's lithographs and sculptures of loving, protective, and mourning mothers are hauntingly illuminating emblems of war's brutality and of the tenderness that might be peace. But in a poignant memoir,[37] the historian Sara Friedrichsmeyer reveals that after a "painful intellectual struggle" Kollwitz realized that "the values she espoused as a woman and mother could in no way be interpreted to support war." Kollwitz had to *learn* to stand against the German state and to reject its abstract military ideals.

Kollwitz sent her younger son to the first world war with flowers and a copy of *Faust*. It was partly her son's death that made her increasingly skeptical of military honor and loyalty to *patria*. But it was also the memory of his "sacrifice" and her desire to honor it that made it nearly impossible for her to accept her own growing antimilitarism. According to Friedrichsmeyer, Kollwitz's diaries reveal "an almost paralyzing bewilderment as she tries to balance loyalty to her son's memory with the horrible reality of the fighting." She *sees*, Kollwitz writes in her diary, only the "criminal insanity" of war, but thoughts of her son lead her to *feel* loyal to the army and the state for which he fought.

Friedrichsmeyer traces Kollwitz's halting, vacillating progress to antimilitarism. At first she can copy into her diary only the antimilitarist remarks of others; slowly she dares to criticize in her own words the abstract ideals of sacrifice and patriotism that she once found so moving. By the end of the first world war, Kollwitz was joining public demonstrations and writing open letters, first attacking the government's last desperate efforts of recruitment, then protesting German militarism, and finally renouncing war itself. Shortly after the war, Kollwitz declared herself committed to nonviolence, which, as she wrote to her daughter-in-law, "was not passive waiting" but "work, hard work." This new commitment provoked new conflicts as Kollwitz tried to reconcile her long-standing fervent support of revolutionary movements with her distrust of the violence they endorsed. Because of her public antimilitarist, socialist, and anti-Nazi sentiments, Kollwitz lost her teaching position and atelier when Hitler cam to power and was forbidden to exhibit her works. But she couldn't prevent her grandson's fighting and dying in Nazi Germany's army, nor do we know that she even tried to persuade him to refuse to serve or to attempt to escape.

In 1938, when she was seventy-one years old, Kollwitz created a small bronze sculpture called *Tower of Mothers* that depicts a circle of defiant mothers, arms outstretched, joined to protect the children massed behind them. This sculpture epitomizes the maternal antimilitarist works that have made Kollwitz a heroine of feminist peace politics. But none of the lithographs or sculptures adequately expresses their creator's internal conflicts and intellectual as well as emotional struggles to see and to act. It is Kollwitz's conflict, learning, and hard work, even more than her achievement, that I find inspiring.

Notes

1. To avoid clumsy repetition, I use the term "soldier" to stand for anyone in the military. I mean no insult to the air force, navy, marine corps, coast guard, or any other branch of service.

2. Randall Jarrell, "The Death of the Ball Turret Gunner," in *The Complete Poems* (New York: Farrar, Straus and Giroux, 1969), p. 144.

3. Klaus Thewelweit, *Male Fantasies* (Minneapolis, University of Minnesota Press, 1987), p. 176.

4. Jarrell, "Losses," in *Complete Poems*, p. 145.

5. Thewelweit, *Male Fantasies*, p. 62.

6. Adrienne Rich, "Natural Resources," in *The Fact of a Doorframe: Poems Selected and New, 1950–1984* (New York: Norton, 1984), p. 264.

7. Shakespeare, *Othello*, I, iii, 167–68.

8. Tim O'Brien, *If I Die in a Combat Zone* (New York: Dell, 1979), p. 52.

9. O'Brien, *If I Die*, p. 146.

10. David Marlowe, "The Manning of the Force and the Structure of Battle, Part 2: Men and Women," in *Conscripts and Volunteers, Military Requirements,*

Social Justice, and the All Volunteer Force, ed. Robert K. Fullinwider (Totowa, NJ: Rowman and Allenheld, 1983), p. 190.

11. Marlowe, "The Manning of the Force," p. 191–92.

12. Marlowe, "The Manning of the Force," p. 191. Nancy Hartsock has written in a profound and illuminating way on the connections of war and masculinity. See [Chapter 7]. . . . Judith Stiehm has also written extensively and in very interesting ways on the masculinist ideology of the military. See *Bring Me Men and Bring Me Women: Mandated Change at the Air Force Academy* (Berkeley: University of California Press, 1981) and *Arms and the Woman,* forthcoming.

13. Plato, *Republic,* 543a, 521d.

14. The phrase "techno-strategic rationality" is Carol Cohn's, and she has enunciated it in numerous talks. See "Sex and Death in the Rational World of Defense Intellectuals," *Signs,* vol. 12, no. 4, pp. 687–718. The notion of a "language of warriors" comes from Freeman Dyson, *Weapons and Hope* (Princeton: Princeton University Press, 1984). Dyson compares the language of warriors with the language of victims.

15. Jean Bethke Elshtain, "Reflections on War and Political Discourse: Realism, Just War, and Feminism in a Nuclear Age," *Political Theory* (February 1985), pp. 49–50.

16. Cohn, "Sex and Death," p. 691.

17. Cohn, "Sex and Death," p. 711.

18. Olive Schreiner, *Women and Labor* (1911; London: Virago, 1978), p. 173.

19. Virginia Woolf, *Three Guineas* (New York: Harcourt Brace/Harvest, 1938), pp. 105, 109. Woolf, however, did not deny her love for her country. Rather, she said that she would use her patriotism, "this drop of pure, if irrational emotion, to give to England first what she desires of peace and freedom for the whole world."

20. East German Women, *Radical America* (Jan.–Feb. 1983), p. 40.

21. Tatyana Mamanova, *Women in Russia* (Boston: Beacon Press, 1984), p. xiii.

22. Helen Caldicott, *War Resister's League Calendar,* 1981.

23. Lewis Thomas, *The Youngest Science: Notes of a Medicine Watcher* (New York: Viking, 1983), pp. 236–37.

24. Chinua Achebe, "Refugee Mother and Child," from the section "Poems on War" in *Beware, Soul Brother* (London: Heinemann, 1972), p. 12.

25. Simone Weil, *"Iliad:* Poem of Force," Pendle Hill Pamphlet no. 91, Wallingford, PA, p. 32.

26. Anne-Marie Troger, "German Women's Memories of World War II," in *Behind the Lines: Gender in the Two World Wars,* ed. Margaret Higgonet, Jane Jenson, Sonya Mitchel, and Margaret Weitz (New Haven: Yale University Press, 1987), p. 286.

27. Hiroshima survivor, cited in Bel Mooney, "Beyond the Wasteland," in *Over Our Dead Bodies: Women Against the Bomb,* ed. Dorothy Thompson (London: Virago Press, 1983), p. 7.

28. Anna Shaw, speech to Women's Peace Party, 1915.

29. Virginia Woolf, *Mrs. Dalloway* (London: Penguin Modern Classics, 1973), p. 96.

30. Toni Morrison, *Sula* (New York: Plume Books, 1973), p. 8.

31. Virginia Woolf, *Letters*, vol. 6, ed. Nigel Nicholson (London: Hogarth Press, 1980), p. 464.

32. Jean Bethke Elshtain, *Women and War* (New York: Basic Books, 1987), p. 101, Chap. 3.

33. Elshtain, *Women and War*, pp. 101–2.

34. I first read this slogan in Leila Rupp, *Mobilizing Women for War* (Princeton: Princeton University Press, 1978), p. 115. I then learned from Claudia Koonz, *Mothers in the Fatherland: Women, the Family, and Nazi Politics* (New York: St. Martin's Press, 1987), that the phrase is from a recruitment poster and that German women themselves were more reluctant than women of other industrial countries to take up war work.

35. Reported in Hilary Wainwright, "The Women Who Wire Up the Weapons," in *Over Our Dead Bodies*, p. 144.

36. Adrienne Rich, "Natural Resources."

37. I am obviously very much indebted to Sara Friedrichsmeyer's paper "'Seeds for the Sowing': The Diary of Käthe Kollwitz," in *Of Arms and the Woman*, ed. Helen Cooper, Adrienne Munich, and Susan Squier (Chapel Hill: University of North Carolina Press, 1989). All citations in these paragraphs on Kollwitz are from this article. Claudia Koonz, in *Mothers in the Fatherland*, suggests that Kollwitz's resistance to the Nazis was only partial (see p. 317). Of various efforts to make sense of women's complex relation to militarism and war and at the same time to criticize militarism from a feminist and women's perspective, I have found especially useful Chapter 11 . . . and Jane Roland Martin, "Martial Virtues or Capital Vices? William James' Moral Equivalent of War Revisited," *Journal of Thought*, vol. 22, no. 3, Fall 1987. I have also been influenced by Anne Marie Troger's discussion of women's victimization in "German Women's Memories of World War II."

FIVE

Bringing Artemis to Life
A Plea for Militance
and Aggression in
Feminist Peace Politics

ADRIENNE HARRIS _____

Joanna Russ's feminist science fiction novel *The Female Man*[1] has at its center a utopian women's community. This is a universe of women living peacefully and playfully. The ancient conflicts of power and possessiveness, the bedeviling problems of child care and work have been resolved. Miraculously, wit, work, sex, play, and individuality survive. But this world of women clings to a myth about its origins. Half the population died of a plague that mysteriously only carried off men Without guilt, violence, action, or intention, this peaceful world of women arose. In truth, this genial, gentle world is the outcome of a sex war, and one figure in the novel, Jael, epitomizes this war. She is a manhater, armed with retractable, stainless steel fingernails, a woman who murders men, particularly men in power. Jael is a sacrifice to the future, essential to change, but anachronistic and dangerous to the utopian culture she has been instrumental in bringing about.

The Female Man plays on an old opposition of peaceful women and warlike, aggressive men. There are many ways to read the rupture or disjunction in the novel. Women find a utopian peace, but the aggression that enables change will be obliterated in denial; the price of peace is the eradication of men; or to achieve peace, to preserve life, women must repress and deny the angry, destructive parts of self.

The novel works through a series of contradictions that are echoed and preserved in many historical and contemporary women's peace movements: peace won by sex war; women's peacefulness in the absence of men; feminine styles of thought and feeling in opposition to masculine ways of being and doing. These contradictions are the ground of this chapter.

Historically, women's peace parties built a brilliant politics on the traditional opposition between men who make war and women who wait receptively to repair and weep. Throughout this century, women took the power they had in the domestic sphere, enlarged on it, moved this power into the public world, and claimed the force of moral motherhood to organize opposition to wars. Sometimes women's peace parties sought genuinely to embody these feminine virtues and sometimes strategically and consciously to manipulate them.

The waiting, reacting woman represents peaceful rest. Although she may technically be mother, wife, sister, lover, or moral guide and critic, she waits always in the position of *mother*, as the one to whom return is made, as the mirror that reflects the bravery and valor of military men. Mothering, nurturance, and life as the "angel of consolation" make woman the one in whose name war is made and danger suffered, the one who holds the place for virtue and love, while men do the dirty work of violence and death. Even as critic, she acts as mother.

Contemporary feminism now raises a series of questions for pacifism and traditional women's peace politics. Does the opposition of peaceful woman and war-making man solidify rather than dissolve militarism? Are women in a privileged relation to peace? Is this peacefulness a natural or social construction? Is the peacefulness of women constructed upon passivity and repression as well as upon nurturance and empathy? How much have the traditional reflectiveness and passivity of female socialization soaked into and marked peace practices, thereby acting as a subtle but debilitating undertow to political lives and structures?

Peace movements guided and infused with *feminist* ideology and theory do rehabilitate activity and militance into their practices and actions. This chapter makes a contribution to that process by addressing the question of women's militance from the perspective of psychoanalytic feminism. I want to move the argument through three realms. First, I use feminist psychoanalytic theory to illuminate women's dilemma with regard to aggression and assertiveness. Second, I draw on French feminist theory to frame this dilemma as a problematic relationship to language and speech. Third, I explore the work of Julia Kristeva and the Russian linguist Mikhail Bahktin to suggest the liberatory power and potential for diversity in language.

Psychoanalytic Feminism

It is worth taking a moment to ask why psychoanalysis is such a powerful constitutive force in social and personal life. It seems unlikely that the excavation of infantile and unconscious experience will be adequate to the task of dismantling state power and the swollen military system. Psychology and psychoanalysis, used critically and self-critically, are necessary although not sufficient to an understanding of patriarchal culture and militarism.[2] As Juliet Mitchell noted more than a decade ago, psychoanalysis must be taken seriously as the most subtle and deep reading of the way patriarchy is inscribed in psyche.

Using both feminist theory and psychoanalysis, I argue that the opposition between masculine war-making and nurturing peaceful women, so crucial for the peace movement historically, is now, seen through the prism of contemporary feminist thinking, deeply problematic. Women have remained too exclusively tied to the ancient mythology of woman as nurturer, preserver of life, and symbolic representation of nature. Artemis and Athena, mythic representations of women of mind and action, wisdom and authority, women embodying the idea of *woman for herself*, have been diminished and neglected.[3] These are the figures and mythic creatures that a feminist peace politics revives in our imagination, our art, and our political practice.

At the level of personal life, the opposition of aggression and peace-ableness is organized as a radical separation of thoughts or feelings, a primitive defense against experiences imagined as dangerous to self or other. This defensive splitting plays a crucial role in the construction of gender. There are splits among styles of being, aspects of subjectivity, the phenomenal experience of speech, action, and identity named as masculine or feminine. Men are enjoined to represent such "masculine" features of self as assertiveness, authority, dominance, and reason. A feminist psychoanalytic reading names these features *phallic*, intending that term to indicate socially derived entitlements—the power to speak, to represent authority, to name desire. Women, on the other hand, are inserted in the social semiotic of the family and the larger community as Other, as object, as one barred or kept from action and power.

I will build on two traditions within psychoanalytic thought that address the origins of this dichotomy in early experience, its investment with questions of masculinity and femininity, and the maintenance of these splits in adult lives and social formations. The first wave of feminist theory used psychoanalysis to argue that early symbiosis and merger with a maternal figure, who is both longed for and feared, shaped the particular defenses of adult men and women and contributed to the construction of sex role identity.[4] Questions of gender identity, then, are wrapped around and implicated in the process of separation and in-dividuation that characterizes the first years of life. Jessica Benjamin has built on this work to show how these processes of differentiation—"an impulse for differentiation," as she has termed it—arise differently for male and female in the earliest negotiated experiences of parent and child.[5]

Another tradition in feminist psychoanalysis, primarily developed in France, sees the crucial structure maintaining female silence and marginality as women's conflictful, impeded relationship to language.[6] Women in their personal lives and in their intellectual and political work struggle to recuperate action and militance, but this must be linked to a new feminist discourse, a new relationship to language. Language, in this view, is a force for social control. This perspective requires a shift in our conventional ideas about language and how it functions. Words, sentences, the act of speaking, are never simply neutral carriers or representations. Rather, language as a formal system and as a mode of communication is shaped by the dominant ideology in any culture, shaped by the forces of domination and power. Language, in this view, inherently acts as a force for law and order, expressing, among other themes, the dominant forms of patriarchy in our culture. In this way, language would be inhospitable to female aggression because language is set up, in its structure and in its content, to manage female passion, not to express it.

The French analyst and philosopher Luce Irigaray, through a critical examination of Freud's work on femininity, shows how the psychoanalytic interpretation of female development constrains women to silence through the apparent eradication of feminine desire, action, longing. She has set up a chain of associations: father, law, interpretive discourse, language, and Freud; these structures shape and proscribe feminine action and desire. *Female libido*, a term erased from analytic discourse, is assumed by Freud to disappear from the female psyche as well.[7] The woman "leaps" up to the maternal place, the position of one to whom the desiring man returns, a position of one who is penetrated and dominated. Irigaray has tracked a connection between objectifying women and silencing them.

Women and Militance

In so many accounts of women's experience, the dilemma and concern about militance or aggression are central. In clinical work, many women do not make distinctions among being active, being aggressive, being competitive, and being destructive or angry. These conceptually and phenomenally discrete experiences blend and smudge. When a woman fails to make these distinctions, many projects involving mastery, creativity, and achievement may acquire some taint of destructiveness or rage, feelings she experiences as dangerous and forbidden. Very often her social surroundings collude with this judgment. Prohibition on the expression and sometimes even the consciousness of aggression or militance generalizes to many related but actually distinct phenomena. In the conduct of many activities and intense experiences, including working creatively and skillfully, visibly having power, arguing a position, or making a personal demand, a woman comes to feel she has gone too far.

Although the imagined consequences of anger or aggression differ in each woman's case, some retaliatory consequence rides hard on the heels of female assertiveness, whether in dream, fantasy, or actual experience. Some women cast the net of inhibition so tightly that their capacity to work and to act in the world is gravely compromised. Others act, try their strength, but undo the efficacy through depression or even more serious acts of self-sabotage. For other women, the negative undertow appears in fantasy and imagined retribution.

A young artist goes to arrange for the first public show of her work. A triumph and afterward a fantasy: All her former advisers and professors circle her in a hostile assault on her work. How deeply the prohibition on activity and creativity bites. In the very act of making art, she experiences fear of the excitement of creative work itself. She will stop herself in anxiety if the experience is too intense. She is afraid that her art reveals her excitement and her greed as well as her vulnerability. She is also afraid that if the work is good, she will be hated. Unbearably, she will become the object of envy. As she struggles with these demons, she continues an intense and passionate encounter with work. It would be a mistake to see her struggles as only a conventional tableau of masochism. Rather, in the deep demands of creative work, we see the emergence of a conflict many women experience—about entitlement and aggression. In the imagination of this woman, a shadow falls across the experience of pleasure, particularly pleasure in activity.

Activity and Aggression
Between Mother and Daughter

I want to locate women's difficulties with aggression in the traces of the relations between mother and daughter. Feminist excavation of a girl's early bond with her mother reveals a complex and contradictory situation.[8] Nancy Chodorow and Dorothy Dinnerstein have drawn attention to the early mother-child tie as a primary site for the construction of gender. The intensity of this first bond with the mother, the bounty and terrible power wrapped up in our maternal imagos, the relative unavailability of the father as a source of identification for the girl all compromise and impede a girl's move toward autonomy and separation.

The bonding and shared identification between mother and daughter can yield up a double message: intensity and commonality, on the one hand, but a shared legacy of negativity, self-doubt, and depression on the other. The early experience of mother may be one of power and authority, but this is undermined steadily, for mother and daughter, in the context of the larger culture and often within the family. If a daughter grows up defensively distanced from her aggression and anger, if her commitment to her own separateness and autonomy is silenced and her ambivalence about nurturance and femininity unacknowledged, this becomes her psychic legacy to her daughter. If, when she mothers, this ambivalence toward both nurturance and aggression maintains its unconscious hold, the early experience of separation provided for her daughter may be problematic. Thus, in the reproduction of mothering a foreclosure on action is also reproduced, and this foreclosure is at the heart of mother-daughter relations, leaving traces of envy and anxiety in its wake.

A complex story emerges if we listen to how women imagine the consequence of their anger or aggression. Women frequently report that they fear the destruction of the object of their anger, that retribution will arise because their anger could do so much damage. I am going to pursue Donald Winnicott's thinking on this matter because he makes so much of the constructive features of aggression.[9] My argument is also clearly indebted to U.S. interpreters of Winnicott, particularly Emmanuel Ghent and Elsa First, and to Jessica Benjamin's work on differentiation.[10]

Winnicott produces prescriptive developmental theory. A child needs to have an aggressive and active engagement with another person that is handled nondefensively, that is, without retaliation or collapse. The aggressive feelings, the destructive, angry, often dangerous-feeling impulses seem then to be contained by the other person, usually the other. This encounter with a person is crucial for the recognition of boundaries between self and other. The object of this anger or destructiveness must survive it, and that nondefensive survival releases the child to experience herself as *subject* and to experience other people as *objects* who are themselves *subjects*. This experience breaks the illusion of omnipotence, the fantasy of destructiveness, the belief that fantasy is as powerful as action, and creates *externality* for the child. There is something or someone outside, an Other whose action operates independently of the child's action or wish. The containing experience establishes this Other as different. The sensitive handling of the child's aggression acts as a crucible of real relatedness and thereby establishes different but related subjectivities.

Winnicott's views on the importance of destructiveness and aggression for development are couched in dramatic language—the importance of awareness by the mother of her hatred for the baby and by the child of hatred for the object. Empathy is not sufficient to provide for both separation and recognition of the Other's subjectivity.

From psychoanalytic accounts and from empirical work in developmental psychology, we can draw ample evidence that both a child's aggression and parental management constitute a robust and pervasive sex difference. There is much more monitoring and supervision of a girl's aggression. For many young girls, aggression is handled in a way that compromises the movement to separateness and autonomy.[11] Because most mothers are women, we can see the transmission of this defensive structure across generations as mothers' conflicted histories with aggression impact on the handling of daughters' aggression, which may take the form of destruction and rageful outbursts or active striving.

A failure in this developmental transition requires a defensive distancing from anger and aggression, which in fantasy remain too dangerous, too devastatingly omnipotent. This is the curious paradox. Failure to trust in one's own efficacy and a deep inhibition in work and many activities coexist with the inner conviction that one is dangerous and destructive.

This contradiction is one to which women are particularly prone not solely because of the dilemma of separation from the maternal figure. The acts that would lead the girl toward an experience of separateness and boundedness are often coded as masculine. Irigaray, reading Freud, notes the fate of a girl's activity, her early experiences of longing, desire, "phallic" excitement. Women exist in an impossible position. Activity is to be given up in the disastrous discovery of shared "castration" with the mother. If women's active striving remains, it can only be present as masculine, or phallic, and thus these strivings remain in the adult women as pure pathology, the disorders of envy or hysteria. Femininity is a "secondary" formation dictated from "prescriptions useful to masculinity."[12]

Irigaray criticizes psychoanalytic theory for its role in silencing women as actors, as desirers. She also speaks of the inner world and psychic reality of many women. The consequences of this social and psychic process can be read in many clinical accounts in which a woman entering the terrain of activity, often of creative enterprise, is debilitated by anxiety and shame. This response seems to look in two directions, to involve two different processes. On the one hand, activity, with its implications for individuation and separation, leads away from mother. Esther Menaker has analyzed female masochism as a defense that holds in place the guilt and ambivalence a woman experiences at the prospect of separation from her mother.[13] For many women, simply being active establishes a difference from the receptive, reflecting mother. Difference is then often imagined to be an act of cruelty or abandonment. A daughter may feel that difference evokes her mother's envy. There is also danger from another direction—an imagined punishment for movement into forbidden, male, father-dominated terrain.

The young painter in my earlier example reported two dreams as she continued to prepare for her first show: "I am standing in a room with my husband and this friend who is a painter. He's lounging in a bathtub. Each man has taken off his penis and hands it to me. Both are erect and I am holding them, thinking about which is bigger, comparing them." For this young woman, the man in the bathtub was a figure she deeply envied. Like the male painters who dominate the art world she longs to enter, he seemed self-satisfied, self-directed, free to act as he wished, feeling naturally empowered to paint and to be at ease. Taking the penis from her husband, which she grasped in her hand like a paintbrush, could signify empowerment. Yet she spoke about the anxiety of female empowerment in the context of the deadly opposition of the sexes. In a system organized around presence and absence, when one has, the other lacks. Her strength and ambition will diminish those of her husband. One phallus circulates between a man and a woman. She gets the phallus only when it is given to her. The phallus is offered not appropriated. She is still the recipient relying on the gift, not on her own activity and effort.

In the dream, there is a surplus in the phallic economy. We may read this as an attempt to solve the dilemma, the wish that there could be two desires, two active, striving subjectivities. The other solution represented in the dream is repression, for the figure of the painter lying in the bathtub may stand for this woman's empowered, active "male" self, still submerged. In the symbolic material of this dream we see how women still struggle for a language and a representation of their desires. This is the heart of Irigaray's indictment of Freudian theory. There is as yet no language for female libido or female power that can challenge or provide alternative to the symbol that stands for the very idea of sex—the penis.[14]

Certainly there is as yet no clinical language, no theoretical apparatus within psychoanalysis to claim activity as a gender-free experience. The woman who holds out for activity, who refuses to give up action for receptivity and pleasure in passivity, who maintains an identification with her father or some masculine character is definitively pathologized. The familiar and damning construct of "masculine protest" is her lot in psychic life. "Penis envy" is her organizing principle.

Penis envy is, for Irigaray, a necessary construct in patriarchal culture. In patriarchal psychoanalysis, it is required to maintain and valorize the phallus. Marie Torok touches on the importance of this construct for women in a somewhat different way.[15] It is not, she feels, bedrock psychic material, the experience beyond analysis, but rather the representation of a defense. In the descriptions women give of the envied penis or its symbolic substitute, it is already idealized. It is an imaginary phenomenon, a part-object, a representation. In that sense, as idealized, it is a projection of the strength, desire, and potency that women feel barred from. The experience that is envied is that of feeling naturally entitled to pleasure, action, and growth. This is not Karen Horney's position, in which penis stands for social power; rather, the penis stands for socially constructed power that men experience as a natural, even biologically based power. The nexus phallus/penis is the site where the social is reproduced as the biological.

The painter's second dream:

I'm standing in a large room in the house I grew up in. There is a large white rug and one chair. Like a chair my father had and sort of like one my husband has. I have this beer I'm drinking and I spill beer out of this long-necked bottle and watch the stain spread across the rug. It makes this large rectangular patch. My mother comes from the kitchen. I think she's going to clean up the stain. There is going to be a party and my mother tells me to go into the kitchen to make the tuna fish salad, to prepare for the guests.

The mother arrives to stop the making of paintings, to stop the daughter from encroaching with stains, messes, spills, and her creativity upon the terrain of the father. Mother calls her daughter to the task of making food for guests, back to the old, safe, mother-identified position of nurturance. And the tuna fish? The painter said it was something her mother made that she particularly loved, a favorite food of childhood. In this minor detail of the dream, I think we see the poignancy of the constrictions upon mother and daughter. The food is for guests. As women, we have not been able to imagine our own creativity fueled and fed by mother love. This is also a dream brimming with the smells and stains of sex. Pleasure, too, for this woman must be compromised and inhibited. To assume authority or creativity, to be responsible for the functions of desire or action, is to encounter two dilemmas: the guilty movement away from the mother and the danger in straying into forbidden, masculine terrain.

Envy functions in a terrible double action here, maintaining the woman in an oscillating, punishing, contradictory dynamic. We might track envy, in fact, as the underside of female action and aggressivity. Envy is the moment when action is subverted and collapsed. In response to the frightening maternal imago, a woman may take up various defensive stances to ward off the unbearable feelings that arise from being the object of envy. I will refuse to be different, refuse to be active, refuse to leave my mother with her passivity, her depression, her disappointment.

Turned in the other direction, toward a culture that masculinizes activity and biologizes the phallus, the worm turns as it were. Now the subject of envy, positioned as a subservient in the hierarchy, a woman is caught up in the corrosive and impotent rage at male entitlement to action assumed as a natural privilege. Envy is the placemark of submerged feminine action, the sign of angry capitulation to gender placement and gender politics.

Reparation

At the level of peace politics, I argue for the development of the nonmaternal. The maternal position, despite its pacifist practice and its vulnerability to love and loss, is incomplete, insufficient for the task of peace. Elsa First's reading of Winnicott on mothering brings to our attention a curious but necessary dimension of that activity: maternal hatred. "A mother must be able to tolerate hating her baby without doing anything about it."[16]

There is perhaps nothing more terrifying and destabilizing than the idea of maternal hatred or maternal aggression. The fact of maternal malevolence and destructiveness is, in my clinical experience, almost beyond assimilation by a young child. The awareness of mother as dangerous and destructive seems constantly to threaten the child's inner world. The idea of danger from such intimate close quarters shatters the very structure of thoughts, the flow of ideas. We count on mothers (and on the maternal principle in analysts) to absorb aggression, to manage and maintain the illusion of safety and control. Where is hatred to be placed?

Winnicott bravely calls down the mythic goddess figure, the primordial mother figure both wise and terrible, and we must bravely follow his idea of the developmental necessity, the cleansing possibility, of maternal hate. This is a hatred not dulled into depression nor expressed as sadism, but a hatred based on the mother's wishes, needs, fantasies as separate from the child's. This hatred is necessary for the child's development, but also for the mother's. A rereading of analytic texts, an infusion of analytic understanding of aggression, and a feminist-informed understanding of mothering will transform maternal practice. This transformation will be crucial for the continued evolution of feminist peace politics, which lean on and use maternal practice.

The deliberately provocative use of the word *hatred* highlights its importance as a balance to the enveloping symbiotic tie of "primary maternal preoccupation." What must be acknowledged here are the irreducible differences between maternal love and female autonomy. This makes of women's mothering a place of deep ambivalence, but an ambivalence that, if acknowledged, promotes separation and growth for both participants and, if unacknowledged, may compromise development. At the mythic level, it is the dialectical union and nonidentity of Artemis and Demeter, the duality of women's experience in which her private pleasures, thoughts, and imaginings, her active self, coexist with the intensely projective, encompassing, and empathic connection to a child.

A postscript on the artist. She works hard at painting and struggles with her terror in creative work and ambition. In her dream life, a series of images unfold, self-representations that mark a shift in her accommodation to her own activity. In one dream, a very fat woman flings a grand brushstroke across a canvas that the dreamer has been painstakingly producing. The stroke of paint finishes the painting wonderfully. The painter's association to the fat woman is a woman who has pleasure without guilt. Later, in another dream, the artist's husband muscularly throws a set of bookcases around a kitchen, opening up space, giving her more room for her studio. She is terrified. A glass object, a wedding gift, smashes to the floor. Her power will damage the marriage. Later, she dreams a monkey is in her studio. It is an elegant white creature with red and blue zigzags cut in its fur. She calls to her husband, "A monkey is playing in my studio." He tells her not to worry. She is exhilarated, and anxious.

To encourage and permit this integration of love and hate on a political level, a feminist peace practice would promote a pacifism grounded not solely in maternal concern but in a more conscious appropriation and recognition of hatred and aggression as aspects of self. Accepting ambivalence, validating the integration of masculine and feminine parts of self, and feeling less terrorized and anxious at the prospect of women's aggression and power offer the hope of a pacifist practice based on self-knowledge, not denial and repression. The integration of militance and nurturance, of maternal and nonmaternal, of woman for herself and woman as mother could create at the cultural and intrapsychic level the conditions for pacifism. At its heart, pacifism entails the incontrovertible recognition of the humanity and subjectivity of the opponent. The split in our culture and in ourselves, which gender socialization constructs and exemplifies, stands in the way of developing such practices.

Women and Collective Experience

At the heart of feminist peace politics, indeed of most feminist practice, is a commitment to the collective experience of women. Women's practices and women's attributes are idealized and often identified with nature.[17] The women's movement has always luxuriated in the discovery of common experience, of emotion-based, mother-connected, woman-identified forms of life and being. This has been a necessary healing. In the developed, political, and social forms of feminist practice, many of these elements continue to enrich political life, but in tension with the requirement to support and nourish difference and real heterogeneity. The refusal of hierarchy is not necessarily the refusal of difference. Feminism, as it is being practiced at Greenham and Seneca, provides an important alternative to the valorizing of hierarchical leadership and conventionally masculine models of political organization.

In fact, feminist peace politics critiques the concept of hierarchy by undermining and deconstructing military discourse. The language of militarism is preoccupied with penetration, accumulation, and hierarchical control. But this militarized control is illusion, based on an illusory sense of omnipotence. The emperor truly has no clothes. This illusion of control and rational planning is maintained in many ways, including the use of gender stereotyping. The inability to see the other person, the women as subject, maintains in patriarchal culture and its discourses the fiction of *opposite* sexes, in which woman is reduced to mere reflection. This fiction of opposites actually denies difference. This structural and psychic blindness maintains men and masculinist culture in a solipsistic universe, an imaginary relation with self in which women are a necessary fiction, useful only as the mirror for masculinity. The stakes are not just peace but reality. If we accept the opposition of peacemaker/woman and warrior/actor/man, we accept a perverse universe, where difference, heterogeneity, and respected Otherness are impossible. Feminist practice is teaching us that hierarchy is no guarantee against regression and the loss of individuality and boundaries.

Yet the psychoanalytic accounts of early separation and individuation do provoke questions for feminist process, which surface in the organizational forms and activities of feminist and woman-based groups, such as the peace camps. The passion and idealization of woman-based political groups must indeed pull some of their appeal from an idealized longing for the fused symbiosis of mother and infant. But the idealization of woman-to-woman experience may also be a defense against the more tumultuous and conflict-laden experiences of separation, particularly for mother and daughter. In women's political groups, we may find remnants of the unconscious undertow of envy and guilt that seems a part of many women's move toward individuation. It is difficult for women to gain access to speech. It is also difficult for women to struggle through conflicts and differences without hostility. Sara Ruddick's analysis of maternal practice points to women's great strengths in managing conflict,[18] but this strength exists in the *mediation* of other's conflicts. Women are often less adept and less comfortable when the conflict involves their own interests.

In woman-based or separatist peace actions and practices, there is often a tension between personal action and responsibility to the collectivity. Personal endeavors of individual women may be denounced as elitist or male identified. The particular conflicts women may have with their own activity and intensity may turn into a lethal and hostile rejection of activity and enterprise in other women. This is a tricky matter because the critique of hierarchy and the creation of a process designed to break the silence and disenfranchisment of many women constitute one of the most important developments in feminist practice. But the repressive structures that silence women and pull for passivity are insistent and not always conscious. A psychoanalytic consideration of the feminist group process invites questions. We need to examine closely our political forms and practices so that we can determine how we may have perpetuated the repression of women as we are attempting to free ourselves for action and transformation.

The Struggle for Language

In many contexts, social groupings, and institutional forums, women report difficulties in speaking, difficulties in being heard, in naming desires, in speaking authoritatively, in being taken seriously. Feminist theory defines this practical dilemma as an outcome of patriarchy that is reproduced in the very structure of language and discourse. Political practice in the women's movement has sensitized women to power differentials in argument and public speaking, to struggles for self-expression and presence in political discourse.

The theoretical argument that men and women are situated differently in respect to language is stated most canonically by Jacques Lacan.[19] His claim is that women are excluded and objectified as Other not *from* language but *by* language. The distinction is subtle but important. Language is formed and shaped by the culture in which it develops. In patriarchal cultures, language, like all cultural forms, will be imbued, soaked, invested, and structured with this dominant ideology. Language, in its many forms and functions, is thus one format for the operation of law and order under patriarchy. Language, in this way of theorizing, is a subtle and somewhat insidious cop, policing what we say, how we say it, and by what authority we express ourselves. To follow this argument, then, language, in its very form and function, operates as a barrier to women. Woman's silence, her repression and her separation from her own desires and capacities for growth, are kept in place through the operations of language.

Language, from this perspective, is a powerful force in cultural and political life, and one of its crucial operations is to establish, for each gender, a position in respect to speaking. There are rules of access and empowerment. Language is thus one source of state power. Women are barred by fiat from speaking as "subject," and this exclusion is carried in the very structure and form of language.

Now, in Lacan's rather baleful vision, no one really inhabits and controls language. If women are kept as Other, as outsider, as the object of desires, never the subject of their own sentences, men also suffer a displacement. Men must struggle to represent desire and authority, without, of course, ever fully appropriating language. The law touches all speakers. What law, exactly? Well patriarchal law certainly, a system of thought and political power in which gender hierarchy and gender privilege prevail. But also, a linguistic law, an aspect of all language— it is in the character of language that it distorts and expresses, that it is both formal and public, private and personal. We must all borrow the public system of speech to communicate, and in acquiring the skill that distinguishes our humanity, our inner experience is distorted and changed. Language acquires us as much as we acquire it, and in that inevitable process, all people's subjectivities are distorted and split.

Nonetheless, the phallic hegemony established and maintained through language endows men with greater authority than is afforded to women. The feminine text, viewed negatively, is a hysterical, disorganized eruption. This theoretical position has led to a creative but troubled discourse in literature, and in psychoanalysis, in an effort to develop what may be broadly described as female authorship, the speaking "I" of women's experience. In *écriture feminine* (these feminine forms and modes of writing), the old stereotype of the feminine is rehabilitated. In this feminist aesthetics, woman artists and writers stake a claim on the terrain of the unconscious, the emotional, the sensuous as the particular province of women's experience.

We can see forms of *écriture feminine* in the political practice of feminist peace groups—that is, in the disruption of linear, standard, critical argument and orthodox styles of protest. There is an unmistakable aesthetic and style of women's peace demonstrations: weaving wool around the gates at Seneca; levitating the Pentagon; using magic, songs and incantation, witches' chants, bread and flowers in response to guard dogs and chains. The theater and aesthetic of women's peace politics parallel the explorations in literary texts of a discourse that envelopes and welcomes silences, gaps, and rhythms and of a prosody connected to a women's body and to her lived experience.

It is a daring but problematic strategy, worked out in theory and in practice. In stressing the fluid, anarchic, labile forms of knowing, writing, and speaking, women activate many standard stereotypes of the feminine but seek to rehabilitate and transform them. Women are reaching for another access to language, another discourse not bound in the crippling forms of patriarchy, but frankly subversive.

Julia Kristeva is a crucial figure in this tradition. Her particular gloss on semiotics is to see discourse as a site that fuses the semiotic and the symbolic, where the inchoate, latent, primary process experience (primarily a discourse of child body to maternal body) erupts into and enters the symbolic forms of language.[20] Women participate in this discourse as dissidents by virtue of their exclusion from their own subjectivity in language and by their more primary access to the semiotic. A feminine presence in discourse leads to a reappropriation of the body, female pleasure, and action. The life, activity, and practice of women in the peace camps are just such an appropriation conducted through language and political action.

A different way of thinking about language and its potential for change and development arises in the work of the Russian linguist Bahktin.[21] Bahktin takes the same situation, in which Lacan reads unapproachable phallic hegemony established through language, and imagines it differently. This situation, an inevitable, inherent feature of language, is the unbridgeable gap between subjectivity and speech, between desire and its signifiers. Lacan endows language with a codified deadness. In his view, language is a closed system in which women, subjected to speech, are barred through the very structure and organization of language from speaking as subjects. What has been mystified is the origin of the power that maintains a species trait—language—as the special preserve of one group within the species—men. For social power, invested in the authority of the father, enforces male privilege in respect to language. This power is masked in code. The social origins of this power are neutralized and at the same time universalized by being set in the structure of language. This is an intricate ideological operation to disguise the social as the structural and to embed this patriarchal structure in the deepest reaches of mind and unconscious process.

Bahktin, following Ferdinand Saussure's distinction between *langue* (the formal system of language) and *parole* (the acts of speaking), focuses on *parole*, on speech, as it carries the ensemble of social relations, ideology, power dynamics, and context. For Bahktin, as for Lacan, there is an irresolvable difference between mind and world, I and Other, self and the markers for self. When we have shared experience with another person, this is an artifact of systems of shared reference. The public character of language is what brings an individual's experiences into apparent conceptual unity. Bahktin is caught up with the paradox of the universality of uniqueness. No one is fully present in and through language, a situation that demoralizes, decenters, but simultaneously offers the possibility of expansions in awareness and in meaning.

Speech, whether oral or literary, is always dialogic. There is always both a speaker and a listener. Any text, however produced, is a social event, a multivoiced dialogic experience limning a horizon "pregnant with possibility." Speaker and listener can never be fused into one identity, and words cannot exhaust meaning. Text is thus a place for the encounter and engagement of multiple subjectivities. Dialogues and multiplicities of meaning reverberate in every act of speaking or writing. The inevitability of other consciousnesses, other readings, other meanings enriches and expands subjectivity. Speech engages all the participants in a vital encounter with the ambiguities and contradictions embedded in meaning itself. Through this process, the possibility of respect for difference is opened up.

In discourse there is always an active "struggle against the necessity of forms." Because consciousness and expression cannot exhaust each other, language merely sets a particular border on consciousness, holding the personal, fluid, chaotic, and specialized meaning in dialectical tension with the formal system. The volatility in words makes language a site for creativity, imagination, and shifting perspectives. The capacity of language to provide altering perspectives as different subjectivities enter the struggle with words for expression makes it an astonishing tool for the sharing of consciousness, the expanding of alternate perspectives, not organized as polar opposites but as genuine heterogeneity. Language is the meeting place of Otherness, of plurality.

Let us not sanitize the idea of struggle for meaning, replacing Lacanian phallic rigidity with a Bahktinian vision of language as the all-encompassing, mediating mother. Language is a place for aggression and disruption. Speech is a site for volatility and hatred and refusal to accommodate. Feminist peace politics in many actions and many situations has made and validated a "feminine text," but not in a docile and conventional form of pacifist practice. Throughout many decades, this pacifism has evolved a unique form of militant nonviolence. These practices are altering political discourse, capitalizing on the subversive nature of women's experience, making militance that roars and heals. Look for the fierceness and the sensuality, the strength and militance mixed with care and gentility. The history of women and in particular of modern feminist peace practices contains much experimentation and development of political actions that integrate love and hate through the use of political discourse in which subversion and connection reverberate.

I close this chapter with three witnesses of such political action. One is a feminist reading of a prefeminist movement, and two are contemporary feminists describing the unique forms of feminist nonviolence.[22]

Amy Swerdlow on the disruptive appearance of Women's Strike for Peace at the HUAC hearings in 1962:

> The first witness at the Committee kept talking about what she saw when she saw her children's Wheaties and no one could get her off that subject. Well, after her testimony the first day, the *Washington Post* ran a cartoon which showed members of the Committee sitting at their tables saying to each other, "Which one is subversive? Women or peace." . . . Every time a witness was called, all the women in the hearing room stood up and the witness was presented with flowers which changed the entire atmosphere of this Committee which usually was very menacing, very dour to something very celebratory. And there were women there sitting feeding their babies bottles, at that time they didn't breast feed in public—but it was a circus.

Gwyn Kirk on the women at Greenham:

> The camp is there without permission so even by going to the camp, you are involving yourself in an action. . . . Beyond that there have been lots of actions to do with blockading the gates to the base, trying to stop the construction vehicles going in and out to build the missile silos. And cutting through the fence, trying to breach the security. To undermine the whole idea that there is any security with nuclear weapons around. Women have climbed over that fence, cut through it, gotten on to the base. They've written peace signs and symbols over the very long runway. They've written peace signs on all the little huts that the guards sit in. They've stolen official documents out of offices. They've gotten into the control tower, basically saying with their bodies and their lives, we don't give you any authority to do this.
>
> I remember on one occasion watching the police, in utter exasperation, trying to keep a gate open when women were blockading it. Three or four women were just moving backwards and forwards between the gateposts, threading woolen yarn backwards and forwards. Every time the police moved forward to break it, they patiently knotted yarn together again. And all the time they were singing and moving backwards and forwards, really quite slowly and deliberately and in a somewhat provocative way. But the police were so furious that all they had to react against was something as insubstantial as woolen thread.

On another occasion women went over the fence for a picnic on April 1st. And they decided to go dressed up. The idea was of a teddy bear's picnic. So they were in theatrical costume. They were teddy bears and pandas. Someone was a witch. There was a hot pink rabbit.

Sometimes women sing a lot. And keen, which women used to do at funerals and now it's only done in very remote parts of Western Ireland and Scotland. And I remember once a police officer saying, "I wish you'd stop making that noise. It really gets to me."

And, finally, Isabel Letelier on women's actions in Chile:

This group of Women for Life, they are really the best examples of creativity, imagination to organize non-violent, active non-violent rallies. For instance, they held one day democratic rights, in the streets and they decided to have elections and they brought ballot boxes to many, many shantytowns. It was done in many places around the country. In Santiago the women put the ballot boxes in the street and people would vote for democracy and after they had voted, they would give them a little sign that said I voted for democracy. The police didn't like this at all and came with water cannons and with the tear gas and with some terrible gas that makes you vomit. . . . Women have learned how to protect themselves against this tear gas and against the vomit gas. What happens is that sometimes the military overdo it. They throw too much of this and even they are affected by the poisonous gases. So in the last rally women came to the soldiers and taught them to protect themselves using lemon and ammonia and water and salt and they didn't know what to do. The soldiers felt terrible.

That was rare. We are not talking about the enemy the way Gandhi talked about the British. These are people that have been trained in the National Security doctrine and they have this horrible concept of the enemy as within the people. Therefore they don't hesitate in hurting you right away. In November 1986, there was a huge rally which was called "For Life." We are More. Somos Mas. And this was an extraordinary rally where women met—there were columns of women marching from the different sectors of the city. So they got together in a place where they started reading litanies in which they said There is more of us. Somos Mas. For life. For democracy. For freedom. For full employment. Somos Mas. And the police came and they brutally repressed the whole group. With the water cannons. The water cannons are filled with filthy water. The smell is really unbearable and the tear gas and the vomit gas. Everytime they arrested a woman, a whole group would follow that woman and if they throw her in a police car, the whole group would get into the police car.

Notes

1. Joanna Russ, *The Female Man* (Boston: Beacon Press, 1987).

2. Psychoanalysis is in a dialectical relationship of mutual influence, infusion, and support with what the historian Jacques Donzelot, *The Policing of Families* (New York: Pantheon, 1976), has called the "psy" apparatus. This apparatus, an array of theory and practices deployed in education, social science, pediatrics, and psychiatry, establishes normative structures and forms for personal life, in particular the psychic life and social life of women. These values, normative structures, and practices are used as social control both externally in cultural and institutional forms and internally as aspects of psychic life and subjectivity.

3. A number of feminist scholars have been working on an analysis of images of women in myth. See Merlin Stone, *When God Was a Woman* (New York: Dial Press, 1976); Margo Adler, *Drawing Down the Moon* (Boston: Beacon Press, 1981); and Starhawk, *Dreaming the Dark* (Boston: Beacon Press, 1982).

4. Nancy Chodorow, *The Reproduction of Mothering* (Berkeley: University of California Press, 1978); and Dorothy Dinnerstein, *The Mermaid and the Minotaur* (New York: Harper Colophon Books, 1976).

5. Jessica Benjamin, *The Bonds of Love: Psychoanalysis, Feminism, and the Problem of Domination* (New York: Pantheon Press, 1988).

6. Luce Irigaray, *The Speculum of the Other Women* (Ithaca, N.Y.: Cornell University Press, 1985), p. 85, quoting Freud in "the dissolution of the Oedipus complex" (*SE*, 11, p. 176). For Irigaray, castration is a psychic event that befalls women through the denial of their desires. According to this view, desire is male, a process that "casts women out of a primary metaphorization" (p. 84).

7. Ibid., p. 84.

8. See Jane Flax, "Mother-Daughter Relationships: Psychodynamics, Politics and Philosophy" in Hester Eisenstein and Alice Jardine, eds., *The Future of Difference* (New Brunswick, N.J.: Rutgers University Press, 1980). Also see Jessica Benjamin, "A Desire of One's Own," *The Bonds of Love.*

9. Winnicott's theoretical papers on the concept of "good enough mothering," creativity, play, symbolization, and the role of hatred in development can be found in the collected papers published as *Playing and Reality* (London: Tavistock Publications, 1980); *Through Paediatrics to Psychoanalysis* (New York: Basic Books, 1975); and *The Maturational Processes and the Facilitating Environment* (New York: International Universities Press, 1965).

10. Jessica Benjamin, "The Bonds of Love: Rational Violence and Erotic Domination," in Eisenstein and Jardine, eds., *The Future of Difference.* Elsa First analyzed the role of hatred in development in a paper read to the New York Freudian Society on March 15, 1985. Emmanuel Ghent, "Masochism, Submission and Surrender" (Paper presented at the New York University Postdoctoral Program in Psychoanalysis Colloquium Series, New York, October 1984).

11. A major review of sex differences is found in Eleanor Maccoby and Carol Jacklin, *The Psychology of Sex Differences* (Stanford, Calif.: Stanford University Press, 1974). For a critical account of the study of sex differences, see Julian Henriques, Wendy Hollway, Cathy Urwin, Couze Venn, and Valerie Walterdine, *Changing the Subject* (London: Methuen, 1984).

12. Irigaray, ibid., p. 120. Here Irigaray addresses the contradictions in Freud's treatment of femininity: the exclusion of women from any position of empow-

erment in respect to desire and the confusion in respect to proposed explanations of this lack of empowerment. Irigaray notes that in Freud's explanation of feminine character, a consideration of the social dimension of women's situation is strikingly absent.

13. Esther Menaker, *Masochism and the Emergent Ego: Selected Papers of Esther Menaker*, ed. L. Lerner (New York: Human Sciences Press, 1979).

14. Irigaray, ibid., p. 58. Here Irigaray notes the singularity of representation for sexuality—the phallus (and sometimes, concretely, the penis)—as the sole metaphor for sexuality. She critiques the theory's patriarchal appropriation of desire and pleasure for masculine experience alone.

15. Marie Torok, "The Significance of Penis Envy in Women," in Jeannine Chasseguet-Smirgel, ed., *Feminine Sexuality* (Ann Arbor: University of Michigan Press, 1966).

16. Winnicott, *Through Pediatrics to Psychoanalysis*, p. 202; also see pp. 204–218.

17. Separatist politics has been attacked by critics using new work in psychoanalytic theory. Jeannine Chasseguet-Smirgel offers a politically conservative reading of the relation of individual ideas and the function of groups. She draws on a construct in Freud's metapsychology, the ego ideal. Chasseguet-Smirgel sees the formation of the ego ideal as a defensive response to the first separation from a powerful, engulfing mother. The experience of blissful fusion is lost and with it the sense of infantile omnipotence. This omnipotence is then defensively projected onto the world (the ego ideal) as represented in a person, a politics, a utopian vision. The power or pull of any group lies in its embodiment of the ego ideal. Groups pull for regressed and primitive behavior in which personal identity dissolves in fusion to the group itself. The group is unified by a refusal of difference. Jeannine Chasseguet-Smirgel, *The Ego-Ideal* (New York: International University Press, 1985). (Her view of the ego ideal is different from the classical view, which connects the ego ideal to the superego or to processes set off by the child's negotiation of the power dynamics and proscriptions of the Oedipal crisis.)

Christopher Lasch has energetically taken up this concept as a cudgel to gender-based groups. He continues to conduct a blanket condemnation of feminist practices and to pursue the familiar masculinist paranoia in which all connections among women are problematic and regressive, indeed dangerous for patriarchy. Lasch outlines this position in his introduction to Chasseguet-Smirgel's *The Ego-Ideal*, and in his own book, *The Minimal Self* (New York: Norton, 1984).

18. Sara Ruddick, "Maternal Thinking," *Feminist Studies* 2, no. 3 (1985), pp. 342–367.

19. Jacques Lacan's analysis of the relation of language and sexual difference is developed in a number of essays in *Ecrits* (Paris: Seuil, 1966), in particular, "God and the Jouissance of the Woman," and "Fonction et champ de la parole et du language en psychanalyse." His work is discussed in two introductory chapters by Juliet Mitchell and Jacqueline Rose in a collection of Lacan's essays, *Feminine Sexuality* (New York: Norton, 1982).

20. Julia Kristeva discusses Bahktin's work in "Word, Dialogue and Novel," an essay reprinted in Julia Kristeva, *Desire in Language* (New York: Columbia

University Press, 1980), pp. 64–91. Her treatment of semiotic process and mother-child discourse is also developed in this text.

21. Bahktin's work is available in the translated essays credited to V. N. Volosinov but in fact written by Bahktin, *Marxism and the Philosophy of Language* (New York: Seminar Press, 1973), and in *The Dialogic Imagination*, ed. Michael Holquist (Austin: University of Texas Press, 1981).

22. Transcripts of interviews conducted for a radio documentary, *Woman as Peacemaker*, broadcast on IDEAS, the Canadian Broadcasting Corporation, October 1986.

SIX

Our Greenham Common
Feminism and Nonviolence

GWYN KIRK _____

> Living at Greenham seems like a challenge, an adventure. It makes few compromises with mainstream society, it is an alternative, an outdoor community of women. Living up against the fence means that there is no switching off—the terror is on our doorstep. We experience autumn, winter, spring and summer as we've never experienced them before. . . . From our alternative reality, the world from which we come looks pale and comfortless. We have to transform it. Not by reforms, but by revolution.[1]

In August 1981 a small group of women organized a peace march from Cardiff (South Wales) to Greenham Common, a virtually unknown U.S. Air Force base in England, 125 miles away, as a protest against the decision made by the North Atlantic Treaty Organization (NATO) to site ninety-six U.S. cruise missiles there. They arrived on September 5. Some decided to stay. Others had to go home, but more women came, doubtless never imagining that what was soon called Greenham Common Women's Peace Camp would still be there more than eight years later, an inspiration to countless thousands of people in Britain and around the world.[2] In Britain, *Greenham* has passed into everyday language, a term both complimentary and pejorative. It is a symbol of hope, a style of creative, nonviolent direct action, an organizational process, a network of women's peace groups, a politicizing experience, a certain kind of woman, a style of clothing. The word represents strength, courage, imagination, persistence, confrontation, marginality, deviance, and stigmatization. In the nearby town of Newbury many people call the camp women "the smellies." Some people said the women poke their babies' faces through the wire fence surrounding the base and throw live cats over the fence to frighten the military, although the people who said this did not see it themselves.

Throughout the first winter (1981–1982) women lived relatively comfortably in tents, caravans, and tipis, with a portacabin office and a large shelter for a communal living room and meeting space. Nevertheless, Newbury District Council forbids any structures on Greenham Common, and since these early months this regulation has been rigorously enforced for long periods of time. Women have had to live out in the open or at best take shelter under sheets of plastic, sleeping in Gortex sleeping bags in the winter. At times they have lived in old vans or "benders"— small shelters made from bent over branches covered with plastic tarps. They cook over open fires. There is one cold water tap, no electricity, and no telephone. A major part of life at the peace camp is taken up with sheer survival: tending fires, drying out bedclothes, keeping food dry, ensuring that everything is compact and mobile so that if there is an eviction women can move their belongings in minutes—before the bailiffs destroy them.

Since the initial march from Cardiff, there have been literally thousands of protest actions against cruise missiles at Greenham Common, at 102 U.S. military bases and facilities in Britain, and in towns and cities throughout the country. Two actions at Greenham involved thirty thousand and forty thousand women encircling the nine-mile perimeter fence. Other actions have been much smaller—vigils, repeated blockades of the gates, women cutting the fence and going onto the base time and again.

Women have maintained an unbroken, round-the-clock presence, surviving the bad weather of nine winters, harassment, evictions, arrests, imprisonment, and attacks by vigilante groups. Looking through the fence, we can see the missile silos and the day-to-day military routine, never forgetting their dreadful purpose.

Cruise missiles are first-use nuclear weapons. Each one is sixteen times as lethal as the bomb dropped on Hiroshima. As ground-launched weapons, the missiles at Greenham are allegedly vulnerable to attack because their location is fixed and known. To counteract this, the U.S. military plans to disperse them at times of "international tension" to secret firing positions in the countryside. Since March 1984 cruise missile convoys of twenty-five or more armored vehicles, with a heavy, British police escort, leave the base periodically on maneuvers.

In theory the convoy is supposed to "melt into the landscape." In practice it is clearly visible from the ground and from surveillance satellites. We can expect the Soviet Union to go to a nuclear alert every time the convoy leaves the base at Greenham. What no one knows is whether this is an exercise or the real thing and if there are nuclear or conventional warheads on the missiles. Such operations are, in their very ambiguity, aggressive and highly dangerous.

Whenever this happens, Greenham women join a wide network of peace groups—Cruisewatch—that track the convoy, publicizing its route and deployment site. Forty-four deployments occurred at roughly monthly intervals between March 1984 and February 1988. People stopped the convoy hundreds of times en route to its launch sites. They painted peace signs on the windshields. Once, a woman cut the air brake cable on a launch vehicle. Another woman caused a support vehicle to break down by putting a potato up its exhaust pipe. Women have climbed up into convoy vehicles and ridden along in them. The military has not been able to move the convoy in secret or without opposition, and military leaders admit this.[3]

Some women have come to Greenham because it is a women's community. Others make the campaign against nuclear weapons their prime concern and downplay feminist issues. Thousands have been drawn to Greenham during the years, and many have been profoundly changed by their experiences. The peace camp extends and develops traditional peace protests and demonstrations because it is a women's action, protesting in original and creative ways. But more crucially it involves leaving home, literally and metaphorically, speaking out about our anger, fear, and hope—being independent women.

Greenham is down to earth, heroic, moving, hilariously funny, and jarring. It is visionary and utopian with a timeless quality that is both very old and prefigurative of a simple, peaceful, postnuclear society. The consumerism and false sophistication of the industrial world are largely irrelevant. Without clocks and regular schedules, time itself seems highly compressed and very drawn out. The basic living conditions and simplest technology, together with the close friendships and womanmade culture of songs and rituals, are reminiscent of preindustrial ways of living. They also anticipate a time when the earth's resources are truly shared, when people in industrialized nations will live more simply, recognizing that peace cannot be achieved at the expense of other people's poverty, illness, starvation, and oppression.

Greenham is one of the most exciting political developments in Britain in recent years, completely outside (and its very existence a critique of) party politics. It also offers a challenge to left-wing political groups with their male-dominated agenda and hierarchical style and to the British peace movement, which narrowly defines peace as disarmament.

The history of the peace camp does not seem linear; rather, it seems more like a rhythmical process, ebbing and flowing as the tide. The original camp at Yellow Gate has moved from sites near the fence to sites near the main road and back again several times due to evictions.[4]

In March 1984 the road up to the base was widened in an attempt to move the women, in what was described at the time as the eviction to end all evictions. Since October 1984 there have been evictions almost every day, yet women are always there. The peace camps at the different gates develop and evolve. Some have closed several times and reopened. There are times of reflection and reassessment and a slow working toward the next development. There are times of bitter argument and division, times of rejuvenation and times of holding on.

In this chapter I look at Greenham as an example of feminist nonviolence. In Chapter 14 I discuss the Greenham network as a political form.[5] I have separated these two strands for clarity and emphasis, but this somewhat arbitrary division unfortunately cannot reflect the interconnectedness between these aspects. I use Greenham in a broad sense to mean the peace camp and the many women's peace groups and projects associated with it. I have been involved in this network since February 1982 and have participated in many of the actions and discussions mentioned here, although I have not lived at the peace camp for any length of time. (I use "we" when describing actions I was involved in and "they" when discussing those I heard about or observed.) For me, as for so many others, Greenham has been an extremely important focus, forging, however falteringly, a distinctively feminist peace politics.

Nonviolence as a Way of Life

I see nonviolence not just as the absence of violence but as a total approach to living, an ideal to aim for and a strategy for change. In Gandhi's words: "The first principle of nonviolent action is that of noncooperation with everything humiliating."[6] Nonviolence means refusing to support a system based on cynicism, greed, and utter contempt for human life. Nonviolence applies to how we relate to one another, how we spend our time and money, as well as how we conduct our campaigns. It involves a dignity and power that come from inner conviction; a belief in ourselves, our creativity, and intelligence; and a belief that people can change and grow. It is a commitment to openness, a celebration of life.

Nonviolence is not meekly turning the other cheek, nor is it a routine tactic—a mass demonstration on a Sunday (perhaps outside a government building where no one is at work) with civil disobedience on Monday for those who want to get arrested.[7] However sincere and inspiring these actions may be, this is a caricature of nonviolence as a philosophy of life.

Without questioning the "success" of violence, many people deride nonviolence as naive and utopian, assuming that it cannot be effective or that it will have to be abandoned when the "real struggle" begins. Yet we cannot achieve peace through violence. It is a fundamental contradiction in terms. We are saying that nonviolence is a possibility, that nations as well as individuals can settle differences without resorting to violence—and must, given the potential devastation of nuclear technology. We undermine our argument if we use violence ourselves. In saying this, I am not telling other people how to judge their own experiences. Some situations are so oppressive that violence may be the only option for immediate survival. But nonviolence is not simply a white, middle-class luxury, a privilege of so-called liberal democracies, as is sometimes made out. At root, it is truly oppositional.[8]

A Feminist, Nonviolent Practice

There are important overlaps between feminism and nonviolence.[9] At Greenham, women have brought a challenging assertiveness to nonviolence by expressing themselves unequivocally in confronting the police and the military. Feminist nonviolence is strong, empowering, and fun. Nonviolent actions include singing and keening or being silent; decorating the fence surrounding the base with photos of our family and friends, children's drawings, toys, clothing, colored ribbons, balloons, prayers, and poems; growing tomatoes in a shopping cart so that they are instantly movable in an eviction; softly calling out names of women we want to remember alongside the fence at dusk; cutting the fence and getting onto the base; painting messages on the roads; obstructing cruise missile convoys; wearing a badge that says "War is menstruation envy"; changing the sign R.A.F. Greenham Common to read OUR Greenham Common.

*   *   *

On March 8, 1983, International Women's Day, a group of women handed out "peace pies"—small cakes, each with a message about peace—outside the Bank of England in London. They had posters linking the squandering of vast resources on weapons with famine and malnutrition, particularly in the Third World. This action had a gentle atmosphere. It is unusual to be given something nice by a stranger in the street, and the action generated constructive conversations about peace and disarmament with passersby. On May 24, 1983, International Women's Day for Disarmament, women at a supermarket made the point that as taxpayers each family spends £18 (approximately $30) a week on arms. They walked around the supermarket with two shopping trolleys, one full of cardboard bombs and missiles and the other with

£18 worth of groceries. To highlight the government's war plans, another group hammered crosses into the lawn in a local park, designated as a mass burial ground in the event of war. Others held a "die-in," blocking traffic at a busy intersection for four minutes, the warning time we would get before a nuclear attack.

I want to discuss six principles of feminist nonviolence in some detail: assertiveness, enjoyment, openness, support and preparation, flexibility of tactics, and resistance.

ASSERTIVENESS

As women we often respond to events rather than defining them from the outset, or we hold back from saying what we really believe. By contrast, the aim of nonviolent direct action is to make a strong, clear statement. This includes each woman's ideas and convictions, the means employed to make that statement, the action, and the ways of dealing with its immediate consequences. We set up the situation on our own terms and keep the initiative by not allowing anyone to undermine our resolve. We choose temporarily to set aside feelings of fear, nervousness, embarrassment, or anger. Nonviolent action feels very strong to the participants, with a powerful unity of thought and feeling.

This is an important contrast to how many people (including some feminists and some left-wing activists) see nonviolence—as passive, reactive, and self-denigrating. It is important to distinguish between the surface appearance—women lying down in the road, for example—and the underlying reason for it. Although we appear to be surrendering our bodies, we are in control. We make a conscious decision to take part, and we can choose to leave.

So much of patriarchal thinking involves false polarization, including the ostensible polarity of being aggressive or being a victim. A nonviolent approach shows the narrowness of this conceptualization. Trying to understand and communicate with people who are against us does not mean that we have to demean ourselves. Being nonviolent in an action does not mean making things easy for the police or letting their violence against us go unchallenged. If they hurt us, we can say so clearly and loudly.

By blockading the gates at Greenham, women confronted the men who were building the cruise missile silos with the reality of what they were building and the police with the reality of what they are "protecting." At the first full blockade (March 21–22, 1982) women yelled to the police who were dragging other women out of the road to stop being used by the U.S. military; to stop defending the U.S. Army against British women; to think for themselves. This yelling culminated in shouts of, "We are ashamed of you! We are ashamed!" Another time, during a ten-day action in September 1984, women pushed the perimeter fence over in several places. A group of U.S. soldiers was called out in the middle of the night to fix it. They worked in silence, lighted by truck headlamps, as if on stage, while women on the outside of the fence kept up a stream of remarks, asking them why they were at Greenham or in the military at all; what their mothers, wives, and girlfriends said about it; if they knew how many kitchen tables could be made from the new timber they were using to shore up the fence. Women are constantly challenging the police, politicians, judges, and the military, telling them to take responsibility for what is happening at Greenham Common.

ENJOYMENT

Women's nonviolent action is celebratory and life affirming and expresses our power, creativity, and imagination. Singing, music, colorful decoration, costumes, and jokes are important elements. Sometimes actions are planned to celebrate a particular day or season: the spring equinox, the full moon, or Halloween.

Some people who come to nonviolent direct action from nonfeminist traditions and who see it as an expression of religious faith for which they are prepared to suffer are not always comfortable with women's assertiveness. Yet nonviolent action *is* a confrontation. It isn't nice, although the confrontation can sometimes be effected in a humorous way. On April 1, 1983, a group of women in costume went over the fence at Greenham for a picnic on the base—they were dressed as teddy bears, pandas, a jester, a witch, and a hot-pink rabbit. Before being arrested they were escorted by the police and the soldiers, stiff-backed in their dark uniforms and camouflage jackets, theoretically in control. Beside them the women lolloped along, skipping and hopping, thoroughly enjoying themselves. Some people active in the labor movement deride this kind of action as whimsical, frivolous, indulgent, yet women undermined the authority of the military much more effectively than by shouting slogans. It was also great fun—a good example of politics that enlivens and feeds the participants, as it must if we are to keep at it and not burn out.

Another time women locked the two main gates of the base together with a Kryptonite bicycle lock (in what amounted to an unintentional Kryptonite commercial). In their attempts to cut through it, the Ministry of Defense police who guarded the gate resorted to larger and larger wire cutters—the largest pair had handles at least three feet long—but hardly put a scratch on the lock. In exasperation, four of the police shoved the gates so hard they came right off their hinges and collapsed on the ground still locked together, an apt metaphor for the bigger-and-bigger-weapons approach, which ultimately wrecks everything.[10]

OPENNESS

A commitment to openness is another important aspect of nonviolence. We have nothing to hide or be ashamed of. It is our business to make public and visible what goes on at military bases, weapons factories, and academic institutions doing military research. This does not mean asking police permission to do an action, or discussing details in public, with strangers, or on the phone (which may well be tapped). In planning the fence-cutting action of October 29, 1983, women from the peace camp worked out the main points and visited women's peace groups around the country to ask them to take part. The action was billed as a Halloween picnic, but women who were planning to participate knew that at four o'clock different groups would all start cutting down the fence.[11] When faced with the reality of the base, women are often prepared to take unanticipated risks at Greenham, but there should be no "hidden agendas" for actions. Each woman should know what is planned, so she can decide what part she wants to play and make the necessary preparations, practical and emotional.

As it happened, one thousand women cut down at least two miles of the fence in several sections. About one hundred fifty were arrested, although probably everyone had expected to be arrested. The police and military apparently thought women would invade the base (a good example of their logic being different from ours) and were waiting inside. We had agreed beforehand not to go onto the base, and neither the military nor the Ministry of Defense police have jurisdiction outside it. Most of them had to stand there and watch, shouting into their walkie-talkies, "They're cutting down the fence! They're cutting down the fence!" The civil police were hopelessly outnumbered on the outside, which explains why so few women were arrested. The police managed to confiscate some wire cutters, but most women hid their wire cutters in packs or under their coats to be used another time.

Openness with one another is important in a coordinated action like this and in small affinity groups, but it is not essential in looser situations. At the ten-day gathering of ten thousand women (September 20–30, 1984), groups at the different gates took whatever initiatives they chose— organizing meetings, workshops, vigils, and blockades of the gates and on the main road near the base and shaking the fence. Some women went into the nearby town of Newbury (mainly hostile to the peace camp) with signs on their backs saying who they were and why they supported the camp.[12] The underlying assumption was that groups would not undermine each other's actions, and although this could not always be foreseen, it worked in practice.

The principle of openness encounters a dilemma in regard to the news media.[13] Mainstream media people want advance notice of an action but will not guarantee to be there unless they are convinced it will be "newsworthy" (which proves a very limited conception). The risk in telling them the details is that they may jeopardize the action altogether. For example, forty-four women climbed the fence and danced on a half-built missile silo on January 1, 1983. They decided to do this at dawn and contacted women photographers they trusted. This was partly for publicity but more because photographers provide some protection from possible police violence. There was no guarantee that mainstream newspapers would use photos from freelance photographers, however. So after much discussion a couple of women contacted journalists in London to try persuading them to travel the sixty miles to Greenham in the early hours of New Year's Day without giving away all the details in advance. This strategy was successful, and the gamble certainly paid off in terms of worldwide TV coverage of women dancing on the silo, but the cavalcade of press vehicles, headlamps blazing, driving up a track to the base shortly before dawn was hardly a subtle approach, and the flashbulbs that went off—despite promises to the contrary—as women scaled the fence alerted the security patrols inside the base and undoubtedly led to the arrest of two women at the fence.

Some peace activists feel that if a woman participates in an illegal action—getting onto a military base and painting peace slogans on the runway, say—she should always take the consequences. This could mean waiting around or drawing attention to herself until the police arrive, thus ensuring arrest. This makes no sense to me. Greenham women oppose the day-to-day operation of a first-use, nuclear weapons base. Being arrested or going to jail may be very useful in attracting publicity for our point of view. But if women can sometimes leave without getting arrested, so much the better. They can do the action again, and if they leave a message of some kind, the military will always know that they were there.

SUPPORT AND PREPARATION

Although the focus of media attention is usually on those who do the blockading or who climb the fence, the support work is equally important to the success of the action. Taking care of each other by providing food and drinks; watching out for people who are cold, upset, or overtired; and giving moral support and encouragement are essential.

So is explaining the action to passersby and reporters and buffering any hostility. In the event of arrests, we keep track of what is happening, note down the numbers of the arresting officers, and contact a lawyer. Someone also goes to the police station and waits until women are released. As blockaders, for example, we can only really concentrate on our roles when we know that others are there, watching, supporting, and ready to intervene if necessary.

The care that goes into planning women's actions is crucial. Detractors and supporters praised the organization for the December 1982 two-day action encircling and blockading the base. Women organized firewood, water, food, portable toilets, parking, road signs, and child care and arranged for lawyers to be there in case anyone was arrested. The planners produced a booklet with a map of the base, details of facilities, notes on nonviolence, legal information, and songs. About three thousand women who took part in the December 13 blockade registered with a coordinating group beforehand. Some women had been meeting together, and a few groups had already taken direct action. The majority had never done anything like it before. But each person had a role to play and was immediately involved in talking through possible consequences with others in small groups to make sure each woman felt confident.

No one is pressured to act in a way she feels uncomfortable with. Every woman must make certain that she is doing what is right for her, not what someone else thinks she ought to do. This is very important because in other contexts we all too often wait to be told what to do.

Because other people only see the result of an action, or the aspects the media deem significant, the planning and support work that make it successful are invisible except for those involved. Many actions may appear spontaneous when they are not. Sometimes at Greenham events are arranged very quickly, perhaps in a couple of hours. The women living at the camps are involved in a twenty-four-hour continuous action, with opportunities to talk things over, get to know each other, and sort out logistics. They often take actions together. Some people describe actions at Greenham as spontaneous, as if they happen as a reflex, without consideration or forethought. This seriously undervalues the thinking and attitudes that women bring to an action, which may not be explicit or obvious but which come from an accretion of experience and past conversations.

FLEXIBILITY OF TACTICS

Nonviolent actions require imagination and flexibility if participants are to respond as a situation develops and keep up the pressure. It is clearly impossible to lay down rules about this. We may decide to finish an action if there seems nothing more to gain, rather than sitting it out until we are dragged away and perhaps arrested. On occasions it is useful for some people to get arrested to show that they are not intimidated. We hope this will increase publicity and support for the point we want to make. But it is never necessary to be arrested to prove our commitment. When getting arrested becomes fashionable, it is time to do something new to keep the confrontation alive. If the police are very angry, we may decide not to provoke them further and agree to move or leave. If they are casual or patronizing, we may continue to confront them. Humming, singing, chanting, or keening may seem appropriate and will reinforce our physical presence through noise. Sometimes complete silence may be better. Our goal is to recognize the dynamics of a situation and keep the initiative.

There is a danger that nonviolent actions such as blockades or die-ins may become a new orthodoxy that is incorporated into what is "allowed," as has happened with rallies and marches. Tactics such as refusing to move when cautioned by the police or going limp on arrest may become new rules people expect to follow, rather than choices to be made depending on the circumstances.

Unpredictability is also important. The authorities simply do not expect to be continually challenged in creative, nonviolent ways. We can always take them by surprise. There are potentially so many of us, and they cannot anticipate what we will decide to do next. In this sense we do not know our own strength.

RESISTANCE

Being nonviolent is no guarantee that no one will be hurt. During blockades at Greenham, police have dragged women and thrown them on the ground, thereby causing severe bruising and sometimes concussion. Some women have had their fingers, wrists, and arms broken by the police, their feet and hands stepped on. Once soldiers were ordered to pull barbed wire out of a woman's hands, knowing she was holding onto it and cutting her badly in the process. The soldiers have a wide repertoire of insults and threats, often sexual and particularly offensive. They are also authorized to shoot women who trespass on the base if they judge this the only way they can make an arrest, which gives the lie to the government claim that the missiles are there to protect *us*. Vigilantes have attacked women, throwing paint, bricks, maggots, and petrol onto their fenders and setting fire to the bushes very close to the camps. These vigilantes drive round the base at night, hooting their car horns, waking women up, yelling abuse and insults. Women's car tires have been slashed and car windows broken. A particularly bad attack occurred around midnight on April 10, 1985:

Hazel and Jane were sitting around the campfire at the newly set up Jade Gate (between Green and Yellow) when two men crept up behind them and attacked them. Both women were taken to hospital. Hazel suffered broken ribs and internal bleeding. Jane was severely cut and bruised. The next day many papers carried the story, but what none of them said was that it seems likely the attackers were American servicemen. (They were young, shorthaired and didn't speak once [so as not to give away an accent?] and the base lights on that stretch of fence mysteriously went out 20 minutes before the attack.)[14]

Since the autumn of 1985 several women have been hurt by reckless drivers of cruise missile convoy vehicles, and other women have been subjected to internal body searches by the police.

Perhaps the most insidious form of harassment is what the women call "zapping"—microwaves or ultrasound that the U.S. Air Force is beaming into the camps.[15] Zapping interferes with brainwave patterns. It is silent and invisible, but the effects are strong and immediate, ranging from mild headaches and drowsiness to bouts of temporary paralysis. Other symptoms are pressure in the ears, vaginal bleeding and miscarriage, burning skin, lack of concentration, depression, irritability, aggressiveness, lack of confidence, a sense of loneliness, panic in nonpanic situations, and loss of short-term memory.

This started in September 1984. It has been worst at Green Gate, which is close to the missile silos, and has often occurred when the convoys left the base or returned. Zapping also happened during large demonstrations and intermittently at other times. Women have been investigating this, doing tests around the base and collecting information from those affected. The government, military, medical profession, and the press have all either denied that zapping could be going on or refuse to take up the issue. They attribute women's symptoms to stress, hysteria, or a cynical attempt to grab the headlines. Of course, it would be extraordinary if the military admitted they were doing this to unarmed women!

The ever-present possibility of violence is coupled with constant evictions. In September 1984 Margaret Thatcher declared her intention to get rid of the peace camp, and since then there have been evictions virtually every day, sometimes violent, with bailiffs beating women up. The authorities may evict a camp several times a day and seize women's personal belongings and useful equipment in a war of attrition designed to intimidate and demoralize women into giving up and leaving.

Women at the peace camp are usually very short of sleep and often completely exhausted, yet they stay and continue to make a mockery of the security of the base (which provides no true security at all) by constantly challenging and resisting what is going on there. They often get into the base in small groups, sometimes night after night. They have planted seeds inside; spray-painted buildings and the long runway with peace messages; climbed into the control tower; driven a U.S. Air Force bus around inside the base; taken official documents from offices and made them public. Women have managed to get into the driving seat of a missile launcher. Once women spray-painted a Blackbird spy plane, ruining its sophisticated radar-proof protective coating. Another time they put a message through the internal base telephone demanding that all planes start taking food to Africa to feed the starving and that the death games stop immediately.

Since cruise missiles arrived at Greenham Common in November 1983, women at the peace camp have been more pressured and threatened than before. In turn they have stepped up their opposition and resistance. Whether they are arrested, whether they are charged, and what sentences they get have all varied considerably. Sometimes they have been thrown off the base, as the least embarrassing outcome for the military, which shows that the line between legality and illegality is not as clear-cut as it is made out to be. The authorities want to wipe out the protest, but they have to maintain some credibility in light of the alleged openness of liberal democracy, and sending women to jail has only made more want to be involved.

New military by-laws came into force at Greenham on April 1, 1985, making trespassing on the base a criminal offense with maximum penalties of £100 (approximately $175) fine or twenty-eight days in prison. Even decorating the fence, a hallmark of Greenham actions, is prohibited.[16] A month before the by-laws came into effect, women planned "a defiant, and silly-as-possible trespass in response,"[17] and on May 25, four hundred women cut their way onto the base. This action was also in solidarity with a woman who had been jailed for twelve months for cutting the fence several times—the longest prison sentence so far.[18] By August 1985 the police had made 1,450 arrests under the by-laws. Many women refused to pay the fine but only spent a few hours in police cells as there simply wasn't room for them any longer. Since then, two women have challenged the legality of these by-laws, arguing that Greenham Common is still legally common land. If their case ultimately succeeds, hundreds of women will be able to sue the police for wrongful arrest.

The nationwide campaign against cruise missiles in Britain has been a campaign of nonviolent direct action right from the start, with women playing a central role. By living outside the base they forced the issue of nuclear weapons and disarmament generally onto the public agenda, so that it had to be discussed and debated. Greenham women and the Cruisewatch network have refused to allow cruise missiles to be deployed outside the base in secret. For military personnel Greenham Common seems to be a miserable posting. Starting in the spring of 1984, millions of dollars were spent improving housing and social facilities there. According to a U.S. Congress Appropriations Committee report: "Transportation problems, the lack of sufficient adequate off-base quarters and cultural barriers create unavoidable negative first impressions. Resulting morale problems could have a serious negative impact on the mission."[19]

Women's enduring presence at Greenham has been remarkably effective in raising awareness of the dangers of cruise missiles and has served as an ongoing forum for determined, powerful opposition to their deployment. As the Greenham experience shows, sustained nonviolent action has enormous potential for challenging the status quo and for empowering those who take part. Women at Greenham have brought a feminist consciousness to nonviolence, expanding and enriching it by incorporating elements of carnival and confrontation. This is what has kept their protest alive, oppositional, and uncoopted for so long.

Notes

1. Barbara Harford and Sarah Hopkins, (eds.), *Greenham Common: Women at the Wire* (London: Women's Press, 1984), p. 5.

2. Cruise missiles have been deployed in Britain against the will of the majority of people, as expressed in opinion polls, and without any meaningful parliamentary debate. The decision was taken by top NATO officials and involved only a tiny handful of British politicians. The campaign against cruise missiles is much broader than the Greenham network and includes peace camps outside U.S. Air Force Molesworth/Alconbury, the second cruise base; many local actions; lobbying, publicity campaigns, and massive demonstrations coordinated through the national Campaign for Nuclear Disarmament. Two hundred fifty thousand people protested cruise missiles in London in October 1983, the largest British demonstration since the campaign for women's suffrage. I refer to cruise missiles in Europe as U.S. missiles not *Euro*missiles, as they are often called in the United States. They are made in the United States, paid for by U.S. taxpayers, and under sole U.S. command in Europe. The Intermediate-range Nuclear Forces (INF) Treaty signed by Ronald Reagan and Mikhail Gorbachev in December 1987 covers 416 ground-launched cruise missiles in Western Europe. It does not apply to thousands of sea- and air-launched cruise missiles to be deployed throughout the Pacific, in Western Europe, Japan, at airbases and seaports in the United States, and around the world in U.S. battleships as part of a U.S. first-strike capability—the plan to fight a nuclear war. But this is not a nationalistic point. Of course, these missiles would be no better or safer if they were British.

3. General Charles Donnelly, Jr., head of the U.S. Air Force in Europe, said of cruise missile maneuvers at Greenham, "The exercises are limited to one five-day period per month because of the expense of providing civilian police

to protect the systems from protesters" (*Aviation Week and Space Technology*, August 5, 1985, p. 47).

4. Landownership near the base is complex. Newbury District Council, the Ministry of Defense, and the Ministry of Transport all owned different sections and could only evict from their own property. When evicted by Newbury District Council, women moved onto Ministry of Transport land a few yards away, and so on. It took two and one-half years, until March 1984, for the three landowners to act together.

5. No brief account can do justice to the complexity of this widespread campaign. Also see Harford and Hopkins, *Greenham Common; Greenham Women Against Cruise Missiles* (New York: Center for Constitutional Rights, 1984); Alice Cook and Gwyn Kirk, *Greenham Women Everywhere* (Boston: South End Press, 1983); Lynne Jones, ed., *Keeping the Peace* (London: Women's Press, 1983); Caroline Blackwood, *On the Perimeter* (New York: Penguin, 1985); Ann Snitow, "Holding the Line at Greenham," *Mother Jones* (February–March 1985), pp. 30–34, 39–44, 46–47; Ann Snitow, "Photographing Greenham," *Frontiers* (Summer 1985), pp. 45–49; Carol Jacobsen, "Peace by Piece" *Heresies*, no. 20 (1985), pp. 60–64; Kalioka, "Greenham Common Wimmin's Peace Camp," *Woman of Power*, no. 7 (1987); news items in *Peace News* (8 Elm Ave., Nottingham 3, U.K.); Beeban Kidron and Amanda Richardson, *Carry Greenham Home* (film and video), and Margareta Wasterstam, *For Life's Sake, Let's Fight* (film), both from Women Make Movies, 19 West 21 St., New York, N.Y. 10010; Gwyn Kirk, *Commonsense* (video), from Greenham Women Against Cruise Missiles, 339 Lafayette St., New York, N.Y. 10012.

6. Quoted in Pam McAllister, ed., *Reweaving the Web of Life* (Philadelphia: New Society Publishers, 1982), p. 118.

7. *Civil disobedience* (from H. D. Thoreau, *On the Duty of Civil Disobedience*) is a term we do not use in Greenham actions. We prefer the term *nonviolent direct action*, which is a much wider concept that is not defined in terms of the state and includes many activities that are not illegal.

8. Much nonviolent direct action has occurred in Third World countries or against highly authoritarian regimes. See accounts from India, Guatemala, and against the Nazis in Europe in Gene Sharp, *The Politics of Nonviolent Action*, (Boston: Extending Horizon Books, 1973) Parts 1, 2, and 3; Alice Partnoy, *The Little School: Tales of Disappearance and Survival in Argentina* (Pittsburgh: Cleis Press, 1986); Marilyn Thompson, *Women of El Salvador* (London: Zed Books, 1986). (In the United States, the civil rights and anti–Vietnam War movements were important nonviolent campaigns.)

9. See Feminism and Nonviolence Collective, *Piecing It Together: Feminism and Nonviolence* (Devon, England: Feminism and Nonviolence Collective, 1983); McAllister, *Reweaving the Web of Life*; Jane Meyerding, ed., *We Are All Part of One Another: A Barbara Deming Reader* (Philadelphia: New Society Publishers, 1984).

10. These actions are shown in *Carry Greenham Home.*

11. Some women thought cutting the fence was violent and thus did not participate. Others argued that the fence had no spirit and did not merit respect:

It served a destructive purpose, protecting a first-use nuclear weapons base and enclosing former public common land. Many women saw cutting the fence as an act of liberation. They could see through a chain link fence and could be sure that no one would get hurt, unlike throwing stones through windows or bombing buildings. These women contended, however, that they were not arguing for indiscriminate destruction of property. The outer fence at Greenham has rolls of razor wire on top of it. In an earlier action women put several thicknesses of old carpet on top of the razor wire and climbed over without cutting the fence.

12. For details of this action see Snitow, "Holding the Line at Greenham."

13. This assumes that women want to get media coverage despite the pitfalls of distorted, unsympathetic reporting. See Cook and Kirk, *Greenham Women Everywhere*, pp. 91–107.

14. Suze da Blues, in *Green and Common Wimmin's Peace Camp* (April-May 1985), p. 19 (mimeo).

15. See Linda Pearson, "Greenham's Unwilling Guinea Pigs?" *Peace News*, no. 2253 (September 20, 1985), p. 8; Louis Slesin, "Zapped?" *The Nation*, March 14, 1987, p. 313; Joseph Regna, "Microwaves Versus Hope: The Struggle at Greenham Common," *Science for the People* (September-October 1987), pp. 21–23, 32. People in the U.S. peace movement took up this issue with U.S. politicians on behalf of Greenham women. As I write this, in March 1988, zapping at Greenham seems to have stopped, although some women feel their health has been seriously affected by it, perhaps permanently.

16. The Official Secrets Act already includes such offenses, with maximum sentences ranging from fourteen years to life imprisonment.

17. Janet and Plankton, "Our Greenham Common," *Peace News*, no. 2242 (April 5, 1985), p. 15.

18. On appeal this was reduced to six months, with six months suspended.

19. U.S. House of Representatives, Committee on Appropriations, *Military Construction Appropriations for 1987*, 99th Cong., 2nd sess., p. 963.

PART TWO

Feminism Challenges Militarism

SEVEN

Masculinity, Heroism, and the Making of War

NANCY C. M. HARTSOCK

Military, strategic, and nuclear issues became prominent during the 1980s as the Reagan administration's military buildup came to absorb more and more U.S. resources and attention. Feminists have been increasingly critical of these actions and have played important roles in peace movements in both the United States and Western Europe, including the Women's Pentagon Actions of 1981 and 1982 and the women's peace encampments at Seneca Falls, Puget Sound, and Greenham Common.

The issue of women and peace has had theoretical impact as well. Feminist theorists have questioned whether women are equally as involved as men in the stress on military preparedness. These theorists have suggested that women's experiences are likely to lead them to be pacifists.[1] Feminist analyses have also included discussions of the gender gap in politics and the extent to which it concerns issues of war and peace.

In this chapter, I want to suggest that there are significant and unexamined issues of gender involved in debates about military preparedness, the theory of deterrence, and the drafting of women. These issues, I believe, are best illuminated by concentrating not on women's supposed pacifism but on some of the sources of men's involvement in the making of war. I should caution at the outset that I do not want to suggest that gender can serve as a complete explanation of the military policies of nations in the contemporary world. Women as well as men have fought in wars, and men fight wars for reasons other than their gender. Nationalism, imperialism, and revolution are also factors in the making of war. Yet there are crucial links between masculinity and the making of war, and I will concentrate on these here in order to illuminate features of our current human predicament.

Manhood and Military Valor

Virility and violence are commonly linked together. For example, in the literature on political power, many social scientists have remarked on the links among virility, potency, masculinity, and domination.[2] These connections appear as well in a satiric 1915 poster titled, "Why We Oppose Votes For Men." Among the reasons given are "because no really manly man wants to settle any question otherwise than by fighting about it," "because man's place is in the army," and "because if men should adopt peaceable methods women will no longer look up to them."[3] The values of traditional masculinity are also systematically invoked in basic training in the military. Recruits learn that to be a man is to be a soldier, not a woman.[4]

The contemporary debate about whether to allow women in combat in the U.S. military also reveals these associations. Judith Stiehm has suggested that an important reason for the opposition to women in combat is that the role of warrior is the only role unique to men in modern society. Thus, in peacetime men lack a way to prove they are men. The inclusion of women would threaten the exclusiveness of the role of warrior and therefore men's identities.[5]

Her argument is well illustrated by the comments of General Robert H. Barrow, until 1983 commander of the U.S. Marines.

> War is a man's work. Biological convergence on the battlefield [by which he means women serving in combat] would not only be dissatisfying in terms of what women could do, but it would be an enormous psychological distraction for the male, who wants to think that he's fighting for that woman somewhere behind, not up there in the same foxhole with him. It tramples the male ego. When you get right down to it, you have to protect the manhood of war.[6]

We can find more recent illustrations in George Bush's note to Senator J. James Exxon of Nebraska during a debate on appropriating more money for the Strategic Defense Initiative (SDI)—"I'm the pit bull of S.D.I., you Ivy League wimp!"—or in General Manuel Noriega's argument that "virility is proven by remaining in power."[7]

But issues of manliness have had more dangerous influence on the politics of war. David Halberstam documented the ways Lyndon Johnson's concern about his manliness influenced his conduct of the Vietnam War.[8] Masculinity is still important in the conduct of warfare. The May 1983 Americas Watch Report on Guatemala indicated that one feature of the "pacification" program was the appeal to masculinity. Thus, according to an unconfirmed but detailed report of a massacre in the town of Parraxtut, members of a civil patrol from a neighboring town were gathered together and told they must be prepared to demonstrate their masculinity. When they arrived in Parraxtut, they were ordered to prove their masculinity by killing all the men in the community. The women were then divided into two groups—young and old, the latter to be killed and the former to be raped.[9]

I will suggest in this chapter that the key to understanding heroic action and masculine citizenship can be found in masculinity as ideology—a set of cultural institutions and practices that constitutes the norms and standards of masculinity, a set of ideals to which few men can measure up. Some, of course, refuse. That masculinity is a cultural construction rather than a matter of raging hormones is well illustrated by the fact that some women do very well at it—Margaret Thatcher comes immediately to mind. But how is the ideology of masculinity constructed? I will argue that masculinity has been centrally structured by a linked fear of and fascination with the problems of death, mortality, and oblivion. These fears and fascinations have emerged in the West in many areas of social life but nowhere more importantly and dangerously than in politics and war.

In particular, I want to suggest that the specific configuration of violence, masculinity, and militarism extant in the modern West represents the legacy of collective efforts by small groups of men—men privileged by their race, class, and gender—to resolve several fundamental problems of human existence. Most centrally, these are (1) how to deal with mortality, (2) how to understand the limits of human power (the power/ fate distinction), and (3) how to define the nature of human relations (or the shape of the human community, as I have put it elsewhere[10]). I propose to begin thinking about these issues by addressing the issue of mortality.

The Centrality of Death

To understand the meaning of death for the masculine actor, who in the tradition of Western political thought has been both of the ruling class and the ruling race, we must analyze the issues raised by the fact of mortality into several distinct assertions: (1) men are dual, both infinite and finite, immortal and mortal; (2) the finite and mortal part can and will cease to exist; and (3) ceasing to exist in turn poses the question of the meaninglessness of human existence, of human nature as a "god-worm."

DUALITY AND MORTALITY

It is in many ways a commonplace to argue that humans are "duplex beings." Many would agree with Ernest Becker's contention that "man is divided into two distinct kinds of experience—physical and mental, or bodily and symbolic," the one, standardized and given, the other, achieved.[11] The self, Becker maintains, finds itself "in a strange body casing and cannot understand this dualism." The impermanence of the body casing or its incompleteness—now male, now female—is confusing. The body, he argues, makes no sense to us in its physical thingness.[12] The body also sentences us to the fate of all that is physical—decay and death.[13]

Human duality, however, as the thinkers I cite have theorized it, is not simply the duality of mind and body. In stronger terms, the duality concerns man's fate as a god-worm[14] or, in yet other terms, the duality of infinite versus finite being, of godlike self-sufficiency versus dependence.[15] Thus, the duality gains a more poignant meaning and significance.

The duality of which these authors speak generates an opposition between the parts—a tension in the dualism—and, in turn, an experience of the self as existing in the context of a tension between opposites. The result, they argue, is that "the human creature has to oppose itself to the rest of nature. It creates precisely the isolation that one can't stand—and yet needs in order to develop distinctively."[16] This is a physical, psychological, and even philosophical reality: "Bodily existence is such that it requires some kind of againstness."[17]

This againstness or adversativeness (Ong's term) becomes a paradigm for understanding our own existence. "In order to know myself, I must know that something else is not me and is (in some measure) set against me, psychologically as well as physically."[18]

MORTALITY, FINITUDE, AND MEANINGLESSNESS

As physical, embodied beings, men come to recognize that they could just as well have been born male or female, or dog, cat, or fish. Moreover, the reality of sexual differentiation itself reminds men of their incompleteness and of their finitude.[19] The result of this finitude and incompleteness, Becker argues, is anxiety because a man has difficulty admitting that he does not stand alone, that he is not in control.[20]

Ernest Becker has stated this problem with the utmost clarity:

What does it mean to be a *self-conscious animal?* The idea is ludicrous, if it is not monstrous. It means to know that one is food for worms. This is the terror: to have emerged from nothing, to have a name, consciousness of self, deep inner feelings, an excruciating inner yearning for life and self-expression—and with all this yet to die. It seems like a hoax. . . . What kind of deity would create such complex and fancy worm food? . . . It takes sixty years of incredible suffering and effort to make such an individual, and then he is good only for dying. . . . He has to go the way of the grasshopper, even though it takes longer.[21]

MASCULINITY AND DEATH

I have argued elsewhere that statements of the human condition such as I have just presented are not gender neutral but reflect masculine experience.[22] I should add here that it is a masculine experience particularly characteristic of European (white) men of the middle and upper classes. Why should this be so? And what is the ground on which I make such claims? I will not repeat these arguments here, but only summarize them. I used psychoanalytic theory, as developed by theorists such as Nancy Chodorow, to argue that men's lives have come to be structured by different issues than women's and that hierarchical and dualist modes of thought were generated by this experience.

It is interesting to read G.W.F. Hegel's account of the relation of the self and other as a statement of masculine experience: The relation of the two consciousnesses takes the form of a trial by death. Dualism, I argued, along with the dominance of one side of the dichotomy over the other, marks phallocentric society and social theory. And the gendered roots of these dualisms are memorialized in the cultural overlay of female and male connotations. In terms of the issues addressed here, the female is associated only with the body, not with godlike transcendence. I argued as well that masculinity was associated with a fascination with death. I argued that the masculine self comes to be surrounded by rigid ego boundaries, the self as walled city, and is discontinuous with others. George Bataille has made brilliantly clear the ways in which death emerges as the only possible solution to this discontinuity, the breaking of boundaries and the gaining of continuity with others.[23] Thus, I concluded, in our culture the masculine self, at least as a cultural norm, must be defined by a fascination with death.

This view is corroborated by a number of other female theorists— feminist and nonfeminist. Dorothy Smith notes Alfred Schutz's descriptions of the fear of death as a fundamental human anxiety governing each individual's system of relevance in the working world. He writes that "from this anxiety come[s] . . . the need to attempt mastery of the world, to overcome obstacles, to draft projects, and to realize them." In reply, she states, "I have always stopped short at this assumption, since I do not personally experience this anxiety. Before I learned from the women's movement I used to transform it into a metaphysical statement unsupported by experience, but Schutz does not mean it that way."[24]

Or consider the work of a woman who has spent decades dealing with death and dying. Elisabeth Kübler-Ross's work is about the dailiness of mortality. She argues that "death is as much a part of human existence, of human growth, as being born," that "death is not an enemy to be conquered or a prison to be escaped. It is an integral part of our lives. . . . We are," she states, "finite little beings who could help each other if we would dare to show that we care." Tellingly, in terms of my thesis here, she states that those who value control "are offended by the thought that they too are subject to the forces of death."[25]

This is in profound contrast to thinkers such as Bataille for whom even the life-giving force of sexuality is reinterpreted as death. Indeed, women philosophers in general seem to have been more concerned about life than death. Consider, for example, Hannah Arendt, who bases her discussions of the human condition not on mortality but on natality.[26] More recently, Mary O'Brien has called attention to the importance of birth for structuring human consciousness and social relations and has argued that although death has been central to masculine philosophy, feminist philosophy must be a philosophy of birth and regeneration.[27] Finally, Virginia Held has made a powerful argument that birth should not be viewed as a natural process but as "an event as meaningful for all that is distinctively human as is the event of human death."[28]

My argument that preoccupation with death and oblivion is not a gender-neutral phenomenon gains further support from the work of Walter Ong on contest and sexual identity.[29] He argues that masculinity is fundamentally defined by agonistic activity, by ritual combat of different sorts, and moreover that this combat must be continually repeated because masculinity is never finally achieved but must be continually earned.[30] The opposition that grows from human duality takes, among others, the social form of contest. Ceremonial and ritual contest, he argues, is not a gender-neutral practice; it is much more essential to the development of masculine identity than feminine identity. Although I do not consider what he has to say about the winter-pasture flocking habits of turkeys of much utility, what he says about human behavior seems to make more sense (although not the particular sense he wants to make). Contest and combat are central to masculine identity.[31] Relying on Robert Stoller's analysis, Ong concluded that femininity is the natural state. The young male must grow away from this state. Men must establish themselves as men against a background of femininity that is simply there.[32]

How does this need for adversativeness, for contest, affect my claim that in Western culture, masculinity for the dominant group of men is essentially defined by death? It leads to the definition of masculinity by its fascination with death in two major ways. First, the contest—the Greek agon—shades into war. Thus, among males in some cultures, "even war can be a kind of game, perhaps seasonal, in which killing is an objective only half-heartedly or incidentally achieved. The ancient Greeks called off their wars for the Olympic games and resumed them again immediately afterward; psychologically the wars and the games were somewhat equivalent."[33]

Second, the culturally defined process of differentiation for boys requires a struggle against the encompassing figure of the mother. Stoller's account of the problems posed by symbiosis anxiety can help us in formulating how masculinity is fundamentally connected with death. The defining ideological characteristic (one that profoundly affects social practice) is a fascination with ceasing to exist—that is, with death. If the fear is indeed as he has described it, then we can understand why the accusation of effeminacy is the worst possible blot on a man's masculinity. The fundamental fear, Ong holds, is that of absorption into the other, the female, the mother.[34] The problem, Ong asserts, is that because everyone, including you, suspects that you are female, there must be a constant struggle, if you are a male, to prove that you are not.[35]

If these are the problems faced by the middle- and upper-class European/white men who have shaped the dominant outlines of Western culture, then we can understand how Ernest Becker could claim that the idea and the fear of death haunt "the human animal like nothing else."[36] And we can understand how those who make this claim would strike a popular chord in our culture. (Becker, after all, won a Pulitzer Prize for his book.)

Heroism

What solution have men developed to the problem of meaninglessness posed for them by death? This is, after all, a problem inherent in human existence. For the last three thousand years of Western history, heroism has been the answer the men who have controlled societies have given to the problems of masculine embodiment; it has been an ideal they put forward as the highest human (*sic*) achievement. As Sarpedon puts it in the *Iliad*, a man becomes a hero because he cannot be a god.[37]

Heroism can fulfill this function because

all men are born to die, but the hero alone must confront this fact in his social life, since he fulfills his obligations only by meeting those who intend his death. . . . To die for something . . . is better than to die for nothing—and that is, after all, the alternative. In accepting death he shows himself searingly aware of it. The hero is in a sense rescued from mortality; he becomes godlike in status and immortal in memory. At the same time he is uniquely conscious of his own mortality.[38]

The construction of heroism is nowhere so clear as in the *Iliad*. By focusing on it here, I intend to say something not only about the reading of the poem but also and more importantly about the construction of heroism and its bearing on our contemporary situation.

THE HOMERIC WARRIOR-HERO: FACE TO FACE WITH DEATH

Homer's epic sets the stage for a precarious community inhabited by heroes and later by citizens. In the *Iliad*, the battlefield and military camp form the stage on which the action takes place. This stage is inhabited solely by men, and heroism is the supremely masculine role.

As the best of the Achaeans, Achilles carries in his person the clearest instance of the problems and possibilities of the hero. His honor defines his very being. The highest good for the warrior-hero is not a quiet conscience but rather the enjoyment of public esteem and, through this esteem, immortality. Honor, or *timē*, is central.

The hero's honor (and thus his immortality in *kléos*, or poetry) is attained through the excellence of his *biē*, or "might." Both the centrality of force and the contradictory situation it creates for the hero are marked by the fact that he confronts and overcomes death and mortality by means of his own death. His position is unique because although all men are born to die, the warrior's social role is defined by the fact that he must go to meet those who would kill him.

The power of his achievement is indicated by the fact that he transcends the condition of both men and gods: "Men die, while the gods live forever; the hero, however, does both."[39] The hero gains his power and immortality through death, and this feat cannot be matched even by the gods because they cannot die. Heroism in combat, then, gives meaning to a world profoundly structured by death. Yet despite its tremendous cost, it remains a meaning only temporarily and tentatively rescued from the meaninglessness introduced by death.[40]

Heroism as we find it in the *Iliad* is not a simple solution to the problem of death but rather a complex construction that requires several steps to be successful. In order to understand heroism we must pay attention to each of the separate steps required to constitute it. First, it requires the exclusion of women as participants in the important action. Second, it requires establishing a zero-sum competition between the men, a competition for honor. One man's win must be at the same time another man's loss. Boasting, ritual combat, definition of the community as a whole by opposition and rivalry, a stress on the importance of potency, strength, and force—all are aspects of the construction of the masculine community by competition.[41]

Third, heroism requires a heroic action. And heroic action in itself is a complex construction that consists of deliberately facing the cessation of existence, a flirtation with death. A man cannot (in the *Iliad* literally) do great deeds without acting in a situation so dangerous that it threatens his continued existence. We might even argue that the presence of such a threat is a centrally defining feature of heroic action. Related, heroic action can take place only in the presence of a separation from daily life, necessity, and production. War-making is of necessity a destructive rather than constructive activity. It (traditionally) takes place at great emotional (and often physical) distance from the mundane work of production and reproduction. Moreover, heroic actions can take place only in the presence of or at least for the approval of an all male community that has its secrets from the women.[42]

Fourth, heroism requires abstraction. The word means "to draw from" or to take one aspect of a larger whole. The hero must focus not on the totality of his existence or on his opponents as full human beings. The individual moment, the present, is important, not the future; the particular task, not the war; the functions of things, not their purposes; the part, not the situation in its entirety.

The purpose of this complex construction is the denial of death by means of a second, homosocial birth, a birth that overcomes the defects of the original, heterosexual birth. Whereas the first birth, from the body of a woman, is a death sentence, the second, through the bodily might of the man himself, leads to immortality. I believe we can find these patterns in a number of the classic texts of Western political thought, just as (I will argue) we can find it in the work of contemporary nuclear strategists. For us, however, the *Iliad* represents the beginning of this construction.

Achilles as hero is best in war. He recognizes that "in assemblies, other men are my [his] betters."[43] But he is the best of the Achaeans because he is the best in war, which is the supreme, and even necessary, test of manhood.[44] Each of the foregoing moves is made and each is important for the *kléos* of Achilles.

THE EXCLUSION OF WOMEN

Women must be excluded not necessarily from the scene but rather from participation in the action. In the *Iliad*, as in the mind of General Barrow, women are what a man fights for, not beside. Women are, in fact, the cause of the fighting. The war, after all, was ostensibly fought for Helen, despite the presence on the field of men there for their own honor rather than her retrieval.[45] Indeed, the *Iliad* begins with a quarrel about Briseis, the girl who was Achilles' share of the booty and whom Agamemnon took from him. This quarrel sets the *Ililad* in motion. It is because of this that Achilles refuses to fight, that the Greeks are driven back, that Patroclus dies. Women, or the female, also serve as a kind of symbol of being insufficiently masculine. Thus, cowards turn into women[46] or run to the arms of their women.[47] Paris's worthlessness as a warrior is made evident by his frequent presence among women.[48]

There are, however, some female figures on the battlefield—the goddesses who manipulate events and men. It is in fact Athena who makes it possible for Achilles to kill Hektor. She appears to Hektor during his confrontation with Achilles as his own brother with an offer of assistance.[49] And it is she who returns Achilles' spear to him after he has tried and failed to kill Hektor. Thus, despite the fiction that the only actors are men, goddesses, although not real women, play important roles.

ZERO-SUM RIVALRY FOR HONOR

The world of the *Iliad* is organized by competition and rivalry. Honor, or *timē*, is central. Thus, Achilles can ask, "Why should I fight, if the good fighter receives no more *timē* than the bad?"[50] The primacy of honor is memorialized in Achilles' withdrawal from the battle over Troy because he feels his honor has been offended and in his choice between his "two destinies." He chooses to stay and fight to win glory and immortality in the memory of men rather than return home to enjoy a long life.[51] Yet the issue is not simply the gaining of honor; honor must be gained at the expense of another losing his fame and honor. Moreover, the honor of the warrior-hero depends importantly on the ranking of his fellow contestants. The greatest victories are those won from the greatest warriors.

Finally, the honor the ancient heroes seek is defined by potency. Achilles' honor and immortality, his status as the best of the Achaeans, in poetry and song are attained through the excellence of his *biē*, rather than *mêtis*, or "craft."[52] We should not fail to note that the choice of Achilles is not simply that of the poet; but since the poems were the documents of a centuries-old oral tradition, the choice of Achilles represented a cultural choice of generations of listeners about who was the best hero.[53]

Rivalry over honor is the central structuring feature of the *Iliad*. Thus, Agamemnon feels that his honor requires that he have some prize of his own after Chryseis, his booty, is ransomed. It is, he says, "unfitting" that he should go without.[54] He is concerned to have the trophy that will show his rank. Achilles, later in the story, is concerned not to submit to Agamemnon, and this in turn leads to the death of Patroclus. Thus, when Agamemnon sends Odysseus as the head of a delegation to Achilles to offer gifts, including Briseis as well as other women captives, a choice of land, and a choice of his daughters to marry, Achilles recognizes that to accept would be to recognize Agamemnon's power, to put himself into a subordinate position, and this he refuses to do. Agamemnon himself had said it when he gave his message to Odysseus: "Let him give way. . . . And let him yield place to me, inasmuch as I am the kinglier/and inasmuch as I can call myself born the elder."[55]

The rivalry appears also in the form of boasting, in which the factor of comparison, of who is best, becomes overt.[56] The boasting is closely related to other forms of competition and combat. Success in combat is the clearest proof of honor and greatness, but the hero must claim his honor, must "make himself by asserting himself."[57] Thus, the final confrontation between Achilles and Hektor includes ritual boasting. Achilles tells Hektor that he will soon be killed by Achilles' spear. Hektor replies that the speech from Achilles was simply to make him afraid and that in turn Achilles will have to drive the spear into Hektor's chest as he runs courageously forward.[58]

The nature of the fracture lines within a community defined by rivalry and competition for honor is well illustrated by the quarrel between Achilles and Agamemnon, which is the source of much of the action in the *Iliad* as they constitute their relationship on the basis of *éris*, or "strife." Indeed, it could be argued that what holds the community together—the collective practice of strife in war—is a central aspect of the community itself.[59] Some Homer scholars have argued that the constitution of the community by strife is not entirely negative, and others have even given some positive evaluation to war. On the battlefield, Redfield argues, the warrior has a tightknit community of "those who are ready to die for one another."[60] The community is only guaranteed by the valor of the warriors.[61] Indeed, Redfield argues that combat is the crucial social act on which the survival of the collectivity depends.[62] Thus, although war is an unhappy task in the beginning, the prestige of the warrior endows war with some positive value. Nagy treats war as more negative but holds that competition, "that most fundamental aspect of most Hellenic institutions—including poetry itself," represents a more positive form of the same thing.[63] My own rereading of the *Iliad* indicates that the heroes were far less willing to die for each other than for their *kléos*. Achilles, after all, quits the war because his honor has been offended, and Odysseus is at one point abandoned by the other Greeks and left to make his own way out of the battlefield.[64]

HEROIC ACTION

The exclusion of women and the definition of the community by rivalry and competition set the scene for heroic action, the doing of great deeds, preferably in the context of deliberately facing death. As Hektor puts it so clearly when he recognizes that Achilles will succeed in killing him: "Let me do some big thing first." In the *Iliad* this requires the hero to confront the possibility of his death as well as move away from concern with everyday life.

Although combat is clearly a confrontation with death, it is less apparent how it is separated from daily life or why this is significant. Daily life, the search for subsistence, acts as a reminder that we are mortal, bodily beings and thus reminds us that we are all born under a death sentence. The separation of heroic action from daily life is obvious. But it is worth noting that in combat, men confront other men (and gods) but not the natural world. Nor do they generate new resources; they despoil resources others have created. Moreover, excellence in combat requires that the warrior cease to think of the future and stake everything on the success of the moment.[65] Thus, the ethic of the hero is not only out of scale with daily life but runs counter to it.

The point of heroic action is to do some great thing, and daily life is rarely a context in which we can perform such deeds. (One is reminded of Hannah Arendt's statement that after a brilliant heroic act that sums up one's life, why live on?) Heroic action, then, must be disconnected from necessity, especially from concern with daily subsistence and thus from bodily, mortal existence. Because it is bound up with facing the possibility of failure and death, heroic action is itself extraordinary, and the role of the hero becomes extraordinary.

ABSTRACTION

Heroic action can take place only in a world of abstracted parts. The hero must cease to see the man he fights as a whole person and instead see him only in partial terms. In the *Iliad*, this abstraction takes (what is for us) a peculiar form. Commentators on the Homeric poems are unanimous in their assessment that the characters and actors in these poems have no inwardness and seem to operate as a set of interconnected but not integrated parts. Thus, we find a series of references to emotions and body parts that treat them as somewhat independent and autonomous from the self. Indeed, the *Iliad* does not contain a real concept of self in a modern sense. Agamemnon's response to Achilles' insults in Book

I is an anger that "fills the heart to the rim."[66] The spirit of a man may "stir him," or a man may "give way to his proud heart's anger."[67] To die is described as the "breath crossing the teeth's barrier."[68] And when Hektor flees from Achilles, he is described not as running but as "moving his knees rapidly."[69]

Not only do the heroes experience themselves as collections of body parts, but when they are uncertain or in doubt, parts of themselves become alien. The monologues of the hero must be experienced as dialogues. Thus, when Odysseus is in the midst of the battle, he is unsure of whether to run away with the rest of the Achaeans or to stand and fight, and he is presented as speaking to his "great hearted spirit," a definite other to whom he addresses the question: "What will become of me?" But then he turns to wonder why his "heart debates" these things.[70]

In addition, the emotions are sometimes seen as detached entities responsible for *atē*, a kind of temporary insanity or clouding of the normal consciousness in which the hero behaves in ways he cannot adequately explain. Within the person of the warrior-hero, a part becomes externalized and may take the form of a dichotomy between the person and supernatural and alien forces that may overcome him from time to time.[71]

SECOND BIRTH

The purpose of heroism is the overcoming of death and the attainment of immortality. The heroes give birth to themselves in an all-male community and do so in such a way that they will not die. Ironically, of course, they attain this immortality through the vehicle of their physical death. Both Achilles and Hektor face the choice of two destinies: to turn away and live a long life in obscurity or to stay and fight, which means death in the near future and everlasting glory. Achilles, given the choice, chooses to stay and fight. And Hektor, when he recognizes that his end is near, says, "Let me at least not die without a struggle, inglorious, but do some big thing first, *that men to come shall know of it*."[72] It is through these choices for early death and a vicarious life through the memories of men that meaning is rescued from the meaninglessness introduced by death.[73] The hero's death is the source of his power.

The hero can defeat death and defy the limits of human power only when the possibility of a humane community is sacrificed. This strategy poses enormous difficulties for solving each of the fundamental human problems I mentioned at the beginning of this argument: Community comes to be defined by conflict and domination; mortality is denied through the death of some members of the community; and the limits of human power are denied by claiming that death is not real, that one can indeed live forever.

Contemporary Issues

That the foregoing is not simply an archaic vision, but one influential in our time, is supported by evidence from several different spheres. Consider the answer a Homer scholar such as James Redfield gives to the question: "Why do we care about these stories, which are so far from us and which anyway are not true?" As recently as 1975, he wrote that Homer's poem seems "uniquely true to the phenomena of experience, including my own experience. . . . [It] seems to me, more than any other, to embody the mature understanding a true man should have of his world . . . [and so] in describing the Homeric world view, I have also intended to praise it."[74]

That the same attitude obtains at the level of popular culture was evident in a recent television interview with Evel Knievel—a motorcycle daredevil who is a caricature of masculinity. When asked why he did such dangerous motorcycle stunts, he said, "When Evel Knievel gets out there he's only got one competitor, the toughest one of all. His name is death and I've beat him every time."[75]

Nor is this simply the understanding of a motorcycle stuntman. Ernest Becker's book, which I have used extensively, was praised by book reviewers (quoted on the back of the paperback edition) as "magnificent," a "rare masterpiece," a "work of electrifying intelligence." Clearly it is a work that speaks to the deep concerns of many men. Ernest Becker argues that "our central calling, our main task on this planet, is the heroic."[76] Even society as a whole should be understood as a "vehicle" for heroism.[77] And Becker recognizes as well that heroism is "first and foremost a reflex of the terror of death" since we admire most the courage of those who face their own extinction. This is the greatest victory we can imagine. Thus, death is the "real 'muse of philosophy' from its beginnings in Greece right through Heidegger and modern existentialism."[78]

*   *   *

Let us return to the issues broached at the outset of this chapter. The masculine political actor as he appears in the *Iliad* is indeed most at home in agonistic and competitive settings, whether the battlefield or the agora, where he can pursue the attainment of glory, honor, and immortality in the memory of men. The calm and rational consideration of the best actions for the community as a whole are of less concern to him than his own status within it. Rather than war being politics by other means, political action as it appears in these texts is simply war by other means. Through this war, citizens, not-yet-citizens, and warriors attain and celebrate manhood.

These central elements of heroic action reappear in contemporary ideologies about the conduct of politics and war. Let me stress here that these are ideologies dominant in our culture—ideologies that are put forward and subscribed to by the ruling group of white men at the top. The realities of politics and war for those at the bottom are quite different. Yet these ideas have profoundly influenced the contemporary conduct of foreign policy. Let us look at each element in turn.

First, the exclusion of women is an obvious feature of our contemporary world. Women are excluded from combat by law; recruits to military service are urged not to behave like women, even if they are women; and cowards or doves have been referred to as women by figures such as Lyndon Johnson during the Vietnam War.[79] This is, of course, contradicted in reality by the fact that women have been combatants in every war in the twentieth century (and many before that), that women serve in modern militaries, and that some female heads of state have acted to defend their national honor.

Second, contemporary foreign policy has legitimated issues of honor and preeminence. Thus, John McNaughton, assistant secretary of defense during 1965, summed up U.S. aims in Vietnam as 70 percent to avoid a humiliating defeat, 20 percent to keep the territory away from the Chinese, and 10 percent to permit the people of Vietnam a better way of life.[80] We can also recall President Richard Nixon's stress on peace with honor. More recently, we have seen George Bush in Lebanon, saying in language more appropriate to a street corner brawl than a reasoned foreign policy, "We're not going to let a bunch of insidious terrorists shake the foreign policy of the United States."[81]

Third, as to heroic action flirting with oblivion, we need only point to the history of brinkmanship in the foreign policy of the 1950s. And in regard to contemporary nuclear strategic thinking, Carol Cohn has recently documented the ways in which the ability to coolly face the possibility of nuclear war gains a person respect and a hearing. World leaders are as concerned as Hektor about "doing some great thing," if not before they die, before they leave office. They are to be remembered not in story and song, but rather in the history books.

The fourth aspect of heroism, abstraction, takes a very important, albeit different, form in the modern world. We find, for example, General Barrow talking about "biological convergence" on the battlefield. Or we find defense intellectuals discussing such things as "clean bombs," "surgical strikes," "strategic bombing and targeting" and discussing human death as "collateral damage." According to Carol Cohn, in 1984 the State Department said it would no longer use the word "killing," much less "murder," for human rights violations in countries with which the United States was allied. Instead the State Department now refers to "unlawful or arbitrary deprivation of life."[82] Elaine Scarry has noted similar sorts of abstractions and reversals. She has described the ways real injury disappears in war—at least as constructed in the language of the commanders. Thus, incendiary bomb operations in North Vietnam were named Sherwood Forest and Pink Rose. In addition, in the language of warfare, soldiers disappear and weapons become subjects; tanks receive "massive injury," whereas the deaths of soldiers and civilians "produce results."[83]

Fifth, the search for immortality, or second birth, surfaces in our political leaders' desire to have their "place in history," as so many of them put it. In addition, images of male birth have been important in the history of war—most recently, in the development of the atomic and hydrogen bombs. The atomic bomb was referred to as "Oppenheimer's baby," and when scientists wondered if it would work, they put their concern in terms of questions of whether "the baby would be a boy." When Henry Stimson informed Winston Churchill of success, the note read, "Babies satisfactorily born," and when the first hydrogen bomb test was a success, the telegram read, "It's a boy."[84] Carol Cohn has also noted that this terminology links this "birth" to the creative powers of god: The first atomic bomb test was called Trinity—the father, son, and holy spirit—an invocation of the male forces of creation.[85]

Conclusion

For Achilles and Hektor, there could be no complete manhood without war. General Barrow's remarks, nuclear discourse, and the remarks of many of our political leaders make it clear that similar views are still extant. Yet today, when the destructive power of our weapons could destroy life on earth, we cannot defend such a vision of politics and war. Human survival may well depend on breaking the linkage of masculinity with both military capacity and death.

Notes

1. Sara Ruddick, "Pacifying the Forces: Drafting Women in the Interests of Peace," *Signs: Journal of Woman, Culture and Society* 8, no. 3 (Spring 1983), pp. 471–489. Jean Bethke Elshtain argues a position similar to Ruddick's in "Women as Mirror and Other," *Humanities in Society* 5, nos. 1-2 (Winter-Spring 1982);

she contends that women must be the pacific Other—must neither remain naive nor innocent, but must oppose a world where murder is legitimate (p. 42).

2. See David Bell, *Power, Influence, and Authority* (New York: Oxford University Press, 1975), p. 8.

3. Reprinted in *Radical America* 15, nos. 1-2 (Spring 1981), p. 147.

4. See Ronald Eisenhart, "You Can't Hack It Little Girl: Psychological Agenda of Modern Combat Training," *Journal of Social Issues* 30 (1974), pp. 13–23; Robert Lifton, *Home From the War* (New York: Simon and Schuster, 1973), pp. 15, 244.

5. Judith Stiehm, "Implementation of Women's Integration into the U.S. Military Academies" (Paper presented at the 1978 Meeting of the American Political Science Association, New York), p. 12. She also notes that a frequent response to the suggestion that women become combatants is the statement, "It just isn't right," coupled with an inability to elaborate on this statement. She suggests that because women are frequently present on the battlefield, we must conclude not that men don't want them there but that they don't want women on their side (pp. 2, 7).

6. Michael Wright, "The New Marines: Life in the Pits," *San Francisco Chronicle*, June 27, 1982. Not only gender is evoked in these statements, but some aspect of sexuality or the erotic. Guns, we know, function as virility symbols. The peculiar terminology employed by the chair of the Joint Chiefs of Staff when he testified before the Senate Armed Services Committee provides an additional suggestion of the salience of such connections. He stated that "deploying a new manned penetrator should be a top priority" and added that he believed the United States "must continue with the development of a manned penetrating aircraft to succeed the B-52." Statement from *New York Times*, January 29, 1981. (E. V. Spelman called this to my attention.)

7. See *New York Times*, September 28, 1987, B6. (Thanks to Ruth Mandel for calling this to my attention.) For Noriega's remark, *New York Times*, March 21, 1988, A1.

8. David Halberstam, *The Best and the Brightest* (New York: Random House, 1972), pp. 51–52, cited in Marc Feigen Fasteau, "Vietnam and the Cult of Toughness in Foreign Policy," in Deborah S. David and Robert Brannon, eds., *The Forty-Nine Percent Majority: The Male Sex Role* (Reading, Mass.: Addison-Wesley, 1976), p. 191.

9. *New York Review of Books*, June 2, 1983, excerpt from the May 1983 supplement to the Americas Watch Report on Guatemala.

10. This is an argument I have made in some detail in *Money, Sex, and Power: Toward a Feminist Historical Materialism* (New York: Longman, 1983).

11. The first quoted phrase is from Walter Ong, *Fighting for Life* (Ithaca, N.Y.: Cornell University Press, 1981), p. 32. The other phrases are from Ernest Becker, *The Denial of Death* (New York: Free Press, 1973).

12. Becker, ibid., pp. 224–225.

13. Ibid., p. 31.

14. Ibid., p. 58. On this point also see James Lewton Brain, *The Last Taboo* (Garden City, N.Y.: Doubleday, 1979), Chap. 6.

15. Becker, ibid., pp. 63, 107.

16. Ibid., pp. 153–154. Ong, *Fighting for Life*, pp. 31–33, makes a similar point.

17. Ong, ibid., p. 15. Also see Becker, ibid., pp. 99, 104.

18. Ong, ibid., pp. 15–16. Ong argues that the Greek contest system can be found at the roots not only of modern academic practices but even of formal logic (pp. 21, 29). He suggests that contest may even have been essential to intellectual development (p. 28).

19. Becker, *The Denial of Death*, p. 41. This idea is something I cannot pursue here, but I have been struck with the extent to which issues of sexuality and issues of death are formulated in congruent terms. On this point also see Brain, *The Last Taboo*; and George Bataille, *Death and Sensuality* (New York: Arno Press, 1963).

20. Becker, ibid., p. 55

21. Ibid., pp. 87, 269.

22. Hartsock, *Money, Sex, and Power.*

23. Bataille, *Death and Sensuality.*

24. Dorothy Smith, "A Sociology for Women," in Julia Sherman and Evelyn Beck, eds., *The Prism of Sex* (Madison: University of Wisconsin Press, 1979), p. 150.

25. Elisabeth Kübler-Ross, *Death: The Final Stage of Growth* (Englewood Cliffs, N.J.: Prentice-Hall, 1975), pp. x, 1, 5.

26. See my discussion of her in Chapter 9 of *Money, Sex, and Power.*

27. Mary O'Brien, *The Politics of Reproduction* (Boston: Routledge and Kegan Paul, 1981).

28. Virginia Held, "Birth and Death" (1987, mimeo), p. 1.

29. I have a number of disagreements with Ong's approach that should be noted here—most importantly, his efforts to locate the roots of the gender differences he notes in sociobiology. In addition, he ascribes far too much actual (as opposed perhaps to mythic) power to women. Even the fact that a woman commonly "takes" her husband's name is something Ong describes as an aggressive act (*Fighting for Life*, p. 73). He insists that the "I" exists in a state of "terrifying isolation" (p. 196). In each case, he is unclear about whether his descriptions are meant to apply to humanity as a whole or to the major topic he is addressing in the book—the dynamics of men's lives. Nevertheless, he provides a great deal of evidence for the positions I take here.

30. See ibid., p. 98.

31. He confuses maleness and masculinity (ibid., p. 64) when he talks about how from the beginning of any mammal's life, masculinity involves living in a state of adversity, in opposition to a "permanently hostile" environment—initially the female environment of the womb.

32. Ibid., pp. 65, 70. See Robert Stoller, *Sex and Gender: On the Development of Masculinity and Femininity* (New York: Science House, 1968).

33. Ibid., p. 62.

34. Ibid., p. 71, cf. Stoller's similar point, *Perversion* (New York: Pantheon, 1975), p. xii.

35. Ibid., p. 103.

36. Becker, *The Denial of Death*, p. ix.

37. Homer, *Iliad*, trans. Richard Lattimore (Chicago: University of Chicago Press, 1951) 9.310–328.

38. See James Redfield, *The Tragedy of Hector* (Chicago: University of Chicago Press, 1975), pp. xiii, 101; Redfield argues that through his own death, Achilles, more than any other Greek confronted the meaning of his own death. Also see Gregory Nagy, *The Best of the Achaeans* (Baltimore, Md.: Johns Hopkins University Press, 1979).

39. Nagy, ibid., p. x.

40. Redfield, *The Tragedy of Hector*, pp. 103, 126, 184, returns repeatedly to the problem of meaninglessness.

41. See ibid., p. 33 (on Book 9); and Nagy, *The Best of the Achaeans*, pp. 9, 11, on these points.

42. See, Hom. *Il.* 1.542. What is the significance of the Bohemian Grove in our own time?

43. Hom. *Il.* xviii, 105–106 (Redfield, *The Tragedy of Hector*, p. 12).

44. "There is no complete manhood without war. War is thus both terrible and necessary to happiness" (Redfield, ibid., p. x).

45. Helen is self-described as a "nasty bitch, evil intriguing" (Hom. *Il.* 7.344); also see Sarpedon's statement.

46. Hom. *Il.* 2.235; 7.96; 8.163.

47. Hom. *Il.* 6.81.

48. Hom. *Il.* 8.769 (Redfield, *The Tragedy of Hector*, p. 121).

49. Hom. *Il.* 21.230–249.

50. See E. R. Dodds, *The Greeks and the Irrational* (Berkeley: University of California Press, 1951), pp. 17–18, citing Hom. *Il.* 9.315ff.

51. Hom. *Il.* 9.411–416.

52. See Redfield, *The Tragedy of Hector*, p. 12, citing Hom. *Il.* 18.105–106.

53. See Nagy, *The Best of the Achaeans*, p. 41. I do not mean to detract from Homer's achievement in writing a splendid version of the oral tradition.

54. Hom. *Il.* 1.119.

55. Hom. *Il.* 9.158–161. Interestingly enough, Odysseus fails to repeat this part of the message, but Achilles clearly understands what giving way will mean. Given the zero-sum nature of the rivalry, he cannot give in. This zero-sum situation appears again and again—finally in Hektor's situation when he faces Achilles: "I must take you now or be taken," he says (21.253).

56. Nagy, *The Best of the Achaeans*, p. 45.

57. Redfield, *The Tragedy of Hector*, p. 129.

58. Hom. *Il.* 21.255–285; also see the boasting in Book 1. See Ong, *Fighting for Life*, pp. 110–111, who notes that especially in a masculine agonistic context, boasting can serve as a kind of public self-nurturing treatment. This treatment can be self-administered or can be given by other men as tribute. Thus, bragging or boasting is the oral equivalent of ritual physical combat. In this context it is interesting to note the significance of Nagy's contention that boasting is related to prayer.

59. But see Redfield's very different argument on this point (*The Tragedy of Hector*, p. 99).

60. Ibid.

61. Redfield, *The Tragedy of Hector,* pp. 99–100. One wonders how the warriors could come to have prestige unless war or combat already had a positive value.

62. Ibid., p. 118.

63. Nagy, *The Best of the Achaeans,* pp. 309–310.

64. Hom. *Il.* 9.404.

65. Ibid., p. 124. Also see Gray, *The Warriors* (New York: Harper & Row, 1959).

66. Hom. *Il.* 1.103–105.

67. Hom. *Il.* 1.200–201.

68. Hom. *Il.* 1.409.

69. Hom. *Il.* 21.144.

70. Redfield, *The Tragedy of Hector,* p. 21, n. 22. Also see Hektor's internal debate as he faces Achilles.

71. I owe this point to Dodds, *The Greeks and the Irrational,* Chap. 1. But I do not subscribe to his argument that this represents a way to deal with shame because it seems a far more pervasive aspect of the Homeric world view.

72. Hom. *Il.* 20.304–305 (italics mine).

73. Redfield argues that "the heroic vision is of meaning uncertainly rescued from meaninglessness" (*The Tragedy of Hector,* p. 103).

74. James Redfield, *Nature and Culture in the Iliad* (Chicago: University of Chicago Press, 1975), p. xiii. This is the same choice made by the ancient Greeks. See Nagy, *The Best of the Achaeans,* p. 41.

75. Evel Knievel, television interview, Baltimore Channel 13, January 1983.

76. Becker, *The Denial of Death,* p. 1.

77. Ibid., p. 2.

78. Ibid., p. 11, citing Jacques Choron, *Death and Western Thought.* In this, he is supported by O'Brien, *The Politics of Reproduction.*

79. On these points, see Judith Stiehm, *Bring Me Men and Women* (Berkeley: University of California Press, 1981); Halberstam, *The Best and the Brightest.*

80. Fasteau; "Vietnam and the Cult of Toughness," p. 186.

81. *New York Times,* October 27, 1983.

82. Carol Cohn, "Sex and Death in the Rational World of Defense Intellectuals," *Signs: Journal of Women in Culture and Society* 12, no. 4 (Summer 1987), pp. 690–691.

83. Elaine Scarry, *The Body in Pain* (New York: Oxford University Press, 1985), pp. 66–67, 74–75.

84. Cohn, "Sex and Death," p. 700.

85. Ibid., p. 702.

EIGHT

Emasculating America's Linguistic Deterrent

CAROL COHN

> If we continue to speak this sameness, if we speak to each other, as
> men have spoken for centuries, as they have taught us to speak, we
> will fail each other. Again . . . words will pass through our bodies,
> above our heads, disappear, make us disappear.[1]

In the January 16, 1982, *Los Angeles Times*, Robert Scheer reported that
T. K. Jones, a Deputy Under Secretary of Defense in Ronald Reagan's
administration, told him that it would take the United States only two
to four years to completely recover from an all-out nuclear war with
the Soviet Union.

> If there are enough shovels to go around, everybody's going to make
> it. . . . You can make very good sheltering by taking the doors off
> your house, digging a trench, stacking the doors about two deep over
> that, covering it with plastic so that rain water or something doesn't
> screw up the glue in the door, then pile dirt over it. . . . It's the dirt
> that does it.[2]

Somehow, not everyone found this reassuring.

Jones's statement and others like it emanating from the Reagan
administration during its early years led me, like so many others, to
turn my attention to the danger of nuclear war. I started to read nuclear
strategy as well as mainstream and radical critiques of U.S. nuclear
policies. I began teaching college courses about the issues raised by the
threat of nuclear war and eventually started doing workshops with
teachers that addressed the nuclear threat. But no matter how deeply I
immersed myself in the subject, one question stuck with me, nagged
in the back of my mind, unanswerable. No matter how much I learned,

no matter what analytic frameworks I applied, no matter what I understood about the "military-industrial complex" or international politics or the functioning of bureaucracies, no matter what I knew about men's reasons for going to war, finally, I still could not understand it. How could men so blithely plan strategies for nuclear war?[3] How could they justify having and preparing to use even a single nuclear weapon, much less the tens of thousands of nuclear weapons that now threaten to decimate the planet? The question repeated itself again and again: "*How* can they think this way?"

For the past four years (1984–1988) I have been attempting to find the answer to that question by reading the writings of, and doing participant observation in the world of, nuclear defense intellectuals.[4] First listening, and then learning to converse in their specialized "technostrategic" language, I began to discover a world of professional discourse that is, I think, a significant part of the answer to that question. As a participant in their community, I became immersed in a discourse that not only removes its speakers from the realities of nuclear war but also justifies the existence of masses of nuclear weapons and, I became convinced, makes their use much more likely. Thus, I became engaged in the project of analyzing nuclear strategic discourse itself. This chapter is a small piece of that larger project.

I have three primary objectives in this project. The first is to describe, analyze, and explore the effects of technostrategic discourse—the language and ways of thinking that defense intellectuals have developed to speak about nuclear weapons, strategy, and warfare. It is a discourse of critical importance because it is the one used to research, theorize, debate, and publicly represent U.S. nuclear weapons policy decisions. As such, it functions both intellectually and sociopolitically; it defines and limits the *way* nuclear weapons are thought about, *who* may be heard as a "legitimate" speaker in the discussion, *what* may be "credibly" said and *what* must remain unspoken. Perhaps even more critically, this discourse not only dominates public debate about nuclear weapons issues but also debate about U.S. "security" policies. To an outside observer of the professional and political debates about U.S. security policy, the discourse would appear to have colonized our minds and to have subjugated other ways of understanding relations among states, the women, men, and children who live in them, and the planet itself.

My second objective goes beyond describing and understanding this discourse. Stated in the strongest possible terms, I wish to render this discourse "impotent and obsolete" (to borrow a phrase from Ronald Reagan). I wish to expose its limits and distortions, its underlying assumptions and values, and the vast gaps between what it claims to do and what it actually does, so as to break its stranglehold on our scholarship, our policy decisions, our national political processes, and our imaginations. I wish to examine and unravel the methods, procedures, and claims that constitute this kind of thinking and thus expose the ways in which a discourse that claims to be rational, objective, realistic, and universal is, in fact, anything but.

My third objective is to foster the development of more truly realistic, effective, and humane ways of thinking about international security and cooperation. I see the deconstruction and delegitimation of technostrategic discourse as a necessary, but not sufficient, condition for this project. A crucial step is the juxtaposition of ways of thinking from other disciplines, other political traditions, and other cultures, as well as ways of thinking that arise from the experience of nondominant groups within this culture. My goal is not to put forth a fully developed and unified policy alternative but rather to open some new space and make some new connections.

Contemporary feminist theory is an invaluable tool in this project, especially that strain of feminist theory that takes as its object of scrutiny discourses produced by men.[5] This kind of feminist work aims to explore the discourses' underlying assumptions, methods, procedures, and techniques of theory development, their use of criteria and methods of inclusion and exclusion; and the ways in which these discourses work and how they exert their dominance.[6] This work is a method, a *strategy*, whose goal is to destabilize, delegitimize, and dismantle patriarchal discourses—to render their systems, methods, and presumptions unable to retain their dominance and power and thus to open spaces for other voices to be heard. Destabilizing and interrupting patriarchal discourse are seen as the prerequisites for establishing new paradigms and different theoretical tools and for creating systems of knowledge based on different values and interests.

Feminist theory is among those that recognize that all knowledge is "interested," and partial; that no knowledge is without a point of view; that different knowledge is produced by different people in different positions; and that any knowledge is a function of the knower's lived experience in the world. Women, and others who occupy different positions in the world than do the producers of dominant discourses, may be therefore especially able to recognize and articulate exactly what gets included in and excluded from those discourses. Discovering the absences and gaps and understanding how these silences function to structure and make patriarchal discourses possible are crucial elements of the strategy of feminist theory and ones with exceedingly important policy implications.

Persephone Descends

I started my journey as a student in a summer program designed to teach college teachers about nuclear weapons technology, strategy, and arms control; the program was taught by nationally eminent defense intellectuals, nearly all of whom had spent time as Washington policy advisers.[7] In the early stages of listening to the experts' "technostrategic" language, I was most struck by the utter absence of the burning, explosive, flesh-tearing, radiation-poisoning, life-annihilating devastation of nuclear war. In its stead, I heard an abstract, euphemistic, acronym-ridden language that in no way enables or requires its speakers to be aware of the graphic reality behind the words. In this world, there is no incinerating of cities, only "countervalue" attacks. Nuclear warheads aimed at a small number of military targets, which also cause 36 million immediate human deaths (and many more fatalities as the days pass) are part of a "limited counterforce exchange." The fatalities are "collateral damage." A nuclear war in which tens of millions of people are killed, rivers and seas and cropland poisoned for decades to come, is referred to as a "sub-holocaust engagement."

The discourse is not, however, utterly devoid of graphic imagery. In lectures and conversations (rather than in written texts), some vivid images and metaphors do appear, but they are sexual and domestic images that serve to turn attention away from the brutal realities of war and toward the titillating or the comfortable and familiar features of daily life.[8] Images of the body appear, but it is not the human body vaporized, shattered, burned, or torn. Rather, metaphors of the body are used to describe the technological artifacts of weaponry or the opponent's military forces as a whole. So "smart" weapons have their own "eyes," "ears," and "brains"; there are "new generations" of weapons and "families" of weapons systems; forces can be "crippled" and weapons can be "disabled" or even "killed," while human death is reduced to "collateral damage." The ragged, charred flesh and bone of women, men, and children disappears, replaced by concern for the "vulnerability" of hard metal implements of destruction.[9]

Pleasures and Dangers

As I learned to speak and think in technostrategic terms, I realized that the absence of human beings and communities, and their fate in a nuclear war, is not simply a matter of words and images. Nuclear strategic thinking is not *about* people, communities, or even nation-states. The subjects, the referents, are the weapons themselves: numbers of weapons, characteristics of weapons, and hypothetical capacities of weapons.

Nuclear strategic thinking is a calculus of the relation of one set of weapons to another. As such, it is utterly bankrupt of possibilities for thinking about peace or meaningful security.[10]

However, as I started speaking technostrategic talk, I learned something else as well: It is enormously seductive, both intellectually and socially. It is, in some sense, fun to speak, as you master arcane concepts, learn to speak coded sentences of acronyms, and converse in language that few understand—a language understood almost exclusively by those with power. Mastery of the language is not only satisfying in itself; it also enables you to feel like a member of a secret and powerful club. Perhaps most importantly, mastery of the words, control of the concepts, seems to carry over to the weapons themselves; in being able to manipulate the theories, you come to feel as though the whole situation is under control.

Another source of intellectual seduction is the rule-governed complexity of the theory. Given the ways in which the euphemistic and abstract language does *not* connect the speaker to the grotesque realities of nuclear war, nuclear strategic theory becomes simply one more baroque, abstract, conceptual system. There are endless ways of manipulating the theory, models to build, puzzles to work through. For those attracted to that kind of complicated abstract thinking, it can be very satisfying. Instead of nuclear war being its subject, this highly stylized theory becomes its own subject.

The longer I stayed in the world of nuclear defense intellectuals, the more I became enmeshed in the logic of technostrategic discourse. I went through an intense phase of learning to use technostrategic logic against itself, to show that particular new weapons systems made no sense *even within* the logic and assumptions of nuclear planners. But as I became more able to do this, as I engaged in conversations with defense intellectuals in which I could use my knowledge of technostrategic logic to question their arguments and rationalizations, I discovered something else. When I pushed a defense intellectual on a particular point, when I could show I knew that even within the mathematical calculus of weaponry, a weapons system made no sense, he would often slide from the technostrategic level of nuclear discourse to a different, less precise and intricate, more amorphous level—a level I call the axiomatic. When I could point out, for instance, that MX missiles in a "vulnerable" basing mode could not carry out the strategic function for which they were supposedly designed (as "second-strike counterforce" weapons), the response would be something like, "Yes, but it's important to demonstrate our resolve, and stay the course." Or, "Yes, that's true, but anything that complicates an attacker's plans is good." In other words, the particularity of the technostrategic justification for the weapons system disappeared and was replaced by a generality that could be used to fit nearly any situation.

What I began to see is that even within the community of nuclear planners and politicians, technostrategic analyses, with all their (to me) crazy logic, are finally almost irrelevant in regard to nuclear decision-making; they do not describe the actual criteria upon which nuclear decisions are made.[11] Nor do they even provide meaningful and internally consistent justifications. Instead, they function as a gloss over a set of much more primitive, ambiguous, contradictory axioms that constitute the core dogma of the nuclear world. It is these axioms, rather than the rationalistic technostrategic analyses and calculations, that defense analysts and politicians invoke when they are called upon to justify weapons decisions. The axioms may include technostrategic jargon, but even when they do not, they appear somehow to draw upon and be the outcome or conclusion of the more scientistic level of the discourse. That is, they do not appear as empty slogans; instead, they somehow call forth the aura of scientific logic and technical rationality that surrounds the more abstruse level of technostrategic discourse.

Among the most frequently invoked axioms are the two previously mentioned: Anything is good if it "complicates an attacker's plans" or if it "demonstrates our will/our resolve/our willingness to stay the course." Other axiomatic "goods" are weapons systems or political moves that "enhance" or "strengthen deterrence"; "enhance U.S. credibility"; "deny the Soviets the potential for coercion"; "enhance crisis stability"; "protect our vital interests"; "put at risk that which he [the Soviets] values most."[12]

Falling Flat on Their Axioms

Let me leave aside, for the moment, the question of why any of these should be taken as axiomatic. (Because most defense intellectuals leave that question aside permanently, I feel that leaving it aside for a few paragraphs is a relatively minor offense.) Instead, let us examine two of the salient characteristics of these axioms. First, even viewed from *within* a technostrategic framework, one major characteristic is immediately striking—the axioms provide no real criteria for discrimination. This is problematic from the standpoint of the intellectual integrity of nuclear discourse and belies its claim to offer meaningful, rational guidance in nuclear weapons policy decisions. But this characteristic is highly useful for the discourse's political legitimation functions.

The axiom that something is good if it "strengthens" or "enhances" deterrence is a good example. It is very difficult indeed to think of any new weapons system that would not "strengthen deterrence," if strengthening deterrence means doing anything that makes the nuclear arsenal more efficient at retaliating, or if it means having weapons systems at every "rung of the ladder of escalation" (so as to deter through "escalation dominance"), or if it means doing anything that makes a nation's opponents less certain of the efficacy of their attack. How, then, does this axiom provide any criteria for discrimination between more and less useful weapons systems?

The nearly infinite expandability and plasticity of the concept of deterrence mean that this axiom can be used to justify and legitimate nearly any weapons system, virtually independent of whether or not the weapon performs a "necessary" strategic function or whether it even has the functional capabilities claimed for it.

Looking at the Strategic Defense Initiative (SDI), or Star Wars, is instructive. No one in the nuclear bureaucracy except, apparently, President Reagan, believes that Star Wars could perform its supposed function—to replace mutually assured destruction with "mutually assured survival"—yet many support it. Their real reasons for support are, no doubt, legion, including loyalty to the president; the desire for research funding; a desire to "get the Russians" (either by using a Star Wars phase of the nuclear arms race to destroy the Soviet economy or by having a system in place that would make a first strike against the Soviet Union more feasible).[13] Nevertheless, the most often heard public justification for supporting Star Wars is not any of these. Rather, it is that SDI would "enhance deterrence." Hypothetically, SDI would provide a defense for some of the United States' "vulnerable" land-based intercontinental ballistic missiles (ICBMs) (but none of its cities), which would strengthen the country's ability to retaliate against a nuclear attack. (Deterrence was, of course, the very thing that Star Wars was supposed to replace by providing a "leakproof" defense against nuclear weapons.) The fact that even without a Star Wars system, the United States would still have the capacity to retaliate with bombers and submarines, even in the entirely hypothetical case of all U.S. ICBMs being destroyed, is ignored. After all, if the Soviets not only had to contend with bombers and submarines but also had to deal with some remaining ICBMs, that would "complicate their plans," another axiomatic good.

The axiom that something is good if it "demonstrates our will/our resolve/our willingness to stay the course" functions in similar ways. It, too, fails to provide any grounds for discrimination, except by automatically framing the cancellation or scaling back of any weapons program as bad. This axiom can be used to justify deploying any weapons system developed and keeping it in place once it has been deployed (even if its initial deployment was "only as a bargaining chip for arms control negotiations"). The axiom can justify deploying weapons systems that do not work. Here, Pershing II missiles provide an example; it "made sense" to deploy them in Western Europe, despite the fact that the United States had not finished testing them and did not know whether they would fly, because it "demonstrated our resolve" (as well as U.S. commitment to our NATO allies, another amorphous axiomatic good).

If failure to provide meaningful grounds for discrimination is a characteristic of these axioms that should be troubling from an insider's point of view, from an outsider's point of view there is an aspect that should, I believe, be even more striking, and troubling. I refer simply to the fact that these axioms are taken as axiomatic—apparently without anyone feeling the necessity to explain or justify them. "Something that enhances deterrence is good," and one does not stop to question whether deterrence in fact needs to be enhanced or whether the current U.S. capacity to kill hundreds of millions of people, as well as the social and ecological communities that support them, might not be sufficient. Even if it were concluded that deterrence did need to be strengthened, one does not stop to ask whether the particular weapons system in question is the best one to do so. Nor does one stop to ask whether something other than weapons systems (and, for liberals, negotiations about them) might best strengthen deterrence. The potential efficacy of the massive U.S.-Soviet "peace hostages" exchange program suggested by anthropologist Ken Smail, for example, is not compared to the deterrence-strengthening value of a new missile.[14]

Demonstrating our will, our refusal to let ourselves be "pushed around," our "willingness to stay the course" are all equally axiomatic, unquestionable goods. No one would suggest that it is a good thing to be a "sissy" or to reconsider and change our mind about a given course. (It is, after all, "a *woman's* prerogative to change her mind.") Showing that we are committed to being the strongest nation in the world and that we are even willing to make sacrifices and injure ourselves to demonstrate this are equally obvious courses of action; everyone knows that to acknowledge or display vulnerability, or even a tiny weakening of will, is to invite attack.[15] At the very least, one is asking to be taken advantage of.

Of States and Men

I could go on through the rest of the axioms, but at this point the third striking characteristic of these axioms should already be clear: We are in a realm where gender is just below the surface. The state embodied in these axioms, and throughout nuclear strategic discourse, bears an uncanny resemblance to a familiar ideal image of masculine identity. It is strong, stable, rational. It devotes tremendous resources to deterring any encroachments of its carefully defined and defended borders. It knows that the job of protecting its interests and getting what it needs falls to it alone. It can depend on no one, and it acts accordingly. It is no sissy. It makes a decision and sticks to it. It would never make the mistake of supposing that vulnerability might incite care, rather than attack.[16] It is capable of "putting at risk that which he [the enemy] values most"—which is, of course, "his" biggest missiles.

There may be precious little intellectual reason to repeatedly invoke these axioms; they may be next to useless in providing a definable set of criteria for rational action, but they have the power to evoke emotional resonances that are apparently compelling for the men who formulate and justify nuclear policy and for much of the public. What we have then, I believe, is a whole level of technostrategic discourse that derives its appeal and power not from its intellectual precision, force, or utility but from its emotional valences.[17]

Whatever the limits of the first level of technostrategic discourse, this second, axiomatic, level is yet more problematic. It partakes of none of the first's methods and rules of logic, of its technical rationality (for all its flaws), and yet it manages, overtly at least, to attain some measure of seriousness, of legitimacy, through its association with that first scientistic level of the discourse. Its public legitimacy stems in part from its apparent adherence to the highest standards of one ideal version of masculinity—the coolly objective, rationally calculating mind, unclouded by passions. While at the same time, its "felt truthfulness" and its power as a motivator come from the ways it taps into much more emotional masculine identity issues—without ever having to acknowledge that it is doing so.

This is, I think, the key to technostrategic discourse's power as a system of legitimation. It has at its core a set of terms that are so abstract and malleable, so imprecise and ambiguous, as to be nearly infinitely flexible in their applications and thus all but meaningless; it can be used to legitimate almost any weapons system or policy. Yet it *seems* precise, inevitable, objective; the discourse's *own* legitimacy comes from its air of science, math, and technical rationality. At the same time, its power stems from the emotional resonance of the issues embodied within its axioms.

A recent booklet by Robert Jastrow and James Frelk is an exquisite example of the phenomenon I have just been describing. Ostensibly a technostrategically based argument for SDI, the argumentation is mostly on the level of amorphous phrases and ambiguous axioms. Yet it is quite successful in mobilizing technostrategic discourse's aura of scientific rationality and objectively rooted imperative. One of the devices it employs to do so is the use of charts and graphs, a very common technique in defense briefings and propaganda. This medium of representation, which we associate with complex mathematical and scientifically derived information, is transmuted into graphics that present information without meaning. Often graphs do not even have their axes labeled, nor is there any indication of why the comparisons displayed on the charts should be considered significant.[18] Yet what they show feels worrisome. They look scientific, yet they do not so much transmit meaningful information as evoke and manipulate an emotional response. (In this sense, they might be considered microcosms of much technostrategic discourse.)

The booklet contains a variation on one of the classic nuclear arms charts. It compares U.S. and Soviet missile size: the erect, mammoth Soviet SS-18 towers over the thick but stubby MX and the puny pencil-thin Midgetman (even the name is an embarrassment).[19] There is no accompanying text. Presumably the import is clear. But in case there is any doubt, the booklet's title would serve as an interpretive guide: "How the Soviets Emasculated America's Deterrent."[20]

Impotence and Obsolescence

Broadly speaking, the pamphlet presents a set of concerns about the destructive power of nuclear weapons and a set of goals—in Ronald Reagan's words, to "render nuclear weapons impotent and obsolete"— and it urges upon the nation the vigorous pursuit of an SDI program. I have, in a sense, the same concerns and goals, but I would suggest a different acronym and a different course of action. In the place of SDI, I propose EALD. I know this is not the perfect acronym because when pronounced, it sounds uncomfortably close to "yield," with all its inappropriately unmasculine connotations. However, until I get this worked out, the acronym is still probably less inflammatory than the course of action itself: Emasculating America's Linguistic Deterrent.

I offer this as a vastly less expensive and far more feasible and effective alternative to Star Wars. The less expensive aspect must be obvious. As to more effective, it is not nuclear weapons that SDI would hypothetically render impotent and obsolete but only ballistic missiles. (Reagan's fantasy SDI, even if it could ever work, would be no protection against nuclear explosives on bombers, cruise missiles, or in suitcases.) I believe that rendering technostrategic discourse impotent and obsolete would not only achieve the SDI program's goal but would, in fact, render all nuclear weapons impotent and obsolete.

I am only being partly facetious when I say this. The key is in the political, intellectual, and military legitimation functions of technostrategic discourse. In military terms, nuclear weapons are already impotent and obsolete in the sense that no one has ever figured out a military use for them; there is no way for a nation to use them and accomplish its goals in battle without damaging itself at the same time. Thus, it might appear hard to rationalize having three thousand of them. But technostrategic discourse, by creating an "as if" world in which it appears that nuclear weapons of almost every conceivable size and characteristic are useful, legitimates their existence. In so doing, it obfuscates the fact that they are militarily impotent and obsolete and so enables them to have a political potency that they would not otherwise have. This is, I think, the most important legitimation function of technostrategic discourse and the central reason why we must render the discourse itself impotent and obsolete, or "emasculate America's linguistic deterrent."

This point requires some elaboration. The assertion that nuclear weapons are already impotent and obsolete in military terms is not the raving of some lunatic peacenik but a widely accepted truth in the defense establishment. I was recently at a dinner with former secretary of defense Robert McNamara and about one hundred other defense intellectuals. McNamara, addressing these men who spend their days thinking about "extended deterrence," "living with nuclear weapons," and "credible" scenarios for nuclear war fighting, said, "No one has ever developed a plan to initiate the use of nuclear weapons with a high probability of advantage to the initiator."[21] He challenged them to disagree. No one could, although a few attempted to throw a protective shield over this very naked statement.

However, to say that nuclear weapons are already impotent and obsolete in military terms, does not, of course, mean that they cannot and will not be used. They have already been used to attack Hiroshima and Nagasaki. As Daniel Ellsberg has pointed out, they have also been used many times in the precise sense that a gun is used to threaten someone in a holdup.[22] In fact, I would argue that the actual physical use of bombs becomes more likely with the elaboration of technostrategic discourse—a symbolic system devoted to working out "credible scenarios," be they in the service of a genuine desire to deter nuclear weapons' use or to "prevail" in a nuclear war. Here, again, the McNamara event was very interesting. When McNamara laid down his challenge to the crowd, one very prominent long-time presidential science adviser argued with McNamara, saying, in essence, "Well, there are certainly lots of people who work at making plans for the use of nuclear weapons, and lots of people believe that such plans exist." (Both of which are true.) McNamara replied, "Yes, and that's my second point. The first is that there's no plan that wouldn't lead to unacceptable damage and destruction of the nation, however you wish to define that. The second: The perception that there *is* such a plan is dangerous, because you'll get some president or other person with power who *believes* those plans exist and so will order them to be used."

But if nuclear weapons are already impotent and obsolete in the sense that they are militarily unusable, they are certainly not impotent and obsolete in the political sense. And that is the key. Technostrategic discourse solves the fundamental problem nuclear weapons create for the political establishment. Nuclear weapons have tremendous explosive power, but if they are not militarily usable, that power is of little value to the state that possesses it. That is, a weapon that is militarily unusable is exceedingly difficult to translate into political power; it is exceedingly difficult to manipulate to attain political advantage, to coerce, or to dominate. It appears only as an empty threat. Technostrategic discourse solves this problem by creating a symbolic system in which it is possible to posit the use of nuclear weapons. In creating a body of doctrine that enables us to "think about the unthinkable," this discourse rescues nuclear weapons from the never-never land of unusable weapons and places them squarely back in the realm of political power. Once there exists a body of doctrine purporting to contain ways to use nuclear explosives as weapons in warfare, even if it is "only as a deterrent" (because the essence of deterrence "working" is that the other side has to believe that its opponent is actually willing and likely to use the weapons), nuclear weapons become politically usable.[23]

The forty-odd year development of technostrategic discourse has, I would argue, been an attempt to develop ways not so much to "think about the unthinkable" (because there is precious little thinking about the weapons, much less humans, going on; instead there is abstracting, quantifying, manipulating, modeling, programming), but to make it more possible to "use the unusable." The development of nuclear strategic theory, as with any other strategic theory, has had the goal of deriving political power from the manipulation of military assets. That nuclear weapons are not actually usable military assets is a fact that vanishes in the realm of technostrategic discourse.

Technostrategic discourse, in creating a conceptual system that theorizes the use of unusable weapons, enables them to be translated into political power. Thus, *it legitimates the very existence and proliferation of nuclear weapons themselves, as well as the entire regime of nuclear-armed organized peacelessness built around them.*[24] It legitimates the commitment of tremendous financial and intellectual resources to their research and production; their integration into U.S. military forces; the vast complex of corporations that make higher levels of profit on military manufacturing than in any other area; the concentration of information and power into a few "classified" hands that is so antithetical to democracy; the U.S. status as a global superpower that may be expected to intervene in the affairs of virtually any other nation. In other words, the very existence of this discourse serves to legitimate not just the physical explosives and "delivery systems" (the missiles, bombers, submarines) but also their whole symbolic and institutional integration into national life and identity.

If my analysis of the functions of technostrategic discourse is correct, exposing it for what it is and delegitimating it become enormously important and potentially very powerful. If we can *publicly* render that discourse impotent and obsolete, we are destroying a crucial part of the structure of justification for nuclear weapons' continued existence, as well as most of the arguments mobilized to support each new weapons appropriation bill, and the systematic set of illusions created by that symbol system that do, I believe, make it far more likely that nuclear weapons will be used. If we could expose and unravel this discourse that justifies the unjustifiable, the political barriers to nuclear disarmament would start to crumble.

Notes

1. Luce Irigaray, "When Our Two Lips Speak Together," *Signs* 6, no. 1 (1980), pp. 69–79.

2. Scheer quoted these lines and others from his fall 1981 interviews with Jones in *With Enough Shovels: Reagan, Bush & Nuclear War* (New York: Random House, 1982), pp. 18 and 23. T. K. Jones was the Deputy Under Secretary of Defense for research and engineering, strategic and theater nuclear forces.

3. Here, and throughout the text, I use the term *men* not in its inclusive sense—to mean men and women—but in its exclusive sense—to mean adult males. We now know that even when "men" is used in its "inclusive" sense, what the reader or listener sees is, in fact, not men and women, but men. This is the image I want my readers to have; more specifically, the image should be of white men. Nuclear strategists, members of the defense intellectual community, and the nuclear bureaucracy in general have always been and are still now virtually all white males. The number of women who have had important roles can be counted on the fingers of one hand. Without at this point speculating on the reasons, or the effects, what can be said with absolute accuracy is that this is a white male realm.

4. When I use the term *defense intellectuals* I am not using it simply to refer to men who use their intellectual skills to think about military matters. Instead, I am referring to a particular professional community whose members recognize each other as such, even though there is no formal set of definitions or criteria for membership. In the depiction that follows, I will attempt to delineate the

characteristics they share, although, of course, any particular individual may differ from this "ideal type."

Defense intellectuals can be characterized not only by what they think about but also by how they think about it and toward what ends. The "what" is "defense" policy (what was once called war or military policy), and in the particular subgroup I studied, it is most often explicitly nuclear policy.

The "how" is, first of all, within an assumptive framework that accepts the goals and means of current U.S. national security policy as legitimate: the use of military force and coercion is seen as a fundamental tool of foreign policy, to be used when "our vital interests" are at stake. Their "realist" assumptions include a vision of the world that is bipolar, with the nations of the Southern Hemisphere largely ignored except as they can be seen to figure in East-West conflict. They also include a view of nuclear arsenals as inevitable; the problem is not how to get rid of them but simply how to live with them, how to "rationally manage" the problems they create and the power they promise.

Another aspect of "how they think" is that they talk, write, and think within a special framework of description and analysis, which has "deterrence theory" as its cornerstone; they create and participate in the discourse I call "techno-strategic." The methods they employ can be characterized as a rationalized mathematical calculus utilized to assess military capabilities. Mathematical modeling techniques, including linear programming, game theory, and systems analysis, play an important role in defense analysis.

The "towards what ends" is that defense intellectuals aspire to be "policy relevant." That is to say, they wish to develop ideas that can have an effect on U.S. defense policy, including arms control. This implies, then, that they not only accept the national security framework but also that they most often gear their suggestions to be fairly conservative, not deviating very far from the status quo. What one might "ideally like" is set aside in favor of hard-nosed assessments of what it might be possible to get, and there is widespread acceptance of the "fact" that one will often have to trade off a lot to get it.

5. The discussion that follows draws closely upon Elizabeth Gross, "What Is Feminist Theory?" in Carol Pateman and Elizabeth Gross, eds., *Feminist Challenges: Social and Political Theory* (Boston: Northeastern University Press, 1986), pp. 190–215.

6. See, for example, Sandra Harding and Merrill Hintikka, eds., *Discovering Reality: Feminist Perspectives on Epistemology, Metaphysics, Methodology, and the Philosophy of Science* (Dordrecht, The Netherlands: D. Reidel, 1983); and Pateman and Gross, ibid.

7. This was the 1984 MIT/Harvard Summer Program on Nuclear Weapons Technology and Arms Control. My participant observation went on to include a year as a visiting scholar at the Center of International Studies at the Massachusetts Institute of Technology; participation in the MIT/Harvard Summer Program on Nuclear Weapons Technology and Arms Control for a second year, this time as a lecturer; attendance at courses, special lectures, and discussions in the defense studies programs at both MIT and Harvard; interviews of graduate students and professors in both programs; attendance at numerous professional conferences; and interviews of men and women in the military.

8. I have written at length about the sexual and domestic imagery I found in technostrategic talk in "Sex and Death in the Rational World of Defense Intellectuals," *Signs* 12, no. 4 (1987), pp. 692–699.

9. For a discussion of the functions of imagery that reverses sentient and insentient matter, that "exchange[s] . . . idioms between weapons and bodies," see Elaine Scarry, *The Body in Pain: The Making and Unmaking of the World* (New York: Oxford University Press, 1985), pp. 60–157, especially p. 67.

10. I have written in much greater detail about these early stages of listening to and learning to speak the language in "Sex and Death," pp. 687–718.

11. For a more fully developed argument on this point, see Carol Cohn, "Nuclear Discourse in a Community of Defense Intellectuals: The Effects of Techno-Strategic Language and Rationality and Their Role in American Political Culture" (Ph.D. diss., Union Graduate School, 1988), Chap. 5.

12. The use of "he" when referring to the Soviet Union is a frequent practice among defense intellectuals and is reflective of what I call the "unitary masculine actor problem" in strategic thinking. It seems to me that this linguistic practice facilitates technostrategic thinking's failure to confront the complexity of the functioning of the nation-state that is deemed the "enemy" and to reduce it to a single male person—a rational male actor who perceives actions in the same way that U.S. strategic professionals do, who is locked into a "rational" male competition for power. At the risk of stating the obvious, this invites dangerously inappropriate and inaccurate understandings of and responses to the Soviet Union.

A related phenomenon is the use of the first person plural pronouns "we," "us," and "our" when referring to the U.S. government, decisionmakers, or armed forces. A defense intellectual might say, for example, "If he hits us with his SS-18s, we can still hit him back with our SLBMs and bombers." The potential reality of government leaders giving orders to devastate each other's homelands is filtered through the image of men besting each other in a fist fight; it becomes a personal contest. This usage also characteristically conflates the identity, actions, and interests of individual citizens with states or sectors within the state. It is common to speak of "defending our vital interests," for example, as though a citizen's vital interests are identical with those of the state, the state's identical with those of a particular industry. Using the term *our vital interests* makes it extremely difficult to ask, "Whose?" and "Why exactly are these interests so vital?"

In this chapter, I have attempted to avoid such usage, except when I am writing in the voice of defense intellectuals.

13. A first strike against the Soviet Union would theoretically be more feasible on the following grounds: If the United States had an effective "decapitating first strike" capability (highly accurate and powerful missiles that could supposedly destroy underground Soviet command and control centers, as well as missiles in their silos), Washington would have to expect the Soviets still to be able to launch a very small percentage of their missiles. With nuclear weapons, a "very small" number is not small enough—they would still cause what is dispassionately referred to as "unacceptable damage." But an SDI system that was utterly

inadequate to deal with the whole Soviet missile force might be sufficient to "mop up" the remaining missiles that were launched before they hit the United States. At the risk of stating the obvious, this scenario is as ridiculous as any other I have dealt with in this piece. But its ridiculousness does not matter once inside the imaginary world of technostrategic planning.

14. Smail is one of several authors who have suggested that the placement of a substantial number of U.S. citizens in the Soviet Union and Soviet citizens in the United States would be a significant deterrent to U.S.-Soviet nuclear war. But he has developed this idea more extensively than most. Whereas others have suggested exchanges at the scale of 1,000 or 10,000, Smail calls for exchanges of up to 1 million citizens, who would each live and work in the other nation for two years at a time. He chooses 1 million to show that even with such a high number, when you cost out this "deterrent" program, it is still less expensive than many of the military means currently employed. Smail has also done some important linguistic reclamation work. He explores the historical and cultural uses of the term *hostage* and finds that current usage runs counter to what the term has traditionally meant. Although we think of hostages as people taken against their will, in order to force another person or nation to meet a demand, typically the meaning is quite different. In instances of agreement between nations of approximately equal power, hostages have been exchanged—given rather than taken—as a pledge pending the fulfillment of the agreement or treaty to which both sides have already assented. Participation has been voluntary. The hostages were seen as surrogates for those making the pledges and often were the kin of the political and military leadership. Thus, as Smail says, hostages have typically been "emissaries of trust" rather than "pawns of fear." J. Kenneth Smail, "Building Bridges Via Reciprocal Hostage Exchange: A Confidence Enhancing Alternative to Nuclear Deterrence," *Bulletin of Peace Proposals* 16, no. 2 (1985), pp. 167–177.

15. The importance for strategic signaling of the willingness to even engage in "self-mutilation" in the service of "demonstrating our resolve" was suggested to me by game theorist Barry O'Neill (personal communication, November 12, 1986). For example, in this framework, U.S. insistence on deploying Pershing II and cruise missiles in Western Europe was in some sense all the more powerful and useful because of the Western European peace movement's protest against it; to the extent that it created problems for NATO governments, and thus had some costs to the unity and stability of the NATO alliance, U.S. insistence on deployment despite those costs and U.S. willingness to "accept" the injuries should have demonstrated to the Soviet Union even more strongly than before U.S. commitment and resolve.

16. Sara Ruddick, "Maternal Thinking," *Feminist Studies* 6, no. 2 (Summer 1980), pp. 342–367, provides an account of the way in which the practice of mothering develops a very different attitude toward and way of thinking about vulnerability, which is wonderfully suggestive for thinking about the role of gender in technostrategic thought.

17. For a discussion of the psychodynamic development of this particular version of male gender, see Nancy Chodorow, *The Reproduction of Mothering:*

Psychoanalysis and the Sociology of Gender (Berkeley: University of California Press, 1978); Dorothy Dinnerstein, *The Mermaid and the Minotaur* (New York: Harper Colophon Books, 1977); and Evelyn Fox Keller, *Reflections on Gender and Science* (New Haven, Conn.: Yale University Press, 1985). Keller's exploration of the relation between the construction of a particular gender ideal and the construction of a realm of intellectual inquiry is fascinating and provides a model of the kind of analysis of the technostrategic project that I have only hinted at in the last few paragraphs.

18. For an excellent, comprehensive critique of this and other "games defense analysts play," see Stephen Van Evera, Michael Salman, and Kevin J. Sullivan, "Analysis or Propaganda?: Measuring American Strategic Nuclear Capability, 1969–1987," in Lynn Eden and Steven Miller, eds., *Nuclear Arguments: The Major Debates on Strategic Nuclear Weapons and Arms Control* (Ithaca, N.Y.: Cornell University Press, forthcoming).

Since September 1981, the Reagan Department of Defense has been putting out a glossy, illustrated annual book called *Soviet Military Power* as a part of its propaganda campaign to justify the administration's massive increases in arms expenditures. The charts and graphics provide many illustrations of precisely the kinds of games and distortions Van Evera et al. detail, and, indeed, some of their examples come from editions of the book. According to Nicolas Lemann, the charts in the first edition played a significant role in turning Caspar Weinberger into a hawk (Nicholas Lemann, "Caspar Weinberger in Reagan's Pentagon: The Peacetime War," *The Atlantic Monthly* [October 1984], pp. 72–94). This thought becomes all the more disturbing after reading Tom Gervasi, *Soviet Military Power: The Pentagon's Propaganda Document, Annotated and Corrected* (New York: Vintage Books, 1987), an annotated version of the April 1987 *Soviet Military Power*, in which Gervasi corrects the distortions, exaggerations, and outright lies in the document as well as identifies "the hidden assumptions used to produce incomplete and misleading comparisons of military power" (p. vi). It is an invaluable resource for anyone who wants to learn how to decode U.S. government statements on U.S. and Soviet military power.

19. Charts like these have played an astonishingly prominent role in nuclear weapons political discourse. They started appearing in U.S. government pub-lications in the late 1970s. Around that same time, a major missile manufacturer gave every member of Congress a plastic desk ornament—a neat row of paired missiles, the bright red Soviet ones towering over their puny blue U.S. counterparts. More recently, a government chart upended a new Soviet Typhoon ballistic missile submarine in order to compare its length to the height of the Washington Monument! (Fiscal Year '83 Annual Defense Department Report, *Soviet Military Power*, Appendix p. 57, as cited by Van Evera et al., "Analysis or Propaganda?") One does have to wonder what strategically important information this image is meant to convey.

20. Robert Jastrow and James Frelk, "How the Soviets Emasculated America's Deterrent" (Washington, D.C.: George Marshall Institute, 1987). I am grateful to Josie Stein for calling this booklet to my attention.

21. Robert McNamara, Harvard Avoiding Nuclear War Faculty Group Dinner, Harvard Faculty Club, Cambridge, Massachusetts, November 18, 1987.

22. Daniel Ellsberg, "Call to Mutiny," in E. P. Thompson and Dan Smith, eds., *Protest and Survive* (New York: Monthly Review Press, 1981).

23. Daniel Ellsberg, a former strategic planner, clearly articulates one of the ways nuclear weapons can be used politically without their detonation. He lists twelve "uses" of nuclear weapons since Hiroshima and Nagasaki, and in each case, it is the *threat* to detonate them that is seen to constitute a use, just as a thief "uses" a gun when he holds it to the head of a victim and asks for money. The weapon is being used, whether or not it is ultimately fired (Ellsberg, ibid.).

The desire to use nuclear weapons in this way is the sort of truism that is absolutely taken for granted within the strategic community, although largely hidden from the public. We are treated to torrents of rhetoric about the defensive purposes of the U.S. military and the (nuclear) deterrent functions of U.S. nuclear weapons, while the experts know that the purposes of the country's armed forces include, preeminently, "armed suasion." The armed forces need not be "used" in the sense of being literally sent into combat; their overt display at the appropriate location is often sufficient. A 1978 Brookings Institution study finds 215 incidents between 1945 and 1975 in which the United States used the display of arms or armed forces for political purposes. The authors discuss the purposes of each display, and their analysis classifies the uses of arms or armed forces according to whether the purpose was to "assure, compel, deter, or induce." (It should be unnecessary to point out that this is language that comes as close as possible to laundering U.S. actions of political content; alternative images—coercion of a weaker nation, pursuit of imperial interests, intervention in and manipulation of another nation's internal politics or economy—seem very far away indeed.) Other factors analyzed in the study include whether the weapons were conventional or nuclear and what the political popularity of the president was at the time of the "incident" (Barry M. Blechman and Stephen S. Kaplan, *Force Without War: U.S. Armed Forces as a Political Instrument* [Washington, D.C.: The Brookings Institution, 1978]).

24. The phrase "organized peacelessness" comes from West German peace researcher Dieter Senghaas, who uses it to refer to "a structure of ceaseless unrest, of permanent prewar mobilization and protracted conflict which the whole practice of deterrence does not so much resolve as lock in place" (Dieter Senghaas, *Abschreckung und Frieden: Studien zur Kritik organizierter Friedlosigkeit*, as cited by Bradley S. Klein, *Strategic Discourse and Its Alternatives* [New York: The Center on Violence and Human Survival, 1987], p. 6).

NINE

We Speak for the Planet

BARBARA OMOLADE

As women of color live and struggle, we increasingly realize that it's time for us to speak for earth and its future. We have heard the voices of white men who speak for earth and its future. When we look at the hunger, despair, and killings around us, we see what white men who speak for earth have done. Their weaponry and visions speak clearly of a future of more and more war.

Science fiction films record and mirror the white man's vision of future life on planet earth in which he has assigned himself centrality and placed people of color at the periphery and margins. In his future visions the lands of people of color and the ways and beliefs of their ancestors and progeny will no longer exist. Earth will be populated primarily by white men, their machines, a few white women, and even fewer people of color. These movies reflect a future in which the planet (earth) will either be devastated by war or made irrelevant, for Western civilization will be able to continue on spaceships or satellites, as Huns become Cleons, Pygmies become Ewaaks, Egyptian rites become Vulcan mysticism, and our ancient First World wisdom becomes the property of an eight-hundred-year-old, nonhuman named Yoda. In this future world people of color will have been divested of their cultures and disconnected from their communities. Women of color will be like Lieutenant Uhuru, communications specialist of the *Starship Enterprise* under Captain James Kirk, functioning within the culture and machines of Western man.

The messages of enlightened Western scientists present us with another vision of the future. Futurists such as Fritjof Capra and Alvin Toffler tell us that Western civilization, using a combination of advanced technology and nuclear physics and matching Western scientific advancement with Eastern mysticism, will enable Western civilization to survive and advance. Although these scientists warn of the limitations and dangers of Western domination and violence and recognize the virtues of non-Western culture, they still envision a world based on Western assumptions of progress and technology. They don't include people of color as creators and participants in the creation of new dimensions to the human experience in the future.

Peace activists also fail to see people of color as initiators and creators and make assumptions about our limited abilities to work for peace and fundamental social change. Those opposed to nuclear weaponry and stockpiling project an equally disturbing politic and vision, which excludes people of color. The antiwar and antinuke organizers and their supporters have gathered millions to march and demonstrate against nuclear war and for a nuclear freeze as if only nuclear war threatens humankind. They have cleverly abstracted the technologies and apparatus of nuclear war and the existence of military conflict from the cultural and historical context that created that path in the first place.

Recent efforts by Soviet leader Mikhail Gorbachev and President Ronald Reagan to limit nuclear testing, stockpiling, and weaponry, while still protecting their own arsenals and selling arms to countries and factions around the world, vividly demonstrate how "peace" can become an abstract concept within a culture of war. Many peace activists are similarly blind to the constant wars and threats of war being waged against people of color and the planet by those who march for "peace" and by those they march against. These pacifists, like Gorbachev and Reagan, frequently want people of color to fear what they fear and define peace as they define it. They are unmindful that our lands and peoples have already been and are being destroyed as part of the "final solution" of the "color line." It is difficult to persuade the remnants of Native American tribes, the starving of African deserts, and the victims of the Cambodian "killing fields" that nuclear war is *the* major danger to human life on the planet and that only a nuclear "winter" embodies fear and futurelessness for humanity.

The peace movement suffers greatly from its lack of a historical and holistic perspective, practice, and vision that include the voices and experiences of people of color; the movement's goals and messages have therefore been easily coopted and expropriated by world leaders who share the same culture of racial dominance and arrogance. The peace movement's racist blinders have divorced peace from freedom, from feminism, from education reform, from legal rights, from human rights, from international alliances and friendships, from national liberation, from the particular (for example, black female, Native American male) and the general (human being). Nevertheless, social movements such as the civil rights–black power movement in the United States have always demanded peace with justice, with liberation, and with social and economic reconstruction and cultural freedom at home and abroad. The integration of our past and our present holocausts and our struggle to define our own lives and have our basic needs met are at the core of the inseparable struggles for world peace and social betterment.

> The Achilles heel of the organized peace movement in this country has always been its whiteness. In this multi-racial and racist society, no all-white movement can have the strength to bring about basic changes.
>
> It is axiomatic that basic changes do not occur in any society unless the people who are oppressed move to make them occur. In our society it is people of color who are the most oppressed. Indeed our entire history teaches us that when people of color have organized and struggled—most especially, because of their particular history, Black people—have moved in a more humane direction as a society, toward a better life for all people.[1]

Western man's whiteness, imagination, enlightened science, and movements toward peace have developed from a culture and history mobilized against women of color. The political advancements of white men have grown directly from the devastation and holocaust of people of color and our lands. This technological and material progress has been in direct proportion to the undevelopment of women of color. Yet the day-to-day survival, political struggles, and rising up of women of color, especially black women in the United States, reveal both complex resistance to holocaust and undevelopment and often conflicted responses to the military and war.

The Holocausts

Women of color are survivors of and remain casualties of holocausts, and we are direct victims of war—that is, of open armed conflict between countries or between factions within the same country. But women of color were not soldiers, nor did we trade animal pelts or slaves to the white man for guns, nor did we sell or lease our lands to the white man for wealth. Most men and women of color resisted and fought back, were slaughtered, enslaved, and force marched into plantation labor camps to serve the white masters of war and to build their empires and war machines.

People of color were and are victims of holocausts—that is, of great and widespread destruction, usually by fire. The world as we knew and created it was destroyed in a continual scorched earth policy of the white man. The experience of Jews and other Europeans under the Nazis can teach us the value of understanding the totality of destructive intent, the extensiveness of torture, and the demonical apparatus of war aimed at the human spirit.

A Jewish father pushed his daughter from the lines of certain death at Auschwitz and said, "You will be a remembrance—You tell the story—You survive." She lived. He died. Many have criticized the Jews for forcing non-Jews to remember the 6 million Jews who died under the Nazis and for etching the names Auschwitz and Buchenwald, Terezin and Warsaw in our minds. Yet as women of color, we, too, are "remembrances" of all the holocausts against the people of the world. We must remember the names of concentration camps such as *Jesus, Justice, Brotherhood,* and *Integrity,* ships that carried millions of African men, women, and children chained and brutalized across the ocean to the "New World." We must remember the Arawaks, the Taino, the Chickasaw, the Choctaw, the Narragansett, the Montauk, the Delaware, and the other Native American names of thousands of U.S. towns that stand for tribes of people who are no more. We must remember the holocausts visited against the Hawaiians, the aboriginal peoples of Australia, the Pacific Island peoples, and the women and children of Hiroshima and Nagasaki. We must remember the slaughter of men and women at Sharpeville, the children of Soweto, and the men of Attica. We must never, ever, forget the children disfigured, the men maimed, and the women broken in our holocausts—we must remember the names, the numbers, the faces, and the stories and teach them to our children and our children's children so the world can never forget our suffering and our courage.

Whereas the particularity of the Jewish holocaust under the Nazis is over, our holocausts continue. We are the *madres locos* (crazy mothers) in the Argentinian square silently demanding news of our missing kin from the fascists who rule. We are the children of El Salvador who see our mothers and fathers shot in front of our eyes. We are the Palestinian and Lebanese women and children overrun by Israeli, Lebanese, and U.S. soldiers. We are the women and children of the bantustans and refugee camps and the prisoners of Robbin Island. We are the starving in the Sahel, the poor in Brazil, the sterilized in Puerto Rico. We are the brothers and sisters of Grenada who carry the seeds of the New Jewel Movement in our hearts, not daring to speak of it with our lips—yet.

Our holocaust is South Africa ruled by men who loved Adolf Hitler, who have developed the Nazi techniques of terror to more sophisticated levels. Passes replace the Nazi badges and stars. Skin color is the ultimate badge of persecution. Forced removals of women, children, and the elderly—the "useless appendages of South Africa"—into barren, arid bantustans without resources for survival have replaced the need for concentration camps. Black sex-segregated barracks and cells attached to work sites achieve two objectives: The work camps destroy black family and community life, a presumed source of resistance, and attempt to create human automatons whose purpose is to serve the South African state's drive toward wealth and hegemony.

Like other fascist regimes, South Africa disallows any democratic rights to black people; they are denied the right to vote, to dissent, to peaceful assembly, to free speech, and to political representation. The regime has all the typical Nazi-like political apparatus: house arrests of dissenters such as Winnie Mandela; prison murder of protestors such as Stephen Biko; penal colonies such as Robbin Island. Black people, especially children, are routinely arrested without cause, detained without limits, and confronted with the economic and social disparities of a nation built around racial separation. Legally and economically, South African apartheid is structural and institutionalized racial war.

The Organization of African Unity's regional intergovernmental meeting in 1984 in Tanzania was called to review and appraise the achievements of the United Nations Decade for Women. The meeting considered South Africa's racist apartheid regime a peace issue. The "regime is an affront to the dignity of all Africans on the continent and a stark reminder of the absence of equality and peace, representing the worst form of institutionalized oppression and strife."

Pacifists such as Martin Luther King, Jr. and Mahatma Gandhi who have used nonviolent resistance charged that those who used violence to obtain justice were just as evil as their oppressors. Yet all successful revolutionary movements have used organized violence. This is especially true of national liberation movements that have obtained state power and reorganized the institutions of their nations for the benefit of the people. If men and women in South Africa do not use organized violence, they could remain in the permanent violent state of the slave. Could it be that pacifism and nonviolence cannot become a way of life for the oppressed? Are they only tactics with specific and limited use for protecting people from further violence? For most people in the developing communities and the developing world consistent nonviolence is a luxury; it presumes that those who have and use nonviolent weapons will refrain from using them long enough for nonviolent resisters to win political battles. To survive, peoples in developing countries must use a varied repertoire of issues, tactics, and approaches. Sometimes arms are needed to defeat apartheid and defend freedom in South Africa; sometimes nonviolent demonstrations for justice are the appropriate strategy for protesting the shooting of black teenagers by a white man, such as happened in New York City.

Peace is not merely an absence of conflict that enables white middle-class comfort, nor is it simply resistance to nuclear war and war machinery. The litany of "you will be blown up, too" directed by a white man to a black woman obscures the permanency and institutionalization of war, the violence and holocaust that people of color face daily. Unfortunately, the holocaust does not only refer to the mass murder of Jews, Christians, and atheists during the Nazi regime; it also refers to the permanent institutionalization of war that is part of every fascist and racist regime. The holocaust lives. It is a threat to world peace as pervasive and thorough as nuclear war.

Women of Color and Development

Women of color speaking from the underdeveloped countries and under-developed communities on the fringes of the so-called developed world are well aware that development has meant war and the violent reor-ganization of our cultures and our lands to produce the resources that will meet the needs, especially military, of multinational corporations and conglomerates. These include cash crops, precious ores and metals, and labor. The world economy is dominated by "11,000 transnational corporations whose production was estimated at $830 billion in 1976. Through their price manipulation they have caused the underdeveloped countries to lose between $50 and $100 billion a year."[2]

Fidel Castro describes the underdeveloped world as follows:

- More than 500 million people are hungry.
- 1.7 billion have a life expectancy of less than sixty years.
- 1.5 billion lack medical care.
- More than 1 billion live in extreme poverty.
- More than 500 million are under- and unemployed, and more than 800 million earn an annual per capita income of less than $150.
- 814 million are illiterate adults (many of them women).
- More than 200 million children do not have schools or are unable to attend schools.
- 2 billion (or about one-half the world's population) lack permanent and adequate water sources.
- More than 1.5 billion depend on firewood for their vital needs.[3]

We speak for a planet whose merchants of war spend $515 billion per year on weapons and in which military expenditures in Third World countries increased from $33 billion in 1972 to $81.3 billion in 1981. These expenditures have risen from 8 percent of the world's expenditures to 16 percent in the last ten years.[4] Women of color represent the majority of the world's people—six-sevenths of whom are people of color and the majority of whom are women and girls—and we "do two-thirds of the world's work hours, receive a tenth of the world's income, and own less than a hundredth of the world's property."[5]

Under the guise of progress, development has robbed women of color of our former status in traditional societies. In these societies we were the primary agrarian work force. Our traditional roles as mother and wife were given high status, albeit in a patriarchal and sexist manner that often rendered these roles inhumanely burdened and unjustly discriminated against. Nonetheless, our primary role in agriculture and trade blunted the full impact of sexism and enabled us to accumulate wealth. In agrarian societies when single-crop, nonedible cash crops have taken over the most fertile lands, usually financed by multinational conglomerates, women farmers, particularly in Africa, have become marginalized, although we grow most of the food for domestic consumption.

When machines are introduced into our underdeveloped communities, we become further underdeveloped because we are denied access to these machines. Money and technology for farm expansion go to men. Mechanized farming uses male wage earners as its labor supply. Women must then farm with dated technology. Money and machines overpower the work of women of color worldwide while we prepare and serve food. We take care of children, the sick, and elderly. We sew garments. We care for shelter.

Men in underdeveloped countries have developed only those sectors of the society that benefit themselves. They ride in cars while women walk or ride in lorries. They turn on water from faucets in their homes, while most women walk to public spigots and wells. They sit and meet while women work and do. They make weapons by signing papers ordering production, and white male workers in the developed sectors manufacture them. They sell the weapons to each other and those men of color who rule developing nations by diverting their countries' resources and monies from food, shelter, and education into monies for weapons. Their wives and lovers have labor-saving devices—washing machines, refrigerators, dishwashers, and freezers—while the majority of the women, men, and children in the world starve or are malnourished.

In developed countries, if women of color can find work at all, we work for the lowest wages, in the most labor-intensive areas of the economy. We also prepare and serve food and care for children, the sick, and the elderly. (Traditionally we worked for wages as domestics, caretakers, and lower echelon factory workers.) Women of color have been employed in public-sector jobs as buffers between the poor and powerless and the state. We work in welfare agencies, nursing homes, prisons, hospitals, and schools.

In the United States, Native American, Afro-American, Afro-Caribbean, Asian, Latin, and immigrant women from the Third World live at the bottom of all quality-of-life indicators. We recoil in horror as armies of the police occupy our neighborhoods and declare black and Hispanic men criminals to be shot on sight, with questions asked later. We watch the miseducation of our children and social workers' attempts to destroy the strengths of our families. The destruction of the black mind is an everyday occurrence. The continued existence of sweatshops and cash crops for illegal immigrants is an integral part of the U.S. economy. It is common for men to beg and for women to live out of shopping bags while young people live in abandoned buildings or on the streets. It is ordinary for there to be madness, murder, and mayhem in our daily lives. We live terrified, not only of ultimate war but of how we "gonna make it one more day, how we gonna keep on keeping on."

In an article entitled, "Peace, Disarmament and Black Liberation," Damu Imara Smith asks us to consider the following:

> As we lose in our fight for jobs with decent pay and stand in long
> unemployment lines, let us remember the MX missile, funded at a cost
> of $2.4 billion for FY 1983. As we lose our fight against dilapidated,
> rat infested slum housing, let us remember the 2.2 billion dollars for
> Phoenix and Sparrow air to air missiles. As we lose in our fight to put
> shoes on our children's feet and adequate clothes on their backs, let us
> remember the Pershing II missile. As we lose our struggle to put
> enough food on the table, let us think about the Minuteman 3 missiles.
> As we shiver in our homes and apartments this winter because we
> can't pay our utility bills, let us reflect on the Polaris and Poseidon
> missiles. As we witness plant closings, the resulting massive layoffs in
> our communities and the shutting down of day care centers, let us
> think about the SSN-688 nuclear attack submarine built at the cost of
> a whopping $900 million each! As we fall further into debt, let us
> remember the 5 year trillion dollar defense budget and the fact that all
> of the Pentagon's bills are paid while ours aren't. . . . As we protest
> the myriad problems afflicting our communities and society, we should
> always link them with the military budget. We should make it clear to
> those who rule our society that we do understand how huge military
> expenditures affect our daily existence.[6]

Women of color are the present and historic victims of development and militarism. Our work has always represented the underpinnings of each society in which we reside. We make and maintain the life supports that everyone else depends upon, including the elite men who dominate the developed world, deciding when and where to militarily and socially wage war. But the work of women of color is invisible, and, when seen, it is devalued.

Our blood and our ancestor's blood have already been shed in continual war precipitated by the movement of a group of self-defined white men. They named themselves white and declared themselves superior to the darker-skinned people they encountered. They divided the world along racial lines and the biological distinctions of color. Military terrorism has become the method of world domination; capitalism, the method of social organization; and racism, the ideology and worldview that holds together the rational and cohesive system of exploitation and oppression they established and that we live under. Racism is an all-encompassing, economic, social, cultural, political, and military war against a group of people whose physical characteristics have been denigrated and used to divide and isolate them from others. Women of color in the developed and the undeveloped world have come to share the same condition and position regardless of different languages, cultures, and methods of colonization or domination. We are powerless victims, relentless toilers, stigmatized and dishonored by white men, white culture, and often our own men as well. We are victims of untold violence against our person, our children, and our communities. Therefore, we speak against all wars—economic, social, and political—for we and our children are often the first casualties.

A Complex Legacy:
Black Women, the Military, and War

Women of color, such as black women in the United States, have a legacy of resistance to war and enlistment and a legacy of support for war and soldiers. We have cheered black soldiers. We have jeered them. We have benefited from black veterans. We have been their victims. We have become soldiers for a war machine. We have become warriors for peace. Throughout history, black men and women have not been merely victims of wars and holocaust but have frequently supported the U.S. military and collaborated with the holocaust-makers.

Black U.S. soldiers fought against the Mexican people and helped white men extend the borders of the United States in 1848. Black Buffalo soldiers fought against the Sioux, the Comanche, and the Apache and helped "tame" the West. Black soldiers helped conquer San Juan Hill and Puerto Rico, the Philippines and Cuba for the United States. They struggled to fight in World War I—a war that furthered the consolidation of Western colonial powers—and then got lynched when they returned home. During World War II, African, Asian, and Caribbean men went willingly, although some were forcibly conscripted. They helped to defeat fascism and give support to the British, French, and U.S. neocolonial empires. Ironically, while Japanese people were in concentration camps in the United States, many Japanese-American men volunteered to fight for the United States against Japan. Afro-American soldiers integrated the U.S. Army and were then given the dubious privilege of fighting alongside white men against the Koreans. Back in the United States, they could not work next to these same white men. During the same historic periods black people fostered and nurtured kinships with other people of color and resisted attempts by the U.S. military to enlist their support in conquering other oppressed peoples.

From the beginning of New World contact, runaway slaves joined Native American tribes and white indentured servants in common cause for freedom. They fought with the Mexicans and the Cubans and questioned U.S. government policy toward Native Americans. They welcomed Puerto Rican freedom fighters, such as Albizu Campos.

In this century, U.S. overseas empire building and European expansion were viewed by many black people as part of the same process that limited and held them inside the color line within the United States. The white man who lynched and persecuted black people was the same white man who declared war on other people of color and denied their attempts to be free. Before many said, "No Vietnamese ever called me nigger," black people felt, "We didn't lose nothing over there, so we don't belong over there—these are white man's wars." Many stood proudly by the fight of the so-called Mau-Mau, the Kenyan Land and Freedom Army, and the Hindu-Pakistani efforts of Gandhi against British rule. We understood the struggle of the Ethiopians against Italian invasion and raised monies to support them. We volunteered and served in the Spanish Civil War against Francisco Franco and fascism. We saw ourselves as part of the world of brothers and sisters struggling for a liberation far bigger than any single national effort for freedom. This struggle, beyond the ideologies of either communism or capitalism, was for a new day for the people of the planet.

There were also daily and practical struggles for family and community survival that made the conflicting legacies of simultaneous collaboration and resistance to U.S. wars and the military even more complex and intricate. Black women, in our relationship to our men (fathers, brothers, mates) and our children, were concerned with immediate and long-range, personal and political liberation, survival, and struggle.

During all these wars, black women were happy that black men were soldiers. We lined the streets of Harlem when our men came back from overseas. We cheered and dated soldiers, "who sure looked good in those uniforms." Being in the army made black men more desirable, for black soldiers were seen as responsible, disciplined, and ready to take their rightful place in U.S. society. They had demonstrated that their manhood equaled the manhood of the white man. After all, they reasoned, military service is the right and responsibility of male citizens. If black men could be in the service, then they could become first-class citizens and their women could be supported and protected.

Black men as well as other men of color have always had difficulty earning enough money to support their families and obtaining self-respect and social status within a racist or colonial system. Economic discrimination in the form of black male unemployment and under-employment has been a form of economic war against men of color at home. It has been a useful way for the ruling elites to protect and promote the armed services as a means of employment and personal advancement. Soldiers received tangible benefits when they returned home. Many black soldiers were given economic opportunities, loans, and, of course, status. They were more desirable mates, more respectful sons, more responsible church deacons, more reliable workers—at least that was the hope and the belief.

My father was a noncombatant in the Navy during World War II when the black community was still fighting for the right of black men to fight. He used his GI Bill benefits to make a downpayment on a house in Brooklyn and to gain a stable job. He was a civilian worker in the navy for twenty years. He was able to provide a stable childhood for my sister and me. Some men who came back, such as Amzie Moore and Medgar Evers, were determined to become fighters for justice for black people in this country, although most returning black soldiers hoped that they would be treated individually as citizens and men.

The Vietnam War exposed and illuminated for many of us the contradictions of people of color—the oppressed in one country living in one part of the world fighting people of color from another part of the world who were struggling for their own self-determination and freedom in their own countries. Many black men arrived in Vietnam and realized too late—in the midst of the white man's bullets at their backs and the Vietnamese in front of them—that they were the cannon fodder for the whites against the Vietnamese. Some realized that black people had no war with the Vietnamese. The pain of these contradictions drove many to drugs and madness.

My cousin John Francis died in Vietnam, but his brother survived it. He came back a killer who neither repudiated nor regretted his killing of the Vietnamese child in the tree. When he lamely told me, "It was me or him," I cringed because he was a gentle, country boy cousin from North Carolina. He is now a cop in Norfolk, part of the American dream, married, divorced, children here and there. Can the murders he committed in Vietnam leave his memory or his life? Does my cousin beat his wife? Does he terrorize his children? Are the prisoners he arrests in Norfolk only a reliving of his treatment of the "VC"? My cousin is just one of many men of color whose material successes seemingly prove that the military is a road to "upward mobility of our people"—although at the price of the blood of Vietnamese women and children.

But the Vietnamese were not the only victims of U.S. soldiers. By 1974, Max Cleland, the head of the Veterans Administration, reported that "an estimated 125,000 Vietnamese vets were serving time in America for crimes committed since their discharge from service . . . [and] around one in five Vietnam-era veterans has some kind of problem that he hasn't been able to deal with, that has kept him from entering the mainstream of society. It can be lack of education, unemployment, drugs or alcohol or a personal problem."[7] The highest percentages of unemployed veterans are black and Latino men. Far too many vets continue perpetrating the horrors of their war experience on our communities and on our bodies.

Women have had to care for Vietnam vets unable to cope with civilian life. Some of these women have been shot, beaten, and maimed because the vets thought they were the VC. Their position was very similar to that of the women and children of Vietnam. Both occupied the same position and condition in relationship to those who dominated and those who committed violence. Unless former Vietnam veterans recognize and repudiate their heinous crimes against Vietnamese women and children, they can never learn to love and respect women of color, although they might give them material support. Men of color who as soldiers in Vietnam committed acts of atrocity, ignorance, and oppression cannot use fighting a war in someone else's country as an excuse or rationale for their actions.

Economic possibilities and patriotism offer only partial explanations for the participation of men of color in the war. The U.S. myth of a rugged frontiersman, detective, or police officer fighting against nature and the savages to gain a golden treasure, to rescue the troubled maiden, or to reach glory for the fatherland has captured the minds and hearts of many men and women of color. Male chauvinism and the relationship between manhood and the military have blinded men and women of color to our backward roles in Vietnam and other wars.

Many women of color hope that the army will make men out of their men but fail to realize that "the purpose of basic training is to dehumanize a male to the point where he will kill on command and obey his superiors automatically."[8] The obedient participation of black soldiers from the United States and other Caribbean islands in the invasion of Grenada has sadly proven that black soldiers will fight other black people in their own country. Military operations in Central America have been no lesson to Chicano and Puerto Rican soldiers to resist participating in denying the people of these Central American countries their rights of self-determination. Men and women of color hope for manhood and the promise of better lives as a result of employment in the armed services. But a congressional black caucus reports

> the total effect of a black serviceman's encounter is that when he leaves he is usually in worse condition than when he entered. He has generally received little training (especially for non-military technology or jobs) . . . has been subject to harassment and discrimination at the hands of his superiors and he too often winds up with a less than honorable discharge which guarantees that his civilian life will be at least as difficult as his former life. In 1979, although Blacks were only 43% of army personnel, they comprised nearly 51% of the army prison population, and they received nearly 40% of all less-than-honorable discharges.[9]

Nevertheless, black women are being encouraged to join the military for better economic opportunities. The June 1984 issue of *Essence* magazine, along with an article on black women millionaires, featured an article, "Careers in the Military for Black Women." According to the article, the 2 million people who work in military operations and the $231 billion military budget constitute the largest government operation. The article continues: "Although the military is a good place to develop job skills, think long and hard before you enlist. The military helps to develop career direction and personal discipline, but you will be expected to adhere to military regulations and codes of conduct. . . . Also the job you perform and skills you acquire are determined primarily by military rules."[10] But one navy lieutenant, a former research biologist states, "The advantage of a military career has given me the opportunity to get my master's degree without a financial strain and to switch careers."[11] Nevertheless, only 2 percent of military personnel and 1 percent of military officers are black women.

The careerism implicit in this black woman's assessment of her naval career is the message of the ad campaigns for the "new armed services." The ads avoid the issue of war and avoid the dangers of enlistment in a "peacetime" army. They aim directly at offers of training, college, and careers. But increasing numbers of U.S. service personnel are dying while patrolling the Persian Gulf, while barracked in Lebanon, while sitting in West Germany. Others have been called for military alert in Honduras and Panama. Regardless, the finality of death and "peacetime" wars, the development of a fascist personhood, and the misdirection of our human resources should be sufficient reason for women and men of color to resist enlistment, the draft, and draft registration.

Nonetheless, every day black women encourage our men, especially our sons, to enlist as an alternative to unemployment and street crime. Black mothers know that the system offers little possibility for our manchildren. Young black men who are not in college or employed will increasingly become prey to a negative life of petty crime and drugs. Without economic self-sufficiency these men will have to be housed, fed, and taken care of by their lovers, mothers, or wives, which creates a tense and painful predicament of dependency for both.

Few black women can live outside the dilemmas posed by this predicament. Which war zone does she protect her son from: the military or the street? Either can render him an addict to drugs and violence. Will the military prepare him for a better job or leave him a personal wreck? Either choice confronts her and her son with systemic and systematic limitations beyond their control. They are surrounded by the walls of an economic and political system that simply has no place, no room for him, an ordinary black man, other than jail or the army. Black motherhood is stretched to become continuous care of her sons through adulthood. What are the limits of her resources and her ability to care?

Lovers and wives of black men wonder how will we live with our men. Both the military and the street cripple and confuse. Will the military ultimately keep them from the street? Will it exacerbate or diminish their personal and economic problems?

All women wonder, if there is a war—will he be drafted? Will it be like Vietnam? Will he be killed or maimed? Who are we fighting anyway? What are our choices anyway? In answering these questions, black women have had to make agonizing decisions, frequently separate from the powerful legacies of resistance and collective political struggles.

Black Male Warriors and
the Antiwar Movement

Cleveland Sellers, an organizer with the Student Nonviolent Coordinating Committee (SNCC), explained his refusal to be drafted in the Vietnam War this way:

> The central question for us is not whether we allow ourselves to be
> drafted, for we have resolved that this shall not happen by any means.
> But rather the central question for us is how do we stop the
> exploitation of our brother's territories and goods by a wealthy hungry

nation such as this. . . . I shall not serve in this army or any others that seek by force to use the resources of my Black brothers here at the expense of my brothers in Asia, Africa and Latin America.[12]

Sellers connected his resistance to a worldwide brotherhood fighting exploitation. He was, in turn, connected to the movement for justice and equality being shaped and waged by both black men and black women in the South.

The first civil rights movement protest of the Vietnam War was circulated in a July 1965 leaflet of the Mississippi Freedom Democratic party newsletter of McComb, Mississippi. Among the five reasons the leaflet listed for black noninvolvement in the war were:

1. No Mississippi Negroes should be fighting in Vietnam for the White Man's Freedom, until all the Negro People are free in Mississippi.
4. No-one has a right to ask us to risk our lives and kill other Colored People in Santo Domingo and Vietnam, so that the White American can get richer. We will be looked upon as traitors by all the Colored People of the world if the Negro people continue to fight and die without a cause.[13]

In January 1966, SNCC issued the following statement expressing its disagreement with U.S. foreign policy and affirming its involvement in the black people's struggle for liberation and self-determination in this country: "Our work, particularly in the south, taught us that the U.S. government has never guaranteed the freedom of oppressed citizens and is not yet truly determined to end the rule of terror and oppression within its own border. . . . Where is the draft for the Freedom fight in the United States?"[14]

SNCC's statement expressed what many men and women of color felt. Because Julian Bond endorsed it, he was refused his seat in the Georgia House of Representatives. Because Muhammad Ali refused to fight, he risked his heavyweight boxing title. Thousands of black men and other men of color refused to go and went AWOL in the United States and in Vietnam.

SNCC's position was part of a national response by black people to the war. This response included Malcolm X's growing internationalism and his attempts to raise the question of black human rights within the United States at the United Nations. He tried to develop independent political alliances between black people and progressive Third World governments. Martin Luther King issued public denunciations of the war and demands for a cease-fire, as well as a radical demand that ministers give up their ministerial exemptions to protest the war by becoming conscientious objectors: "These are the times for real choices and not false ones. We are at the moment when our lives must be placed on the line if our nation is to survive its own folly. Every man (*sic*) of humane convictions must decide on the protest that best suits his convictions, but we must all protest."[15]

That movement was strong and far reaching because it was, as the leaflet in McComb suggested, part of a national movement to fundamentally change this country, particularly regarding the treatment of its "black citizens." The civil rights–black power movement (1955–1972), which at times involved seventy thousand to one hundred thousand actively organized black people yearly in sit-ins, boycotts, demonstrations, jailings, was not simply to end segregation but to challenge and transform the system. Those who made the challenge discovered, often with their lives, the interlocking infrastructure of repression and duplicity in this country.

This organic and holistic movement originated in the black communities of the deep South and in the black communities of the North. The southern communities amassed hundreds of thousands to resist the tyranny of local government power in the hands of racists. The northern movement mobilized hundreds of thousands to resist segregated school housing; to demand jobs; and to build independent black institutions, such as the Nation of Islam and black schools.

The free speech movement of white college students began as an effort to support the Freedom School Movement in Mississippi. It grew from the questions white and black college and high school students were raising about the relationship between the university and high school and their responsibility to end injustice and inequality. These students challenged the neutral, "objective" centers of so-called learning. The people's law movement grew from the twenty-five-year-old legal challenges of black lawyers to segregation. The free clinic–people's health movement came from clinics organized during many demonstrations and campaigns in the South. Federally funded day care and the Head Start concept developed from efforts begun in Mississippi during the civil rights movement. Second-wave feminism was developed, inspired, and initiated by white women working and learning from powerful black women and men. And yes, white men such as Tom Hayden and Staughton Lynd were also inspired and taught how to organize by black organizers in the southern movement. They then returned North to become leaders of the anti–Vietnam War and the peace movements, which in turn were given impetus and power by the leading national spokesperson for peace in the post–World War II era—Martin Luther King.

After learning from and following black leadership, many white peace activists began to dominate the issue, neither remembering nor articulating their black connections. Some would ignorantly ask, "Where are the black people? Why aren't they interested in 'peace' issues?"

Black people originated the modern peace movement from an organic and holistic movement for social change that we developed and led. The obliteration of the true history of our movement has enabled whites to ruthlessly ignore what black people have done to solve some of the problems of war and peace. This ignorance has reinforced white chauvinism and blinded the white activist to his/her accurate history and historical role in movements for social change.

Women Warriors

Black and brown men said, "Hell no, we won't go!" White men joined them, white women were discovering their own power, and black and brown women warriors said, "Continue to struggle to free us all—to break our chains." Every demonstration, organizing effort, or act of defiance was surrounded by women who encouraged, urged, demanded *freedom*, with peace and love.

Rosa Parks refused to move and was jailed. Fannie Lou Hamer and Annelle Ponder were beaten in jail for daring to be citizens. Septima Clarke lost her job because she was a member of the National Association for the Advancement of Colored People. Teenage girls were hosed. Annie Pearl Avery snatched the menacing billy club from the hands of a southern sheriff. Old women were handcuffed and still they wouldn't stop.

The actions of these warriors were reflected in the refusal of Chicano women in lettuce fields to work, in the demands of Puerto Rican women in New York and San Juan for liberation, in the marches of Asian women, and in the protest by Native American women at Wounded Knee. And still they wouldn't stop. Everywhere there was space to say, "No!"—women of color hollered it, chanted it, and, if silenced, glared out our protest against all the evils and demons that limited and tied us down.

Our strength to "keep on keeping on" comes not from weapons but from the power of our prayers and visions—of peace, love, and freedom. Often we don't join *the* organization or the movement of men or of white women because our time, our moves, our ways are creatively complicated and cumbersome, woven ways of holding everything together around us. For underneath the conflicts between resistance and collaboration, the wholeness and connectedness of all things are understood by women warriors—for only if we survive, by any/all means available, can we resist. Women of color warriors are constant warriors who dig in bare earth to feed the hungry child, who pray for health at the bedside of the sick when there is no medicine, who fashion a toy to make a poor child smile, who take to the streets demanding freedom, freedom, freedom against armed police. Every act of survival by a woman of color is an act of resistance to the holocaust and the war. No soldier fights harder than a woman warrior for she fights for total change, for a new order in a world in which she can finally rest and love.

Everywhere women of color gather we realize a common concern, a common agenda for the planet, and a common practice to achieve the reality of liberation. We are sisters; at last we have found each other. For many women of color who have traveled and spoken with other women of color, sisterhood is a living reality.

In Israel, the Palestinian woman eloquently pointed at the same brownness of our skin.
In China, women treated me like their daughter.
In Jamaica, poor women gave my children sugar water.
An Indian woman shared her poetry and stories of womanhood with me.
When Puerto Rican women speak Spanish I find myself listening with my heart.
A Sioux Medicine woman gave me the ring from her finger and the earrings her mother made for her.
They all said to me,

We are your sisters, at last we have found each other.[16]

We will meet again and again—to fulfill a remembrance, to become stronger warriors, to "organize, before it's too late." We will speak as best we can, as truthfully as we must, for the billions of women and children and their men throughout the world who can not yet come forward to say:

I am the woman who holds up the sky.
The rainbow runs through my eyes.
The sun makes a path to my womb.
My thoughts are in the shape of clouds.
But my words are yet to come.[17]

We reach out knowingly, for we are your sisters; at last we have found each other. Our visions and our warriorship speak for and claim this planet, earth, for we have a precious covenant with our ancestors, our brothers, our sisters, and our progeny to "lay down the swords and shields" of the "masters of war," so we can "study war no more."

Notes

1. Ann Braden, "A Call to Action," *Southern Exposure* (Waging Peace Issue) 10, no. 6 (November–December 1982), p. 3.

2. Fidel Castro, *The World Economic and Social Crisis* (Report to the Seventh Summit Conference of Non-Aligned Countries, Council of State, Havana, 1983), p. 142.

3. Ibid., p. 196.

4. Ibid., pp. 203–204.

5. United Nations Decade on Women Report.

6. Damu Imara Smith, "Peace, Disarmament and Black Liberation," *Southern Exposure* 10, no. 6 (November–December 1982), p. 16.

7. L. C. Dorsey, "Broken Promises, Shattered Dreams," *Southern Exposure* 10, no. 6 (November–December 1982), p. 14.

8. Victor de Mattei quoted in Helen Michalowski, "The Army Will Make a Man Out of You," *Southern Exposure* 10, no. 6 (November–December 1982), p. 18.

9. Dorsey, "Broken Promises, Shattered Dreams," p. 14.

10. Dari Giles, "Careers in the Military for Black Women," *Essence* (June 1984), p. 26.

11. Ibid., p. 26.

12. Cleveland Sellers, "Hell NO," *Southern Exposure* 10, no. 6 (November–December 1982), p. 55.

13. "The War in Vietnam: A McComb, Mississippi, Protest," in Joanne Grant, ed., *Black Protest* (New York: Ballantine Books, 1968), p. 415.

14. SNCC, "Statement on Vietnam, January 6, 1966," in Grant, ed., *Black Protest*, p. 417.

15. Martin Luther King, "Beyond Vietnam," in Grant, ed., *Black Protest*, p. 425.

16. Barbara Omolade, untitled (unpublished).

17. Nancy Wood, ed., *War Cry on a Prayer and Feather: Prose and Poetry of the Ute Indians* (New York: Doubleday, 1979), p. 89.

TEN

Women and the Economics of Military Spending

LOURDES BENERÍA and REBECCA BLANK _____

Military spending constitutes a large and growing component of both the United States and the world economy. In a book concerning the relationship of feminism to issues of war and peace, it is appropriate to discuss the economic impact of these military dollars, with a focus on how the growth in the military sector is affecting women's lives.

One of the most prominent aspects of feminism has been the push by women toward equal economic opportunities: access to jobs, equal wages, similar career possibilities, and equal economic protection in the form of pensions, unemployment insurance, and so on. As we shall see, the military sector of the U.S. economy remains one of the most male dominated sectors in terms of employment and jobs. This is true of armed services personnel as well as the employment generated by the military in its purchases of goods and services. In addition, military spending tends to compete with spending on other forms of public goods, and increases in military budgets typically mean decreases in domestic social programs. This has a particularly harmful effect on women, especially those heading households, who are disproportionately poor and who often must rely on various government transfer programs. This chapter will analyze these economic impacts. Although much of our focus will be on the United States, we will also make comparisons to other countries.

Feminism is more than just a call for equal opportunity. In a broader sense, feminism presents an alternative vision of how people relate to each other and how they shape and participate in their society. As such, a feminist viewpoint raises normative questions about social priorities and the economic role of the military in society. We will conclude with a discussion of some of these wider issues.

Military Spending and the U.S. and World Economies

The U.S. military budget in 1987 was $293 billion.[1] One way to conceptualize the size of this amount is to break it into smaller components; it is the equivalent of each person in the United States (men, women, and children) contributing $1,203 to the military during the year. If we took the military dollars budgeted in 1987 and spread them across time from zero A.D. (1987 years ago), we would have spent $280 *every minute* of that time period.

The dollar amount as well as the percent of the federal budget that goes to the military is growing. During the Reagan administration, military spending increased at annual rates well above inflation rates, thereby absorbing a larger proportion of national resources. In 1980, 22.7 percent of federal expenditures went to military spending. By 1987, the percent had increased to 27.8 percent, with further increases expected.[2] After adjusting for inflation, the United States is spending almost as many dollars on the military today as it did at the height of the Vietnam War.[3]

While military budgets in the United States have been growing, their composition has been changing. The United States is currently buying a very different mix of goods and services with its defense dollars than it was in past decades. In 1972, nearly half of the military budget was used to directly employ military personnel. But this percentage has shrunk to one-third during the 1980s.[4] The recent increases in military expenditures have been almost entirely focused on the development and purchase of weapons and weapons systems, such as the Trident submarine or the MX missile system. As we will see later, this has changed the way in which military dollars impact the economy and has particularly shifted the employment effects of military spending.

Military spending in the United States is particularly concentrated in a few states, such as California, Connecticut, Massachusetts, and Texas. With the recent growth in the defense budget, these states have become more dependent on the arms race for employment and economic growth. But as the rest of this chapter describes, even those of us who are not directly employed by defense dollars are still affected by military spending through its effects on jobs, on government services, and on the growing budget deficit. If only because we are all contributing increasing amounts to the military through our taxes, none of us can claim independence from it.

Compared to other countries in the world, the United States spends an unusually large amount of its resources on the military. A 142-country comparison based on 1982 data ranked the U.S. eighth in per capita military expenditures. The seven countries ranked above the United States were all Middle Eastern states. In that year, when the United States spent $845/person on the military, Israel (ranked fifth) spent $1,301/person, and Saudi Arabia (ranked first) spent $2,579/person. The USSR was ranked eleventh, at $630/person.[5]

Whereas the more developed countries, such as the United States and the USSR, have had large defense budgets for decades, one disturbing international trend is the increase in military spending among the less developed, or Third World, countries. Between 1970 and 1983, military spending as a percent of gross national product (GNP) increased from an average of 4.3 percent to 5.5 percent in 114 less-developed countries.[6] Of course, this means fewer relative resources were available in these countries for agricultural and industrial development and for basic expenditures on food, education, or health.

As military budgets of individual countries have increased, there has also been a large increase in the international sales of military goods. For instance, exports of military goods from developed countries increased from $2.3 billion in 1971 to $24.4 billion in 1980.[7] Included in this trade is a wide range of equipment, from jeeps and fighter planes to ammunition and radar. The less developed countries alone imported a total of $19.5 billion in arms during 1980. It has been estimated that among the twenty Third World countries with the largest foreign debt, arms imports between 1976 and 1980 were equivalent to 20 percent of the increase in debt during that period.[8]

In summary, military expenditures are large in both absolute and relative terms in the United States. They are also growing, with an increasing emphasis on weapons procurement rather than on military personnel. Although the United States maintains one of the largest military sectors in the world, there are other countries that spend more, relative to their size. Other countries have also experienced large increases in military budgets in the last decade. This increase in military spending within countries has also produced an expanding international market in military equipment. In short, we are witnessing a growing militarization of the world economy, with the corresponding channeling of resources away from other uses.

The Employment Effects of Military Spending

There are two ways in which military spending affects employment. First, the military employs people directly by hiring them into the armed forces or by hiring civilians to work for the armed forces. Second, the Defense Department buys goods and services from companies throughout the private economy, and these companies employ people to produce those products. We will refer to this second effect as the indirect employment generated by the military and the first effect as direct employment.

The extent of direct employment varies greatly, depending upon military needs. In 1986, there were 2.2 million active duty armed forces personnel and another 1 million civilians directly employed by the Department of Defense.[9] There is little information available on these civilian employees, but we know the composition of the armed forces. Historically, almost all military personnel have been male. Only during the twentieth century were various women's auxiliaries formed, in which women were allowed to serve directly in various (noncombat) military capacities. Since World War II, these auxiliaries have all been folded into the regular branches of the armed forces. Currently, about 10 percent of the U.S. Armed Forces enlisted personnel are women, as are 10 percent of the officer's corps. These positions are disproportionately filled by minority (black and Hispanic) women. Fourteen percent of the female officers are minority women, whereas 33 percent of the enlisted women are from minority groups.[10]

Nevertheless, although women are actively recruited throughout the military today, there are still clear male/female differentials. As noted, women are not allowed to serve in a variety of positions, either because of a concern that these positions would be too dangerous or because of presumed personnel problems (for instance, only recently have women been allowed to serve on ships during periods at sea). In addition, even though women are recruited, there are still clear assumptions in this country that military service is primarily a male responsibility. Women have never been drafted. The courts have upheld this distinction, ruling that even the recently initiated military registration of young men need not include women.

It is debatable whether increased female involvement in the armed forces is a desirable goal, but it is certainly true that military service provides a set of useful career options. Military service has traditionally been a source of jobs and job training for youth from locations where private-sector job options are low. (It is not by chance that the majority of current recruits are young white men from rural areas and young black men from urban areas, two groups that face high unemployment rates.) Not only do many people receive useful job training and job experience while serving in the military (which gives them an advantage in the job market when they leave the military), but military service frequently provides a number of other long-term benefits. Generous educational support sent a whole generation of (primarily) men back to school following World War II, one reason that male education levels rose relative to female levels during the 1940s and 1950s. The set of social rewards available to veterans have varied, including pensions, housing subsidies, job hiring preferences in civil service jobs, health benefits, and educational support. To the extent that women have historically been excluded from or discouraged from military service, they have not had access to these social benefits.

The indirect employment effects of military spending depend on the mix of goods and services the military buys and the employment demands of the industries that produce those goods and services. The major industry categories that receive the bulk of military spending include aircraft, aircraft parts, shipbuilding, radio and communication equipment, guided missiles, and miscellaneous business services (which is the category where much of the research money is spent). A major recent trend in military spending has been an increase in the purchases of various electronic components. A very high percentage of the cost of new fighter planes or ships is due to electronic guidance, communications, and weapons systems. This has meant a concurrent decrease in military spending in the heavy manufacturing sectors of the economy.

Data available in 1977 indicated that close to 44 percent of military expenditures on goods and services went to the aforementioned six military dominated industries.[11] These industries, plus private ordinance, accounted for 3.3 percent of all civilian employment in 1982. But they included 21 percent of all engineers, 24 percent of all electrical engineers, 32 percent of all mathematicians, and 34 percent of all physicists.[12] Thus, military spending predominantly buys goods from industries that disproportionately employ many highly skilled and often high-wage individuals. In addition, these industries disproportionately employ men, largely because these professions tend to be male dominated. Seventy-seven percent of the employees in these six industries are male, as compared to only 62 percent in the aggregate economy. Twenty-three percent of them are employed in "professional, technical and kindred" occupations (compared to 15 percent in these occupations in the overall economy), mainly in categories (such as engineering) in which women are not equally represented. This means that women are largely excluded from many jobs that may be created by the current increases in defense spending.

There have, of course, been periods in the past when military purchases of goods and services have created new jobs for women. This has been most important during times of major war mobilizations, when the military demands on the private economy were expanding rapidly and the male labor force was being drawn into the armed forces. Women's employment expanded during both world wars in the United States and other countries. Stereotypes about male and female tasks have largely been dropped in periods of war, even in most traditional societies.[13] Yet few of these employment gains were maintained at the end of mobilization; men reclaimed their jobs, and women (not always voluntarily) returned to their traditional roles.

The recent increases in research and development spending by the military have strongly affected those who do research. More than 70 percent of all research funded by the federal government currently involves military projects, and this is an exceptionally high number, both historically and relative to other countries.[14] This means that those interested in non-military-related research areas are having more and more difficulty getting support, while universities are becoming much more reliant on military spending. Graduate students in many scientific areas can find ready support only by becoming attached to military research contracts, and after graduation, physicists, engineers, and computer programmers are finding that more and more of the available jobs are involved with military research.

The indirect effects of military spending on employment and career opportunities for women also include the large number of women who are wives of military personnel. Given the frequent relocation often required of military men, their spouses may have a great deal of difficulty gaining continual job experience or planning for careers.

The total effect of military spending on employment depends on the mix of spending on armed forces personnel and purchases of goods and services. As we noted in the previous section, the 1980s have seen a steady increase in the percent of the military budget that goes into purchases (particularly weapons). This has meant that the employment effects of the recent military increase are occurring in the private sector among a well-educated, predominantly male, and highly paid workforce. Thus, the military budget increases have not been useful in decreasing the high unemployment rates among young workers that existed throughout the 1980s.

Military Spending and Economic Growth

Although the impact of military spending on the job opportunities of any one individual may be positive or negative, many people argue that the net effect of military spending is positive because it induces economic growth, thereby creating jobs and raising productivity. Efforts to decrease military spending (or even to slow down the rate of increase) are often viewed with alarm, particularly in those regions with a high concentration of military spending. Opponents of military budget cuts claim that reductions in the military budget would create high rates of unemployment and a loss of productive capacity that the private economy would not be able to replace. There are several aspects of this argument that deserve examination.

First, as noted, a decreasing amount of military dollars are being spent directly on armed forces personnel. The increases during the 1980s have gone into the purchase of military equipment. This changes the nature of military spending in two ways. On the one hand, the employment effects of military spending have become smaller (far fewer people are employed per dollar spent on purchases than are employed per dollar spent on directly hiring armed forces personnel[15]). On the other hand, many types of military-related production have inherently smaller positive effects on the economy when compared with production for private consumption and other types of government spending. This is because most weapons have low multiplier effects—that is, they do not transmit growth to other sectors, having a low level of ongoing productive uses. When a piece of durable equipment is produced in the private economy— say a tractor—there is an initial economic effect as individuals are employed and materials are bought in order to make the tractor. After the tractor is made and purchased, it continues to generate economic resources; it is used to produce agricultural goods and services, which create further income and employment; and people are employed to operate and maintain it. These economic multiplier effects are low for military equipment because of the way in which it is used. A weapon is built—generating some employment demand and some materials purchases—but then it is typically stored or used only in training exercises. It does not generate an ongoing stream of further production and demand for services. These facts have led many people to conclude that modern forms of military spending contribute less to economic growth and to the generation of income and employment than does spending on private economic goods or alternative avenues of public spending.

An alternative way of valuing military spending in the economy is to ask whether other types of government expenditures could create the same number of jobs as military spending creates. Most research that compares the employment generated by military spending on goods and services with the employment generated by other forms of public spending (on schools, road maintenance, public utilities) finds that military spending is inferior and creates fewer jobs.[16]

Finally, we can turn to other countries that spend much less on military goods and see what impact this has had on their economies. Perhaps the best examples are Japan and West Germany, which are prevented by law from spending large amounts for military purposes. Both of these countries have shown phenomenal economic growth, in part because of massive infusions of economic aid following World War

II. But even in the 1970s and 1980s, when outside aid was minor, both countries maintained healthy economies and high levels of economic growth. Japan in particular has begun to dominate international consumer markets in the production of sophisticated consumer electronic equipment (such as stereos or cameras)—an area that requires many of the same types of skills and training that in the United States are used for the military development of sophisticated weapons systems.

The relationship between military spending and economic growth is related to a policy issue of concern to those who would like to see military expenditures reduced: the issue of conversion. The impact of a significant reduction in the military budget depends on how that budget affects the overall economy and the ease with which those currently working for the military or on military production contracts can be integrated into other jobs in the economy.

The redirection of those sectors of industry that currently rely heavily on military purchases would require serious employment retraining and economic restructuring. To the extent that many employees have skills in areas that are in demand in the private economy, this process is easier. One way of thinking about military conversion is to look at the natural conversion occurring constantly in the economy. We are always in a situation in which some industries are growing and others are contracting. A recent study indicated that between 1979 and 1984 about 11.5 million jobs were lost due to plant shutdowns.[17] At the same time, jobs were also being created; between 1983 and 1984 alone, 3.9 million new jobs were generated in the private economy.[18] Although not all those who became unemployed found one of these new jobs, efforts at industrial retraining and relocation can significantly improve the reemployment options of workers who lose jobs. In general, no more than 3 million workers are indirectly employed by military purchases within the private economy. Even if a conversion process eliminated half of these jobs, this is a small job loss in comparison with the ongoing dynamic changes the economy is constantly experiencing, especially if conversion is accompanied by training programs to facilitate the transition to other employment.

If conversion also implies reduction in the size of the armed forces, then increased job opportunities for young men and women must be created in the private economy or in the public sector. This could occur either through programs designed to stimulate private sector job creation for youth or through the creation of alternative forms of public service jobs. One possibility is the creation of a youth corps designed to work on public works projects.

In any case, conversion *is* economically feasible, even though it is not easy. In order to minimize hardships, it must be accompanied by investment and labor programs that redirect the economy toward non-military sectors. But this task will become more difficult if the military sector continues to expand.

The extent to which conversion is possible depends on our collective social judgment about how much military spending is necessary to provide adequate national defense. Curiously enough, the enormous expansion in military spending that took place during the 1980s occurred under an administration that advocated using the market and the private sector to allocate resources, while pressing for the dismantling of the public sector. Yet, defense or, more specifically, defense-related products (such as tanks) do not have a market with a defined demand level. Unlike the market for cars, the average citizen does not buy military products, and there is no clearly observable level of demand for "defense" that would tell government officials what the size of the military budget should be.

Military production takes place through contracts between the government and private corporations not subject to the scrutiny and pressures of market competition. One result of this system is the higher prices often charged by contractors, generating wasteful spending of tax dollars. This has been widely publicized in recent years, as in the case of Representative Berkley Bedell of Iowa, who bought a $92.44 kit of twenty tools for which the military had paid $10,186.

Thus, economically, there are no limits on the amount of military production a government can demand (unless, of course, the government starts to demand more than the entire economy can possibly produce, at which point all private production has been redirected into the military). Clearly, the limits must be set politically, so the size of the U.S. military budget is determined in a rather complex process of legislative decisionmaking. This means that any analysis of the appropriate size of the military budget must depend on normative judgments about the appropriateness of defense objectives and the value of different military projects relative to other social demands. U.S. defense needs are also related to the country's foreign policy commitments and goals. Thus, as the degree of U.S. involvement in world affairs has increased, the evaluation of military needs has included an increasing international dimension. Ultimately, this requires a political evaluation of society's choices as they are guided by individual and collective values.

Military Increases and Cuts in Social Programs

Even if there are no market constraints on how much money can be spent on the military, there are quite real limits on the total revenue the federal government is able to raise. This means that any increase in one section of the budget must be matched by a decrease in another section, unless taxes or government borrowing is increased. In particular, the current very high level of federal deficits has led many people to call for significant cuts in the budget. This concern with reducing the total size of the federal budget, along with the demand for increases in military expenditures, has meant that all other forms of government spending have come under severe pressure for deep cuts. Most seriously hurt between 1980 and 1985 were domestic social programs, particularly those that provide support to low-income households. The 1981 Omnibus Budget Reconciliation Act, which approved a military budget increase of 9 percent, cut the budget for education, training, employment, and social services by 34 percent.[19]

Although these cuts have had wide repercussions, their impact on women has been particularly large. The "feminization of poverty" has been a much-discussed phenomenon in recent years. Whereas a large number of families are below the poverty line in this country (13.6 percent in 1986), a shockingly high 34.6 percent of female-headed households are poor. Among black and Hispanic women who head households, more than 50 percent are poor. With an increasing number of women heading households (almost one-third of all households are currently female headed), more and more of these women are facing serious economic problems as they try to support their families. Among children, more than one in five lives in a poor household. Among black children, almost one-half are raised in poor families.[20]

These clear inequities in the distribution of income among households mean that women (and children) are particularly hurt by the type of budget cuts that occurred in the 1980s. The point is that women are not just left out of the jobs created by increases in the military budget; they are actively harmed by the other budget cuts necessary to support these military increases. Along with the cuts in actual income support programs, budget cuts for other social services also have repercussions for women. For example, to the extent that women live longer, reductions in health services for the elderly have a gender dimension. Budget cuts eliminating school lunches imply more domestic work. Similarly, the elimination of all forms of public service employment programs, severe cuts in support for urban mass transportation, decreases in legal aid, and so on all have serious effects on low-income households, which are disproportionately female headed. The cost of the recent increases in military expenditure is measurable by rising poverty rates and increased economic hardship.

At the international level, rising military expenditures intensify the problems of economies already under strain. The Worldwatch Institute has estimated that in 1984 the value of international trade in arms exceeded trade in grain ($35 billion to $33 billion) for the first time, thus placing arms ahead of bread in world trade. This group has also estimated that the $980 billion spent worldwide on arms in 1985 represented more than the combined income of the poorest half of the world.[21]

Economic interdependence among countries also implies that military expenditures for a country cannot be considered in isolation. For example, to the extent that budget deficits in the United States resulted in high interest rates during the first half of the 1980s (due to government borrowing), this worsened the debt problem for many Third World countries.

Concluding Comments

Much of this chapter has focused on a set of equity issues relating to the distribution of government spending and its impact on income and employment opportunities for different groups of workers. But equity is not the sole focus of feminism, although it is an important focus. Feminism also addresses issues of human connectedness, emphasizing dialogue and cooperation over dominance and violent confrontation. Thus, as feminists, we repudiate the current massive military buildup, with its capacity for overkill and its threat to life on this planet. In this sense, feminism provides a *strategy for peace* and opposes policies that, beyond necessary defense objectives, focus on a strategy for war. We end this section with some of the questions and ideas that this discussion of the economic forces involved in military spending has raised for us vis-à-vis a strategy for peace.

1. Should the armed forces be the "employer of last resort" for our young people? We see no reason why this should be so; we have argued that alternative forms of government-supported public service might provide similar training and job experience, such as a youth job corps. That so few women find military service attractive should not lead us to find ways to increase women's involvement with the military but rather to look for alternatives that will attract both men and women, providing economic options for the unemployment and the untrained.

2. Similarly, that military spending in the private economy provides relatively few jobs for women does not imply that we should urge more women to become involved in military contracts. Instead, we should be giving serious thought to conversion of the military sector into more employment-creating and growth-generating products. This of course requires serious thinking about how we can best provide an adequate level of national defense, without becoming involved in the economically (and politically) destructive mindset that equates defense with an arms

race involving large monetary expenditures on huge weapons systems. A strategy for peace requires federal budget support of groups attempting to provide workable conversion strategies.

3. We need to be clearer on the links between increases in military spending on the one hand and decreases in social support programs (leading to increases in poverty and economic need) on the other. The full impact of military increases should be more broadly discussed. This is not only a concern within the United States; at an international level it becomes even more crucial. The greater the emphasis on military hardware and military aid to other countries, the less money will be available for education, agricultural development, health programs, and other basic needs in all countries.

4. We must go beyond issues of economic equity and development and ask basic questions about the origins of violence, the military buildup, and human nature. How are aggression and violence related to a cultural emphasis on greed and economic individualism? What kind of social structures can we build that will work toward resolving political and economic conflicts without violence? We think feminist perspectives can be useful in thinking about these issues. The location of women with feminist concerns in many parts of society also means that feminist approaches can have direct influences on social structure and organizational behavior. We simply cannot afford to passively allow our communities and our countries to be blind about the consequences of an unchecked militarization of society. As the Chinese proverb has it, "If we do not change our direction, we are likely to get where we are headed."

The current military buildup is taking place at a time of increasing poverty and belt-tightening programs in many Third World countries. The huge amounts of debt owed to the more developed countries represents a siphoning off of resources from those areas most in need. Inflation, falling real incomes, and unemployment are affecting large sectors of the population in these countries. For women, this means increasing concern about how to manage meager domestic budgets, often done through intensification of domestic work. To the millions of poor households facing hunger, malnutrition, and related problems of poverty, the level of resources spent on military production is sheer madness. At the U.N. Decade for Women Conference in 1985 in Nairobi, women from all continents agreed on the dangers of channeling resources from basic human needs to further escalation of the arms race. As a document written for this conference put it, "Peace cannot be separated from development."[22] This is so for both rich and poor countries.

Notes

1. Office of Management and Budget, *Historical Tables, Budget of the U.S. Government, FY 1988* (Washington, D.C.: GPO, 1987).

2. Ibid.

3. Ibid.

4. Rebecca Blank and Emma Rothschild, "The Effect of U.S. Defense Spending on Employment and Output," *International Labour Review* (December 1985), pp. 677–697.

5. Ruth Leger Sivard, *World Military and Social Expenditures, 1985* (Washington, D.C.: World Priorities, 1985).

6. Ibid. The 114 developing countries include all of Latin America, Africa, and Asia (excluding Japan and Israel), but also Fiji, Papua New Guinea, Albania, Malta, and other middle- and upper-middle-income countries such as Greece, Portugal, Spain, and Yugoslavia.

7. Ruth Leger Sivard, *World Military and Social Expenditures, 1983* (Leesburg, Va.: World Priorities, 1983).

8. Ibid.

9. U.S. Bureau of the Census, *Statistical Abstract of the United States, 1987* (Washington, D.C.: GPO, 1986).

10. Ibid.

11. Blank and Rothschild, "The Effect of U.S. Defense Spending."

12. Ibid.

13. During the Spanish Civil War, for example, women were mobilized for jobs in industry and agriculture they had never held before. As during the two world wars, they performed these tasks with a relatively short training period.

14. Eric Bloch, "Basic Research and Economic Health," *Science*, May 2, 1986, pp. 595–599.

15. Blank and Rothschild, "The Effect of U.S. Defense Spending."

16. Robert W. DeGrasse, Jr., *Military Expansion, Economic Decline* (Armonk, N.Y.: M. E. Sharpe, 1983). Also see ibid.

17. Office of Technology Assessment, *Technology and Structural Unemployment: Reemploying Displaced Adults, Summary* (Washington, D.C.: GPO, 1985).

18. U.S. Bureau of Labor Statistic, *Monthly Labor Review* (Washington, D.C.: GPO, May 1985), p. 61, Table 9.

19. John Ellwood, *Reductions in U.S. Domestic Spending* (New Brunswick, N.J.: Transaction Books, 1982), Table 1.7.

20. All poverty statistics are from the U.S. Bureau of the Census, *Money Income and Poverty Status of Families and Persons in the United States: 1986*, Current Population Reports, Series P-60, no. 157. (Washington, D.C.: GPO, 1987).

21. "Study Says Weapons Costs Strain Economy," *New York Times*, March 2, 1986, p. A8.

22. DAWN, *Development, Crises and Alternative Visions: Third World Women's Perspectives*, written by Gita Sen, with Casen Grown (New Delhi: Institute of Social Studies Trust, 1985).

PART THREE

Women Organizing for Peace: Triumphs and Troubles

ELEVEN

Feminine Behavior and Radical Action

Franciscans, Quakers, and the Followers of Gandhi

PHYLLIS MACK

The first Franciscans, the early Quakers, and the followers of Gandhi: Here are three radical religious movements, widely separated in time and place, but sharing elements that their adherents identified as "feminine." We are all familiar with the gentle, domestic images of Francis preaching to the birds and of Gandhi spinning; these images are so familiar, in fact, that it would be difficult to describe the persona style of these leaders and their closest followers and avoid feminine associations. One thinks immediately of Francis plucking the juiciest grapes to encourage a sick brother to eat, of Gandhi fussing over his family's diet, dispensing garlic to those he decided needed it, and of the Mothers in Israel who were the earliest Quaker missionaries. One of Gandhi's adopted children wrote a biography of him that she called *Bapu—My Mother.* Margaret Fell called George Fox "our dear nursing father." The most intimate term that the Franciscan brothers used to address the founder was "mother."[1]

The reaction of many modern observers has been to dismiss such stories as anachronistic at best and at worst as a crass distortion of spiritual truth: trite, cloying images of great men that obscure their essence, cheapen their memory, and turn the stuff of religious genius

An expanded version of this essay appeared in *Signs, Journal of Women in Culture and Society* 11, no. 3 (Spring 1986), pp. 457–477. © 1986 by The University of Chicago. All rights reserved.

into material for children's legends, mass entertainment, or plastic figurines to hang from rearview mirrors. One biography of Francis contended that "the truth lies deeper, in his hard character, and the abrasion of that character on his times." Current Quaker scholarship stresses the hard, Puritan core of early Quakerism against its softer, mystical aspect. A recent newspaper article on Gandhi reminded New York moviegoers that Gandhi was not simply a nice man with fine ideals but a remote, oriental ascetic.[2] Feminine behavior has also been discussed as an aspect of the neurotic underside of the leader's personality (Gandhi's ambivalence about his sexuality or his compulsion to dominate the personal lives of his disciples) and as evidence that the moment is culture or timebound and hence irrelevant for us. So Francis's sense of immanence with nature is charming but "medieval," the early Quakers who emphasized prophetic dreams over knowledge and nakedness over status and power were courageous but "primitive," and Gandhi's doctrines of nonviolence and self-sacrifice were inspiring but fundamentally "Indian." Some would also point out that healing is the activity of doctors and scientists as well as nurses and that in their tender care of the afflicted, Francis and George Fox were, after all, imitating the *man* Jesus.

A more creative response to this type of religious behavior is that of anthropologist Victor Turner, who used the concept of liminality to analyze certain cultural phenomena. A person in a liminal condition— say, a young woman undergoing a puberty rite—has no particular status or social definition. She is

> betwixt and between the positions assigned and arrayed by law, custom, convention and ceremonial. . . . Thus liminality is frequently likened to death, to being in the womb, to invisibility, to darkness, to bisexuality, to the wilderness. . . . Liminal entities . . . may be represented as possessing nothing. . . . Their behavior is normally passive or humble. . . . It is as though they are being reduced or ground down to a uniform condition to be fashioned anew.[3]

Turner observed a dialogue between these movements or conditions of liminality or *communitas* and the structured society of everyday life: "It is as though there are . . . two major 'models' for human relatedness. . . . The first is of society as a structured, differentiated and often hierarchical system. . . . The second, which emerges recognizable in the liminal period, is of society as an unstructured . . . community, or even communino of equal individuals."[4] Movements of *communitas* may be brief (the hippies at Woodstock), occur over time (millennarian cults), or be an ongoing ritual or institution within the larger stratified society (puberty rites, monasteries). They often occur at historical moments "when major groups or social categories are passing from one cultural state to another."[5]

In describing the customs of a patrilineal African tribe, Turner observed a double affinity between structure and masculinity, *communitas* and femininity. Even more revealing of Turner's views on the relationship of gender and society is this general description of the dialectic of *communitas* and structure: "Spontaneous communitas is (not) merely 'nature.' Spontaneous communitas is nature in dialogue with structure, married to it as a woman is married to a man. Together they make up one stream of life, the one affluent supplying power, the other alluvial fertility."[6] I don't know how pleased Turner would have been to find himself in the company of feminist theoreticians, but there is clearly an affinity between his own typology and that of Sherry Ortner, who discussed culture and nature in terms of structure and antistructure and who viewed women as occupying an intermediate and ambiguous position between the two.[7] In the remainder of this chapter, I want to explore some aspects of feminine symbolism and behavior in the movements led by Francis, Fox, and Gandhi by relating them to the paradigm of nature and culture, or structure and antistructure. I also hope to build on the theoretical work of anthropologists and historians by redefining the feminine qualities embodied in these three men and their followers and by suggesting a different model of feminine attitude and activity that might be used creatively in our own social and political life.

Feminine Symbolism, Feminine Behavior

Turner actually mentioned Francis and Gandhi as examples of *communitas*; in fact, his typology seems to work neatly as a framework for analyzing all three movements. All occurred at historical moments when social and political structures were in a state of flux or of open conflict: conflict among the papacy, the German princes, and the independent towns in twelfth century Italy; between king and parliament, Anglican and Puritan, aristocracy and laborer in seventeenth century England; between up-holders of caste and social reformers, British imperialists and partisans of home rule in twentieth century India. All three movements set themselves against social and political structures and parties, all were nonviolent, and, to different degrees, all preached poverty.

Francis, Fox, and Gandhi were also aware of a pervading cultural symbolism in which authority and the absence of authority were often expressed in terms of gender. On the one hand, they saw masculine figures of political and spiritual power, whether pope, king, or viceroy. On the other hand, they and their contemporaries saw feminine figures that were commonly used to convey a sense of liminality, that twilight zone where generation and decay, order and chaos meet. Francis knew the polarity of Mary and Eve. Gandhi understood the double visage of the goddess Kali, the mother and devourer of all life, and he surely knew of the attainments of Ramakrishna, the nineteenth century Indian mystic who overcame the illusion of personal identity by dressing and behaving as a woman, so much so that, according to one scholar, he was thought to be able to menstruate by having periodic discharges of blood through the pores of his skin. Fox recorded in his journal the contemporary belief that women had no souls, and he may have also been aware that men sometimes dressed as women during riots—living symbols of disorder—just as Quaker women visionaries were often perceived as living vessels of divine energy.[8]

Given this cultural context, it is not surprising that when Francis, Fox, and Gandhi characterized the condition of the true believer by the symbol of nakedness, they chose to associate this nakedness with aspects of femininity. Francis believed that unity with God was contingent on freedom from possessions. He instructed the brothers to live without hoarding, to follow only the most insecure occupations, and to beg indiscriminately, not only at the houses of the rich. Francis also preached a poverty of intellectual attainment; the friars were to live not only without buildings but without books. He spoke of a learned postulant "in a certain fashion resigning his learning so that he may offer himself naked to the arms of the crucified one."[9] Finally, Francis denied the reality of status in the world and within his own order. The brothers were to rejoice when they found themselves among mean and despised persons, and no one was to take on the office of preacher or minister, "but at whatever hour the command may be given him, he should lay down his office without any contradiction."[10]

Francis expressed all of this not as elements of an abstract economic and social doctrine but in the concrete, feminine image of Lady Poverty, whom his followers came to identify with himself. Appropriately enough, this crusade in the service of Lady Poverty, undermined by many of Francis's contemporaries and by most of his successors, was most vigorously upheld by a woman. Indeed, his disciple, Clare, almost outdid Francis by sleeping on vine twigs with a rock for a pillow. Even after Francis's death, she continued to battle with the pope for the right of her order, The Order of the Poor Ladies, to remain poor.[11] As he became less human and more saintly, the persona of Francis assumed more strikingly feminine attributes; toward the end of his life he even acquired stigmata, a mark of sanctity usually attained by women.[12]

The Quakers believed in a philosophy of the inner light, a state of inner fulfillment that exalted the unity of the spiritual community of believers and denigrated the outward distinctions of wealth, rank, and political power. As such they were less militant than contemporary sects like the Levellers, but they were no less egalitarian. The Quakers met in private houses or in fields. Not only did they abandon the clothing of their rank, which was often considerable; they often abandoned clothing altogether. They counseled against the hoarding of goods. They repudiated formal social etiquette, so much so that many converts were reluctant to embrace the Quakers because of their reputation as a despised sect. Although they often cited scripture to buttress their arguments, they repudiated formal learning as a means of attaining grace.

One way the Quakers expressed this sense of social and intellectual nullity was by casting visionary women as living symbols of Christian nakedness or foolishness, arguing that women should prophecy not just because they were the spiritual equals of men but because "God makes use of the weak." Quakers who attained a state of salvation, or who had acquired the inner light, sometimes wrote as though they had shed the attributes of gender altogether; women declared that they stood before God as men, and men declared, metaphorically at least, they they had become women.[13]

When Gandhi died he owned a loincloth, a pair of sandals, a book, a replica of the three monkeys, and almost nothing else.[14] He advocated a kind of economic populism based on village agriculture and the domestic production of homespun, or *khadi*. He spent much energy considering the uses of human excrement as fertilizer. He opposed formal education, refusing to given his sons training for any profession. He dramatized his negation of caste structure by degrading acts—cleaning latrines and treating Untouchables; by his own nakedness, and by the feminine activity of spinning, which he made his followers practice every day. He articulated these activities and programs as part of a campaign against both the caste system and British rule, but he also insisted that his primary goal was apolitical and spiritual: the negation of all personal desire and the practice of *ahimsa*, "a positive state of love, of doing good even to the evil-doer."[15] He further believed that he could attain this universality by becoming physically and spiritually more like a woman.

> Their love was selfless and motherly, stemming from the demands of childbearing and childrearing. They were more virtuous than men, because they had a greater capacity for suffering, for faith, and for renunciation—in fact, for non-violence. They were therefore better qualified than men to preach the art of peace to the warring world.[16]

Gandhi believed that once he had attained the practice of true *ahimsa*, or "nonviolence," even his sexual organs would change their appearance and come to resemble those of a woman.

The condition of outward and inward nakedness associated with these movements of *communitas* had another, more positive dimension—the image of salvation as a return to the bliss of infancy. By their capacity for simplicity and playfulness, Francis and Gandhi were prototypes of the worshipper as a naked, erring child, wrapped in the loving motherhood of God. By their capacity for nuture and for healing, all three men gave their adherents a foretaste of God's limitless maternal care. Clare once had a vision that she was walking toward Francis:

> When she reached Saint Francis, he bared his breast saying: "Come, take a drink." And having sucked the Saint exhorted her to do so again: which doing what she sucked was so sweet and delightful that she could in no way describe it. And having sucked, that roundness, or the mouth of the pap from which the milk flowed remained in the mouth of the blessed Clare; and if taken in the hand what had remained in her mouth seemed something bright and shining in which all could be seen as in a mirror, in which she saw her own reflection.[17]

For Francis, Fox, and Gandhi, the safety of total immersion in God could be experienced only as the culmination of a process of self-annihilation and the negation of all earthly structures: political, social, mental, even anatomical. Such a radical conception of human nakedness must have been a threatening concept on many levels, and because the soul's homelessness and the sheltering haven of God's love were embodied, for all three men, in symbols of womanhood, it is not surprising that their attitudes toward actual women were ambivalent. True, all three men affirmed the quality of the sexes in "real" life. Francis defied canon law in order to establish the Order of the Poor Ladies, led by Clare, and he maintained relations with Clare's convent in opposition to many of the brothers. He even revered Clare herself as a healer and sent patients to her to be touched.[18] Fox defended the right of Quaker women to preach and to hold independent meetings even against many of *his* own followers; more than three hundred women were active as missionaries or prophets during the latter half of the seventeenth century.[19] Gandhi supported the right of women to work and to enter politics; his advocacy of the validity of Indian marriages in South Africa in 1913 brought women into the political arena for the first time; and he inveighed against the evils of child marriage with as much vehemence as he denounced the evils of caste.[20]

Yet all three men buttressed their support of women by a faith in their own ability to transcend desire and by the belief that women, through humility and chastity, would help them do it. Francis's relationship with Clare was conducted in an atmosphere of complete, out-of-the-body ecstasy. For a long time Clare had desired to share a meal with Francis, who finally consented to her wish; but the food turned out to be the word of God as preached by Francis, and the woods where the two sat was seen by villagers to be engulfed in spiritual flame.[21] Gandhi bowed to the superior humility and chastity of women, but his relations with them were still marked by *his* absolute control; witness his practice of sleeping with naked girls and quizzing them on their reactions to his seventy-seven-year-old presence.[22] The Quakers were accused of sexual immorality by their contemporaries, but one precondition of women's eminence in the movement was the ability of both men and women to contain their own sexuality. Although the Quakers married, it was their policy for couples to preach separately, ministers traveling with others of the same sex. Fox became a loving spiritual husband to Margaret Fell, but when asked by a Puritan whether marriage was only for the procreation of children, Fox answered that he hadn't given the matter a thought: "I judged such things as below me."[23]

In short, although each man affirmed the equality of women—or, more properly, the irrelevance of gender—and although each felt a rich appreciation, even awe, at what he took to be the feminine spirit, all three men believed that they had to sustain a balance of spiritual intensity and emotional distance in their relations with actual women. One of Francis's biographers even implied that Clare was put on earth mainly as a challenge to Francis's virtue: "For saints as for heroes the supreme stimulus is woman's admiration."[24] So it shouldn't surprise us that their contemporaries often felt incapable of such fancy emotional footwork. Many Franciscan brothers opposed Francis's visits to Clare during his lifetime, and the convent was eventually forced to accept a papal rule that made the sisters cloistered nuns.[25] Many male Quakers opposed Fox's establishment of women's meetings by focusing, significantly, on the authority of women over whom they married. Quaker women continued to preach during the eighteenth century but without the institutional buttress of an independent meeting and without access to the meeting for business. Whereas seventeenth century women visionaries were often young, or mothers of young children, eighteenth century preachers tended to be middle-aged widows and grandmothers.[26]

Communitas Reviewed

If we look at the Franciscans, the Quakers, and the followers of Gandhi as expressions of *communitas,* we can see why Turner called them movements of transition. "Spontaneous communitas is a phase," he wrote, " . . . a moment, not a permanent condition. . . . In practice, of course, the impetus soon becomes exhausted, and the 'movement' becomes itself one institution among other institutions—often one more fanatical and militant than the rest, for the reason that it feels itself to be the unique bearer of universal human truths."[27]

By extension we can also see why women are transitional figures in many radical movements, coming to prominence in the early stages of egalitarian fervor and then receding into obscurity with the reemergence of structure. We can even understand why Turner disparaged liminal movements, while asserting the dialectical nature of their relationship to social structure:

> The moment a digging stick is set in the earth, a colt broken in, a pack of wolves defended against, or a human enemy set by his heels, we have the germs of a social structure. This is not merely the set of chains in which men everywhere are, but the very cultural means that preserve the dignity and liberty, as well as the bodily existence, of every man, woman and child. . . . Since the beginnings of prehistory, the evidence suggests that such means are what makes man most evidently man.[28]

In other words, according to this view, cultures need periodic, invigorating doses of *communitas*, momentary affirmations of universal human dignity and oneness as distinct from particular humans with cultural identities and political relationships; but in the last analysis it is the wheel, not love, that makes the world go round. In this context, feminine symbolism might be a reserve ideology, put on ice and treated simply as myth or folklore during some periods, put into practive as a model for human activity in others.[29] Religious women might be a reserve army of spiritual labor, brought in to affirm egalitarian principles and accomplish dangerous ascetic practices and missionary work, laid off when these activities are no longer timely. In England, that would have occurred when the development of patriarchal and liberal theory and practice made communal models and female public authority both irrelevant and dangerous.[30] Perhaps this is how we should understand one Mary Starbuck, who was responsible for starting the Quaker meeting on the island of Nantucket. She and some other women sustained Quakerism on the island during the years when the men were gone whaling. Yet when the meeting finally got official recognition, it was established as a men's business meeting. Modern historical accounts refer to the heroic leadership and self-sacrifice of Starbuck and many other women and then go on to describe the men who were the "real" founders of Quakerism in the American colonies.[31]

This way of thinking about movements of *communitas* and the place of feminine elements within them has the virtue of being clear-cut, even bracing, in its cynicism. But it is also one-sided. Indeed, it *has* to be, given the categories of Turner's typology. Turner described people, institutions, and forms of behavior as wholly one thing or wholly another. He spoke of individuals, rituals, even whole movements as being either structured or formless, hierarchical or egalitarian, aggressive or pacific. The early Franciscans, Quakers, and Gandhians *must*, in this typology, have been movements of antistructure in contrast to their goal-oriented contemporaries—the Dominicans (organized to combat heresy), the Puritans (organized to make England a city of God), or the Congress party (organized to reform Indian politics and expel the British).

Not only does the paradigm of structure/antistructure (or nature/culture) encourage a one-sided interpretation of the material; it may also be sexist in its implications. By defining femininity in negative terms (as a symbol associated with movements that reject prevailing structures) or in terms of global collectivity (as in movements that espouse universal equality and love), this implies that the real driving force in any movement—the organization, the vital energy of the leader, the actual plan for reform of society or spirit—must be associated with symbols of masculinity. This also implies that when movements of *communitas* fail, they do so because of their feminine elements.[32]

But the fact is that none of the three movements failed. Of course, they rejected conventional modes of exercising authority and limiting personal contact. But one of the most arresting things about Franciscans, Quakers, and Gandhians is their worldly effectiveness—the competence and vigor with which these avowedly apolitical, otherworldly, even whimsical people took on the worldly establishment and sustained the life of their communities. Francis, Fox, and Gandhi did not reject goals or programs in favor of a formless, impractical, and cathartic love-in. Instead, they and their followers sought spiritual salvation and social reform by focusing on domestic virtues and personal relationships rather than on formal public authority, church organization, or monastic rule and by adhering to a fluid strategy of negotiation and self-sacrifice rather than an abstract policy that was aggressive, inflexible, and potentially violent. All three groups steered a middle course between the elitism of a revolutionary vanguard and the democracy of a world turned upside down. They cared less about ramifications of doctrine than techniques of communication: Francis, through public preaching and the establishment of a third order; Quakers, through a system of double meetings ("threshing" meetings for the public, silent meetings for Friends); Gandhi, through popular journalism and public demonstrations of *satyagraha* (truth-force). We might say, indeed their adherents did say, that they raised the principle of the interrelatedness of all people to a higher level by successfully projecting the personal, affective relationship of everyday existence into the public sphere.

We need a typology for a kind of political and social behavior that is disordered only in relation to a specific notion of order; one that encompasses the Quakers' skill at providing for their material *needs* alongside their rejection of material *wealth* and Gandhi's orchestration of peaceful political demonstrations alongside his rejection of party politics. Perhaps we should formulate the difference between, say, Puritans and Quakers, by a typology of groups that emphasizes the pursuit of fixed goals through formal organizations that are more or less militant and groups that perceive truth and social harmony as extensions of concrete, personal experience, tending to equate ends with means.

A "Feminine" Model for Activism

Modern theorists have argued that modes of moral thinking that emphasize relationship and concrete circumstance over logic and principle are predominantly feminine.[33] I want to argue that this feminine element of Franciscans, Quakers, and Gandhians is of great relevance for our own political life; greater, perhaps, than their use of traditional feminine symbolism or their relatively liberated attitudes toward women. I want to focus on one aspect of this feminine moral thinking as a way of grasping their highly creative political style; a typology of thinking and behavior associated, in our own time, with active parenthood.[34]

By active parenthood I am not referring to the traditional feminine symbolism of God as Mother—"Mother" being one who gives unmediated, unquestioning love and nurturance, cutting across the barriers created by ethical standards or social hierarchies. Francis, Fox, and Gandhi were, as we have seen, powerful preachers of God as Mother; but this traditional image of God as Mother, and of motherhood as a source of pure and unending nurturance, was no more the whole essence of Francis, Fox, or Gandhi's truth than it is of any modern parent's.[35] I define parenthood not only as a way of feeling but as a way of thinking and not only as a state of being but as an active discipline. Such a parent might be one who strives to be reliable and flexible, combining nurture and judgment. A parent follows a rhythm of feeling and action that shifts from minute to minute, tracking the unpredictable needs and moods of children; but she also seeks to shape and direct that rhythm and to integrate these domestic and teaching activities with her own strictly adult, or public, concerns. More than most educators or psychologists, our archetypal parent is profoundly humble; she recognizes that the most vigilant solicitude and the most advanced theory of childrearing cannot guarantee against emotional or physical catastrophe, nor can they fully explain the catastrophe when it happens. More than most politicians or public leaders, a parent lives with the ambiguity of benevolent authority. In her daily relations with her child, particularly a young child, she is both master and slave. She experiences an awareness of physical power almost continually held in check and learns the resilience that comes from all the blows that are contemplated but not given. She also learns the futility of being the undisputed winner over her child in a battle of wills or of bodies. She controls and coerces one whom she also cherishes and works to set free.

A far more sophisticated typology of maternal thinking has been developed by the philosopher Sara Ruddick. "For me," she wrote,

> . . . "maternal" is a social category: although maternal thinking arises
> out of actual childcaring practices, biological parenting is neither
> necessary nor sufficient. Many women and some men express maternal
> thinking in various kinds of working and caring with others. And some
> biological mothers . . . take a fearful, defensive distance from their own
> mothering and the maternal lives of any women.[36]

Such a parent was Gandhi, whose relations with his biological children were unsuccessful by any standard.[37] Yet Gandhi's behavior toward both his intimate followers and the wider public corresponded to that of our hypothetical parent in at least two ways: his integration of personal, domestic activity with the rhythm of his wider political life and his self-abnegating but persuasive, even humorous posture toward those in authority. Gandhi elevated the tasks of daily life to a holy discipline. He did not leave the cares of the household in order to contemplate higher things, as most other Indian ascetics—indeed most revolutionaries—do. For Gandhi and his spiritual family, truth emerged out of the mundane activities of eating, cleaning, sleeping, even defecating. Days of silent contemplation alternated with periods of domestic busyness. The practice of physical restraint flourished in an atmosphere of total physical intimacy. Personal choices had political significance; hence, Gandhi's policy of blessing only those marriages that crossed class lines.

Gandhi's priority—to respond to particular human needs rather than to the dictates of an abstract program of spiritual growth or political reform—was evident in his ability to work with opponents who disagreed with him.

> In the quest for . . . truth, and in its propagation, it is . . . not
> possible . . . to inflict harm on others. In so behaving, truth itself
> would lose its meaning. He who claims a different version of truth
> from the satyagrahi's must be converted by gentleness. Meanwhile, the
> satyagrahi must re-examine continuously his own position—for his

opponent may be closer to the truth than he is. . . . The objective . . . is to win the victory over the conflict situation—to discover further truths and to persuade the opponent, not to triumph over him.[38]

Now the Quakers: In 1665 Joan Whitrowe, a Quaker preacher living in London, was commanded by God to go to Bristol and call the people to repentance. She went on foot, wearing sackcloth and ashes, and returned the next day to her husband and family, including a year-old baby who was still nursing.[39] That Joan Whitrowe, and many other Quakers, chose to record and make public these personal aspects of their experience indicates that for them, daily life was not merely something to be transcended in martyrdom or in an ecstatic trance. On the contrary, the Quakers, like the followers of Gandhi, placed great stress on the integrity and emotional warmth of their personal relationships, both as a reflection of the harmony that flowed from the presence of the inner light and as a message to the wider community.[40] Hence, the importance of providing for the economic needs of poor Friends and the importance Fox placed on the institution of marriage, giving the women's meeting authority to determine the spiritual readiness for marriage of every couple who was so inclined. Quaker prophecy itself was in many respects a cooperative and collective effort. Many writings, often done in prison, were composed and signed by several people. Numerous accounts of sufferings mention a Friend who accompanied a prophet to prison, although she had felt no inward call to preach herself.

Although these collective experiences were certainly emotional and cathartic, they were not undisciplined or unconscious. The Quakers evolved highly successful methods of determining what they called the "sense of the meeting" in order to achieve true consensus—the resolution of a problem with no winners and no losers—and these methods are still in use today.[41] The Quakers also evolved strategies for collecting and dispensing charity and for negotiating for the release of prisoners. More importantly, they displayed an unusual and very successful combination of humility and assertiveness toward those in power. The Quakers were avowedly apolitical, but they ignored laws that offended their principles. They preached nonviolence, but they also aggressively courted martyrdom and tried to fill the prisons with their adherents. They also exhibited a fine sense of the power of propaganda, establishing a meeting for sufferings that collected and published details of outrages perpetuated by the government on Quaker victims. Alongside all this energetic pacifism, the meeting began a program of legal education, recruiting lawyers to negotiate with the magistrates for the release of prisoners.[42]

We find a similar integration of personal and public life, although less fully articulated, in the career of Francis. Francis hated money and status not only as barriers to spiritual freedom but as obstacles to brotherhood; obstacles he overcame for himself when he kissed a leper—the ultimate outcast. Although drawn to a life of asceticism and isolation, Francis decided, after God had spoken to him through Clare, to live in the world and preach. He also established the Order of the Penitents to accommodate those whose family commitments obliged them to live in the world but who aspired to the ideals of Franciscan poverty.[43]

Surely part of the appeal of Francis, Fox, and Gandhi to their disciples was based on their ability to be simultaneously figures of authority and of intimate association. Surely the public achievements of all three men stemmed from their ability to present a model of behavior toward those in power that was both pliant and heroic. I have suggested that the model of structure and *communitas*, or nature and culture, is less helpful in appreciating these qualities than the model of parenthood because a successful parent has to be both hard and soft; she integrates the most minute, even degrading details of daily life into an overall conception of adulthood toward which both she and her child must strive. For many children, she is also a link between the private world of home and the wider, public world in which she earns their living. Consciously or not, a parent synthesizes both nature and culture, *communitas* and structure, as she experiences the trials and pleasures of a single day.

It seems appropriate and satisfying to bring domestic habits of thought and behavior into the intellectual sphere, as Francis, Fox, and Gandhi brought them into the sphere of social life and politics. It is also gratifying to resurrect these particular movements; indeed, *any* movement that challenges structures of authority and advocates egalitarian behavior is bound to attract women, who have never really shared in creating those structures. It may also be that at this historical moment, when conflicts bred by the structures of nation or class seem likely to threaten our very existence, many of us might be especially receptive to movements that devalue structure and hierarchy and offer creative techniques of nonconfrontational public behavior. The problem for contemporary feminists or peace activists is not that we are too bourgeois to comprehend or imitate the achievements of these radical men and women of the past but that we are too secular. We tend to overlook or discount the fact that the energy and inner self-assurance of Francis or Clare or Gandhi as they confronted those in power sprang from their submission to an even higher power—that of God; and that their ability to sustain unformalized relationships among their adherents, even for one lifetime, sprang from their faith in the existence of a spiritual realm that transcended time itself. Those of us who reject the traditional male model of the narrow-minded, rigid, loveless revolutionary may try to coopt their political style without reference to their religious faith. In doing so we still face a problem of authority: of sustaining cooperation and unity of purpose when our deepest convictions make us critical of power vested in others, even when those others are our heroes, and distrustful of power vested in ourselves.

Parents, especially those in modern, middle-class, permissive households, confront this problem of authority every day of their lives, whether they choose to think about it and regardless of whether they are successful in solving it. I think that the ordinary, unheroic experience of parenthood may have much to offer as a source of insight in thinking about our public behavior, at a time in our history when it seems particularly urgent to consider forms of political interaction that work to mediate, rather than escalate, conflict.

In arguing for the political potential of parenthood, both as a symbolic system and as a source of behavior techniques, I am all too aware that my own ambivalent emotional reaction to the concept of motherhood is shared by many other contemporary feminists. Even my use of the (hopefully) more neutral term *parenting* is bound to arouse mixed emotions from those of us who have devoted much of our personal and intellectual lives to deconstructing the mythology of woman as a nurturing, sacrificial mother. In this chapter I have also attempted to deconstruct the myth of motherhood but in a more positive direction; I have suggested that parenting is an intellectual and ethical activity, not merely an emotional or instinctual one, and that the skills in conflict resolution acquired by many parents have an affinity with those we seek to exercise as peace activists. The women who successfully challenged Congress in the Women Strike for Peace movement are one example of this, as was the behavior of Chilean women and children as they created new family forms and new modes of political activism from within their jail cells.[44]

Certainly I have no wish to espouse the sanctity of motherhood or to resurrect those Victorian feminists who tried to turn the whole world into a living room or even to imply that parents have a monopoly on compassion. Just the opposite: The behavior of Francis, Fox, and Gandhi— only one of whom was a biological parent, and a bad one at that— suggests that "feminine" domestic habits of thought and activity may be transposed into the public sphere by both women and men; we might even speculate that these feminine modes of behavior gained moral and political credibility for Francis, Fox, and Gandhi just because they were being used creatively by men. In either case, I suggest that we would do well to contemplate the virtues of these partisans of nonviolent public behavior and that we can find affinities with their compassionate activism very close to home, as we move to embrace our own political and spiritual struggles.

Notes

1. On Francis, see John Holland Smith, *Francis of Assisi* (New York: Charles Scribner's Sons, 1972), especially p. 185. On the Quakers, see Jeanette Carter Gadt, "Women and Protestant Culture: The Quaker Dissent from Puritanism" (Ph.D. diss., UCLA, 1974), especially p. 99. On Gandhi, see Ved Mehta *Mahatma Gandhi and His Apostles* (New York: Viking Press, 1976), especially p. 97.

2. On Francis, see Smith, ibid., p. 1. On the Puritan aspects of the Quakers, see Hugh Barbour, *The Quakers in Puritan England* (New Haven, Conn.: Yale University Press, 1964). On Gandhi, see Martin Green, "Coming to Terms with the Gandhi Who Stands Behind 'Gandhi,'" *New York Times*, January 30, 1983, sec. 2.

3. Victor Turner, *The Ritual Process: Structure and Anti-Structure* (Ithaca, N.Y.: Cornell University Press, 1969), p. 95.

4. Ibid., p. 96.

5. Ibid., p. 111–112.

6. Ibid., pp. 115–120, 140. Turner maintained that this association holds only where public authority and inheritance patterns follow male lines.

7. Sherry Ortner, "Is Female to Male as Nature Is to Culture?" in Michelle Rosaldo and Louise Lamphere, eds., *Women, Culture and Society* (Stanford, Calif.: Stanford University Press, 1974).

8. Joan Mowat Erikson, *St. Francis et His Four Ladies* (New York: Norton, 1970). On Ramakrishna, see Mehta, *Mahatma Gandhi*, p. 182; and Christopher Isherwood, *Ramakrishna and His Disciples* (New York: Simon and Schuster, 1964), pp. 112–113. On the Quakers, see Phyllis Mack, "Women as Prophets During the English Civil War," *Feminist Studies* 8, no. 1 (Spring 1982), pp. 19–47.

9. Malcolm D. Lambert, *Franciscan Poverty* (London: Allenson, 1961), pp. 39, 49, 62, 65. Also see John Moorman, *A History of the Franciscan Order from Its Origins to the Year 1517* (Oxford: Clarendon Press, 1968), Chap. 7.

10. Lambert, ibid., p. 50.

11. Ibid., p. 73; Moorman, *A History of the Franciscan Order*, pp. 36–37.

12. Caroline Walker Bynum, *Jesus as Mother: Studies in the Spirituality of the High Middle Ages* (Berkeley: University of California Press, 1982), pp. 172n., 192, 257.

13. Mabel Brailsford, *Quaker Women, 1650–1690* (London: Duckworth, 1915), especially 160f, 254. Mack, "Women as Prophets," pp. 29, 37–38.

14. Louis Fischer, *The Life of Mahatma Gandhi* (New York: Harper & Row, 1983), photograph.

15. Mehta, *Mahatma Gandhi*, p. 183.

16. Ibid., p. 182.

17. Quoted in Erikson, *St. Francis*, p. 90.

18. Moorman, *A History of the Franciscan Order*, pp. 36–37.

19. Gadt, "Women and Protestant Culture," pp. 2–3; Mack, "Women as Prophets," p. 24.

20. Mehta, *Mahatma Gandhi*, p. 126.

21. Moorman, *A History of the Franciscan Order*, p. 38.

22. Mehta, *Mahatma Gandhi*, pp. 90–97. Gandhi defended himself: "I am amazed at [the] assumption that my experiment implied any assumption of woman's inferiority. She would be, if I looked upon her with lust. . . . My wife was inferior when she was the instrument of my lust. She ceased to be that when she lay with me as my sister" (p. 191).

23. Gadt, "Women and Protestant Culture," pp. 108–109.

24. Paul Sabatier, *Life of St. Francis of Assisi*, tr. Louise Seymour Houghton (New York: Charles Scribner's Sons, 1935), p. 148.

25. Rosalind B. Brooke and Christopher N.L. Brooke, "St. Clare," in Derek Baker, ed., *Medieval Women* (Oxford: Basil Blackwell, 1978), pp. 275–287.

26. Dictionary of Quaker Biography (mss.), Friends House, London. Survey by the author.

27. Turner, *The Ritual Process*, p. 112.

28. Ibid., p. 140.

29. For an interesting discussion of this phenomenon in another culture, see Philip Carl Salzman, "Ideology and Change in Middle Eastern Tribal Societies," *Man* (N.S.) 13, pp. 618–637.

30. For an interesting discussion of this idea, see I. M. Lewis, *Ecstatic Religions* (Harmondsworth, England: Penguin, 1975), pp. 3ff.

31. For example, see Rufus M. Jones, *The Quakers in the American Colonies* (London: Macmillan, 1911), p. 280.

32. Turner's analysis of Francis was exclusively devoted to his views on poverty. Turner emphasized Francis's "deficiencies as a legislator" and his inability to make a rule for the order that would stick (p. 142).

33. Carol Gilligan, *In a Different Voice* (Cambridge, Mass.: Harvard University Press, 1982). Sara Ruddick, "Maternal Thinking," *Feminist Studies* 6, no. 2 (Summer 1980), p. 346; and "Pacifying the Forces: Drafting Women in the Interests of Peace," *Signs: Journal of Women in Culture and Society* 8, no. 3 (1983), pp. 471–490. Jean Bethke Elshtain, *Public Man, Private Woman* (Princeton, N.J.: Princeton University Press, 1981), Chap. 6, is also relevant, although my conclusions are very different from the ones she drew.

34. The following discussion is not an argument for biological determinism, nor is it a discussion of the family or of parenting as social institutions. If anything, the Lutherans and Puritans put the family more at the center of their theology than the Quakers did. Luther emphasized the spiritual importance of marriage and Calvin the importance of the patriarchal father as the family emissary to God. But it is also true that women have traditionally been associated with childrearing and that the bulk of the historical literature on the family quotes men, not women. It is therefore impossible to say, at this point, what elements of child care are unique to the modern, middle-class family and what elements were shared by the cultures of medieval or early modern Europe or of India. It would be more accurate to say that Francis and Fox prefigured

certain types of behavior that have become generally true of modern, middle-class parents in the West.

35. Although male Cistercians in the twelfth century depicted God the Mother in the conventional way I have described, a number of thirteenth century women mystics did not. The men associated engendering and authority with fatherhood and nursing with motherhood. They also saw maternal love as "automatic" and "ethically irrational" (Bynum, *Jesus as Mother,* p. 122, 158). The nuns saw it differently; for Gertrude of Helfta, "Frequently God as mother means . . . discipline and testing. A mother sometimes . . . for its own good, denies a child something it wants" (pp. 189–190).

36. Ruddick, "Maternal Thinking," p. 346. She asked, "Do women, who now rightfully claim the instruments of public power, have cultures, traditions, and inquiries which we should insist upon bringing to the public world?"

37. Erik Erikson, *Gandhi's Truth* (New York: Norton, 1969), "The Past," and p. 243.

38. Joan V. Bondurant, *Conquest of Violence: The Gandhian Philosophy of Conflict* (Princeton, N.J.: Princeton University Press, 1958), p. 33. Ruddick said, "Mothers in particular have . . . developed a theory of conflict quite distinct from the militant's account of just wars. Although physical and psychological violence is a temptation and a frequent occurrence in maternal practice, mothers nonetheless learn in a daily way to choose peace over combat and, if peace fails, to fight most battles without resorting to violence. The theory of conflict that maternal thinkers develop bears remarkable similarity to that of pacifists. Both refuse to separate means from ends; both wish to treat 'enemies' as opponents with whom one struggles . . . and to seek reconciliation rather than victory" ("Pacifying the Forces," p. 482).

39. Joan Whitrowe, "The Humble Address of the Widow Whitrowe to King William," (n.p., 1689), pp. 9–13.

40. Howard Brinton, *Friends for 300 Years* (New York: Harper & Bros., 1952), especially pp. 62–65.

41. Bondurant, *Conquest of Violence*, pp. 221–223; Gadt, "Women and Protestant Culture," p. 319; Brinton, ibid., Chap. 6.

42. Arnold Lloyd, *Quaker Social History, 1669–1738* (Westport, Conn.: Greenwood Press, 1979), pp. 83–85.

43. *The Little Flowers of St. Francis* (New York: Dutton, 1951), pp. 36–37; Sabatier, *Life of St. Francis*, p. 156; Moorman, *A History of the Franciscan Order,* p. 40f.

44. Amy Swerdlow, "Ladies Day at the Capitol: Women's Strike for Peace vs. HUAC," *Feminist Studies* 8, no. 3 (Fall 1982), pp. 493–520. "From its inception, the WSP was a non-hierarchical participatory network of activists opposed both to rigid ideologies and formal organizational structure" (p. 495). The WSP rejected other peace groups for their internal purges of Communists and for their hierarchical bureaucratic structure; they were also more successful than these groups in confronting and intimidating the House Un-American Activities Committee. On Chilean women, see the speech by Gladys Diaz, published by the Women's International Resource Exchange.

TWELVE

Pure Milk, Not Poison
Women Strike for Peace
and the Test Ban Treaty of 1963

AMY SWERDLOW _____

This chapter will examine the motherist rhetoric and tactics of Women Strike for Peace (WSP), a grass-roots, middle-class women's peace movement of the 1960s, in the context of the contemporary debate among scholars and activists regarding the relationship of female culture to radical politics and to the empowerment of women.[1] This debate, in its most polarized form, pits the concept of female difference against the feminist goal of sexual equality. For feminist peace activists, a crucial question today is whether separatist peace groups, which make their appeal to women on the basis of their special connection to life preservation and moral guardianship, do not in the end undermine women's political power and even the cause of peace by reinforcing a gender system that encourages male violence in the family and the state. Simone de Beauvoir, who was a leading proponent of the equality over difference viewpoint, put it this way shortly before her death:

> Women should desire peace as human beings, not as women. And if they are being encouraged to be pacifists in the name of motherhood, that's just a ruse by men who are trying to lead women back to the womb. Women should absolutely let go of that baggage.[2]

For the most part, historians of women who have been examining political movements based on traditional female culture have found that

Revised version of a paper delivered at the Seventh Annual Berkshire Conference on the History of Women, Wellesley College, June 21, 1987.

difference and equality are not opposite categories and that posing one against the other is both ahistorical and undialectical. Feminist historians studying women's political activism have shown that in different cultures, classes, and ethnic groups, in places as diverse as Europe and Africa, the United States and Latin America, groups of women have moved from private family concerns to militant political action when they perceived a threat to their maternal responsibilities and rights. Despite a dialectic in motherist movements of the Left that politicizes women's family role, transforms housewives into political thinkers and leaders, and elevates women's sense of self and sisterhood, most of these movements, whether for bread, social justice, or peace, are usually short-lived and leave an ambiguous legacy in terms of political culture and feminist consciousness.[3]

Women Strike for Peace fits this picture, with some important exceptions that were shaped by the specific political and gender consciousness in the United States in the 1940s, 1950s, and 1960s. WSP emerged in 1961, at the end of a long period of political and sexual repression, when there was little visible protest against the cold war and U.S. policies. The movement played an important and recognized role in the campaign for the test ban treaty of 1963 but retreated into relative obscurity by middecade. Although the women of WSP continued to be politically active, working passionately and militantly against the Vietnam War, they were overshadowed, ignored, and sometimes ridiculed by the young men who took over the leadership of the antiwar movement later in the decade. Unlike the young women of the New Left who resisted marginalization and trivialization in the peace and antidraft movements and went on to found their own movement for women's liberation, WSP accepted for itself a secondary, supportive, helping, and enabling role in the anti–Vietnam War movement, one to which its members were accustomed.

The story of WSP provides fresh evidence that traditional female culture can be a source of strength, commitment, passion, and creativity for women's movements of the Left. Female culture can serve to mobilize a deeply felt critique and alternative vision of political institutions, along with fresh forms of dissent and social interaction. Although radical movements based on traditional culture have, in the past, rarely addressed issues of gender inequity or sexual oppression, they are not static and change with historical developments. The WSP experience reveals that when a motherist movement encounters a rising feminist consciousness, as WSP did in the late 1960s, its unquestioned acceptance of the sex-role system is shaken, and its general political protest begins to include specific gender demands.[4]

The Birth of WSP

Women Strike for Peace burst upon the U.S. political scene on November 1, 1961, as a radioactive cloud from a Soviet nuclear test hung over the U.S. landscape and the United States was threatening to hold its own series of atmospheric explosions. In response to their fears of nuclear fallout and the total destruction of the planet by accident or male design, an estimated fifty thousand women in more than sixty cities walked out of their kitchens and off their jobs in a one-day, nationwide peace strike.[5] The slogans of the strike addressed issues of particular concern to women. "Pure Milk Not Poison" and "Let the Children Grow" were most widely used. A placard that hung from the neck of a little girl sitting in a baby buggy expressed the motherist assumptions of the strikers: "I want to grow up to be a mommy some day."

The November 1 peace strike was the largest coordinated national female peace action of the twentieth century. After a decade noted for its regressive politics of nostalgia and containment—containment of the Soviets, the bomb, dissent, and women—the sudden appearance of middle-class female peace strikers so shocked and puzzled the media and public officials that WSP became one of the biggest news stories of 1961 in terms of coverage by press, radio, and TV.[6] What shocked the media was that the strikers were, as *Newsweek* put it, "perfectly ordinary looking women, with their share of good looks," the kind "you would see driving ranch wagons, or shopping at the village market, or attending PTA meetings." What further puzzled reporters and politicians was not only that respectable women were "acting up" but also that they seemed to have emerged from nowhere, as they belonged to no unified, identifiable organizations, and their leaders were totally unknown as public figures.[7]

The women who struck on November 1, 1961, were an ad hoc group responding to a hastily drafted call from a handful of Washington, D.C., women who expressed the concerns, fears, and anger of women like themselves across the country in a language and style with which they could identify. The strike was organized in only six weeks through female networks such as Christmas card lists, car pool and PTA telephone chains, the League of Women Voters, and peace group mailing lists. The organizers of the strike had met as members of the Washington, D.C., Committee for a Sane Nuclear Policy (SANE). They were alienated by SANE's hierarchical structure, its focus on lobbying instead of direct action, its exclusionary policy toward Communists and former Communists, and its unwillingness to make the issue of nuclear fallout its central concern. They were brought together by Dagmar Wilson, a successful children's book illustrator, who, for the purposes of the strike, identified herself as an outraged housewife and mother.

Wilson and four of the five initiators whom I knew personally when I was a WSP activist and whom I have since interviewed recalled that they sensed it was time for women, ordinary housewives and mothers, to take direct political action because men, both on the Right and the Left, could no longer be counted on for leadership or rational behavior in the face of an unprecedented threat to human survival. The following declaration of the organizers met with instant and enthusiastic response:

> We don't want chairmen, boards, committees, long serious meetings.
> We just want to speak out loudly, to tell our elected representatives,
> that they are not properly representing US by continuing the arms race
> and increasing the threat of total destruction.[8]

The founders were convinced that the old hierarchical, abstract, ideological politics was leading the world to destruction and that they wanted no part of it. The only piece of social philosophy expressed in the call to strike identified the Washington initiators more with the conventional culture of domesticity than with traditional radical politics. "Nations disagree as families disagree," the women proclaimed. "Women believe that nations can solve differences as families do without killing each other." This theme of social housekeeping, used by women reformers since the nineteenth century, would be invoked frequently by WSP in the years to come. Nevertheless, the leaders of the movement had no conscious historical memory of either the words or deeds of their pacifist foremothers. They arrived at this formulation from their own political and maternal experience.

Most of the women who joined the strike in November 1961, and those who participated in the national movement that grew out of it, came from liberal to leftist political backgrounds, having been associated with Quaker, pacifist, New Deal, socialist, anarchist, or Communist causes in the years before World War II. Many would have identified themselves as antiwar and antifascist in the 1930s and 1940s, even though they may have not been politically active. The majority were college-educated women in their thirties and forties who had been employed outside the home before, during, and immediately after World War II.[9] Unlike Jane Addams, Emily Balch, and Alice Hamilton, who led the Women's Peace party and the U.S. delegation to the international women's peace conference at The Hague in 1915, the leading activists of WSP were not professional women.[10] Most had succumbed to societal pressure after the war and the advice of the Freudian baby doctors and child-development specialists to retire from the work force to become resident housewives/mothers. They had been convinced that full-time care of a child by its biological mother was the only way to raise the well-adjusted, productive, achieving children who would be capable of building the postwar world of justice and peace to which they were committed.[11] The women of WSP had grown to adulthood in an optimistic, if difficult era, marked by depression and war. They shared the liberal and radical assumption of the 1940s that society could be reordered in the interest of social justice and peace through the direct efforts of ordinary people of goodwill like themselves. As socially concerned women, WSPers viewed motherhood as more than a responsibility to the private family. They saw it as a service to the world community and to social progress. In its global outlook, WSP was different from nonpolitical, local, mothers' groups that organized to win a traffic light for their neighborhood or to protect their children from drunk drivers.

Dorothy Dinnerstein has described the psychological process of depoliticization and privatization that drove socially conscious radicals out of national politics in the 1950s. According to Dinnerstein, people like the WSPers spent the 1950s traumatized by the horrors of Stalinism, McCarthyism, and, I would add, the Nazi holocaust. They lost their optimism and their capacity for social connectedness. In this condition, Dinnerstein suggests, they withdrew, "more or less totally, more or less gradually, more or less blindly into an intensely personalistic, inward turning, thing and place oriented life."[12] What the women of WSP withdrew into, with society's blessing, was the manageable sphere of home, children, and local community. When their children no longer required full-time care, many WSPers were propelled by their earlier social, political, and humanitarian concerns to become active in Parent-Teacher Associations, the League of Women Voters, the liberal wing of the Democratic party (many had campaigned for Adlai Stevenson), and church or temple reform groups. Some were already involved in peace groups such as SANE and the Women's International League for Peace and Freedom (WILPF); others were returning to school and to part-time work. But very few of those who served as key women in WSP were employed full-time outside the home. It took the escalation of the nuclear arms race, and the example of the civil rights sit-ins in the South, to give WSPers the sense of urgency and possibility that is necessary for political movement.

At a time when cold war dissenters in the United States were dismissed by the press, the public, and political leaders as either "commies" or "kooks," the image projected by WSP of respectable middle-class, middle-aged mothers picketing the White House to save the children helped legitimize a radical critique of the cold war and U.S. militarism. By never seeming to threaten the political or gender system, WSP was able to gain support from the president of the United States, who had been elected on a cold war platform but was also interested in building a constituency for a nuclear test ban. At a press conference in 1962 he stated that he thought WSPers were sincere, that he knew there were many of them, and that he had received their message. In an interview published in seven women's magazines shortly before his death, John Kennedy made an appeal for motherist peace activism even more eloquent than that of WSP when he stated, "The control of arms is a mission we undertake particularly for our children, and our grandchildren, and they have no lobby in Washington. No one is better qualified to represent their interests than the mothers and grandmothers of America."[13]

The "key women" of WSP understood that the projection of a traditional, respectable, middle-class image was essential for attracting a positive, or at least a benign, response from the media. They knew what Todd Gitlin has since pointed out: that only through sympathetic media coverage can a movement reach the attention of the public it wishes to recruit and the eyes and ears of those in power. But the WSP image was not inconsistent with the thought and consciousness of the movement's leaders and rank and file. When questioned by the press about the sexual rebellion implied by WSP's Lysistrata-like action, Dagmar Wilson, who became the spokesperson for the strike and for the movement that later emerged, reassured the public that WSP posed no threat to the sexual status quo. "Our organization has no resemblance to the Lysistrata theme or even to the suffragettes," Wilson told a reporter from the *Baltimore Sun*. "We are not striking against our husbands. It is my guess that we will make the soup that they will ladle out to the children on Wednesday."[14]

Wilson was not dissembling. She worked in her home as a children's book illustrator in order to assure a well-run household and be available to her children when they returned from school. She certainly intended to make the soup her husband would dispense. In the years to come WSPers often complained to each other that their housekeeping duties were neglected during particularly active protest periods, but they blamed only themselves, or the nuclear crisis, for this neglect. Little or no help was expected from husbands or children. A Smith College alumna of the WSP generation spoke for WSP women when she described her consciousness as a student, "We were concerned about the big problems about peace and poverty but changing our personal lives didn't occur to us."[15]

WSP Tactics

I have been asked frequently if the founders of WSP were as naive as their rhetoric. The answer is no. Neither they nor their rhetoric was naive. WSPers chose to use simple language, the mother tongue, because the old political rhetoric that many knew from their youth had not served them, or society. Convinced that professional politicians, scientists, and academics were, for the most part, leading the world to extinction, WSPers gloried in their own exclusion from the system. Most of the women learned by the time the movement was six months old that they already knew more about the dangers of radioactive isotopes than the men in Congress and even some members of the Atomic Energy Commission. Later in the 1960s, they mastered the draft laws and knew the details of all the disarmament treaties, but they chose to translate them into the womanly language the lady next door and the working class mother could understand.

WSP political tactics never mimicked male forms. In organizing national and international direct actions, WSPers often used the informal house-wifely techniques developed in their daily practice managing households, running church luncheons, organizing bake sales, League of Women Voters forums, and car pools. At one White House demonstration the New York women carried hundreds of feet of dishtoweling, on which thousands of women had inscribed their signatures in opposition to the nuclear arms race. The dish towel, a city block long, was affixed to the White House gate. Even some WSP women were embarrassed by the use of what they perceived as a degrading image. But for most of the WSP it was a symbol of the powerlessness *and* the potential power of women. At another demonstration the women attached pictures of their own children to their spring hats, using these symbols instead of words as political slogans. Maternal language was also employed consistently in WSP's internal rhetoric and metaphor. An example is a statement in the Los Angeles newsletter on the occasion of WSP's second anniversary. *La Wisp* declared:

> We all know what two year olds are like—loveable, busy, noisy, but not easy to get along with. WSP is a typical two year old. We've gotten some of what we wanted but we want more. A partial test ban treaty is not enough.[16]

WSP demonstrations were dramatic, playful, and photogenic. As Jean Bethke Elshtain has pointed out, WSP, in its confrontation with the House Un-American Activities Committee (HUAC), employed the grand destructive power of a politics of humor, irony, evasion, and ridicule. WSP used a form of guerrilla theater more akin to classic comedies of reversal than to tragedies riddled with plots, violence, and victories bought at terrible costs. Indeed, many political reporters perceived the HUAC investigation of WSP as a battle of the sexes, rather than a confrontation between two conflicting political ideologies. A report in the *Vancouver Sun* was typical of many others:

> The dreaded House Un-American Activities Committee met its Waterloo this week. It tangled with 500 irate women. They laughted at it. Kleig lights glared, television cameras whirred, and 50 reporters scribbled notes while babies cried and cooed during the fantastic inquisition.[17]

Russell Baker commented:

> If the House Un-American Activities Committee knew its Greek as well as it knows its Lenin it would have left the women peace strikers alone. Instead with typical male arrogance it has subpoenaed 15 of the ladies, spent several days trying to show them that woman's place is not on the peace march route, and has come out of it covered with foolishness.[18]

There was also more of an antimale element in WSP than one would have expected from women who had come out of the popular front politics of the 1930s and 1940s. Their anger at men was not confined to men in power. They were tired of dealing with male leaders of the peace movement who ignored their ideals and feelings. In fact, they refused to consult them when the movement planned its guerrilla theater against HUAC. Jean Bagby, one of the WSP founders, wrote in *Liberation* in 1963 a response to the historic memo from Casey Hayden and Mary King raising issues of women's oppression in the New Left. "As I remember," Bagby wrote, "Women Strike for Peace was founded for many of the reasons laid bare in the 'Sex and Caste memo.'"

> We shared a wonderful sense of freedom to be ourselves, bring up the kookiest ideas and experiment with activities other groups might consider silly. In our meetings, especially in the early days . . . we had a spirit and enthusiasm unmatched by anything in our previous experience. . . . It was great working without men! . . . It seemed to us that other organizations invariably suffered from the hierarchical, formalist, impediments we so briskly ignored. Our naive, disorganized methods seemed to annoy men of all ages.[19]

Despite their domestic language and imagery, the WSP leadership displayed a high level of political acumen in the campaign for the test ban: a sense of the strategic moment for pressure, a talent for research, self-education, and public relations unexpected of nonprofessional women of their time. I. F. Stone, the brilliant independent radical journalist, stated in 1970 that he knew of no antiwar or radical organization of any kind in the United States that had been "as flexible and intelligent in its tactics, and as free from stereotypes and sectarianism in its strategy." In 1970, Stone was apparently as insensitive to the issue of sex-role stereotyping as were WSPers.[20]

From its inception, WSP viewed itself as a participatory movement of women who were consciously opposed to tight organization and top-down leadership. As each group was autonomous, the women often duplicated efforts and crossed wires, but they preferred overwork to "formalist hierarchical impediments." Influenced by male standards, WSP was apologetic about its much-debated, innovative format, which members referred to as "our un-organization." The women defended their rebellion against hierarchy as energizing but showed little understanding of their theoretical contribution to feminist political culture. WSPers, as middle-aged women, were too diffident, too fearful of being presumptuous, to theorize or even to assert that their political tactics came from considered thought. Everything WSP did seemed spontaneous, pragmatic, practical, inspirational; and for the most part it was. What the women did not understand was that they were building theory in the feminist mode—in the process of struggle, combining observation, experience, and emotion.

The Nature of WSP Political Action

The women of WSP possessed a dual consciousness: maternal and political. Their opposition to the test ban treaty did not arise solely from maternal concerns, nor did those of Phyllis Schlafly, who testified against the test ban treaty at the Senate hearings on ratification:

> I appear here as a mother who is eager to have her five small children have the opportunity to grow up in a free and independent America, and because I do not want my children to suffer the fate of children in Cuba, China, and the captive nations.[21]

WSP opposition to the acceleration of the nuclear arms race came from a long-held commitment to social justice and peace, but the women were moved to public action by pressing maternal concerns. After years of sacrifice of careers and personal goals to raise healthy, "well-adjusted" children, WSPers were outraged by society's break of faith with them. What was particularly offensive was the contradiction between the way motherhood was praised and celebrated by opinionmakers and the media and the realization that mothers were powerless to defend their children. My own years in WSP as a "key woman" and editor of its national publication (from 1970 to 1973) convinced me that WSPers operated out of political or religious convictions that transcended the perspective of motherhood, but for the moment when their maternal practice was most under attack, they rallied to defend it. They made the most of mothers' rights and responsibilities because that was the only way in which they could be heard. And they found that working in a separatist motherist movement was empowering and fun. It was a pleasure for the women to be heard, respected, and admired and to work with others on an equal basis.

Given its double vantage point of radical politics and female culture why was WSP so lacking in feminist consciousness? A Pentagon officer commenting on a paper I gave at a meeting of the Society of Historians of Foreign Relations refused to believe that women who may have been Communists were not feminists. He did not understand it was precisely because they came out of the Left that they were not feminists. I noticed that in WSP the women who had been in or close to the Communist party had even less knowledge of the women's rights movement than did those with liberal or anarchist backgrounds. In the socialist parties in the 1930s and 1940s, the issues of economic crisis, fascism, and war superseded gender, and popular-front rhetoric celebrated motherhood and female self-sacrifice. WSPers were not moved to research the Women's Peace party or the early years of WILPF because they lacked historical consciousness, as did the other political movements of the 1960s. For WSP the Nazi holocaust and the atom bomb had made history irrelevant.

Having no feminist insights and experience to build on, WSP was unable to offer a feminist critique of the bomb and the war. We in WSP, and I include myself, had neither the language nor the analytical tools to make a connection between woman's secondary status in the family economy and her political powerlessness or between domestic violence and state violence. All we could do was forward women into the political struggle in a period of political and gender repression and demand that we be represented on disarmament negotiating teams and all governmental bodies dealing with issues of health, life, and death. Equal power in all areas of life was not even a dream, let alone a demand.

Without setting out to do so, WSP did help to change the image of the good mother from passive to militant, from silent to eloquent, from private to public. In proclaiming that the men in power could no longer be counted on for protection, WSP exposed one of the most important myths of the militarists—that wars are waged by men to protect women and children. By stressing international cooperation among women rather than private family issues, WSP challenged the key element of the feminine mystique—the domestication and privatization of the middle-class white housewife. By making recognized contributions to achievement of a test ban, WSP also raised its participants' sense of political efficacy and self-esteem. WSP's rejection of male political culture prompted the movement to create a nonhierarchical, participatory, playful style of radical politics that foreshadowed the structurelessness of the feminist movement, the consensus form of decisionmaking now used in the antinuclear movement, and the emotional, poetic, self-empowering guerrilla theater of the Women's Pentagon Action. One of WSP's greatest achievement was the way in which its motherist struggle against the bomb made clear to its participants and to the public that the personal is political and that the private and public spheres are one.

Notes

1. See Ellen DuBois, Mari Jo Buhle, Temma Kaplan, Gerda Lerner, and Carol Smith-Rosenberg, "Politics and Culture in Women's History: A Symposium," *Feminist Studies* 6 (Spring 1980), pp. 26–64. Also see Kathy Kahn, "Gender Ideology and the Organizers," *RESIST* (December 1980), pp. 1–2; Ellen Willis, *Village Voice*, June 23, 1980; Judy Houseman, "Mothering, the Unconscious and Feminism," *Radical America* 16 (November-December 1982), pp. 47–61; Jean Bethke Elshtain, "Women, War and Feminism," *The Nation*, June 14, 1980, p. 1; Dorothy Dinnerstein, *The Mermaid and the Minotaur: Sexual Arrangements and the Human Malaise* (New York: Harper Colophon Books, 1976), pp. 207–228; Micaela di Leonardo, "Morals, Mothers, Militarism: Antimilitarism and Feminist Theory," *Feminist Studies* 11 (Fall 1985), pp. 599–618; and Barbara Steinson, "The Mother Half of Humanity: American Women in the Peace and Preparedness Movements in World War I," in Carol Berkin and Clara Lovett, eds., *Women, War, and Revolution* (New York: Holmes and Meier, 1980), pp. 259–284.

2. Alice Schwartzer, "Simone de Beauvoir Talks about Sartre," *Ms.* (August 1983), p. 37.

3. Barbara L. Epstein, *The Politics of Domesticity* (Middletown, Conn.: Wesleyan University Press, 1981); Blanche Glassman Hersh, *The Slavery of Sex* (Urbana: University of Illinois Press, 1978); Mari Jo Buhle, "Politics and Culture in Women's History: A Symposium," *Feminist Studies* 6 (Spring 1980), pp. 55–64; Ruth Bordin, *Women and Temperance: The Quest for Powerful Liberty, 1873–1900* (Philadelphia: Temple University Press, 1981); Temma Kaplan, "Female Consciousness and Collective Action: The Case of Barcelona, 1910–1918," *Signs* 7 (Spring 1982), pp. 545–566; Sara Ruddick, "Preservative Love and Military Destruction: Some Reflections on Mothering and Peace," in Joyce Trebilcot, ed., *Mothering: Essays in Feminist Theory* (Totowa, N.J.: Rowman and Allanheld, 1984); and Carol Gilligan, *In a Different Voice* (Cambridge, Mass.: Harvard University Press, 1982).

4. This, as Maxine Molyneux has pointed out, is a central aspect of feminist politics. See Maxine Molyneux, "Mobilization Without Emancipation? Women's Interest, the State, and Revolution in Nicaragua," *Feminist Studies* 11 (Summer 1985), p. 232.

5. The U.S. wire service Associated Press reported on November 2: "The radioactive cloud from Russia's mighty nuclear explosion was following the

expected path but was picking up speed as it headed toward Alaska" (*Sacramento Union*, November 2, 1961). In San Francisco, the California State Health Department reported that "slightly radioactive rain" was falling (*Newsweek*, November 13, 1961, p. 22). Also see *Los Angeles Times*, November 2, 1961; *Los Angeles Mirror*, November 1, 1961. The figure of 50,000 women was an estimate based, according to Washington founders, on reports from women in sixty cities across the country. In order to verify this figure I tallied the highest numbers reported either by strike groups or local papers and could arrive at a total no greater than 12,000. Nevertheless, this was the largest women's national peace action of the twentieth century.

6. For a brilliant analysis of the connection among the cold war, McCarthyism, and the feminine mystique, see Elaine Tyler May, "Explosive Issues: Sex, Women and the Bomb in Postwar America," in Larry May, ed., *Promise and Peril: Rethinking Postwar American Culture* (Chicago: University of Chicago Press, forthcoming).

7. *Newsweek*, December 13, 1961, p. 21.

8. "Dear—, The other night I sat with a few friends," Draft of call to strike, Washington, D.C. (Swarthmore, Penn.: WSP Document Collection, Swarthmore College Peace Collection, September 22, 1961, mimeographed).

9. Sixty-five percent of the women had either a B.A. or a higher degree, at a time when only 6 percent of the female population older than 25 had a B.A. or more. Seventy-one percent of the WSP women were suburb or city dwellers, with the highest concentration in the East Central states, the West Coast, and the Midwest, and with low participation in the Mountain states and the South. The WSPers were concentrated in the twenty-five to forty-four bracket. Only 5 percent of the group were "never marrieds." Of the married women, 43 percent had from one to four children younger than six; 49 percent had from one to four or more children older than eighteen. Sixty-one percent of the women involved in the WSP were not, at the time of the questionnaire, employed outside the home. Nearly 70 percent of the husbands of the WSPers who responded to the survey were professionals. Only 4 percent of the WSPers were members of professional organizations. Thirty-eight percent of the women who responded claimed to belong to no other organizations or at least did not record the names of any other organizations in response to questions concerning community activities. Forty percent were active in a combination of civic, race relations, civil liberties, peace, and electoral political activity. Boulding concluded that many of the WSPers were nonjoiners. As for their goals in joining the WSP, the Boulding survey revealed that 55 percent gave abolition of war or multilateral disarmament as their primary goals, and 22 percent gave nonviolent solution of all conflicts, political and social. This indicated that the majority were not committed pacifists. The remainder chose as their goals a variety of proposals for world government or limited international controls, such as a test ban treaty. As to their reasons for taking part in WSP activities, 28 percent said they had joined the movement because of concern about fallout, testing, and civil defense; another 4 percent were motivated by the Berlin Wall crisis; but 41 percent listed no specific event, just an increasing sense of urgency about

the total world situation and a need to make a declaration of personal responsibility. Elise Boulding, *Who Are These Women?* (Ann Arbor, Mich.: Institute for Conflict Resolution, 1962).

10. For a history of the Woman's Peace Party and the Hague Conference, see Marie Louise Degen, *The History of the Woman's Peace Party* (New York: Garland, 1972).

11. See Benjamin Spock, *The Common Sense Book of Child Care* (New York: Duel Sloan and Pearce, 1945); Lawrence K. and Mary Frank, *How to Be a Woman* (New York: Bobbs Merrill, 1954); and Ashley Montagu, "The Natural Superiority of Women," *Saturday Review*, September 27, 1958, pp. 13–14.

12. Dinnerstein, *The Mermaid and the Minotaur*, pp. 259–262.

13. Commenting on a WSP march at the White House on January 15, 1962, the president told the nation in his regularly scheduled news conference that he thought the WSP women were extremely earnest: "I saw the ladies myself. I recognized why they were here. There were a great number of them. . . . I understand what they were attempting to say; therefore, I consider their message received" (*New York Times*, January 16, 1962). In November 1963, seven of the largest mass circulation women's magazines published an interview with the president regarding women's role in the campaign for nuclear disarmament. He was asked if groups like Women Strike for Peace embarrassed him, and he replied, "Some groups may be more controversial than others but I think they are probably very good too. . . . There is great pressure against peaceful efforts. . . . These women's groups, working for peace and disarmament are very valuable; because they help balance off that pressure" (*Woman's Day* [November 1963], pp. 37–39, 141–142).

14. *Baltimore Sun*, October 29, 1961.

15. Eileen Eagan, *Class, Culture and the Classroom: The Student Peace Movement of the 1930s* (Philadelphia: Temple University Press, 1981), p. 149.

16. *La Wisp* (Swarthmore, Penn.: WSP Document Collection, Swarthmore College Peace Collection, November 1962), p. 9.

17. *Vancouver Sun*, December 14, 1962.

18. Russell Baker, "The Ladies Turn Peace Quiz into Greek Comedy," *Detroit Free Press*, December 16, 1962.

19. *Liberation* (December 1966), p. 33.

20. I. F. Stone to National Office, Women Strike for Peace, Washington, D.C., reprinted in *MEMO* (Special Commemorative Issue) (Swarthmore, Penn.: WSP Document Collection, Swarthmore College Peace Collection, April 1970).

21. "Testimony of Mrs. Phyllis Schlafly, Fairmont, Alton, Illinois," *Hearings Before the Committee on Foreign Relations, United States Senate, Eighty-Eighth Congress.* (Washington, D.C.: U.S. Government Printing Office, 1963), p. 906.

THIRTEEN

Seneca Women's Peace Camp
Shapes of Things to Come

RHODA LINTON _____

In the spring of 1983, when I heard that antimilitarist activity by women at the Seneca Army Depot might be planned, I knew I would participate. My only prior involvement with women's peace activity was the two-day 1981 Women's Pentagon Action (WPA) in Washington, D.C. At that event, I was so struck by its difference in method from other demonstrations I had attended that, collaborating with a friend, I wrote about it in an article published in *Socialist Review* in 1982.[1] I also knew that my interest was in the *women's practice* more than in the substance of the cause—stopping deployment of the Euromissiles that the depot was strongly suspected of harboring (a suspicion that has since been confirmed).

As I live only twenty-five miles from the encampment, I could easily maintain involvement. But this proximity has also made participation difficult, given that mine is a small rural township very similar to Romulus, the village in which the encampment is situated. Negative feelings about the encampment have run very high in these villages, and my work and personal relationships have been affected. Four generations of my family live in my town, including my parents, siblings, nieces and nephews, and grandnieces and grandnephews. As far as I know, no one in my family has ever had positive feelings toward the encampment, with the exception of my mother. But she had difficulty maintaining a positive interest as the media image of the camp participants began to shift from sincere but harmless, naive, female peaceniks to traitors and Communists, crazy witches, perverted lesbians. The steady escalation of purposeful illegal actions (civil disobedience) also caused

239

an erosion of my mother's belief that this happening was a good thing. My participation in the Ithaca Women's Affinity Group civil disobedience action at the big August 1, 1983, demonstration, which was duly noted in an article on the front page of the local newspaper, contributed to the town's hostility toward me.

During the weeks of summer 1983, I felt a constant anxiety that intermittently surfaced as fear for my physical safety. Indeed, I usually went alone to the camp for evening general meetings and then participated in actions at the main gate that followed the meetings. Being stopped by police patrols on the way to or from the encampment after dark, although never anything but friendly, added to the anxiety/fear. I was usually a woman alone in the car, and I never knew until the last moment, when the red lights started flashing, that the fast-approaching headlights in the rearview mirror were those of police rather than of pickup trucks filled with Veterans of Foreign Wars (VFW) members out to harass women from the camp.

Many people at work approached me with what were, from their perspective, reasonable questions and (mainly) reservations about whether anything good could come out of such an outrageous effort. Maybe we were "only hurting our cause" by choosing this place, or having a women-only camp, or using *civil disobedience* as a tactic. I had trouble replying in a civil fashion to such comments because most people were only able to perceive a small part of what was going on. Unless I made a huge effort all the time, I couldn't convey enough about what I saw as the reality. I often gave up in frustration and even took to staying away from work because it was too much to have to "justify" myself day in and day out about something so important to me.

At the same time, I felt very nourished by and excited about the experience I continued to have during my time at the encampment, especially as new ways of living together and of carrying out our social change work constantly unfolded in front of my eyes and ears and mind and heart. This high level of awareness, this constant fear and hope and joy and frustration, this anxiety and anticipation, frame what I have learned from this experience.

When I wrote about the methodology of the 1981 WPA demonstration in Washington, I did so strictly as a participant uninvolved in its planning or preparation. I saw and felt the effect of feminist theory on organized political practice. As a long-term local participant at Seneca, although by no means a central figure, I have seen the internal workings of the encampment as well as its external effects, both locally and further abroad, on myself and others. This provides me with a much richer view; but this very complexity makes description and analysis more problematic, particularly when I attempt to describe various parts of the dynamic while keeping the whole in the forefront. The parts out of context, without the whole, lose their power.

The Women's Encampment: Theory, Practice, and Goals

As an "ongoing demonstration," the Women's Encampment for a Future of Peace and Justice (WEFFPJ)[2] intentionally incorporates into its "permanent protest" (a term used about the Greenham Common Women's Peace Camp in the film *Carry Greenham Home*) a *reaction* to our militaristic society and a *proactive*, visioning approach to the camp's ends and its means. The effort of the WEFFPJ to envision, create, and practice new ways for individuals to live in the world, while directly and constantly addressing the U.S. contribution to the threat of nuclear annihilation of that world, is an especially fertile context for investigating the relationship between theory and practice. At the camp, theory is examined through practice—that is, through the interaction of structure and process. Practice often demands a decision a minute at times, whether or not the theory is complete and in place. In such settings, theory is revealed through the immediate action taken. In fact, such practice forces theory to emerge. We may sometimes be horrified by the theoretical meanings revealed, but this process does make visible our contradictions and push us to decipher and face the meanings of our actions. This process also provides us with an immediate context in which to change our practice, to see where our theory doesn't work, and to try fitting theory and practice more closely. This is clearly articulated in the WEFFPJ *Resource Handbook's* introduction.

> The women's encampment is an action to bring women together to protest the Cruise and Pershing II missiles. It is inspired by the women's peace camp at Greenham Common, England, and those protesting all over Europe. Women from all parts of the United States and a variety of backgrounds will gather in a large outdoor camping area to say No to war and Yes to life. We will conduct workshops on such topics as racism, sexism, social and economic justice, non-violence, homophobia, women's history, feminism, military conversion and conflict resolution. We will explore our common ground and difference as women of color and white women, as lesbians and straight women, as differently abled women, and as old and young women.
> There will be protests and civil disobedience actions at the depot throughout the summer. AUGUST 1st HAS BEEN CHOSEN FOR A LARGE ACTION INCLUDING A NON-VIOLENT CIVIL DISOBEDIENCE ACTION.[3]

In its broadest sense, Seneca's goal was envisioned as saying "No to war and Yes to life." This goal took two specific forms: to stop deployment at the depot of Cruise and Pershing II missiles, which was scheduled for fall 1983, and to create an alternative way of living based on women's experiences. These goals required for their realization a *living structure* that could initiate specific processes and produce specific results, both internally (processes for living that would produce a feminist, nonviolent governance system for the camp) and externally (processes for creating and staging nonviolent acts of confrontation of the military at the Seneca Army Depot). The results were purposefully structured protest demonstrations at the same place during a long period of time and the connection of these direct actions with new ways to govern ourselves in community (that is, building the operating structure through which the action is accomplished).

The tension created by the interaction between direct confrontation and community governance has a trampoline effect; ideas jump on and change in shape and dimension. Combining diverse women's experiences with such structural aspects as varying lengths of stay, size of groups, varying capabilities and expertise, particular interests, goals, approach, open group process, and joint community maintenance tapped individual difference to create a fabric strengthened by its many and diverse origins— a crazy quilt existence. One of the many strong chants heard frequently at Seneca expresses it like this:

We are the old wimmyn
We are the new wimmyn
We are the same wimmyn
Stronger than before![4]

The learning that takes place in this exposure to difference, which is not a common feature of most women's lives in this society of divisions, thrills and energizes individuals, cracks open thinking and attitudes, pushes back the boundaries of women's limiting horizons. I think this internal effect is one of Seneca's most important contributions to feminist method.

The Governance System

Two aspects of the camp's beginnings—the operating structure and the decisionmaking process—shaped the fundamental nature of the endeavor. Both relate to the governance system as it was visioned and as it evolved.

The operating structure—that is, an ongoing demonstration—made possible a new level of direct action, with both planned and unplanned consciousness-raising activity. The structure gave rise to external products (constant confrontation at the depot, attempts at community "outreach," media coverage, publicizing of the existence of the camp through women's networks, and so on) and internal organizational development (decisionmaking structure, innovative group processes including the incorporation of the affinity group as an integral structural unit, changing expectations about present and future ways to live, ways for participants to take responsibility for exchange of information and so on).

The decisionmaking process as it had evolved by the time of the official closing of the camp in early September 1983 (after two months of peak operation, including the August 1 mass demonstration in which three thousand women participated) grew out of the operating structure. The interaction of the two aspects provided the thread that bound them together even as they collided and emerged in new forms.

Barbara Deming describes an experience she had at the camp when there were 3,000 women there that embodies this complex interaction.

> What most moved me was the fact that in spite of the differences among us, and in spite of our numbers, and in spite of the fact that our population kept shifting—new women arriving all the time, others having to leave, the small staff and a few stubborn volunteers the only long-term inhabitants—the commitment was to making decisions by consensus. And this process was not abandoned. . . . Ways kept being found to enable this [real listening] to happen. More and more of these ways need to be invented—and are being invented.[5]

She tells of one specific meeting called to decide "whether in encounters with the press and with people from the surrounding towns we should try to play down the fact that many of us were lesbians."[6] This was one of the most volatile issues to camp members and to local people. The meeting started out with hard-line opposing views and consensus seemed unlikely. But acting on the suggestion of a participant to break into smaller circles of like opinion, including a middle-ground group, and create a circle within a circle, each group taking its turn, the discussion proceeded.

> Without fear of judgement now, because speaking with those with whom we felt most at ease (sic)—while the others listened in. And so speaking more deeply than before. When we formed one large circle again, the talk was no longer strained. . . . And consensus, to the astonishment of all, I think, was reached easily.
> . . . I remember especially of the final round of this meeting the look on the face of a neatly-dressed church woman—as she told us that she'd never before given any thought to the subject of lesbians or

homophobia. "But," she said, "I do want to open myself to new thoughts." I think that the form we had chosen for this meeting had helped her to want just that. The look on her face was a look of grave surprise.[7]

The entire encampment was governed by a set of "respected policies." Respected policies were presented to newcomers, along with other information, in an orientation handout. As of an early handout (July 22, 1983), the policies were listed as follows:

Respected policies have been reached by consensus in the national planning committee meetings (before the encampment opened and/or at general meetings here. They were arrived at after much discussion. Please, if you have concerns, find out the history of the decision. As of 7/22, they stand.

1. This is a WOMEN'S ENCAMPMENT. Children are welcome although conditions may be rough, and boys up to age 12 are welcome. Men are welcome in the reception area only and are invited to do support work off the land.
2. The Women's [sic] Encampment for a Future of Peace & Justice is committed to support nonviolent actions of both a legal and illegal nature. The guidelines for nonviolent actions as stated in the handbook are respected policy.
3. The land was purchased to create a safe and legal emcampment [sic] and we are committed to trying to keep it safe and legal.
4. We respect the Earth and the land and resources which make up our encampment. Therefore:
   * We recycle trash by placing it in properly desiganted [sic] containers.
   * Cigarette butts, which are plastic, need to be put in butt cans or regular trash cans, not on the ground.
   * We gather only dead wood for firewood.
   * We use designated paths to avoid unnecessary compacting of soil.
   * We conserve water.
5. The camp is everyone's responsibility. Women's work energy, whether physical, spiritual, emotional or rational, is needed for smooth running of our camp.
6. For our safety and the earth, FIRES in designated fire pits only. Please make sure all fires are completely out because it has been a very dry summer. Fires should never be left unattended. Coleman stoves are only to be used in kitchen area.
7. The refrigerators in the house are for staff and medical use only. Cold storage pits are back near the kitchen area.
8. Read the handbook. It contains information which will help us all.
9. Anybody taking photographs or taping should ask subjects if they mind first.

10. Shirts should be worn between the barn and the street and at the first set of sinks (where we are visible from the road) and when women are working on the pavillion roof or over by where the Amish family's property where there are no trees (where we might insult them).

11. Actions should not be taken on the depot's back fence where it adjoins our land as this might endanger the safety or legality of other women on the land.

12. As a rule, we will take only quiet actions at the depot's front gate after 5 P.M. This is to avoid alienating people who live near the gate and cannot sleep with our noise. Exceptions can be made for special actions and these should be brought up at a general meeting beforehand.

13. – The consumption of alcohol is restricted to Amazon Acres (anytime) and Heartland only after 9 P.M.
    – No smoking at general meetings. Smoking or no smoking in small meeting and other workshops will be determined by group consensus.

14. We do have a resolution to the flag issue: that is, we encourage any women who wants [sic] to create a personal statement to do so by putting her message on a piece a [sic] material not larger that [sic] a pillowcase. we [sic] arrived at this resolution to support the diversity of women at the encampment.

15. 13 hugs a day, minimum. (Staff need more.)[8]

This list of governing policies reflects the diversity of women's voices in the camp. Some of the most complex issues come from a rising collective feminist consciousness. For example, how to relate to men is reflected by (1), both in setting an upper age limit after which male children cannot stay on the land and in setting geographical limits on the presence of men at the same time as inviting their support in specific ways. Additionally, what is known as the "bare breast" question, the policy referring to the wearing of shirts in (10), includes an extensive range of issues connected to the sexual objectification of women, including the double standard revealed by the freedom men have to be bare chested in public and the constraints on women not to be, on the threat of being arrested for "lewd and lascivious behavior."[9] Both issues have special significance for lesbians, many of whom, struggling to raise male children, find their exclusion at a certain age counterproductive and, struggling to establish their own place in a predominantly homophobic society, find these constraints and their implications insulting and out-rageous.

Other policies appear that, although representing serious ecological concerns (for example, [4] and [6]), sound as if they might have come from a signboard at the local state park or, more likely, from women's old and beloved Girl Scout manuals. The respected policies are a wonderful representation of the things that we know from past everyday life, things we have learned as women in this historical era, and things we are striving to know. The latter is evident in (2), (3), and (11), which concern ways to combine safe, legal and illegal, nonviolent approaches, and in (9), (12), (13), and (15), which address conscious respect for others. The attention to difference among women is made explicit in (14), which categorically states that the resolution of "the flag issue" (to be described) is intended "to support the diversity of women at the encampment." This mixed document, then, elicits mixed reactions—some of it is somewhat prissy and hardly begins to indicate anything new; yet the very mixture is new. This putting together of the old and the new is one of the camp's unique contributions to feminist method.

WORK WEBS AND DAILY SCHEDULE

One aspect of the operating structure planned for the summer program included the formation of work webs (all women were expected to contribute three hours of work per day) and a general daily schedule. According to the orientation handout, the work webs were security, garbage/recycling, child care, food prep, dinner cleanup, greeters reception, garden, healing/emotional support, office/clerical, general maintenance/construction, media, and process.

Work webs, which had "weavers" to keep some continuity (women who provided a coordinating function but who rotated the function to avoid unintentional leadership creation), some of whom were paid staff and others who were staying long periods without pay, met daily at 9 A.M. to decide what work needed to be done and how the group would proceed to do it. At first camp planners hoped that women would attach to only one web for the duration of their stay so that there would be an ongoing core of women to really learn what needed to be done in specific areas and women would have an opportunity to build some skills. But women seemed to prefer trying different jobs, and thus in many cases the weavers were the only continual members of work webs and had more information than others about how the camp really functioned.

Weavers, faced with new workers every day, many of whom preferred to be told what to do and get it over with, felt the limits of their patience taxed, and at times it was much easier to assign tasks. As a result, work webs did not always function by group decisionmaking, and sometimes this system became a burden on the energy and momentum of other camp activities. For example, the functioning of the work webs was affected by the number of women living at the camp at a given time.

Fewer women staying at the camp, for example less than fifty, did not reduce the need for twenty-four-hour-a-day security coverage. But with less than fifty women, almost everyone had to volunteer to do frequent security shifts. I remember some general meetings in which all of us at the meeting held ourselves hostage until enough women volunteered to do security and put their names on the security clipboard (sign-up sheet). This functioned to take the spirit out of actions planned to follow the general meeting.

Other daily planned activities included racism workshop at noon on the dome tent; orientation for newcomers and other visitors at 2 P.M. on the front lawn; and general meeting at 7 P.M. after the evening meal. The general meeting was more often than not followed by an action at the main gate (we usually walked about a mile along a two-land road, through the village of Romulus, to the main gate and back the same way after an action). One other regular session was a twice-weekly offering of civil disobedience training from 10 A.M. to 4 P.M. on Tuesdays and Saturdays. All regular sessions were increased in number as needed— for example, extra civil disobedience training, as well as peacekeeper training, was done prior to major actions. Extra orientation sessions could be held for large groups arriving after 2 P.M. Once, when a group of about forty women and men on a bicycle trip from Buffalo arrived, they were given a special orientation, and another time when two big buses pulled up on the road in front of the camp and more than one hundred women and children, who had been riding for two days from Minneapolis, piled out, amid great excitement, they were given a special welcome and orientation on the front lawn.

In addition to the regular planned activities, there were one-time planned activities and/or theme times. The August 1 mass demonstration was one example, as was the planning of special events, such as participation in the opening of the National Women's Hall of Fame and Convention Days in nearby Seneca Falls, which included a parade and an event called "The Faces and Phases of Women"; a day's walk along the Underground Railroad as part of a weekend focusing on women of color; a weekend for "Women of Faith"; and a week focusing on "International Links in the Peace Movement."[10] Although not an activity per se, the bulletin board (BB) was an integral, planned part of the operating structure's internal communication system. Women learned to check the BB between meetings as all current information, including planned and unplanned activities, as well as any messages from or to individuals were posted there by everyone with anything to say. The BB was, in effect, the regular "camp crier." In addition, during emergency situations (either of individuals, groups, or the entire camp), camp members would volunteer or be recruited to verbally carry necessary immediate messages throughout the various areas of the camp.

Although some structure was planned prior to the existence of the camp, it also evolved along with the camp as a direct result of the commitment to open participation and decisionmaking, a unique and crucial feature. I use the term *unplanned* to indicate the aspects not specific to the original plan, but in one sense nothing could be truly unplanned because part of the plan was to provide a place and way of being where any and all women could bring their "energies, ideas, skills, experience and knowledge"[11] and merge them into the camp. "Your activities will be ongoing with other planned actions, including leafletting, vigilling, local outreach, and civil disobedience. . . . Spontaneity is encouraged and last minute programming will be entered as time permits. However, advanced scheduling is recommended and appreciated."[12] Part of the plan was to provide time and space for the *unplanned*. These two categories, planned and unplanned, can be used to distinguish the parts of the camp that were in place from the beginning and those that were created as the camp evolved.

The operating structure was a semipermanent framework for camp life governed by some general and some specific policies; that is, although a general structure was planned and in place, there was a lot of freedom to change it on an ad hoc basis. In general, this operating structure provided a community governance system within which an amazingly smoothly running group life took root and flourished. In fact, the relative lack of disaster amid chaotic conditions was a definite measure of the system's viability and potential for other settings.

Some of the same features that were the foundation of the structure's creative success, of course, also made it difficult to sustain. For example, by summer's end, the interaction of the process and the structure resulted in one of the camp's most agonizing debates—whether the camp should continue as a permanent structure. This question, which undoubtedly entailed the most conflicting and painful process, clearly stretched the endeavor to the limit. Many individuals were pushed past the breaking point, causing them to leave the group. The type of decisionmaking process and the women's capacity for innovation based on need—which included endless individual go-rounds, careful attention to feelings via the use of group meeting "vibes" watchers, and intentional release of tension through such mechanisms as circling, silence, singing, dancing, and "rage circles"—made such discussions possible and, eventually, productive. The following is a description of this decisionmaking process and its evolution during summer 1983.

DECISIONMAKING

Consensus was viewed by the women who planned the camp as the ideal decisionmaking process from the beginning of the formulation of the WEFFPJ. Such decisionmaking was considered one aspect of a nonviolent approach to social change. References in the *Resource Handbook* to other groups using nonviolence—including Mahatma Gandhi in South Africa and India; women's suffrage in Britain; the labor, civil rights, and anti–Vietnam War movements in this country—connected the camp's approach to other political struggles.[13] Many feminists identified this process with their experiences in consciousness-raising groups, and other women, who came with experience as religious pacifists and as participants in other peace movement organizations, had long histories of using the consensus process.

The formal procedures used at the encampment were described in the *Resource Handbook,* and an overall view of the process was outlined as follows:

> The fundamental right of consensus is for all people to be able to express themselves in their own words and of their own will. The fundamental responsibility of consensus is to assure others of their right to speak and be heard. Coercion and trade-offs are replaced with creative alternatives, and compromise with synthesis.[14]

If an individual could not support a specific decision, the consensus process provided several ways to express objections, which were:

> *Nonsupport* ("I don't see the need for this, but I'll go along.")
> *Reservations* ("I think this may be a mistake but I can live with it.")
> *Standing aside* ("I personally can't do this, but I won't stop others from doing it.")
> *Blocking* ("I cannot support this or allow the group to support this. It is immoral." If a final decision violates someone's fundamental moral values they are obligated to block consensus.)
> *Withdrawing from the group*

> Obviously, if many people express non-support or reservations or stand aside or leave the group, it may not be a viable decision even if no one directly blocks it. This is what is known as a "lukewarm" consensus and it is just as desirable as a lukewarm beer or a lukewarm bath.

> If consensus is blocked and no new consensus can be reached, the group stays with whatever previous decision was on the subject [known as a "fallback position"][15]

The roles needed to conduct this process and the tasks of the people who filled them were:

1. Facilitator—aided the group in defining decisions that need to be made, helped group members through the stages of reaching an agreement, kept the meeting moving, focused discussion to the point at hand, made sure everyone had the opportunity to participate, and formulated and tested to see if consensus had been reached. Facilitators helped to direct the process of the meeting, not its content.
2. Vibes watcher—someone besides the facilitator who watched and commented on individual and group feelings and patterns of participation.
3. Recorder—took notes on the meeting, especially of decisions made and means of implementation.
4. Timekeeper—kept things going on schedule so that each agenda item could be covered in the time allotted for it (if discussion ran over the time for an item, the group might or might not decide to contract for more time to finish up).

All members of the group were also reminded that

even though individuals take on these roles, all participants in a meeting should be aware of and involved in the issues, process, and feelings of the group, and should share their individual expertise in helping the group run smoothly and reach a decision. This is especially true when it comes to finding compromise agreements to seemingly contradictory positions.[16]

The *Resource Handbook* also specified the group member attitudes needed for the consensus process.

Responsibility: Participants are responsible for voicing their opinions, participating in the discussion, and actively implementing the agreement.
Self-discipline: Blocking consensus should only be done for principled objections. Object clearly, to the point, and without putdowns or speeches. Participate in finding an alternative solution.
Respect: Respect others and trust them to make responsible input.
Cooperation: Look for areas of agreement and common ground and build on them. Avoid competitive, right/wrong, win/lose thinking.
Struggle: Use clear means of disagreement—no putdowns. Use disagreements and arguments to learn, grow and change. Work hard to build unity in the group, but not at the expense of the individuals who are its members.[17]

The *Handbook* described further procedures for dealing with consensus decisionmaking in large groups, including randomly breaking down into small groups for discussion of proposals, relaying questions for clarification through a spokesperson, regathering as a whole to see what issues of disagreement had emerged, and continuing this cycle until consensus was reached. The *Handbook* suggested that representing conflicting opinions in the small groups would enable a full discussion to take place.

THE FLAG ISSUE

Within the context of this decisionmaking procedure, women of the encampment conducted their everyday communal life. Many members were familiar with the procedure and its flow and brought innovative features to its use, such as when raising her hand to be recognized to speak, a woman would indicate, by raising one finger, that she wanted to make a point about process and, by raising two fingers, that she wanted to address the issue under discussion. Of those women who were unfamiliar with consensus, many made great efforts to learn and use it; others who were unaware of the process, and who did not read the *Handbook*, operated in a variety of decisionmaking modes. Very early in the summer, however, the decisionmaking process was tested in a unity-defying case known far and wide as "the flag issue." Before the opening ceremonies on July 4, a local man offered to give a U.S. flag to the camp to be flown in some conspicuous location—similar to the displaying of flags throughout the local village and town. This man's motivation was questioned but quickly became irrelevant as the camp began to deal with a decision about whether to fly the flag. This decision revealed the camp's underlying philosophy regarding such basic issues as the politics of national versus international governance, the place of patriotism, and the role of citizenship. We could hardly have conceived of a more volatile or controversial issue, yet no one had anticipated either the immediate explosive emotional and political response or the endlessly negative repercussions to the camp both internally and externally.

Time to theorize leisurely about the issue did not exist; a decision had to be made. Being in a practice setting meant that action was required, whether the participants were sure what they did was "correct" and "consistent with our theory" or not. Many hours of discussion by a huge group of women led to the development of a new process by which debate was delegated to small subgroups representing the two basic positions, with a third subgroup of women who saw both sides and could attend to the process needs of the ongoing discussion group.

Through this process a solution was reached that incorporated both sides of the debate—all women were encouraged to make flags from all nations, including the United States, not to exceed the size of a pillowcase. These flags could then be carried in marches and be flown, en masse, from "clotheslines" tied among the many trees on the front lawn of the camp. I remember seeing a friend of mine from Sweden as she sat among many U.S. women in the backyard on the day of the opening of the camp joining in the creation of colorful communication of the unified spirit of the day. This decision also inspired some women to spend long hours during the next month creating a fantastically beautiful set of flags of all nations, which were carried in the mass march on August 1.

The women did not have the luxury of stopping everything they were doing to deal with this crisis. When the whole group could not come to consensus, another way to carry on the process had to be found in order to free up most of the women to continue the ongoing maintenance of camp life. This situation produced an innovative solution.[18] Resolutions in form (creation of a new process) and in content (decision about a specific substantive issue) were arrived at as a matter of necessity. This necessity pressured the group with a time limit within which to sort out the pros and cons of the position and produced a process that allowed women to enlarge their understanding and to take new positions.

The flag experience brought everyone close together by succeeding at reaching a solution that represented a new view of the issue itself (that is, the U.S. role in the worldwide arms race and commitment to global citizenship) and by developing and learning to use a new decisionmaking technique, to conceive a new possibility. The group also was able to take this initiative action on its own terms instead of reacting to external demands (for example, fear of social disapproval and reprisal in the local area). Unfortunately, the media either did not, or chose not, to understand this resolution and continued to sensationalize the issue by saying the women refused to fly the U.S. flag. This, of course, fed local citizens' beliefs that we were all Communists and thickly in cahoots with the USSR.[19] Because of this public view of "the flag issue," a great deal of energy was expended on a continuing basis, both internally and externally, to clarify the decision and action.

PROBLEMS WITH THE PROCESS

Although there was a commitment to open decisionmaking by those present at the time as a basic ideological and practical tenet, several events brought out the feeling that it somehow seemed wrong for whomever happened to be passing through, many for very short periods of time, to determine the fundamental philosophy of the camp or to set precedents that could quickly drain the at-that-time meager and uncertain coffers.

At one time a woman, traveling in her car near the camp, was stopped by the police for some reason. She was taken to jail because she could not immediately produce the proper vehicular documents. It seemed a clear case of harassment of a peace camp member by local authorities. Women at the camp at the time, notified by the camp crier, immediately called a meeting and decided they wanted to provide her with bail money. In this urgent situation, in which no policy existed, the question of accountability between individuals and the peace camp quickly spilled over into debate about taking responsibility for our sisters, declarations about commitment to sisterhood, and the real implications of the peace camp.

Around the same time, some women from the camp were arrested for nudity at a local public beach. This occasioned another emergency need for bail money and another discussion about camp policy on individual-organizational accountability. As far as I know, both emergency situations were resolved by taking up collections from those women present at the time. But this resolution allowed the structural and process questions raised to remain unresolved.

BIRTH OF THE PROCESS WEB

As a result of incidents such as these, which arose frequently, a new work group was formed called the process web. This web's job was to figure out how to address the various questions raised during the operation of the camp. The process web constructed the decisionmaking flowcharts in Figures 13.1 and 13.2. These can be useful as documentation of the developing camp governance system. The development of the process web started during a long meeting during the week directly following the opening of the camp[20] and was in effect as early as July 22, 1983. Although there is no date on these charts, I was at the camp at least twice weekly during that period and first saw them on the pavillion bulletin board on August 26, 1983.

Figure 13.1 indicates who made which decisions as well as what the entire structure of the operation looked like. This figure includes who was involved at what level and an identification of off-land components. Questions/issues that arose were decided by those units of participation directly affected (A–F). With the exception of nonemergency hiring and firing and nonemergency long-term policy, all other decisions were made either by camp participants only or, as in the case of policy additions and deletions, in combination with the regional extended-family meeting.

8-26-83

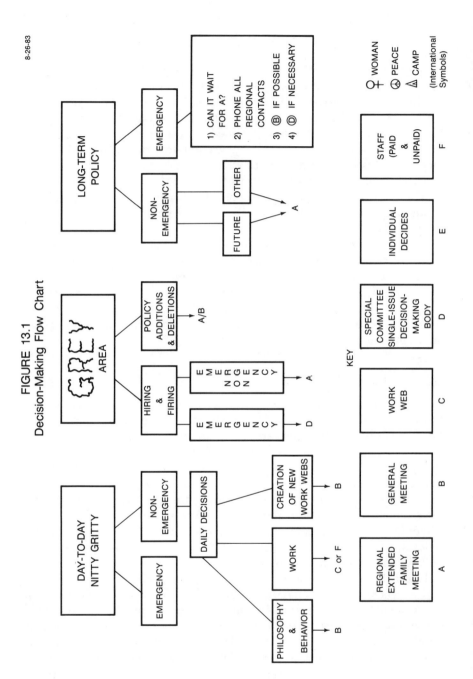

FIGURE 13.1
Decision-Making Flow Chart

FIGURE 13.2
The
Decision-Making
and
Process Web
Bulletin Board

THERE IS A LOGBOOK OF
ALL DECISIONS THAT
HAVE BEEN MADE AFTER
AUG _____ KEPT IN OFFICE
IN THE HOUSE.

FINANCIAL DECISIONS

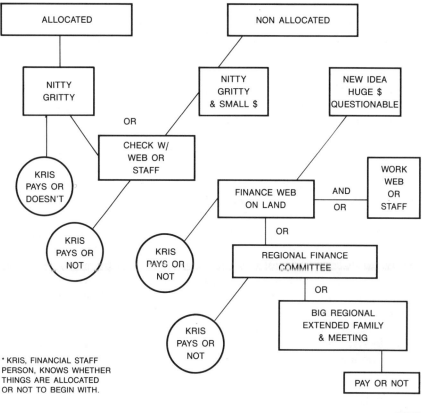

* KRIS, FINANCIAL STAFF
PERSON, KNOWS WHETHER
THINGS ARE ALLOCATED
OR NOT TO BEGIN WITH.

8-26-83

According to the figure, with the exception of the gray area, no resolution was advanced as to who would make emergency decisions, whether day to day or long term. An apparent resolution about the issues described previously, however, does appear in the figure; that is, the general meeting (B) was designated as the appropriate unit to make "daily decisions" about day-to-day, nitty gritty philosophy and behavior. This resolved the conflict between those women at the camp for short periods, who believed in their right to be involved in decisions that affected the camp's attitudes or philosophical position, and those women who either were involved in the planning and the original vision or who were involved as long-term residents.

Unfortunately, although the figure identifies the individual woman as a camp unit (E), it fails to include information as to when the individual (E) decides anything on her own.[21] According to the figure, as decisionmakers women were a collective presence, not individuals. A curious omission in the designation of participating units is the affinity group, especially given that it was an integral part of the structure of ongoing life at the camp, indeed, even the *basic* unit of many direct actions. These characteristics indicate that the conception of the camp as a whole unit, with centralized administrative responsibility for overall management, set the scene for participants to relate to its maintenance as individuals but to relate to its decisionmaking processes as members of groups. The only exception to this shown in the figure is the staff. For example, women joined workshops or work webs as individuals. Women could join actions, however, as individuals or as members of affinity groups.

An interesting example of another kind of participating unit, which didn't occur often but could be built on in the future, was the large preorganized group, such as the one hundred plus women and children who came together from Minnesota. This group came for a week prepared to fit into the camp's structure on three levels: as individuals, who could choose to attend workshops of their choice, to sign up for work webs, and so on; as affinity group members, who had actions planned for small units as well as actions planned in which they hoped all women at the camp would join; and as a total unit, as the women from Minnesota who came to share, to learn, and to return home to enrich their local struggle with Seneca experience. They created a women's peace camp on the doorstep of Sperry Rand.

FINANCIAL DECISIONMAKING

Figure 13.1 indicates that the decisionmaking body with the broadest powers was the camp general meeting, with full authority in the area of day-to-day life, including philosophy and behavior (except work plans) and emergency hiring and firing, plus potential for policy additions and deletions. The figure does not, however, address situations in which such questions were connected to finances. One issue in which philosophy and finance frequently converged in general meetings was that of support for Greenham. I remember several times when women visiting from

Greenham spoke of the situation there and asked for money to be sent in support. Sometimes a can would be passed around immediately, and sometimes there would be discussion about formalizing some way to send money from "the camp." Usually there was confusion in such discussion because those who did not know about the financial structure of the camp wanted just to decide in the present group meeting to authorize money to be sent to the sisters who inspired us. Attempts at explaining financial decisionmaking were often received in such group discussions as anti-Greenham or as evidence of bureaucratic, male, establishment ways of operating.

According to Figure 13.2, financial decisions followed a pattern of their own. Allocated funds (by whom was not mentioned) were automatically dispersed by a designated staff person. She, together with web workers or other staff, could also decide to spend "nitty gritty & small $" from nonallocated funds. Although the existence of "or" in several connecting links lent some uncertainty, it appears that the only other financial decisions made on the land were about other nonallocated funds decided either by the finance web or that web plus another work web and/or staff person. All other financial decisions about non-allocated funds were made by women in the Regional Finance Committee, the members of which might or might not be on the land at any given time, or by meetings of the Regional Extended Family, which were generally held on the land on a frequent but not regular basis during summer 1983.

This connection of philosophy and finance, as for example in the entry "new idea, huge $, questionable," was the volatile combination that produced the debate about whether the encampment should continue after summer 1983. The philosophy question in that debate had to do with vision and purpose, and the finance question had to do with what should be done with a rather large balance that came in toward the end of summer, mainly from the thousands of women who had come to the camp.

The Impact of Decision Process on Organization

Although processes that evolved from decisionmaking during the summer were sorely tested in a seemingly endless number of marathon meetings held throughout the Northeast that fall, I think one methodological result of this effort overshadows all others: that in an organizing effort, the final product (the organization), if it survives, will almost certainly be determined by its initial conception. Many organizers, of course, purposefully manipulate various activities, people, and stages of the organizing effort to accomplish precisely that goal. This did not happen in the WEFFPJ. What was visioned and indeed occurred was a summer during which hundreds of women with many and varied resources to share came from many places to the Seneca Women's Peace Camp to confront the military and to explore living together in new ways.

As summer ended, the focus shifted to a winter of very few women surviving through hard, frigid months with no indoor plumbing and an ever-hungry wood stove, while struggling to reconceptualize the purpose and meaning of the effort. Off-land women within driving distance offered definite, but sporadic, participation and support. I think this defiance of organizing dogma was a result of the camp's original and absolute commitment to open decisionmaking within a nonhierarchical, purposefully pluralist structure. Generally speaking, those women who were involved very early on, in the planning and early stages of fundraising and implementation, many of whom had commitments requiring them to leave the land by September, were more likely to be in favor of closing the camp as it had evolved to that point, a generally undisputed "success." Because their vision was rooted in an open decisionmaking process, however, they did not have control of that decision. In addition, a contradiction inherent in this position was their early decision to sow the seed of permanence through purchase of the land.

Other women, who had become involved as participants on the land and who were free and willing to stay on through the winter in a very different sort of atmosphere, believed the camp should continue to evolve its purpose by remaining open, although no one at that time quite knew what that would mean. But only a few short months before, no one knew what an ongoing demonstration, a permanent protest throughout a whole summer in camp form would mean either. Consensus decisionmaking required a resolution that reflected basic agreement of all participants.

The actual resolution was a compromise that included philosophy and finances. The primary share of the unexpended balance of money was allocated to be redistributed to other peace groups, some of which had helped to raise the money in the first place; and the land, plus a small share of the unexpended balance to be used primarily in improving the house and establishing a fund for land taxes, was allocated to continue the camp. One result was, in effect, a "withdrawing from the group" by many long-term participants, especially those from the large cities and geographically distant areas, from the ongoing camp.

Another contradiction to established organizing experience about the camp regarded the notion that organizations tend to get more bureaucratic the longer they exist. The apparent lack of structure and plan for the winter's activities and beyond, and the philosophy and lifestyles of the women who were free and willing to stay on, which tended more toward anarchism and cultural feminism, were in fact part of the problem for those who questioned the continuation of the camp.

Conclusion

The development of the governance system at Seneca during its first summer of operation represented an exciting social experiment. Its moments of triumph were interspersed with moments of frustration, doubt, and disillusion, but although difficult, and at times even counterproductive, as a living critique of group and community governance, the Seneca camp was a harbinger of something new. The WEFFPJ was clearly a contributor to the emerging outlines of what constitutes commonality in feminist practice. In a women-only context, the camp tests such features as:

- Nonhierarchical governing structure—to move away from the domination/subjugation mode but not into the "tyranny of structurelessness"[22]
- Consensus decisionmaking—to embody the values of every woman's life experience, understanding, and expectation of commitment to group decisions
- Commitment to struggle with alternative modes and processes— to insist on openness to dynamic development through incorporation of "unplanned" activities and major decisions by open participation
- Intentional seeking of diversity and difference—to see diversity and difference as essential components from which to derive an inclusive understanding of women's lives as well as to enrich our experience and knowledge
- Establishment of a specific practice site—to struggle with philosophical and practical issues of on-land/off-land relations in a practice setting

Epilogue: June 1988

The women of Seneca in 1983 set external and internal goals for their work. They intended to confront the U.S. military about its Euromissile policy and to create an alternative way to live based on women's experience. Certainly Seneca women confronted the military. Many will claim that Seneca, as a part of the peace movement worldwide, played a part leading to the signing of the Intermediate-range Nuclear Forces Treaty. Certainly, Seneca women created an alternative way to live based on women's experience. It wasn't smooth, it wasn't easy, and it was only occasionally perfect. In a woman-only context of ever-shifting, often threatening, unfamiliar reality, we struggled to construct a governance system of respected policies, nonhierarchical structures, and open processes through which decisions were made, community work got done, and the military was constantly confronted in a variety of creative and often surprising and joyous ways. We laughed and we wept; we mourned and we cheered. We all learned, got angry, grew, and were frightened, exhausted, and exhilarated.

Women will recognize this as a somewhat exaggerated version of the wholeness of our ordinary existence. I think that Seneca's heightened experience tapped into this level of women's commonality. Experiencing this commonness under unusual circumstances, including explicit commitment to the overriding goals of woman-only community and peace, created time and space to explore, accept, and even love the differences that normally divide us. Can we take Seneca's experience into whatever situation we face? Seneca itself continues to be an example. The women of Seneca of 1988, out of the media focus, unheralded by big names, continue to do important work, not only by building women's community for action at a specific military site but also by communicating information about interconnected injustices to a large network of women in the United States and abroad and to other peace and justice organizations. The governance system that was created in 1983, although adapted to changes in the situation, continues to be the framework for this ongoing demonstration of U.S. women's peace activism.[23]

Notes

1. Rhoda Linton and Michele Whitman, "With Mourning, Rage, Empowerment and Defiance: The 1981 Womens Pentagon Action," *Socialist Review* 12, nos. 3-4 (May–August 1982), pp. 11–36.

2. The very long title chosen for the encampment was often misstated. It has frequently been abbreviated by the media and others to the Women's Peace Camp. Several different references are used here.

3. This statement was made on a leaflet printed in spring 1983 and distributed in upstate New York, with the local contact listed as "Women's Encampment, 150 Castle St., Geneva, N.Y. 14456, (315) 789-8610."

4. Natasha Harmon, *Risking: An Exploration of the Feminist Decision-making Process at Seneca Women's Peace Encampment, Summer 1984* (unpublished paper, Hampshire College, 1985), p. 98.

5. Barbara Deming, *Prisons That Could Not Hold: Prison Notes, 1964–Seneca 1984* (San Francisco: Spinsters Ink, 1985), pp. 202–203.

6. Ibid., p. 203.

7. Ibid., pp. 203–204.

8. Orientation handout.

9. The early identification of the bare breast question was revealing of its fundamental importance as an ideological issue. Controversy among camp participants about the issue was continual and included increasing noncompliance with the respected policy governing behavior related to it. As recently as September 1985, two women were arrested on the land as one part of this controversy.

In a conversation with Madeline Remez about Project Elf, a women's peace camp in Wisconsin, I discovered that bare breasts had also been an issue there. In addition it has been an issue at Sisterfire, a women's multiracial music and cultural festival in Washington, D.C., that is open to men.

10. Summer program leaflet.

11. WEFFPJ letter, May 1983.

12. Ibid.

13. *Resource Handbook* (Romulus, N.Y.: Handbook Committee, Women's Encampment for a Future of Peace and Justice, n.d.), p. 39.

14. Ibid., p. 42.

15. Ibid.

16. Ibid.

17. Ibid.

18. Many thanks to Eva Kollisch for her part in the flag decision and for her conversation with me about it.

19. Frequently, a pickup truck would be parked on the opposite side of the road from the front lawn of the camp, with a big sign put up by local people saying, "Did Moscow buy your farm?"

20. Thanks to Dian Mueller for this information, August 1985, at the encampment.

21. Thanks to Alison Jaggar for pointing this out to me.

22. Joreen, "The Tyranny of Structurelessness," in Anne Koedt, Ellen Levine, and Anita Rapone, eds., *Radical Feminism* (New York: Quadrangle Books, 1973), pp. 285–299.

23. Current information can be received by writing to: Women's Encampment for a Future of Peace and Justice, 5440 Route 9, Romulus, N.Y. 14541, (607) 869-5825.

FOURTEEN

Our Greenham Common
Not Just a Place
But a Movement

GWYN KIRK

Women at Greenham or those involved in the women's peace groups associated with the peace camp have tried to work in supportive ways, sharing tasks, skills, and knowledge; encouraging and caring for one another; respecting each other's ideas and experience; and deciding things together, understanding that the best decisions incorporate everyone's truth. Each person acts from her own sense of responsibility, doing what she can. Together we are a decentralized, nonhierarchical, loosely connected network.

This chapter looks at the Greenham network as a viable political form, the organizational basis for the actions mentioned in Chapter 6.[1] Here I concentrate on principles of nonviolent organization: personal responsibility; the value of diversity; nonhierarchical organization and decisionmaking; communication, coordination, and continuity across a wide network; and the value of flexibility. These are counterparts to the principles of feminist nonviolence I discussed earlier.

Personal Responsibility

A central strand of feminist nonviolence is taking personal responsibility for situations rather than thinking of ourselves as powerless victims without resources. In many situations we have the power to withdraw our support at the very least. Often we can challenge the status quo. For many women, taking the first step is the hardest. Isolated at home or at work, it is difficult to know how to begin and vital to have some way of meeting others who share our opinions. In writing about the march from Cardiff to Greenham Common in 1981, Ann Pettitt stressed how tentative the beginnings were and how the few women who initiated the march "had to overcome feelings in ourselves that we were not the right . . . people to make this thing happen."[2]

Greenham has provided a focus for many women on a day-to-day basis and through major actions such as the massive encirclement of the base on Sunday, December 12, 1982. The idea that there might be enough of us to completely surround the base was really exciting but daunting. We calculated it would take about fifteen thousand women, compared to two hundred who had taken part in the previous blockade nine months earlier. Women at the peace camp wrote to several hundred on their mailing list. Each was asked to copy the letter and send it to ten friends, who would also copy it and send it to ten more, and so on, so that many women were drawn into the organizing. When the task was broken down this way, it became manageable and, in the event, highly successful, for thirty thousand women came.

This method shared the work, the cost, and, crucially, the responsibility. No one wasted time or postage writing to someone she knew would be there anyway or who was not interested at all. We contacted friends who might be interested, to whom a personal invitation would make a difference. Everyone's contribution was important to the success of the action, and this followed through to the form it took. There were no "important" people, no platform, and no speeches. Each woman was asked to bring something representing real life to her, to hang on the fence. Thus, we transformed a military base into a nine-mile celebration of life, a living artwork, personal and very poignant.

At the peace camp each woman does what she thinks is necessary, so there are no rosters or lists of who has to do what. Some women decide to live at Greenham for weeks or months at a time. Others may stay for a few days or visit occasionally, taking part in actions, bringing food, raising money for the camp, publicizing actions through writing or photographs.[3] Women living at the camp decide how to organize things there, sharing food, firewood, sleeping bags, water, plastic sheeting, wire cutters, money, and so on. They ask other women to come to Greenham as self-sufficient as possible, bringing food, water, camping equipment, and plans for what they want to do.

This is very unfamiliar to some people, who exclaim in frustration, "Why don't they *organize* something?" To their great credit, women at the camp have not given in to this demand but have created a space that allows many women to ask instead, "What do *I* want to do?" Some feel alienated and do not return, but others become much more autonomous and effective than they would if they merely followed other people's directives.

Anyone is free to initiate an action, talk it over with friends, set up planning meetings, and so on. Sometimes others will have been thinking along similar lines quite independently. Not everyone will be excited by the idea, and no one has to join in if she would rather do something else. If enough women want to put effort into a particular project, it will happen, but no amount of urging will make it work otherwise.

In this kind of organization there is no rank and file. There are no formal leaders whom the authorities can bargain with or sentence to long periods in prison in the hope that the movement will collapse without them. We are not "demo-fodder," but purposive individuals, our own experts, acting for our own reasons. This both transcends and subverts hierarchical power relations. It contrasts with many would-be radical organizations that create the same anonymous, alienated relations among people as obtain in mainstream society. Any serious change requires a change in organizational structures, a vital point recognized by feminist, anarchist, and green politics in principle, if not always carried into practice.[4]

The Value of Diversity

Greenham has brought together thousands of women, many of whom had never been on a demonstration or voted in their lives. Some look to women's tradition as nurturers and mothers, perhaps with a belief in women's spiritual insight and connectedness to the earth and forces of life. Others reject any definition of themselves as caretakers and see the peace camp as part of a wider opposition to all forms of male violence. Some believe that women have innate good qualities that make them better qualified than men to take up the issue of peace, whereas others feel that if women are less aggressive and more caring, this is due to conditioning and experience. On a tactical level, women's actions force the authorities—the government, the police, and the courts—to deal with women, and many women believe that nonviolent direct action is more likely to stay nonviolent if only women are involved.

This diversity of experience and opinion is a source of great strength and richness as well as contradiction, disagreement, and uncreative friction. Each woman has her point of view and speaks for herself. We have been able to work together without always having complete agreement, and this is worth recognizing. Often what passes for agreement in political work is some lowest-common-denominator solution hammered out through many meetings or a correct line imposed by some subgroup.

This space for individuality has been one of Greenham's great strengths, although women do not always show respect for differences. This may have as much to do with lack of knowledge or thoughtlessness as with a lack of generosity. Sadly, some women criticize and put down others for being strong, capable, or articulate, sometimes even without knowing them. Some Greenham supporters play down the lesbian energy and commitment that have kept the peace camp going, arguing that these will alienate a wider public. Lesbian politics are central to many women living at Greenham, and lesbians want their lives and choices to be respected by other women. At the same time, women who are not lesbians want to participate in this movement and to feel that their choices are also respected. These differences have caused conflict and tension among women active in the Greenham network and sometimes have led to destructive polarization. Each person and all aspects of a project are essential to its success. Sometimes women have lost sight of this and have become very wrapped up in their own past. Arguments inevitably consume precious time and energy and leave women feeling ineffective, exhausted, and demoralized. On the other hand, important differences of opinion cannot be ignored or simply "processed" away.

Most women involved in the Greenham network are white and middle class, but of different ages and backgrounds. Many women of color are critical of Greenham and the women's peace movement generally for our failure to integrate issues of racism and day-to-day survival with antimilitarism.[5] In the summer of 1987 this issue came to a head in a series of bitter arguments. A well-publicized split developed between women at Yellow Gate, together with supporters from the Wages for Housework Campaign (a multiracial organization based in London), and women at the other gates and their supporters.[6] Yellow Gate women claimed an antiracist perspective and condemned others on the Greenham network as racist. Also involved were issues of leadership and who had the right to call herself a Greenham woman.

There is much antiracism work to be done in such a racist society as Britain, and many women recognize this. Some are involved, for example, in protesting the British government's vote in supporting apartheid, uranium mining in Namibia, and police harassment of black people and racist attacks in Britain. Other women participate in campaigns to provide facilities of benefit to women, children, and people of color in inner city areas. In 1985 women from the Pacific challenged the "Eurocentricity" and whiteness of the British women's peace movement and urged us to place ourselves on the side of people of color opposing militarism worldwide. For them, to be nuclear free and independent of imperialist powers are two sides of the same coin. Women Working for a Nuclear Free and Independent Pacific formed as an initiative of the peace camp to publicize and protest the terrible plight of Pacific peoples as a result of atomic tests, the use of native land for military bases, and ocean dumping of nuclear waste by the United States, Britain, Japan, and France.[7] In a relatively short time they have done a lot to educate people on these issues.

Personal attacks and polarized argument, such as have gone on at Greenham regarding the issue of racism, make people angry and defensive. Some women have drifted away. Others have been as active as before, but in an embattled atmosphere hardly befitting a peace camp. Many feel that this issue is crucial but deplore the way it has been raised. (I hope that women will get beyond this polarized situation, which has consumed much time and energy, to begin building the multiracial networks we need.)

A Decentralized Network

Many local Greenham groups formed in different towns and cities during the winter of 1982–1983, inspired by the encirclement action at the base. They support the peace camp by fundraising, publicizing, and arranging child care and transport, so that women from their area can visit or stay at the camp. They also initiate their own actions as well as taking part in actions at Greenham.

Other women's peace groups came together independently of the Greenham network, although probably knowing of its existence. Some started with an informal meeting, perhaps watching Helen Caldicott's video, *Critical Mass*.[8] Small, friendly groups give emotional support and encouragement. They also act as local affinity groups, both independent and part of a wider movement.

In the early years the network grew rapidly, involving thousands of women in Britain. More recently it has decreased in size. There were fewer Greenham groups in 1987–1988 than earlier, and they were generally much smaller. Some groups have been more active than others. Some have had bursts of intense activity for a while, and then the women have moved on to other issues. Meanwhile Greenham has continued to draw in newcomers. At a ten-day action in September 1984, three years after the inception of the peace camp, about ten thousand women camped at the base. Many came from overseas, and many of the British women were also there for the first time. During the years a range of arguments have taken their toll, particularly those about racism and leadership.[9] Many women feel that everything they loved about Greenham has been turned on its head. Some who attended an action at the base on December 12, 1987, felt that they were probably there for the last time, but many women are still in contact with each other either through other projects or informally as friends. And new women have continued to come to Greenham.

The peace camp keeps going because enough women have wanted it. The camp has been a permanent focus, a center of gravity that many women have felt themselves part of, and have contributed to, often in different ways at different times. Some women who have moved on may decide to make the Greenham network their focus again in the future.

To describe this as a loose network, open and flexible, is not to say that it is sloppy or badly organized, as some people think, but very much the opposite. It has tremendous strengths, for it draws on every person's ideas, abilities, and energies. This means that an enormous amount can be accomplished, which is very different from centralized, hierarchical organizations in which a leader or committee decides policy and members are urged to attend monthly meetings, annual conferences, and so on. Many people assume that only real bureaucratic organization is valid and authoritative, yet there is no simple correspondence between formal organization and effectiveness, as the Greenham experience clearly shows.

Nonhierarchical Decisionmaking

A commitment to open, egalitarian ways of working has led women's peace groups to adopt some version of feminist group process in which there is space for everyone to talk and a responsibility to really listen to one another.[10] At the heart of this process is consensus decisionmaking. As each person speaks, everyone's understanding of the issue deepens and the discussion opens up possibilities rather than closing them. We are most used to majority decisionmaking in which we choose between competing options. Those who lose have no place in the final decision. They are under pressure to accept, or at least go along with, the majority view against their own judgment. If they are regularly in the minority their situation is intolerable. In consensus decisionmaking no one side wins; a cooperative decision emerges. Everyone can give herself to the decision. We can all rely on each other to participate in whatever has been agreed. This is very different from polarized argument in which we have an investment in being right. Often there is no right. There are many potential outcomes that would all be good.

A safeguard for an individual who strongly opposes a group decision is to block consensus. The onus is on her to state her reasons for this, and the group as a whole has a responsibility to reopen the discussion. If consensus cannot be reached, the one individual can stop the group going ahead, or she can decide to stand aside.

At times a consensus process can be frustrating, time consuming, and manipulative, with an unfortunate emphasis on technique—reminiscent of the "how to's" and "faultfinders" of a garage manual.[11] There seems to be a cultural difference between Britain and the United States, with much more awareness of, and appetite for, consensus process in the United States. Women's peace groups in Britain have evolved their own specific practices, which are generally based on a modified, looser version of consensus process and are more informal than U.S. women's peace group meetings tend to be. There is less reliance on techniques such as setting time limits and less conscious labeling of processes— brainstorming for example. The downside of this is that discussions may ramble on or shy people will not get much chance to talk, but often the meetings seem much more lively and spontaneous.

The driving forces are each person's energy, commitment, and ideas. The group cannot ultimately block individual initiative. Others can advise and warn, point out that a particular course of action may jeopardize what others are trying to achieve, but they cannot stop anyone doing something she really wants to do. Disagreements are often resolved by doing everything that is suggested rather than by trying to choose one proposal over another. Or women plan different actions, perhaps in parallel.

For instance, in November 1983 a group of women who had met each other at Greenham and done actions together there decided to file a lawsuit in New York against Ronald Reagan and others, trying to challenge the legality of the deployment of cruise missiles at Greenham through the U.S. courts.[12] Many people in Britain and the United States supported this suit, although some women at the peace camp did not. They saw it as a waste of time and money and a distraction from their own focus. They saw no benefit in it either legally or politically. Despite these arguments, a group of twenty women or so decided to go ahead with this court case. They were denied a hearing of evidence in court but were able to speak at hundreds of meetings across the United States and to develop an extensive network of U.S. contacts who have supported the camp in many ways. Again, in September 1985, there was an action at Greenham initiated by London Greenham groups that camp women had opposed several times. Women were invited to come to the fence with blankets, to "blank out" the base, and to use the motif of eyes, either on the blankets or the fence itself, to suggest both our watchfulness and our visions. Some women living at the camp full-time felt impatient with what they thought of as yet another symbolic action and wanted more women to take risks, to be more confrontational, cutting the fence, going onto the base, and so on.[13] The action went ahead because the London groups wanted to do it. Those involved would have preferred to have agreement with women at the camp but were not prepared to give them the power of veto. A third example concerned plans for

December 12, 1985, the sixth anniversary of the decision by the North Atlantic Treaty Organization (NATO) to site cruise missiles in Europe. Many women wanted to do actions in their home areas. Others wanted to go to Greenham. These were both good ideas, and women didn't set them up in opposition to each other. The solution was to do both.

A general problem for feminist organization concerns power and leadership. Many women do not want to create organizations with permanent leadership positions and are loathe to admit that some women sometimes take on leadership roles, if only for a while.[14] At Greenham decisions concerning the camp are made by camp women—those who are living there at a particular time. This means that women who have just arrived or who are staying only for a few days have more say than supporters who have been around for years. This is a good way of keeping decisionmaking processes open, but it implies a hierarchy between camp women and supporters who do not live there regularly. Part of the argument between the two Greenhams mentioned earlier concerned who could call herself a Greenham woman and speak about the peace camp in public. In the early years the distinction between women who lived at the camp and those who supported them but lived at home was played down. The slogan was "Greenham women are everywhere." Greenham was as much a state of mind as a place, and anyone who supported the camp or participated in actions there was free to call herself a Greenham woman. During the summer of 1987 some Yellow Gate women claimed that this designation could only apply to women living at the camp; that it stopped the minute they left; and that only women who had lived there for several years could represent the camp at meetings and conferences or to the press. Other women deeply resented this bid to impose a recognized hierarchy and continue to call themselves Greenham women, being careful to make it clear that they speak for themselves, not as representatives of anyone else.

While rejecting centralized, hierarchical structures, we can find ourselves setting up other kinds of exclusiveness based on strong personalities, women who are very articulate or who have been around a long time, cliques of close friends, or new rituals that become ends in themselves. But people in informal groups are only leaders and only have power over us if we give it to them. No process can provide a safeguard against ego tripping, personality clashes, insensitivity, impatience, or deep differences of opinion. This is what we have to work on, although sometimes people seem to think of a process as if it were a commodity, a *product*, the magic ingredient to make things "work."

Feminist nonviolence means listening and caring, but it does not mean being dishonest, indulging women who are demanding or avoiding a discussion we anticipate will be difficult. We rarely come to this task with the skills we need, a fact all too often brought home when difficulties occur. This leads some women to say we must have a formalized structure and hierarchy. Probably what we do need are fewer romantic assumptions that everything will work out just because we are women. Brought up in hierarchical institutions—families, schools, churches—most of us have no models and very little experience of the kind of organizations we are trying to create. In a decentralized network no one will ever know everything about what is happening or who is involved. As a result, trust that others will do their part is needed. In the event, they may do or they may not, but they certainly won't if we don't let them. They might do something very different, but brilliant, that would never have occurred to us.

Communication, Coordination, and Continuity

To coordinate activities, support and inspire one another, we keep in contact with each other through personal conversations; local, citywide, and regional meetings; newsletters; women's newspapers; and peace movement publications. At Greenham there were public meetings on Sunday afternoons in the early months, and the camp served as a unique clearinghouse for information and ideas, with an important coordinating role for the network as a whole. Camp women send out appeals for things they need and urge women to support those who have to go to court or who get prison sentences. Women keep the base under constant surveillance, day and night, and pass on news of what is happening there, particularly concerning cruise missile convoys. The actual monitoring of the cruise convoys off the base is coordinated by CB radio.

There are no phones at Greenham so all communication with women there must be by letter or by visits in person. A number of people in Newbury and nearby villages have acted as contacts, taking phone messages and passing on information. Between the summer of 1982 and summer 1985 there was a series of six Greenham offices in London, at different addresses, with a new phone number each time, and organized by different groups of women. Most were in women's homes and very modest in scale for a national organization, which in a sense the Greenham network is. Many major actions were organized from these small offices on an entirely voluntary basis.

For many women at the peace camp these London offices became isolated and too exclusively the concern of the women working there. For their part, women in the office often felt that their work and support were misunderstood and unappreciated. Problems of sharing information, knowing who could make what decisions, or who the office represented led to bitter arguments, sometimes crudely characterized as London versus the camp as if they were two opposing monoliths. The solution was for another group to start a new office base, which got around these problems for a while, although at the expense of some continuity and experience. Since then different Greenham support groups have helped women at the camp to get out newsletters and information about upcoming actions.

The main issue that ran through the arguments about the London office was power, although the office work was for the most part neither glamorous nor a source of power. It was humdrum and routine and, like housework, often noticed only when it was not done. But women at the office inadvertently became "spokes*men*" for the camp, for example, simply by being on the end of the phone. Reporters want concise, "authoritative" statements, with a minimum of trouble. Loose, non-hierarchical ways of working are unfamiliar to the press, and it takes reporters time and effort to talk to a range of people, which is sometimes genuinely impractical with tight deadlines. A woman speaking for herself, not as a representative of the camp, is a distinction that reporters simply do not seem to understand or appreciate even when it is spelled out to them. The bind is that refusing to talk, for fear of being misrepresented and called a leader, will only result in no publicity.

The importance of maintaining an organization and of continuing to be a political cutting edge presents a dilemma to any movement. A safeguard against the gradual bureaucratic stagnation that often overtakes would-be radical organizations is to have these periodic changes, with different groups coming together to coordinate actions or put out information from time to time. Energy and creativity keep flowing, although each new group has to learn by experience, starting from scratch each time. Such lack of continuity is anathema to conventional bureaucratic organization, although during a period of time many women participate and learn these skills. What they may lose is a sense of the movement's history. They may simply not know how women organized previous actions or handled difficult issues, although this can be picked up gradually by listening to women talk and through our own documentation—film, videos, photos, and written accounts.[15]

The Value of Flexibility

Change and flexibility are essential elements in this way of working. At Greenham things change all the time depending on the seasons, how many women are there and what they want to concentrate on, what the military is doing, and what is happening on the wider political scene. Usually more women live at the camp during the summer months. Sometimes many have to go to court or are involved in actions in other places. Evictions of the camps usually happen in the morning. Women may get on with something else later in the day—writing an article for a newsletter, cleaning up around camp, talking to friends or visitors—only to drop everything immediately to form an impromptu blockade if they see military vehicles coming out of the base. Women initiate actions and also have to react to the actions of the police and military, sometimes at a moment's notice.

Different organizational mechanisms are adopted as necessary, depending on who is available. In the spring of 1985 a night watch coordinator took on the task of trying to see that women came to do night watch at each gate, keeping the base under observation while women living at the peace camp slept. For several winters a number of women have brought hot meals to the camp everyday so that women there do not necessarily have to cook. There is no paid staff to keep things going. At the peace camp women live on donations, which cover basic expenses. Others support their peace activities however they can—through jobs, savings, or social security payments.[16]

Specific circumstances at Greenham also reinforce a decentralized, flexible organization. If there are enough women, there are camps at each of the seven gates in the nine-mile perimeter as well as at intermediate points between them. Camps cannot see or hear from gate to gate, so these small groups automatically have a degree of independence from each other. Some camps are right on the edge of the road, completely open to view, and women have to deal with anyone who arrives there for whatever reason: day visitors, reporters and press photographers, vigilantes, bailiffs, or police.

Decentralized, nonhierarchical organization is potentially very productive and effective, as the Greenham experience demonstrates. It needs a high level of energy and involvement from participants—putting their ideas into action, maintaining a complex communication network, staying engaged. Such an organization must be fluid and flexible, able to respond to changing circumstances as women come and go or as the authorities change their tactics. The peace camp has survived some bitter arguments during the years but also kept drawing new women in. It has undoubtedly maintained its radical cutting edge, although many women have been burnt out in the process. At the core of this kind of organization is the principle of personal responsibility. This continues to be crucial as women grapple with the issues that confront them and the differences that separate them.

The Importance of Greenham
for Feminist Peace Politics

Women have occupied land outside the base with exceptional tenacity, and exhausting and intense as this process has been, it has been highly effective. They have sustained the peace camp for more than seven years under extremely difficult conditions—a remarkable manifestation of women's determination, courage, and love. Greenham has revitalized ideas about nonviolence, and women's continuous presence outside the gates of the base is a constant challenge to the authorities: subversive from the core out.[17]

The cruise missile deployments outside the base give the peace camp a continuing strength and purpose, but the movement has endured because women are involved in a transformative politics, an attempt to live peace now. They are saying no to the violence of the arms race, but at the same time they are also saying yes to creativity, assertiveness, and community among women.

Living at a peace camp or being closely identified with the women's peace movement carries the stigma of being on the outside. Many women have chosen to give up jobs, education, or even close friendships, but they are supported by a new community. This support and encouragement make a woman feel less vulnerable to the system's punishments and sanctions, although women are often fearful of what might happen to them as a result of their opposition and resistance. But they have chosen not to be intimidated by spurious authority that does not deserve respect or support.

Greenham could end at any time, when women do not want to be there or when the authorities make it impossible for them to stay.[18] At the first eviction in May 1982 and subsequently, many people thought the peace camp was finished—not least perhaps because the newspapers were constantly reporting its supposed demise. But Greenham is a movement, not just a patch of ground, and whatever happens, the experience of the peace camp and the actions will live on in women's lives and networks.

As women we have not been brought up to recognize or act on our power. By living at the peace camp women put *their* concerns first. They set aside other responsibilities and give themselves the opportunity to discover more about who they are and what they can do. No one tells them what to do. Perhaps the hardest thing is to get used to being free from familiar routines and commitments, coming face to face with ourselves. Once past this threshold, women who stay at the camp often radiate a new confidence and strength.

Many things hold us back from taking such a step, and it is harder to take for people who have some stake in the system, some place of privilege to hang on to, however small or illusory. We go along with things, not wanting to make a fuss or stand out, afraid of what people might say or what might happen to us. We prefer to assume that those in power, the government and the military, know better than we do or that opposition is pointless because nothing will change.

Being involved in the Greenham network has been highly politicizing for many women. The peace camp started as a protest against cruise missiles, but women gradually recognized the crucial connections among militarism, poverty, racism, hunger, and unemployment and as a result have worked on many interrelated projects: joining other peace camps outside military bases and weapons factories; networking with women's peace groups in other countries; supporting women prisoners; filing a lawsuit against the U.S. government. They occupied the South London hospital threatened with closure as part of Margaret Thatcher's dismantling of the National Health Service. During the year-long miner's strike of 1984 many Greenham women were involved in Women Against Pit Closures groups. Others are active against apartheid, pornography, violence against women, cuts in welfare programs, U.S. intervention in Central America, uranium mining, nuclear power plants, the transport and dumping of nuclear waste or the stockpiling of food in Western Europe to keep prices high while so many people in the Third World die of starvation. Taken together this adds up to a very broad under-standing of peace.

Greenham has been a transformative experience for many women. To try living out principles of feminist nonviolence demands major changes of us, yet to change in far-reaching ways we need some place or community where we can do it in our own way, at our own pace. Creating such transformative settings is a major problem for feminism. The women's peace movement has flourished during the past seven years in Britain, and the Greenham network has been a recruiting ground for feminism like no other. Many women have come into contact with feminist ideas for the first time. They have learned from each other, found new friends and support networks, perhaps come out as lesbians. Many women have been able to grow and develop, to reassess their priorities, their careers, their relationships. They have literally changed their lives.

Greenham has been a model and inspiration for thousands of people. In Britain there have been peace camps outside other bases and military facilities, outside prisons, on sidewalks and in parks, as a focus for protest and outreach. Greenham has also validated women's organizing in other struggles. During the miner's strike women from coal mining communities said they felt able to take a more active role and organize separately as women following the Greenham example. They organized community kitchens and collected food and basic household items from supporters around the country, which was essential in keeping the strike going for such a long time.

Women have also set up peace camps in Sicily, Holland, Denmark, West Germany, Australia, and the United States (at Seneca, Puget Sound, Savannah River, northern Wisconsin, Minnesota, San Francisco Bay, New York City, and Nevada).[19] Some camps lasted for days, others for months or years. At La Ragnatella (Comiso, Sicily), and Soesterberg and Volgel in Holland, ground-launched cruise missiles were the focus. In Seattle, the Puget Sound Women's Peace Camp protested weapons production at Boeing Corporation. In St. Paul, Minnesota, women opposed Sperry-Univac, a manufacturer of weapons components. The peace camp at Alameda Naval Station, California, started as a protest against sea-launched cruise missiles. At Pine Gap (near Alice Springs, Australia) women focused on U.S. military communications and surveillance facilities. Just as any particular base or factory is only a small part of a global patriarchal culture obsessed with killing, the women's peace camps are part of a feminist opposition to all forms of violence and a feminist support for experiments in cooperative living, caring for each other and the land.

There is no formalized communication among the camps, and the circumstances of each place make each one different. Yet there are similarities, making for a clearly recognizable feminist peace politics. The peace camps are a source of information and inspiration, with a rich culture of songs, poems, celebrations. Women are reclaiming ancient matriarchal symbols and festivals long discredited by the Judeo-Christian tradition, creating visions of a future that is life affirming.

Women's peace camps provide a focus for many women who previously had no clear political "home" and this often in the most unpromising circumstances: out of doors, sometimes in remote locations, or beside very busy highways, in the cold of a Midwest winter or the desert heat. Keeping a peace camp going takes sustained work and enthusiasm from many people. But even as short-term ventures, peace camps bring women together and provide a catalyst for future activities. They are part of an evolving women's political culture and practice and for many women a crucial first step in withdrawing support from a warring patriarchy that cannot sustain itself without women's cooperation—however passive or reluctant—and that so many white, middle-class, Western women in particular are complicit in supporting, if only by our silence. Where women have bought the land, as at Seneca, there is a permanent base for any number of projects.[20] In other situations women's peace groups continue to be active even if the peace camp closes.

Paradoxically, Greenham's success may act as a kind of tyranny, an orthodoxy to be copied by others. In some ways Greenham is unique. Britain is a small, densely populated country with at least 160 U.S. military bases and facilities.[21] The peace camp is close to many towns and two hours from London and is supported by a wide network of people who are both within relatively easy reach and who recognize Greenham as a front line. The majority of British people oppose the deployment of cruise missiles at Greenham and deeply resent Britain's vassal status. The cruise missiles are solely under U.S. military command, ultimately the command of the president.

Not everything that has worked at Greenham is necessarily appropriate elsewhere, although the decentralized organization has great intrinsic strengths. Any authentic political practice must grow out of its time, place, and political culture. It is the spirit of Greenham that matters, taking personal responsibility and saying "No," not merely repeating specific details that may not translate to the vast scale of Australia or the United States or the traditional culture of Sicily.

Widening the Web

We live in very dangerous, yet exciting times. The ongoing escalation of the nuclear arms race and the economic systems that perpetuate it are an outrage, controlled by a few rich, white, middle-aged men and their faceless corporations. Never have women's creativity, resistance, and understanding of life been needed more. Our challenge is to continue finding ways to grow, expressing our opposition, building our own networks, affirming our various visions, and keeping our politics *alive*.

The theme of a major action at Greenham in December 1985 was the widening web, making links through workshops and discussions with women struggling for peace and freedom in different ways throughout the world. This time they turned their backs on the base. Three years earlier women first encircled the base. In December 1983 forty thousand women came to Greenham with mirrors to reflect the reality of the base inward. In 1985 they reached out to other women around the world. These three actions encapsulate the development of women's understanding of peace as wholeness—without poverty, hunger, sexism, and racism, where people resolve conflicts without violence and live in harmony with the physical environment.

Greenham women have begun to make important connections across class lines and national boundaries. These alliances need to be strengthened and developed to build a truly multiracial, global women's peace movement. We need to develop a feminist peace politics true to these ideals, where peace is not just an absence of war but the presence of life worth living. The Greenham experience is an important step in this direction.

Notes

1. Chapter 6 overlaps with this discussion and has notes and references that are also useful in connection with this chapter. Note that here, as in Chapter 6, I use "we" to refer to actions in which I participated and "they" to refer to actions I heard about or only observed.

2. Ann Pettitt, "Greenham Common: From Conception to Birth," in *Womanspirit*, no. 36 (1983), pp. 9–11.

3. The peace camp could not survive without the support that comes from women's groups, peace and disarmament organizations, church groups, and trade union branches, who send letters, money, food, firewood, warm clothes, and so on.

4. Greenham is a good example of anarchist/feminist principles in practice, although the women involved would not necessarily accept this designation. Discussions of anarcha-feminism that overlap with much of the discussion are Howard J. Erlich, Carol Erlich, David DeLeon and Glenda Morris, eds., *Reinventing Anarchy* (New York: Routledge and Kegan Paul, 1979); *Quiet Rumors: An Anarcha-Feminist Anthology* (London: Dark Star, n.d.).

5. See, for example, Wilmette Brown, "Black Women and the Peace Movement" (London: Falling Wall Press, 1984); Valerie Amos and Pratisha Parmer, "Challenging Imperial Feminism," *Feminist Review*, no. 17 (1984), pp. 3–19; Barbara Smith, "Fractious, Kicking, Messy, Free: Feminist Writers Confront the Nuclear Abyss," *New England Review/Bread Loaf Quarterly* (Summer 1983), pp. 581–592; Alice Walker, "Only Justice Can Stop a Curse," in Barbara Smith, ed., *Home Girls: Black Feminist Anthology* (New York: Kitchen Table: Women of Color Press, 1983), pp. 352–355.

Another important critique of Greenham comes from feminists who condemn what they see going on there as liberal feminism. They argue that women should be active around issues of immediate concern to women's daily lives: battering, rape, pornography, child abuse, sexual harassment at work, unequal pay and opportunity, limited rights to abortion and so on, rather than an abstract, remote issue such as the possibility of nuclear war. See Radical Feminist Organizing Committee, *Breaching the Peace* (London: Onlywomen Press, 1983); Ruth Walsgrove, "Greenham Common: Why Am I Still so Ambivalent?" *Trouble and Strife*, no. 1 (Winter 1983), pp. 4–6; "Obliteration as a Feminist Issue," *off our backs* (March 1984), pp. 16–17; Ann Snitow, "Holding the Line at Greenham," *Mother Jones* (February-March 1985), pp. 30–34, 39–44, 46–47, argued that Greenham is feminist, despite her initial doubts.

6. See Jane Dibblin, "They Play Such Terrible Head Games," *New Statesman*, November 27, 1987, pp. 20–21; and Beatrix Campbell in *Sanity* (November 1987), pp. 19–21, for one side of this argument. Women at Yellow Gate have published a newsletter and leaflets setting out their side. Their address is Yellow Gate Peace Camp, outside U.S.A.F. Greenham Common, Near Newbury, Berks., U.K.

7. Women's Action for Nuclear Disarmament, ed., *Pacific Women Speak* (Oxford: Green Line, 1987), is available in the United States from Woman Earth, P.O. Box 2374, Stanford, Calif. 94309.

8. *Critical Mass* is not distributed in the United States. *If You Love This Planet* (film) and *Woman Working for Peace* (video) are available from Women Against Nuclear Destruction, 691 Massachusetts Ave., Arlington, Mass. 02174. Also see Helen Caldicott, *Nuclear Madness* (New York: Bantam, 1980); Helen Caldicott, *Missile Envy* (New York: Bantam, 1985).

9. This argument is not the first, nor will it be the last. In any community there are always difficult choices to be made. To put this argument in perspective we can note other issues that have divided women in the past. These include making the peace camp women only and claiming the right to organize women-only actions at Greenham, lesbianism, money, drugs, the U.S. lawsuit brought by Greenham Women Against Cruise, how to care for women who come to the camp ill or very upset, and how to deal with the fact that women had been raped at Molesworth peace camp by men living there.

10. See, for example, Charlene Eldridge Wheeler and Peggy L. Chin, *Peace and Power: A Handbook of Feminist Process* (Buffalo, N.Y.: Margaretdaughters, 1984); Starhawk, *Dreaming the Dark* (Boston: Beacon Press, 1982), Chaps. 6 and 7, Appendix B; *Seneca Women's Encampment Handbook* (Seneca, N.Y.: 1983); Puget Sound Women's Peace Camp, *We Are Ordinary Women* (Seattle: Seal Press, 1985).

11. Good guides are Virginia Coover, Charles Esser, Ellen Deacon, and Christopher Moore, *Resource Manual for a Living Revolution* (Philadelphia: New Society Publishers, 1978); Donna Hawxhurst and Sue Murrow, *Living Our Visions: Building Feminist Community* (Tempe, Ariz.: Fourth World, 1984). For an excellent, wide-ranging discussion of power and process, see Starhawk, *Truth or Dare: Encounters with Power, Authority and Mystery* (San Francisco: Harper & Row, 1987). She talked about consensus process specifically on pp. 183–192.

12. Details about this case, *Greenham Women* v. *Reagan et al.*, 591 F. Supp. 1332 (S.D.N.Y. 1984), *aff'd* 755 F. 2d 34 (2d Cir. 1985), are available from the Center for Constitutional Rights, 666 Broadway, New York, NY 10012.

13. Sometimes people use the phrase *symbolic action* as a put down, although to my mind the distinction between symbolic and nonsymbolic actions is rather blurred. There is a sense in which everything we do is symbolic. In any case there is value in a whole range of actions, many of which may be perfectly legal, and it is not helpful to set them up in opposition to one another. We need actions that will encourage newcomers to participate and to build confidence and experience.

14. Often women are squeamish about leadership and try to pretend that there are no leaders when this is patently not the case. Starhawk, *Truth or Dare*, pp. 268–286, has an excellent discussion of responsible leadership in nonhierarchical and hierarchical organizations.

15. So much of women's history, the information and inspiration of it, has been lost to us. We need to document our work in every possible medium, tell our experience in our own words, and listen to other women talk of theirs.

16. Although set at a very low level, Social Security payments to the unemployed are more widely available in Britain than in the United States. In addition, everyone is covered by the National Health Service. Together these provide something of a safety net that makes it easier to be unemployed and politically active in Britain.

17. Greenham has been criticized by left-wing activists for having no strategy; in terms of an itemized program, top down and given, this is true. Women have redefined strategy in their terms: continual subversion, an accretion of small steps.

18. The revised Public Order Act, 1986, greatly restricts people's freedom to gather in public places. The police have wide powers to ban rallies and demonstrations and harass "organizers," and they can define any small group in a public place as a demonstration.

The Intermediate-range Nuclear Forces (INF) Treaty signed by Ronald Reagan and Mikhail Gorbachev in December 1987 applies to ground-launched cruise missiles in Western Europe. If ratified by the U.S. Senate, and put into effect, the missiles at Greenham should be withdrawn. The timetable for this appears to be at least three years from the time of ratification, during which period the missiles will be maintained in a "fully operational" condition. Maneuvers outside the base will continue as before. Early in 1988 the peace movement was already publicizing government plans to replace the ground-launched weapons with sea- and air-launched cruise missiles. So, despite the INF Treaty, this campaign is far from over. Women have vowed to stay at the base to verify that the ground-launched weapons are indeed withdrawn and to obstruct their maneuvers in the meantime. Some also want to go beyond this to reclaim Greenham Common for some productive, socially acceptable use.

19. This is not a complete list.

20. Women's land projects may also serve this same purpose and provide space for many projects, gathering, learning, and sharing among women.

21. Information about U.S. bases and facilities in Britain is available from Campaign for Nuclear Disarmament, 22-24 Underwood Street, London N1.

If I Can't Dance
in Your Revolution,
I'm Not Coming

YNESTRA KING

These are the words of anarchist feminist Emma Goldman. They also express the politics of the evolving contemporary feminist peace movement—a politics of joie de vivre in the face of the threat to life posted by the many ugly, faceless faces of militarism. It is not only a critical politics but an exemplary politics. There is no orthodoxy or party line to this movement. There is no big national organization. This is an antibureaucratic, creative movement, with an ability to respond flexibly to an ever-changing and continually more dangerous political situation. But this strength is also a weakness because it is very difficult to assess the power and forms of the movement at any one time, to know how many women are actually involved in peace work, and to decide what to include under the designation "politics."

As I was beginning this chapter, I took time out one rainy night to attend a benefit concern for the Maine Irish Children's Program, which brings children of different faiths from Northern Ireland for summers in Maine free of the hate and violence in their own country. Their guiding spirit is an inspired woman named Claire Foley, who told me as she bustled about serving Irish soda bread she had baked, and raffling off an Irish wool sweater she was to knit, that she does not think of her work as political, yet she spends all her time working in her own way for peace in Northern Ireland. This is the way women have traditionally worked for peace, as Amy Swerdlow's chapter (12) exemplifies. It occurred to me as I was driving home and thinking about this woman and the many others like her around the world that to assess the *potentiality* of feminist peace politics, we must include all the activities undertaken by women that move the world toward peace in big or small ways, but mostly in small ways, on a local and often personal level. Many of these activities may not be considered political by the women who carry them out because politics is by definition a big-time, abstract, male enterprise.

That is why one task undertaken by feminism is the intentional remaking of politics from the point of view of women, and here politics has more in common with art than with science. Therefore, an important aspect of this movement is an opposition to bureaucracy, to pontifical political posturing, to the inflexibility and lack of imagination of the world of men in neckties and uniforms. It is the very lifelessness of these institutional creatures and creations that threatens the continuation of life on the planet—so to oppose a culture and politics of death with a culture and politics of life is a requirement of our time. This libidinal politics—by which I mean the spontaneous emergence of a love of life into the public arena—on which the continuation of life may depend, is in its infancy. It is so commonsensical and so utopian that it is not politics in the old sense. And for those of us who are trying to create this new politics, it is like a continual seeking of grace or an attempt to devise a formula for connecting human beings with what is most deeply feeling and most deeply alive in themselves. That's why I have come to call these politics libidinal and to rely on the truthtelling of art, play, and the erotic, none of which has much to do with the instrumentality of politics as usual. Libidinal politics assumes that if people actually knew these parts of themselves, they would transform the social and economic structures that oppress human beings and are killing the planet.

But in attempting to analyze our current political situation from a feminist perspective, and in undertaking the production of an anthology such as this, we are also using another major resource of the movement— the ability of women to think intelligently about the world and ourselves in it. We must make theory as well as we make art and love and babies. Feminist theory is not some abstract academic discipline confined to the university. It is a growing critical and reconstructive view of all of society that originates in the rich life experience of women, both its oppressive and liberatory aspects.

But when we throw out old definitions of politics and standards of effectiveness, it is hard to know when we are on the right track, when we are succeeding in our work. For those of us who have been most active in the radical direct-action wing of the movement, with its emphasis on aesthetic actions and a politics of experience, this is especially difficult. Even as we create an iconography designed to bring people to life— parading with enormous puppets, quilting scenes from daily life, weaving the doors of the Pentagon closed with brilliantly colored yarn, waltzing around police barricades, shaking down fences, spray-painting runways, placing photos of beloved places in nature and children woven in the miles of fencing around military installations, wearing flowers and brilliant colors as we face into the gray and khaki of militarism, opposing machines with handcrafted alternatives—we wonder, Is there time to do this? Is there time not to do this? Is there an alternative? How can we lead decent, meaningful, ordinary lives—the fertile ground for any decent politics—and take responsibility for changing history?

At times the commitment to embodying a participatory, democratic alternative in which everyone is absolutely equal can lead to a maddening obsession with "process" that can be just as moribund as bureaucracy. (See Rhoda Linton and Gwyn Kirk, Chapters 13 and 14, for an account of these processes, and Adrienne Harris, Chapter 5, for an account of some of the problems with the underlying psychology.) A continual quest to live without contradiction—to eat only food that was grown with respect for the land and the people who grew it, to participate only in totally egalitarian relationships, to always tell the truth and to be nonviolent in all interactions (or, as Albert Camus said, to be "neither victims nor executioners"), to never let the smallest act of cruelty pass— such are the daily aspirations of the women who live in the culture of this movement. Yet all of us must make compromises to get through the day, and most women's lives are a mesh of interwoven commitments and relationships to which they are responsible—families, jobs, neighborhoods—and that necessitate these compromises and leave very little time for political activism. Yet, there must be room for these women in the movement. Feminism is first and last the business of giving expression to the hearts of women, so there must be room for women who care about peace, without a full-scale feminist analysis of the world.

I am one of the most privileged of contemporary women, of that generation that came of age just as the exuberant vitality of the New Left was informed by the equal vitality of feminism. The sense of personal and historic possibility of these combined legacies have shaped my entire adult life, and I am without the overwhelming, necessitarian burdens of most of the women in the world. I am a thirty-six-year-old, white, childless (as yet), teacher/writer/artist living in New York City in a multiethnic culture of women much like myself who live intentionally created and creative lives. We are not fleeing bombs, going hungry, or living in desperate poverty. Many of us are politically active in some version of feminist peace politics, and we are often preoccupied with our personal lives in the face of an enormously difficult political situation.

This is especially true as Ronald Reagan ends his second term and we are faced with a Bush presidency, Pretoria announces that it has a nuclear capability, and the ecological crisis, related to the militarist crisis, accelerates in the dissipation of the ozone layer, the greenhouse effect, the cancer epidemic, and the disappearance of hundreds of species of life and thousands of acres of wilderness each year.

So what follows is a personal account of a feminist peace politics that derives from the traditional concern of women with the preservation of life on the planet and from a contemporary feminist consciousness. (See Sally Ruddick, Chapter 4.) We are a hodge-podge of organizations and political actions, some of which are overtly oppositional and political and others of which are reconciliatory in the traditional, womanly mode.

But from my perspective, only through keeping the truths of traditional women's consciousness and intentional feminist consciousness in active tension can we move in the most liberatory and informed direction. It is in the interests of the peace movement that women be empowered by a feminist movement to move more effectively and forcefully into the public world, defining positively the meaning of "woman" for ourselves. But for the feminist peace movement, a feminism that repudiates the traditional life work and experience of women is truncating its own potential by cutting itself off from women who work effectively for peace but do not yet consider themselves feminist.

This dialectic has been visible in several women's political movements and events held during the last ten years. I will start with a political initiative I was personally involved with and which was an important influence on subsequent feminist peace initiatives around the world—the Women's Pentagon Action.

The Women's Pentagon Action: Initiating Feminist Peace Praxis

For many of us, ecological (or green) politics and peace politics are integral, so ecological feminism (ecofeminism) has been a primary informing philosophy for the feminist peace movement.[1] The Women's Pentagon Action was one of the first actions that attempted to articulate this convergence of feminism, ecology, and peace.

Following the meltdown of the nuclear reactor at Three Mile Island, Pennsylvania, a group of feminist activists who had also been involved in the ecological/antinuclear movement met to talk about the relationship between our work in these two movements. We were concerned about the spiraling arms race, the militarization of culture, and the deployment of cruise missiles in Europe. It seemed to us that the meltdown at Three Mile Island and the antivitalist cultural ideology represented by the response to this incident and other ecological catastrophes were intimately connected with the growing militarism and impending election of Ronald Reagan. All of us had been struck by the sexist rhetoric of the Three Mile Island spokesmen, who talked about "cooling her down" and "slamming the rods into the core" and referred to the reactor as "excited." Having watched the courageous leadership of prefeminist women in the ecology and peace movements, we also deplored feminist belittling of traditional women's work and lives and the acceptance by most feminists of the idea that women should work their way into culture defined against nature, rather than challenging that basic dualism itself. Or, as I came to ask the question, "Who wants an equal piece of a rotten carcinogenic pie?"

Given our ecological sensibility, we felt it was critical that women use our socially constructed, historical identification with nature[2] to critique the whole idea of culture against nature and to bring together feminist and ecological understandings. By trying to get out of the trap of being identified with nature in a culture defined against nature, we had dug ourselves into another trap—implicit acceptance of the ideology of antinaturalism, which has been used to denigrate, exploit, and abuse anything or anyone perceived as "more natural" than the dominant white Western bourgeoise male. We did not want to promote the misogynist idea that women should be planetary housewives, but we wanted to make feminist women see that an ecological perspective is basic to our self-interest and to make prefeminist, ecologically concerned women see that they needed feminism as a primary tool of analysis and action. Hence, we were consciously struggling to forge a politic that was true to women and to feminism.[3]

Bringing together our concern with ecology and militarism and our belief that these issues must be understood by feminists as feminist issues, we decided to hold a public conference. We knew that our position implied a rethinking of feminist theory and strategy and a different political practice than that familiar to us in the mixed movements for social justice and in more conventional liberal politics—all male dominated. So we decided to be intentionally naive.

When we issued the call for a conference, we found out that many women had been thinking the way we had, and more than eight hundred women attended the Conference on Women and Life on Earth, held at the University of Massachusetts, Amherst, in 1980.[4] We had not expected such a massive response, and had we not limited registration we would have had twice that number. As we began this work, we did not know what kind of political action would reflect our politics of combining the vantage point of traditional femininity and radical feminist militance. But out of this collaborative process grew the idea for a feminist action at the Pentagon.

So on a cold November day in 1980, women ringed the Pentagon, "making the connections" among war, poverty, ecological devastation, and the oppression of women. In keeping with our analysis, this action had a distinctly feminine and feminist aesthetic, process, and politics. The result was that several decisions were made that explicitly violated the conventional wisdom on political effectiveness and how to organize an action. Because of these decisions the women were thought naive by liberal and Left antiwar people and many other feminists. The first set of decisions had to do with who should call such an action. The action was initiated from the Northeast region by women who had attended the conference and shown an interest in such an action. The initiators decided that the meetings would be open to any woman who wanted to participate as an individual. There would not be the usual organizational and individual endorsements. All women, and men in support capacities, who agreed with a call issued in the name of the group (this was the Unity Statement) were welcome.

At the first organizational meeting, those present also decided that numbers were not as important as the integrity of the message and that the politics should be as inclusive of all heartfelt concerns as we could make it. This was a violation of the tenet that it is more politically effective for an action to express a narrow set of issues so more people can agree—the lowest-common-denominator philosophy.

The group operated by consensus—everyone had to agree on a decision before it could be carried out. The organizers believed that this process, drawn from the Quakers and the antinuclear movement, was most true to the feminist principle of equal respect for each woman regardless of her credentials, notoriety, or status. In theory, it allowed for everyone to make her contribution. It also allowed for a genuine togetherness and enthusiasm for each stage of the process, even though meetings were sometimes long and arduous. This process implied a critique of voting and majority rule as polarizing and as setting up a power dynamic within an organization that leaves many participants feeling disregarded and powerless. The principle of direct participation continued to illuminate these meetings as it later did the Women's Pentagon Action and many actions around the world that drew their inspiration from this one.

One of the most important products of the Women's Pentagon Action was the Unity Statement. It is the best-known articulation of the politics of the feminist peace movement to date and has been translated into many languages including Spanish, French, German, Italian, and Dutch. It was written by Grace Paley, a writer and an activist, in collaboration with action organizers from around the Northeast United States. It was a call to an action at the Pentagon, but it has become an international movement manifesto. In writing this statement, we constantly worked the tension between valuing the traditional lives and work of women and drawing on our feminist analysis and politics. This statement said in part:

> We are gathering at the Pentagon on November 16 because we fear for our lives. We fear for the life of this planet, our Earth, and the life of the children who are our human future. . . .
>
> We have come to mourn and rage and defy the Pentagon because it is the workplace of the imperial power which threatens us all. Every day while we work, study, love, the colonels and generals who are planning our annihilation walk calmly in and out the doors of its five sides. . . .
>
> "We will protect you . . ." they say, but we have never been so endangered, so close to the end of human time.
>
> We women are gathering because life on the precipice is intolerable. We want to know what anger in these men, what fear, which can only be satisfied by destruction, what coldness of heart and ambition drives their days. We want to know because we do not want that dominance which is exploitative and murderous in international relations, and so dangerous to women and children at home—we do not want that sickness transferred by this violent society through the fathers to the sons.
>
> What is it that we women need for our ordinary lives, that we want for ourselves and also for our sisters in new nations and old colonies who suffer the white man's exploitation and too often the oppression of their own countrymen?
>
> We want enough good food, decent housing, communities with clean air and water, good care for our children while we work. We want work that is useful to a sensible society. . . . We respect the work women have done in caring for the young, their own and others, in maintaining a physical and spiritual shelter against the greedy and militaristic society. . . .
>
> We want an end to the arms race. No more bombs. No more amazing inventions for death.
>
> We understand all is connectedness. We know the life and work of animals and plants in seeding, reseeding and in fact simply inhabiting this planet. Their exploitation and the organised destruction of never to be seen again species threatens and sorrows us. The earth nourishes us as we with our bodies will eventually feed it. Through us, our mothers connected the human past to the human future.
>
> With that sense, that ecological right, we oppose the financial connections between the Pentagon and the multinational corporations and banks that the Pentagon serves. Those connections are made of gold and oil. We are made of blood and bone, we are made of the sweet and finite resource, water. We will not allow these violent games to continue. If we are here in our stubborn thousands today, we will

certainly return in the hundreds of thousands in the months and years to come.

We know there is a healthy sensible loving way to live and we intend to live that way in our neighborhoods and our farms in these United States, and among our sisters and brothers in all the countries of the world.[5]

There was much discussion of how to do an action at the Pentagon that exemplified feminist participatory process and made all the connections among the issues in the statement and in the action itself. One of the most unusual aspects of this action was that there were no speakers and leaders in the usual Washington–demonstration style— everyone participated equally. There was no podium or sound stage. The organizers decided that the action should happen in stages that expressed our feelings and ideas about the Pentagon (critical) and the power of women to challenge militarism in all its forms (reconstructive/ utopian).

The first stage was mourning—it began with a procession to the Pentagon through the Arlington National Cemetery, with its rows and rows of tombstones, visible for miles. Then the women made a cemetery on the main lawn of the Pentagon with tombstones from throughout the country remembering victims of war and oppression. The tombstones included remembrance of the named and nameless—Anne Frank, nuns killed in El Salvador, victims of illegal abortion, women dead from radiation, war refugees, rape victims, and more.

One of the most important things about this stage of the action was that it encouraged women to bring their private pain into a public place. The grief of women, a privatized repository of moral feeling, broke into the public space beside the Pentagon thereby subverting the false tidiness of business as usual. The most memorable tombstone was brought by a California housewife who had never been in a political action in her life. She traveled alone from California with her tombstone on which she had written, "For the three Vietnamese women my son killed."

Mourning followed very easily into the next stage—rage. All the stage changes were signaled by twenty-foot puppets and drumming—the rage puppet was red. As the red puppet moved to the center of the graveyard, women spontaneously began to chant, "Shame, shame, shame," shaking their fists and raging at the Pentagon officials gathered at the entrance and looking down from their windows. As the women chanted and drummed a woman emerged from the Pentagon. She had quit her job as a secretary to join the action. She said she had seen many demonstrations before, but none had spoken to her in the way this did.

After rage came empowerment, led by the yellow puppet. Following the yellow and red puppets women moved in two directions to surround the Pentagon, meeting on the other side. These feminist women una-bashedly wove a ribbon of life containing many womanly messages as they went. Woven into this length of yarn, ribbon, and fabric strips were photos of children and other loved ones; beautiful pieces of nature, twigs, and flowers; poems and the names and messages of women who could not be physically present but who were present in spirit.

After empowerment came the final stage—defiance—a civil disobe-dience action taken only by those who were comfortable doing it. The entrances to the Pentagon were woven shut with yarn, and Pentagon police moved again and again to cut through the yarn. As fast as it was cut loose, some of the women rewove the yarn as others sat down in an act of nonviolent civil disobedience. After about an hour of women weaving and police warning, arrests began. About one hundred twenty women were arrested and charged with blocking entrances. Some women were given stiffer charges, and women who pled guilty in court were given unprecedented sentences—ten days in prison for women with no arrest record and a month in prison for women who had been previously arrested demonstrating at the Pentagon.

Only two thousand women took part in this action the first year and four thousand the second year—very small numbers—but the effect of this action was international and lasting. It had a mythic quality—an action that told all the truths, had no identifiable heros, and was beautiful, spiritual, womanly, and feminist. These actions hit a responsive chord in women who had not felt comfortable in other forms of politics and gave women in many places the confidence to go ahead with political initiatives that were deemed "naive" by experienced politicians and activists.

The Women's Pentagon Action provided a model of audacity and imagination that has changed the landscape of public political action and possibility. Throughout the 1980s, hundreds of actions were taken by women around the world in the cause of peace. For most feminist peace activists feminist peace politics necessitates a resistance to all forms of oppression and domination—hunger, violence, racism, soma-tophobia, imperialism, and the devastation of nature—and an insistence on constantly making all these connections in our evolving theory and practice.[6] In many cases the Women's Pentagon Action Unity Statement was a direct influence on the development of this philosophy.

But as has been pointed out especially by women of color in this country (see Zala Chandler and Barbara Omolade, Chapters 2 and 9), the feminist peace movement has reflected the strengths and limitations of women like myself, who are white Americans and Europeans. We have used our freedom from a basic struggle to survive in order to imagine and demand an unprecedented range of options never before available to women, and these ideas are gradually taking root in the particular soils of many nations and cultures around the world. But we could not and should not articulate the relationships between the survival struggles of poor women around the world and our movement, which grew out of ideas about personal freedom that presume a woman has already the means to basic survival. (See Ann Snitow, Chapter 3.) So the United Nations Decade on Women conference in Nairobi, with its themes of development, equality, and peace, dramatically raised our consciousness of the conditions of women in the world.

The United Nations Decade on Women

In 1985, I, along with fifteen thousand other women, attended the United Nations Decade on Women in Nairobi, Kenya. There were many European and American activists from the feminist peace movement who attended this conference, and the experience has profoundly affected our subsequent work—both our understanding of the issues and our political practice.

In Nairobi, the word *feminist* was in the air from Third World women and First World women alike. And many of us from the United States were asked again and again to tell the story of the U.S. feminist movement to excited women from other countries, many of which had no organized feminist movement as yet. At this amazing international conference participants assumed that feminists are prowoman and that any feminist politics and strategy must include the concerns of women who are the poorest of the poor—war refugees, victims of famine, those who must walk hours every day carrying jugs of water on their heads, who must scavenge endlessly for firewood to cook and heat with, and who must do forced labor on farms growing luxury products for the West on their arable lands as their children go hungry. The tension that exists for white Western feminists between "woman" and "feminist" is not so pronounced in the feminism emerging in the Third World as of yet. I don't believe anyone left Nairobi without a visceral and intellectual understanding of the interrelationships among equality for women, the need for feminist development strategies and a redistribution of wealth among countries and classes, and an end to war and the militarization and violence of culture.

Fully half the participants at the conference were from the Third World, a large percentage of those were from Africa, and every aspect of the program reflected this diversity. As official government delegates debated official resolutions, unofficial participants crowded into classrooms at the University of Nairobi to hear women from around the world make these connections in English, Swahili, French, Spanish, and many other languages. Women from Development Alternatives for Women in a New Era (DAWN) gave numerous workshops critiquing development and talking about what it would mean for women to set development strategy. DAWN is a remarkable group of women from India, Tahiti, Kenya, Central America, Bolivia, and other developing countries.[7] Women from the Indigenous People's Network talked about their desire to save their traditional cultures and the need to transform these cultures from within when they are oppressive to women. Women from many countries analyzed foreign policy, criticizing the misplacement of resources and the effect of the militarization of the planet. They paid special attention to the effects of militarism on women, including the forcing of women who live near U.S. airbases into prostitution, the taking of lands, the use of funds that should be spent on food and health care to buy weapons, and the consequences of the international monetary system for women. The International Women's Tribune Center of the United Nations[8] conducted workshops called "Tech and Tools" about appropriate technology for women—ecologically sound, accessible, and inexpensive labor saving for women who live in small villages or rural situations. There was the Peace Tent—a huge circus tent that was a forum for women to talk with each other in a setting that was multicultural, international, hospitable, and spontaneous.

I went to Nairobi as a guest of the Feminist International for Peace and Food, an ad hoc, privately funded international organization that organized the Peace Tent, so I spent much of my time there. The program changed daily and evolved as we went along. There was a small storytelling tent alongside the big tent where women sat in a circle and told their personal stories as their sisters translated. Many issues were discussed—women from monogamous cultures talked with women from polygamous cultures; Kenyan village women and women from New York City shared their lives; many women spoke about contraception, abortion, and sex. In the big tent women from the Soviet Union and the United States had a dialogue on peace; women from Palestine and Israel argued and talked with each other; and everyone listened to panels on international feminism, the political situation in Chile, and international economics. Outside, under their own tree, lesbians from around the world met and talked about their lives. Some of the women were from cultures that did not admit they existed, that had no word for "lesbian." Two of the women who came to these meetings did not know there were other women like themselves in the world. Under another tree the disabled women met, some with congenital disabilities, others the victims of war wearing artificial limbs, and together they drafted a resolution on accessibility. As diverse and wide ranging as the program was, lesbians and disabled women (and possibly other groups I don't know about) were too far "outside" to have an official workshop. Yet they found each other, and they met daily.

One of the most memorable sessions took place in a huge auditorium (with headsets for simultaneous translation) and was conducted by Bella Abzug on the theme, "What If Women Ruled the World?"[9] Parliamentarians from thirty countries talked about what would be different if women were in charge and discussed how legislatures can facilitate the goals of equality, peace, and development. These women were concerned with how to use existing, male-dominated political structures, but what surprised me was that every one of these women assumed that things would be different if women were in charge, and everyone of them talked of the need for women to engage in bold political action outside these structures. They also talked about the limitations of governments as vehicles for change and the difficulties women encountered in being listened to, taken seriously, and being effective in these structures. Every seat in the largest auditorium was filled, and hundreds of women occupied every inch of floor space. Women of different cultures cuddled close together to share the same headset.

This was in contrast to the official sessions in which the U.S. delegation, symbolically headed by Maureen Reagan, consistently attempted to dominate the proceedings. In observing the official proceedings, we could always tell when something important was being debated, even before hearing the discussion, because the women delegates had been replaced by the men in virtually all delegations. The governments of the world did not trust women to speak for themselves even when the issues under consideration related to the welfare of women.

The unofficial forum had a completely different feeling to it—spontaneity, art, laughter, and women constantly making room for more women in already crowded sessions and making sure everyone understood and was heard. The final evening was a celebration of all the cultures of the world, with music, dancing, storytelling, and brilliant costuming held outside on the great lawn of the University of Nairobi. Nairobi was a euphoric experience for those of us fortunate enough to attend. I think all of us came back with a renewed hope that women throughout the world could make common cause with one another and do politics differently if we were given a chance.

Beyond Nairobi

There are other international examples of women taking original political initiatives and engaging in successful political protest under conditions of extreme political repression. Although feminism in the Third World has its own distinctive character, the same contradictions exist between women's organizations that rely exclusively on traditional ideas about women and those that are infused with feminist consciousness.

One such prefeminist group is the Mothers of the Plaza de Mayo, in Argentina, called Las Locas Mamas (The Crazy Mothers).[10] They invented a form of political action appropriate to a situation in which overt opposition and demonstrations as usual were impossible. They protested the "disappearance" of their loved ones by gathering every Thursday at 3:30 at the Plaza de Mayo, wearing handkerchiefs with the names of their missing loved ones embroidered on them, and silently circling the Plaza. They organized as they stood in line together at government offices to register the names of their missing family members. Conventional public forms of organization were not possible in such a repressive state. In fact, more than half of the thirty thousand people who "were disappeared" were people younger than thirty. These women used the sexism of the government, which allowed them a greater modicum of public mobility than the young and male members of their families, to call the world's attention to the repression in Argentina.

Out of this waiting together came "the mothers' movement," also called "the conscience of Argentina." This movement grew to two thousand five hundred members and was responsible in part for forcing the government to hold elections in 1982. But however powerful they were in calling attention to the brutality and repression of the Argentinian government, as an organization they have never been able to move beyond their position as mothers and to take on real political authority. Like the Women Strike for Peace, they have been limited by their prefeminist, motherist stance.

The Chilean Mujeres por la Viva (Women for Life) is a group of fifteen women who come from different backgrounds and constituencies and meet together to call large actions protesting Augusto Pinochet's government. They have been able to get groups to cooperate that would not work together in the past, and the group has been instrumental in the recent huge protests held in Santiago. They are an ad hoc group, they decide things by consensus, and they meet in each other's living rooms. One of their slogans proclaims, "No more because we are more." They use indigenous women's conversation networks to call actions because most Chilean women don't have telephones. In 1984 they successfully organized a protest action of four hundred thousand people in twenty days using these indigenous networks. According to Isabel Letelier of the Institute for Policy Studies, they were able to get opposition groups to cooperate that had never before been able to work together. Such is their moral and political authority.

The Chilean women are consciously wielding enormous political influence, and although they recognize and use the moral authority conferred on them by the old stereotypes, they are also powerful members of trade unions, professions, and other political groups. They have not represented themselves primarily as mothers or traditional women. They have used explicitly feminist slogans connecting the oppression of women and government suppression of free political expression. One of their major slogans, visible in huge banners at demonstrations, is "Democracy in the house, democracy in the country." Clearly they are not subordinating their concerns as women to other political concerns,[11] which points toward an even stronger resolution of the dialectic between women's lives and feminist praxis.

Conclusion: Feminism, Peace, and the Future

The role of women in liberation struggles worldwide is being expanded and publicly recognized. These movements may also be peace movements, if peace is understood as an active state of being in which people have enough to eat, are equal in society, are free to speak their minds, and can take part in politics, art, and every area of society. I would contend that the self-conscious, double-edged militance on the part of women in these struggles—against male domination and for a peaceful society— is a form of feminism. These women are doing (at least) double duty, often struggling against the sexism of their male comrades while fighting alongside these same men in a struggle of cultural and national liberation.

In South Africa women have led the pass law struggles and have used their work situations as domestics to challenge government restrictions on their movements. In Central America, according to Sylvia Sandeval of the Women's Association of El Salvador, the women of each revolutionary situation (Cuba to Nicaragua to El Salvador) have been more feminist than the last in their understanding and demands. She cited the feminist influence on her movement as reflected in its educational campaign about marital rape. According to Sandeval, her organization has held meetings on the subject in many areas of the country—telling women that they are not their husbands' property, that they need not have sex when they don't want to, and that their bodies and their pleasures are their own. Even in the middle of the war zones, amid violence and desperate poverty, these ideas are relevant. According to Sandeval, they help women to assert themselves in their homes and political organizations and to act with sense of their own subjectivity— the core of every feminist philosophy.[12]

Like Cassandra the Trojan seeress, positioned between the ancients and the moderns, between the loyalties of immediacy and family and those of abstraction and state, contemporary women have the ability to see where our world is heading.[13] Cassandra saw the beginning of a historical epoch we may live to see the end of—the beginning of expansionist nation-states, featuring warrior-hero (male) citizens who go to war for territory and power. (See Nancy Hartsock and Carol Cohn, Chapters 7 and 8.) But unlike Cassandra, and all the women who have been silenced, we have reached a historical moment when we can and must be listened to. (See Dorothy Dinnerstein, Chapter 1). Hers was the gift of prophecy; ours is the knowledge of history. Now feminism must learn to ground itself in the critical alterity of women—using the outsider vantage point of traditional women's lives and values as a source of analysis, insight, and political imagination.

We are only beginning to see how women do politics when they are aware of their historical position as women and conscious of the limitations of existing male-dominated political methods and structures for everyone. Nevertheless, some aspects of women's approach to politics are already clear. There is an implicit critique of the state and the impersonal nature of bureaucracy,[14] leading women to act directly, to cut through rhetoric and statistics with flesh and blood reality. Here the feminist movement meets the anarchist tradition of radical direct action and civil disobedience, refusing to respect the system logic of "proper channels," demonstrating resistance with bodies as well as words. Persons socialized as women do not tend to polarize situations; they tend, rather, to negotiate and to allow every individual to find some expression within the totality. Women also take note of the smallest particulars; they think contextually (the "reason" of traditional women's consciousness), which helps ground political movements in the realities of daily life.

In the West, feminist peace politics most represents the political potential of both womanist and feminist worlds and presents a politics that allows connections between white women and women of color in our own countries and in the Third World. These connections are critical to the emergence of a universally relevant, international women's movement that furthers the interests of women and of peace.

As we conclude this volume, there are a number of ongoing activities in the feminist peace movement, and the influence of our work is evident in other movements. For examples, in New York City and elsewhere around the country, Jewish women who have been part of this movement have begun to vigil weekly in front of Israeli consulates to protest the treatment of Palestinians in the west bank. Other women (some of whom are gay and some of whom are not) coordinated the civil disobedience action at the national gay rights demonstrations in Washington in November 1987. These same women held hundreds of trainings throughout the country in the months preceding the action. In fact, when I arrived in Washington the night before the civil disobedience was to take place, I went directly to the church in which the last minute orientation was already in progress. As I entered through a side door, I saw that at the podium virtually everyone presenting from the various committees, the lawyers, and the speakers had been part of the Women's Pentagon Action. The men who took part in the civil disobedience, most of whom had never engaged in this form of political action before, were very explicit in their recognition of the leadership of the women and their gratitude toward the feminist peace movement for our pioneering work in developing a playful public gender critique and a politics of joie de vivre.

Many peace organizations now have feminist task forces. On the other hand, the Women's International League for Peace and Freedom, not originally a feminist organization, is actively engaged in becoming one, assessing its hierarchical organizational structure as well as its political program, as women from the feminist peace movement enter the traditional women's peace organizations. The encampments at Seneca and Greenham continue, other encampments come and go (these are too numerous to mention), and the decentralized nature of the movement ensures that no one knows about all of them. The same is true of the small consciousness-raising/affinity group formations that work for peace in local communities, many of them actively making connections with feminist groups working to end violence against women, linking the causes of rape and domestic violence at home with ecological devastation and militarism. One button features the slogan, "Peace begins at home—stop domestic violence." Another major direction of feminist peace activism is the movement for peace in Central America. The burgeoning green movement has also felt the influence of the feminist peace movement, as women insist on making connections among ecology, feminism, and peace in the political program, process, and actions of the greens.

As we go to press George Bush has just been elected president in a campaign with racist and sexist overtones, which featured such critical issues as the "wimp factor" and the respective heights of the candidates. Presidential politics, conducted almost entirely through the mass media, sunk to new lows as both candidates vied for "media bites," and they and their wives worried about their "images." Never has the political process been so anemic.

The feminist peace movement has been called utopian and unrealistic and snickered at by the "experts." But the deeply ethical orientation of our movement, with its continual conversation about how the world "ought" to be, its respect for each person (and everything alive, human or not), its attempt to link the particular and the universal in theory and practice (to work locally and think globally), and the value it places on a face-to-face participatory political community create an oppositional force with a powerful morality. Potentially, we are a model for remaking politics if we can continue to link issues and constituencies, provide an affirmative vision of a better society, and develop the means to effectively oppose the state without taking on militarist forms or tactics ourselves. The issues of who makes politics, how it's done, and what interests it represents as well as the pressing need for alternative ways of thinking and acting create a context in which the vision, critical thinking, and inventive political process of the feminist peace movement, as represented in this book, have never been more relevant or more necessary.

As I was finishing the conclusion to this book late one August evening, I lay across a bed in a secluded house on the top of a beautiful mountain in Vermont able to think of nothing but a personal crisis. "Peace" seemed like a very remote concern that day, and I was feeling very sorry for myself. As I lay there immobilized there was a knock on the door. I opened it, and in from the black night came a beautiful, dark-skinned woman, about my age, with five small, frightened-looking children. They all had straight black hair and brown eyes, and I recognized their immaculate, ironed clothing as Guatemalan. She said to me in Spanish, "You are the lady who writes about peace?" I said, "Yes," even though that was a lie at that particular moment. She smiled and said, "I am Veronica. These are my children. We have come here from Guatemala, and tomorrow we will go to Canada. I want my children to know they are safe now so I brought them to meet the lady who writes about peace." And one by one she introduced them and pushed them forward to shake my hand. "Gracias, señora," she said. After she left I cried, but this time I was not crying about my broken heart. And I went back to work.

We will continue rocking the ship of state.

Notes

1. For a more complete account of ecofeminist philosophy, history, and politics, see Ynestra King, *Ecofeminism and the Reenchantment of Nature* (forthcoming).

2. Ecofeminism is not a biologically determinist philosophy, and in organizing the Conference on Women and Life on Earth we took pains to make this clear.

3. I wrote in 1980: "Women are the less rationalized side of humanity in an overly rationalized world. Yet we can think as rationally as men and perhaps transform the idea of reason itself. Women are naturalized culture in a culture defined against nature. If nature/culture antagonism is the primary contradiction of our time, it is also what weds feminism and ecology. . . . Without an ecological perspective which asserts the interdependence of living things, feminism is disembodied. There is more at stake in feminist debates over 'the ecology question' than whether feminists should organize against the draft, demonstrate

at the Pentagon or join mixed anti-nuke organizations. At stake is the range and potential of the feminist movement" ("Feminism and the Revolt of Nature," *Heresies* 13 (1980), p. 12).

4. Women and Life on Earth was sponsored in part by the Institute for Social Ecology, then affiliated with Goddard College in Plainfield, Vermont.

5. "Unity Statement, Women's Pentagon Action (USA), in Leonie Caldecott and Stephanie Leland, eds., *Reclaim the Earth* (London: The Women's Press, 1983), p. 15.

6. Alice Walker called the parallel development in black feminism during this same time period "womanist." See Alice Walker, *In Search of Our Mothers' Gardens: Womanist Prose* (New York: Harcourt Brace, 1984). Also see "Cumbahee River Collective Statement," in Zillah Eisenstein, ed., *Capitalist Patriarchy and the Case for Socialist Feminism* (New York: Monthly Review Press, 1978), where Barbara Smith and the other members of the black feminist Cumbahee River Collective also reflected this direction. In fact, as I noted, the feminism of women of color has never capitulated to the feminist versus woman split I have articulated here.

7. See DAWN, *Development, Crises and Alternative Visions: Third World Women's Perspectives,* written by Gita Sen with Casen Grown (New Delhi: Institute of Social Studies Trust, 1985).

8. The Tribune Center is a nongovernmental organization. It is not part of the official United Nations.

9. See Bella Abzug and Mim Kelber, *The Gender Gap 1984* (Boston: Houghton Mifflin, 1984).

10. I am indebted to the participants in the Seminar on Motherist Movements of the Barnard College Women's Center for much of the information in this section. We have met together for several years to discuss the work of "motherist movements" (those that grow out of traditional women's lives and works but are not necessarily feminist) and feminism, including movements that are both feminist and motherist, such as the contemprary feminist peace movement. Of the contributors to this collection, Ann Snitow, Amy Swerdlow, and Sara Ruddick are also members of this group.

11. My information comes from an interview with Chilean exile Isabel Letelier, Director of the Third World Women's Project of the Institute for Policy Studies, Washington, D.C., conducted by Adrienne Harris in the studios of the Canadian Broadcasting Corporation in May 1986.

12. Personal interview with Sylvia Sandeval, Fall 1985, New York City.

13. See Christa Wolf, *Cassandra* (New York: Farrar, Straus, Giroux, 1984), for a fascinating reinterpretation of Cassandra.

14. Kathy Ferguson has developed an anarchist feminist critique of bureaucracy that I very much agree with in *The Feminist Case Against Bureaucracy* (Philadelphia: Temple University Press, 1984).

About the Editors
and Contributors

Editors

Adrienne Harris, Ph.D., an associate professor of psychology at Rutgers University, is a founding member of Group for a Radical Human Science. She has written articles on the psychology of women and on the relations of psychology and ideology and is a psychoanalyst and psychotherapist practicing in New York City.

Ynestra King is a political philosopher, writer, and peace activist. She is a founder of the Womens Pentagon Action and WomanEarth; a long-time feminist and antiwar activist, she has spoken all over the United States and Europe on women and peace and has written on these issues in *Ikon, Heresies, Win, Signs,* and other publications. She is currently writing a book connecting feminism, ecology, and peace, which develops a philosophy of "logical ecofeminism" and is entitled *Ecofeminism and the Reenchantment of Nature.* She lives in New York City.

Contributors

Lourdes Benería, Ph.D., is a professor of city and regional planning and women's studies at Cornell University. She is coauthor (with Masa Roldan) of *The Crossroads of Class and Gender* and is now working on the effect of the debt crisis on household survival and women's work.

Rebecca Blank, Ph.D., is an assistant professor of economics and public affairs at Princeton University. Her research has focused on the behavior and well-being of low-income households, with particular attention to the economic situation of women who head their own households.

Zala Chandler, Ph.D., is a graphic artist and professor of humanities at Medger Evers College of the City University of New York. Her research on women in the Caribbean and Central America is an outgrowth of her position as co-chair of the board of Madre.

Carol Cohn is a senior research scholar at the Center for Psychological Studies in the Nuclear Age in Cambridge, Mass. Supported by a grant from the John D. and Catherine T. McArthur Foundation, she is currently writing a book about the language and thinking of defense intellectuals.

Dorothy Dinnerstein, Ph.D., is professor emerita of psychology, Rutgers University, and the author of the groundbreaking work of feminist theory *The Mermaid and the Minotaur.* She is a long-time activist in a number of different political movements; women's issues, the survival of the planet, and movements for social justice. She is also the author of many articles and a number of scientific papers in cognitive psychology.

Nancy C. M. Hartsock, Ph.D., is professor of political science and women's studies at the University of Washington. She is the author of *Money, Sex, and Power: Toward a Feminist Historical Materialism* (1983) and is currently working on a manuscript entitled *Postmodernism and Political Change.*

Gwyn Kirk, Ph.D., has been a commentator, participant, and supporter of the Greenham Women's Peace Movement in Britain since 1982. She earned her doctorate in sociology from the London School of Economics. Her work life has been a blend of scholarship and activism. She is a founder-member of WomanEarth, a multiracial, multicultural United States women's network committed to an integration of spirituality and politics with parity between women of color and white women. She has coauthored *Greenham Women Everywhere* with Alice Cook (1983).

Rhoda Linton, Ph.D., is an independent program evaluator specializing in women's programs. She is interested in women's organizing and feminist practice. She was a participant in the activities at the Seneca's Women's Peace Camp. She is core faculty at the Union Graduate School of the Union of Experimenting Colleges and Universities.

Phyllis Mack, Ph.D., is a historian who teaches European women's history at Rutgers University. She is the author of *Women and the*

Enlightenment (1984) and is currently completing a study entitled *The Quaker Prophet and Her Audience: Gender and Spirituality in Seventeenth-Century England*, an analysis of visionary women in seventeenth-century England.

Barbara Omolade is on the staff of the City College Center for Worker Education where she both teaches and counsels. She is a consultant for the League of Black Single Mothers and for the Medger Evers College Center for Women's Development. For over twenty years she has been an activist in the civil rights movement and in the women's movement. She is the author of *It's a Family Affair: Black Single Mothers, The Real Deal*.

Sara Ruddick, Ph.D., philosopher, teaches at Eugene Lang College of the New School for Social Research. She coedited *Working It Out* and, in 1984, *Between Women*. Her book *Maternal Thinking: Towards a Politics of Peace* was published in 1989.

Ann Snitow, Ph.D., has been a feminist-activist since 1970, when she was one of the founding members of New York Radical Feminists. She is a literary critic, a professor of literature and women's studies at Eugene Lang College of the New School for Social Research, and coeditor of *Powers of Desire: The Politics of Sexuality* (1983) with Christine Stansell and Sharon Thompson. In another life she wrote a book about Ford Madox Ford, and her articles appear in such places as the *Village Voice, The Nation, Ms,* the *Women's Review of Books, Mother Jones,* and the *New York Times.*

Amy Swerdlow, a founder of Women Strike for Peace, is currently the director of the graduate program in women's history at Sarah Lawrence College. Her chapter in this book is part of a longer work, *Motherhood, Pacifism, and Feminism: The Case of Women Strike for Peace*, forthcoming from the University of Chicago Press.